Other books in ABC-CLIO's On Trial Series

Charles L. Zelden, Series Editor

Voting Rights
ON TRIAL

*A Handbook with
Cases, Laws, and Documents*

Charles L. Zelden

A B C  C L I O

Santa Barbara, California • Denver, Colorado • Oxford, England

Library of Congress Cataloging-in-Publication Data
Zelden, Charles L., 1963–
Voting rights on trial : a handbook with cases, laws, and documents / Charles L. Zelden.
    p.   cm. — (On trial)
Includes bibliographical references and index.
ISBN 1-57607-794-2 (hardcover); 1-57607-795-0 (e-book)
   1. Suffrage—United States.   2. Voting—United States.   I. Title. II. Series.
KF4891 .Z45 2002
342.73'072—dc21   2001006956

07 06 05 04 03 02 01 10 9 8 7 6 5 4 3 2 1

ABC-CLIO, Inc.
130 Cremona Drive, P.O. Box 1911
Santa Barbara, California 93116-1911

This book is printed on acid-free paper.
Manufactured in the United States of America

Contents

Series Foreword

The volumes in the On Trial series explore the many ways in which the U.S. legal and political system has approached a wide range of complex and divisive legal issues over time—and in the process defined the current state of the law and politics on these issues. The intent is to give students and other general readers a framework for understanding how the law in all its various forms—constitutional, statutory, judicial, political, and customary—has shaped and reshaped the world we live in today.

At the core of each volume in the series is a common proposition: that in certain key areas of American public life, we as a people and a nation are "on trial" as we struggle to cope with the contradictions, conflicts, and disparities within our society, politics, and culture. Who should decide if and when a woman can have an abortion? What rights, if any, should those with a different sexual orientation be able to claim under the Constitution? Is voting a basic right of citizenship, and if so, under what rules should we organize this right—especially when the application of any organizing rules inevitably results in excluding some citizens from the polls? What about the many inconsistencies and conflicts associated with racial tensions in the country? These are just some of the complex and controversial questions that we as a people and a nation are struggling to answer—and must answer if we are to achieve an orderly and stable society. For the answers we find to these disputes shape the essence of who we are—as a people, a community, and a political system.

The concept of being on trial also has a second meaning fundamental to this series: the process of litigating important issues in a court of law. Litigation is an essential part of how we settle our differences and make choices as we struggle with the problems that confront us as a people and a nation. In the 1830s, Alexis de Tocqueville in his book *Democracy in America* noted "there is hardly a political question in the United States which does not sooner or later turn into a judicial one" (de Tocqueville, 270). This insight is as true today as it was in the 1830s. In *The Litigious Society,* Jethro K. Lieberman notes that "to express amazement at American litigiousness is akin to professing astonishment at learning that the roots of most Americans lie in other lands. We have been a litigious nation as we have been an immigrant one. Indeed, the two are related" (Lieberman 1983, 13). Arriving in the United States with different backgrounds, customs, and lifestyle preferences, we inevitably clashed as our contrasting visions of life in the United States—its culture, society, and politics—collided. It was to the courts and the law that we turned as a neutral forum for peaceably working out these differences. For, in the United States at least, it is the courthouse that provides the anvil on which our personal, societal, and political problems are hammered out.

The volumes in this series therefore take as their central purpose the important task of exploring the various ways—good and bad, effective and ineffective, complex and simple—that litigation in the courts has shaped the evolution of particular legal controversies for which we are "on trial." And, more importantly, the volumes do all this in a manner accessible to the general reader seeking to comprehend the topic as a whole.

These twin goals—analytical and educational—shape the structure and layout of the volumes in the series. Each book consists of two parts. The first provides an explanatory essay in four chapters. Chapter 1 introduces the issues, controversies, events, and participants associated with the legal controversy at hand. Chapter 2 explores the social, economic, political, and historical background to this topic. Chapter 3 describes in detail the various court decisions and actions that have shaped the current status of the legal controversy under examination. In some cases this will be done through a close examination of a few representative cases; in others by a broader but less detailed narrative of the course of judicial action. Chapter 4 discusses the impact of these cases on U.S. law—their doctrinal legacy—as well as on U.S. society—their historic, sociological, and political legacy.

Part Two, in turn, provides selective supplementary materials designed to help readers to more fully comprehend the topics covered in the chapters of Part One. First are documents aimed at helping the reader better appreciate both the issues and the process by which adjudication shaped these matters. Selected documents might include court opinions (excerpted or whole), interviews, newspaper accounts, and selected secondary essays. Next comes an alphabetically formatted section providing entries on the people, laws, events, and concepts important to an understanding of the topic. A chronology next provides the reader an easily referenced listing of the major developments covered in the book, and a table of cases lists the major court decisions cited. And lastly, an annotated bibliography describes the key works in the field, directing a reader seeking a more detailed examination on the topic to the appropriate sources.

In closing, as you read the books in this series, keep in mind the purposefully controversial nature of the topics covered within. The authors in the series have not chosen easy nor agreeable topics to explore. Much of what you read may trouble you, and it should. Yet it is precisely these sorts of contentious topics that need the most historical analysis and scrutiny. For it is here that we are still "on trial"—and all too often, as regards these matters, the jury is still out.

Charles L. Zelden
Ft. Lauderdale, Florida

Preface

Ⅰt seems so simple. Every year we go to the polls, enter the booth, and flip a lever, mark a ballot, or punch a card to take part in the voting process that lies at the heart of democratic governance. What can be easier than this?

Yet, scrutinized in detail, voting in the United States is anything but a simple or easy task. Even a passing glance at the history of voting rights in the United States presents a picture of a voting system wracked by systematic and chronic vote denial and vote dilution. Complex and convoluted registration rules undermine the voting rights of numerous groups—in practice if not by intention. Out-of-date voting technologies and local control over the election process produce widely disparate election results—empowering some voters while effectively disenfranchising many others. Even the way we organize our elections—employing at-large or mandatory majority vote procedures—repeatedly dilutes the impact of certain groups' ballots, in the process undermining the significance of the act of voting.

For most of our national history, almost as much effort has gone into denying disliked or despised groups the vote—or at least diluting the impact of their vote—as into expanding the franchise. True, over time, the category of Americans able to vote has expanded to include nearly every adult citizen. This is a fact we cannot, must not, forget. Yet, as the 2000 presidential election amply demonstrates, the problems of vote denial and vote dilution are not artifacts from the past—we are still coping with the reality of those problems today, and we will have to do so for years to come.

How can a democratic nation allow such exclusions to happen? Doesn't democracy mean that everyone gets to vote? How democratic can we be, given the existence of widespread vote denial—and the all-too-slow process by which we opposed this denial? Just how healthy are U.S. politics and constitutional government? How healthy can they be? Should they be? Are we in trouble here? Or are the events of the 2000 election simply an aberration already being fixed by legislative initiative?

These are questions central to the health and future of the nation. They are also questions central to this book. If the 2000 election showed anything, it showed that voting really matters in this country—and that we still haven't quite figured out how to make the voting process work smoothly and equitably. In fact, as we explore in detail in the chapters and sections that follow, the right to vote has been "on trial" in the United States almost from the first time a colonial Virginia planter cast a vote to elect a representative to the House of Burgesses. At its root, the debate over who gets to vote is really a debate over the character of the United States—over the forms and functions of American life, society, and culture—and the answers we arrive at define that character.

What follows is the story of the ongoing trial of the character of American life as it has been shaped by means of contracting and expanding the range of those enjoying the franchise—and thus full membership in the U.S. body politic. The intent is to provide a short, engaging exploration of the various forces that have shaped this debate, both in the formation of vote denial and vote dilution and in their erosion (if not elimination yet) by judicial and legislative action.

As with all books in the On Trial series, *Voting Rights on Trial* achieves its goals by means of two interconnected parts. The first is a series of analytical essays, in four chapters, exploring the history, evolution, and effects of voting rights in the United States. Chapter 1 introduces the topic by means of a short summary of the protracted expansion—and occasional contraction—of voting rights from the colonial period to today, pointing out the dilemmas and potentials posed by the ongoing conflicts over the right of all Americans to vote—or not to vote. Chapter 2 explores in detail the many ways that unpopular or feared groups have been denied the vote, depicting extensive discrimination and exclusion. Chapter 3 delves into the progression, over nearly two centuries, by which courts first enforced vote denial, only later to attack it—in the process becoming some of the most ardent defenders of minority voting rights. Chapter 4 analyzes the legal aftermath of the 2000 presidential election, using *Bush v. Gore* as a window into the future of voting rights in the United States.

Part 2 provides supporting materials intended to help the reader explore and understand the issues raised by the narrative analysis in part 1. It first presents a series of excerpted documents, mostly judicial rulings and opinions, chosen to represent the wide range of issues, problems, and concerns faced by the courts in these matters. Next comes an alphabetical glossary of the people, laws, and concepts discussed in part 1. A chronology follows, organizing these same people, events, and concepts over time. Last, an annotated bibliography of selected secondary sources offers help for readers wishing to explore the topic of voting rights more fully.

Read in tandem, the essays and their supporting materials offer the reader a short but comprehensive introduction to the history and issues of voting rights in the United States. The topic is important, and the story—while often frustrating and even enraging—is absorbing. I hope that the book will engage readers and guide them to a fuller examination of the topic. At the least, I hope this book will raise questions about the society and political system we inhabit and foster both thoughtfulness and contemplation (not to mention action) in our roles as citizen and voter. If this book imparts any lesson, it is that this is *our* country, and the success or failure of its institutions depends on us and our willingness to do our civic duty thoughtfully and rationally. Nothing less than the future of U.S. democracy and free government depends on it.

Before moving on, a few words on how this book came to be written are in order. For the last fifteen years I have been exploring the history of the lowest level of the federal judicial system: the federal district (trial) courts. For the last decade, I have been working on a major project analyzing the role of these courts, in particular the federal district courts of the South, in civil rights matters. As part of this study, about two years ago I began to research voting rights litigation in the late twentieth century, a large segment of which took place in the southern federal district courts. This work was largely completed by the summer of 2000. Then came the 2000 presidential election.

As a Florida constitutional historian who knows something about voting matters—and even more important, as one living at the epicenter of events in south Florida—I found myself drawn into the public debate over the election and its aftermath. Commenting on television, radio, and in print, I was forced to delve deep into my earlier research as I tried to explain to the general public the bizarre events of November and December 2000 (not to mention trying to understand these events myself). In the process I started to see the connections between the voting rights litigation I had been studying and the 2000 election controversy. In particular, I came to recognize the common foundations of both phenomena in our nation's history of vote denial and vote dilution. The Florida election fiasco was not an isolated event. The 2000 election in Florida was marred by a pattern of injustice, ineptitude, and inefficiency based in large part on long-standing exclusionary practices in Florida's election machinery and the failure of state officials to comprehend the problems and to heed warnings of an impending constitutional crisis.

This connection between history and current events interests me the most and resides at the center of this study: the link between change over time and the interaction of social conflicts with political forms and events. As series editor, I felt that recent events dictated the need for a voting rights volume in the series, and I took this need as an opportunity to explore more fully my historical interests in vote denial and vote dilution and the litigation process by which each was attacked and largely eliminated.

I should note that this book does not represent the only way to approach the issue of voting rights. Many analytical, theoretical, and statistical studies provide essential insight into the workings (or nonworkings) of our electoral systems. In fact, this book would not have been possible in its present form without the work of many other scholars. Given the need to compress and summarize a complex subject, I have been forced to stand on the shoulders of such works, and I willingly acknowledge my indebtedness to those scholars working in this field—social scientists, legal scholars, and historians.

In particular, I recognize the debt I owe the work of historian Alexander Keyssar and his magisterial and insightful book, *The Right to Vote*. Although much of the work on which *Voting Rights on Trial* was built had already been completed by the time I read Keyssar's book, his examination of the topic helped me to understand the early origins and development of this process and to appreciate better the contexts of later events with which I was more familiar. Any reader wishing to explore the topic of voting rights in more detail would be wise to start with Keyssar's book.

Charles L. Zelden
Ft. Lauderdale, Florida

Acknowledgments

The truism that no book is written alone—no matter what the author's byline says—is very true in this instance. Many individuals and organizations have aided me in the completion of this book. And I am grateful for all of their help and support.

Most of the research and writing for what became chapter 3 was completed during a semester-long sabbatical leave in the spring of 2000. I am grateful to the board, president, and undergraduate dean of Nova Southeastern University for this opportunity and for the financial support of the Farquhar Center's Faculty Development Fund that provided a $1,000 research grant that helped defray costs while on this sabbatical.

Although they did not know it at the time, the students participating in NSU's Legal Studies Capstone Class (1995–2000) served as a sounding board for many of the ideas and interpretations expressed in this book. I am grateful for their willingness to tackle strange new topics and argue over my occasionally odd interpretations.

My colleagues in the Liberal Arts Department at NSU provided not only moral support but a ready ear, a welcoming shoulder, and a critical perceptiveness as I coped with the stresses associated with writing a book. I am especially thankful to the department chair, Ben Mulvey, the department staff (Santa Alemonte, Maria Converse, Eve Figueroa, Isabelle Biamby, Collette Dillon, and Latoya Williams), and to Professors Stephen Levitt, Gary Gershman, Jim Doan, Scott Stoddart, Karen Vance, and Tim Dixon.

I would also like to thank the anchors and news reporters at WTVJ-NBC 6. Although they were unaware of their role at the time, their willingness to employ my services in explaining the 2000 election to their audience (and by the end, I was on television almost every day) was a true genesis of this book. Without their forcing me to dig deeper and put together disparate pieces of data, I would never have thought to write in more detail than I already had on voting rights.

Chandler Davidson of Rice University provided both practical advice and a comprehensive listing of southern voting rights cases (Table Z as described in his book, *Quiet Revolution in the South*) at the start of my research into voting rights. Both provided essential aid in the writing of Chapter 3.

Alicia Merritt at ABC-CLIO is one of those editors who give editing a good name. Not only did she bring the On Trial series to me in the first place (graciously allowing me to modify the series proposal to fit my own interests and understandings), but her ready support in the writing of this book proved invaluable. Thanks are due as well to the rest of the editorial staff at ABC-CLIO for the fine job they did in editing and producing this book.

Longtime friends Lee Walzer, Brad Cohen, David and Heidi Needleman, Robin Sherman, Kevin Petrich, Ric Burns, Connie Killebrew, David Narrett, Connie Anderson, and Judy Harris all provided much needed support and encouragement.

R. B. Bernstein—colleague, friend, and partner in crime—read every word in this book, often more than once. One of the downsides to writing a volume in a series for which you are series editor is that you lose the second pair of eyes that a series editor provides. For this book, Richard was that editor. Without his help, whatever quality this book has achieved would have been vastly diminished.

I would like to thank my family—my mother Janice, my sister Renee, my wife Lynn, and my daughter Miriam—with as strong a thanks as possible. More than anyone else, they had to put up with the obsessiveness that is my normal writing mode. I know that it was often not easy to be around me as I wrote, and I am indebted to their forbearance and support.

Finally, I would like to dedicate this book to my father, Jerome J. Zelden, who died six years ago, and to my daughter, Miriam Ivy Zelden, born about that same time. As a historian thinking and writing about the past in terms of the past, I often lose sight of the true meaning of the topics I study. As a son and father I cannot.

Voting is not just about the past. It is about the present and the future as well. As a son, I now understand the lessons my father tried to teach me—about history, life, and citizenship. My father taught me that the past has real meaning and importance in the here and now and that it is up to us to apply these lessons wisely. For that insight alone, I will be always beholden to him. As a father, the future suddenly means a whole lot more to me than it once did. My vote, and that of everyone else, suddenly is a lot more important than it used to be. I may study the past, but I now worry about the future. Children have a way of doing that to a person. I only hope I can teach my daughter the lessons my father taught me—and help provide her with a world worth living in based on those lessons.

Part One

1
Introduction

The Strange Career of Voting in the United States

November 7, 2000. Election day. As they do every four years, Americans across the nation went to the polls to cast their vote for president. That night, as was also the norm, the television networks began to report the returns. At first things seemed to be going according to the usual script. One by one, moving generally westward, individual states were called for George W. Bush, the Republican, or Al Gore, the Democrat. At the bottom of the screen, a running count of the electoral college vote (whose number is the important one in choosing the new president) showed one of the closest races in modern U.S. history. Then events departed from the norm. Suddenly, Florida (which, based on exit polls, had been given to Al Gore) was pulled off the table and placed in the too-close-to-call category. A few hours later the networks called the state for George W. Bush, only to restore the state to the too-close column once again. By morning, the issue was still undecided. It would remain undecided for the next thirty-six days. In the end it took a controversial Supreme Court decision to pick the winner in Florida and hence the forty-third president of the United States.

The constitutional equivalent of watching a car *almost* fall off the side of a cliff, the 2000 presidential election controversy was predicated on a simple but unavoidable reality: in a number of states, but especially in Florida, the contest between George W. Bush and Al Gore was too close to call without including every single vote. Even-

3

tually, the difference in Florida would prove to be fewer than five hundred votes out of a total of some six million cast (less than a .005 percent difference). It was this closeness that caused all the problems. In a very real sense, the election was a statistical tie; and given inevitable margins of error and technical mistakes, determining exactly whom the people of Florida (and hence the nation) had chosen for president was a nearly impossible task. Nevertheless, both practical politics and the Constitution required that one of the candidates be declared a winner. The question was, Who? Or more accurately, By what standards or means would we determine who the victor was?

No one disagreed that Al Gore received the majority of votes nationwide. Yet under the Constitution, the national popular vote is not the final determinant of victory. Article II, sections 2–4, of the Constitution lay out the methods by which the president is chosen. Under these sections, each state is assigned a certain number of electors in the electoral college, a majority of whose votes are required to win the presidency. Though the *popular* vote within each state determines who gets all of that state's electoral votes, the magic number for victory is 270 *electoral* votes. On November 8, Al Gore had 268 electoral votes while George W. Bush had 246. With neither candidate holding a clear majority in the electoral college, whoever won Florida with its twenty-five electoral votes would be the victor: win Florida, and win the presidency; lose Florida, and all was lost.

Yet with the vote in Florida so close, the normal mechanics of determining the winner broke down. Suddenly, errors and inconsistencies that in other elections would have been irrelevant became the key to victory or defeat: outdated voting methods, undertrained and overwhelmed volunteer election officials, local control of the voting process with its attendant lack of uniform standards as to what was and was not a proper vote—each had its effect on the election's final outcome. Then there were the claims of race-based intimidation and voter fraud, of confusing ballots and outright vote denial. A great shining spotlight was being thrown on the voting process in Florida and, by association, that of the nation as a whole. The picture illuminated was not a pretty one.

For weeks, broadcasters showed the strange sight of local voting officials hand counting disputed ballots, holding outdated punch cards up to the light to see if the voter had intended to vote or not. Chads (the little pieces of card pushed out of the punch card when a voter properly made a choice) became a part of everyday language. Jokes about pregnant chads and hanging chads filled the airwaves on late-night TV. Furious debates over the standards applied to determine what constituted a valid vote clogged the newspapers, daily TV talk shows, and workplace conversations across the nation.

Things did not get any better when the focus moved from the polls to the courts. Not surprisingly, given this nation's predilection to turn to the courts to settle any and all types of disputes, the Florida electoral train wreck sparked dozens of lawsuits. Actions were filed by voters claiming that their votes had been miscounted and that confusing ballots and obsolete voting machines resulted in their "throwing away" their vote by voting twice for the same office (which invalidated that ballot). African Americans objected to numerous instances in which their names were improperly left off the voting rolls, their polling places had been moved without proper notice, or various forms of explicit or implicit intimidation kept black voters from exercising their franchise. The candidates argued over whether, and how, to count (and if necessary recount) disputed ballots. The courts, in turn, struggled with these issues. Appeals were automatic, and remands and reversals contradicting the logic of the courts below were common. Judges yelled at litigants, lawyers, and one another—even if in only the most proper judicial language. Then there was the spectacle of one U.S. Supreme Court justice seemingly prejudging this important case (Justice Antonin Scalia in the Court's order halting the Florida recount); meanwhile other justices were reduced to grumbling that the majority's opinion, in the words of Justice Stephen Breyer, "runs the risk of undermining the public's confidence in the Court itself," of producing "a self-inflicted wound—a wound that may harm not just the Court but the nation" as the high Court, in effect, chose the president of the United States (*Bush v. Gore*, 557).

The 2000 election breakdown taught many lessons: about the impulses and incentives that shape media decision making; about the political sources of judicial activism; about the workings of the Constitution and our constitutional system; about the racial tensions still unsettling this country. Yet, if the 2000 presidential election demonstrated anything, it imparted the contradictory lessons that in the United States every vote counts and yet, at a very basic level, we really do not want all the people to vote (for if we did, why would we make it so hard to vote?). In fact, it is the tension between what we

need (for people to vote) and what we achieve (people either not voting or being kept from voting) in the operation of the franchise that
may be the most important lesson of the 2000 election.

The Florida election controversy did not just happen without
warning. True, the immediate cause of the crisis was one of the closest presidential elections in U.S. history; and when any vote is that
close, problems are going to crop up. Yet underlying the entire mess
was more than 200 years of ambivalent feelings toward popular
democracy and the vote. For most of our national history, almost as
much effort has gone into denying disliked or despised groups the
vote (or at least diluting the impact of their vote) as was made to
expand the franchise. Women, blacks, Hispanics, immigrants, Native
Americans, the poor, and city folk have all faced at one time or
another organized efforts to obstruct their participation in the political process. As historian Alexander Keyssar notes in his magisterial
history *The Right to Vote,* "for much of American history, the right
to vote has been far from universal" (Keyssar, xvi).

The impact of vote denial is huge. Most Americans believe in
democracy as an ideal and assume that the United States is a democratic nation (which they define as one in which "everyone" can
vote). In fact, most picture U.S. democratic institutions as the standard by which all other democracies should be judged. After all, did
we not fight both a Civil War and two world wars to ensure that, in
Lincoln's immortal phrase, government "of the people, by the people
and for the people" would not perish from the earth? That in practice
we may not be governing ourselves consistently with our democratic ideals is troubling. It calls into question the very nature of U.S.
democracy. As Keyssar concludes, whereas "a nation certainly could
have universal suffrage without being a democracy, a polity cannot
be truly democratic without universal suffrage" (Keyssar, xvi).

Counter to vote denial, of course, is vote expansion. Concurrent
with efforts to deny the vote have come campaigns to expand the
franchise. In fact, efforts to expand who can vote have moved step-
by-step with attempts at vote denial. Although the path toward universal suffrage has been filled with periods of contraction as well as
expansion, the result has been a general (if very slow) movement
toward universal suffrage. Individuals and groups who in the past
have been excluded from the franchise now are permitted to vote.
Women, blacks, ethnic minorities, and even the poor, all groups long
excluded from the polls, now have the right to cast their vote—and

they do so in large numbers. True, the Florida example shows that the more subtle problem of vote dilution (rules and procedures that undermine the impact of a particular group's vote) remains an ongoing concern, yet even here the watchword is improvement.

The fight to expand the right to vote has been fought in many ways and on many levels. Women waged national campaigns to get the vote. So did those who promoted the black franchise. Members of these groups, as well as others, fought local campaigns against the formal and informal vote denial common in most localities. Ultimately, four constitutional amendments explicitly expanded the right to vote (the Fifteenth, the Nineteenth, the Twenty-fourth, and the Twenty-sixth Amendments), two others implicitly affected the franchise (the Thirteenth and Fourteenth), and another increased the range of offices for which Americans could vote directly (the Seventeenth).

One of the more significant forums used to combat vote denial and vote dilution, though, has been the courts. Constitutional amendments and congressional legislation are essential if the right to vote is to be expanded successfully to include excluded groups. Yet, by themselves, they change little. Without enforcement, few real changes are likely to be made. It is here that the courts come into play. The judicial branch is the legal enforcement arm of government. It is the job of judges to interpret the law and apply that interpretation to the particular facts of a case. When the federal government attempts to enforce a civil right, it traditionally turns to the courts as part of that enforcement process. The same holds true for individuals who wish to enforce their rights regarding their own personal contexts and situations. Even though other means of expanding the franchise are both possible and necessary, sooner or later the debate over the right to vote usually ends up in the courts.

Of course, historically the courts were often among the strongest *supporters* of vote denial, upholding discriminatory election rules and permitting election officials to exclude particular groups and individuals from the polls. As agents of established society, judges often viewed their job as protecting the status quo—including limits on the right to vote—not changing it. Still, when change came, the courts usually were part of that process. As was seen with the 2000 election (and as is discussed in detail in chapter 3), much of the debate over vote denial has taken place in the courtroom. Litigation allows otherwise voiceless groups to argue their case and seek remedies to their problems. In time, the courts and the nation as a whole did respond positively to such pleas. Often judges took the lead, creating new rights and empowering the franchise of dispossessed or discriminated-against groups. Yet, even when the ultimate solution to the problem was found elsewhere (in statutory change or constitutional amendments), court cases often were key either to defining the issues prior to statutory change or to applying the new rules afterward.

The debate over who can and cannot vote has been "on trial" in this country from the beginning. The essence of popular government—of who we are, as a people and a nation—rests on the outcome of this trial. Although actual court trials are not the only site for this debate, nor always the most important, they do offer a useful window into the issues and solutions that we have found to the dilemmas of participatory democracy—in particular the clash between democracy's need for expansive participation by all in order to be effective and our social and political desire to limit the vote to only the "right" people. Something had to give, and in the hundred and forty some years since the Civil War, court cases have often been the field where it gave way.

The Right to Vote: A Short History of a Contested Right

Participation in the political process is key to the success of a democracy (or even of a democratic republic as is the United States). As noted earlier, democracy without full participation is really not very democratic. Yet the move toward general suffrage has been a long and tortuous journey. For one thing, democracy has not always been the key component of U.S. government. The founding generation, for instance, had serious concerns about the role of democracy in the formation of the new nation. They worried that a government in which every voice had an equal say in shaping the governing process would be inherently unstable, and this instability concerned them greatly. As James Madison noted in *Federalist #10* (one of a series of published essays explaining and defending the Constitution and long considered a window into the perspectives of the Constitution's writers), "democracies have ever been spectacles of turbulence and contention . . . incompatible with personal security or the rights of property." The problem lay in the danger of faction and discord intrinsic to popular government. The dangers of faction, which Madison defined as "a number of citizens . . . who are united . . . by some common impulse . . . adverse to the rights of other citizens, or to the permanent and aggregate interests of the community," strongly motivated Madison and the other supporters of the new Constitution. The 1780s had been a time of conflict and strife. State had competed with state and, along with political infighting within the states, threatened to undermine the nation's experiment in popular government. "The instability, injustice, and confusion introduced into the public councils, have, in truth, been the mortal diseases under which popular governments have everywhere perished," explained Madison. What the nation needed, the Constitution's supporters argued, was stability. Democracy, unfortunately, was unlikely to control the problems of faction and thus provide the stability the nation so badly craved. "Theoretic politicians, who have patronized this species of government, have erroneously supposed that by reducing mankind to a perfect equality in their political rights, they would, at the same time, be perfectly equalized and assimilated in their possessions, their opinions, and their passions." Sadly, this was not the case. "Pure democracy, . . . can admit of no cure for the mischiefs of faction." For, Madison explained, "the form of government Itself" results in "a common passion or interest" on the part of some which, "in almost every case," produces concerted action for personal profit; that is to say, creates a faction. Once that faction became "a majority of the whole," there was "nothing [in a democracy] to check the inducements to sacrifice the weaker party or an obnoxious individual," and hence the instabilities caused by factions. "In general," Madison sadly concluded, democracies have been "as short in their lives as they have been violent in their deaths" (Hamilton 1961, 77–84).

Instead of democracy, the founders turned to republican forms of government in constructing the Constitution and hence the new national government. Republican government does not try to include everyone in the governing process. Rather, it entrusts the governing power to a smaller number of citizens elected by the whole as representatives. It was argued that this body of representatives offered the advantage of space, distance, and reasoned thought. By sifting popular passions "through the medium of a chosen body of citizens, whose wisdom may best discern the true interest of their country," the founders felt that "patriotism and love of justice" would lead such representatives "to sacrifice" their own personal interest to the common good (Hamilton 1961, 77–84). Where this proved not to be the case, the large size and diversity of the nation, combined with the selection of representatives to run the government, still meant that what factions did form would not be majority factions. Lacking a clear majority, factions posed minimal danger to the well-being of the nation as a whole. As Madison goes on to note:

> [T]he influence of factious leaders may kindle a flame within their particular States, but will be unable to spread a general conflagration through the other States. A religious sect may degenerate into a political faction in a part of the Confederacy; but the variety of sects dispersed over the entire face of it must secure the national councils against any danger from that source. A rage for paper money, for an abolition of debts, for an equal division of property, or for any other improper or wicked project, will be less apt to pervade the whole body of the Union than a particular member of it. . . . In the extent and proper structure of the Union, therefore, we behold a republican remedy for the diseases most incident to republican [in this instance meaning *popular*] government. According to the degree of pleasure and pride we feel in being republicans, ought to be our zeal in cherishing the spirit and supporting [the new Constitution]. (Hamilton, 77–84)

The application of a republican, as opposed to purely democratic, form of government under the Constitution had a significant effect on voting rights in the new nation. True, as with a democracy, republican governments depended on voting to determine policies and pick leadership. However, by emphasizing the idea that one person could represent the interests of another, could somehow legitimately speak for another, republicanism engendered an acceptance of less than universal suffrage. This acceptance fit in well with existing voting practices across the nation in 1787. It also would strongly shape future efforts to grapple with the dilemmas posed by living in an increasingly democratic society (which the nineteenth and twentieth centuries would bring) under a republican form of government. Over time, the nature of popular government in the country was going to change, and, like it or not, the franchise was going to have to change with it.

The Eighteenth Century

For most of the colonial period, the power of the ballot was a closely held right. Not only was it accepted without much debate that women, blacks, Indians, and the young could not vote, but also that those men without property (and hence a stake in society) should be barred from the polls as well. Established wisdom held that dependency on others for the necessities of life—food, shelter, clothing— somehow robbed an individual of the independence of spirit necessary to make the sort of selfless decisions so necessary for popular government to keep at bay the dangers of faction. How could one take a stand for the good of all, when the result of this stand might be starvation or homelessness? The common answer was that one could not. Most colonies therefore imposed specific property qualifications for voting. Only those who owned property, especially such tangible property as land, had made the solid commitment to society so necessary if they were to say no to the seductive inducements of faction and greed, the argument went. For only those with property had the economic foundation to take unpopular stands even at the cost of personal losses and attacks. For similar reasons most colonies imposed limits on "outsiders" voting in an election, assuming they would be unfamiliar with its imperatives. It was with this assumption in mind that colonial politicians excluded from the vote women, minors, blacks, and members of Indian tribes. These groups were limited in their ability to own property, and each was felt to lack the necessary independence to vote. (Of course, even where women or free blacks somehow owned property, they were still denied the vote as alleged inherently dependent persons).

It is unclear just how extensive the franchise actually was in colonial America. Estimates vary from most free white males (due to the relative ease of acquiring the necessary property to vote) to a small fraction of the total white male population. The reality falls somewhere in the middle. For one thing, voting rates varied by colony. In some places where land was cheap, most white males could vote. In others, where land was scarce, or where other impediments limited property ownership, the electorate was quite small. In addition, over time the percentage of white males owning land declined as local populations increased. Ultimately, on the eve of the Revolution, only about 60 percent or less of white males voted in elections.

The coming of the Revolution called into question the limited nature of voting. If the primary cause of our rebellion against Great Britain was a lack of representation in the governing process (the popular refrain of those opposed to British rule was "no taxation without representation"), and voting was the primary means of participating in the selection of representation, should not the new nation expand the franchise to include all people? At the very least, should not all white males, regardless of property ownership, be allowed to vote?

Such thoughts troubled a leadership fostered on the idea of a limited franchise. They also came into conflict with their views on the need for a voter's independence to apply the franchise effectively. Not to mention that in expanding the vote, the control over government by those already permitted to vote would be threatened. Still, many Americans argued that the right to vote was just that, a natural right, inherent in citizenship and the ideals of the Revolution ("all men are created equal"). As "The Watchman" wrote in the *Maryland Gazette* in 1776, "the ultimate end of all freedom is the enjoyment of a right of free suffrage" (quoted in Keyssar, 8). More to the point, how could a nation be truly free when it could tax men without their consent?

Most politically active Americans, however, resisted such overtures to expand the franchise. They made several arguments defending restrictions on the right to vote. The first had to do with the quality of the voting public. In line with earlier arguments against expanding the right to vote, those opposed to an enlarged franchise stressed that, without independence, the voter could not be trusted to do what was best for the community. To this point they added the truism that *franchise,* by its very definition as a term, meant a privilege to vote, not a right to vote. This privilege, in turn, could only be entrusted to those who would use their vote wisely. More serious was a concern that the poor, driven by the needs of their poverty, would band together and threaten the wealth of more established members of society—would, in fact, create the sort of factions that political theory and past experience showed led to instability and chaos. Furthermore, some argued, the vote was not as important as one might think. After all, given the common republican values of the community, the poor would still be virtually represented by those who could vote. So why the fuss?

Perhaps the most effective argument against removing property qualifications for voting was the threat that, if one allowed all white males to vote as a matter of right, then by implication one would have to grant the same rights to blacks, women, and even minors. As John Adams argued as early as 1776, "the same reasoning which will induce you to admit all men who have no property, to vote, . . . will prove that you ought to admit women and children; for, generally speaking, women and children have as good judgments, and as independent minds, as those men who are wholly destitute of property." Depend on it, Adams warned, "new claims will arise; women will demand the vote; lads from twelve to twenty-one will think their rights not enough attended to; and every man who has not a farthing, will demand an equal voice with any other, in all acts of state." There "will be no end of it," Adams concluded (Adams 1856, 377–378).

With such dire warnings before them, it is not surprising that new state constitutions, written during the 1770s to encapsulate the spirit and practicalities of the Revolution, chose to limit popular participation in government even while formally expanding the right to vote. Pennsylvania did away with real property requirements, yet limited the vote to only those white adult males who could afford to pay a poll tax; Maryland significantly lowered the amount of property needed to vote, but still retained property requirements; New Jersey abolished landholding as the standard for voting, but replaced it with the prerequisite that the voter own £50 worth of property, personal or real (land). Rhode Island, Connecticut, and Delaware kept their colonial limits, and Virginia and South Carolina made only superficial changes to the franchise. In the end, only Vermont severed a man's ability to vote from his financial circumstances.

On a more positive note, a number of states did away with religious restrictions on voting for Roman Catholics and Jews. Six granted free blacks the tacit right to vote (they had no law explicitly barring blacks from voting) though three others explicitly retained the ban. New Jersey's Revolutionary constitution even enfranchised (by oversight, not on purpose) single women who could meet the property requirement. (Married women still could not vote, for, under the Common Law rule known as *coverture*, they were represented in politics by their husbands.) Underlying all these changes was the reality that for many white males, meeting newly lowered property qualifications was not difficult. Still, when faced with the opportunity to end property-based limits on the franchise, only Vermont chose to act. More significantly, the *formal* limits on women, blacks, and minors remained in place. As the future was to show, informal access to the polls would prove easy to retract.

So events stood throughout the 1770s and 1780s as economic crisis and political chaos shaped the new nation. By 1787, the U.S. experiment in nationhood was at risk. In response, the Federal Convention assembled in Philadelphia to work out a new structure for national governance. Among the issues debated by the Convention was the question of who should, and should not, be allowed to vote under the new national government. Some delegates argued for a wide national franchise. Benjamin Franklin in particular warned that excluding "the lower class of freemen" from the vote was a dangerous decision likely to undermine the "attachment" of the people to the new government (quoted in Keyssar, 23). Most delegates, however, advocated a more restrictive approach to voting. Conservative in their politics and seriously concerned over the instability of the last decade, delegates such as Gouverneur Morris and James Madison held out for a national freehold (land ownership) requirement to vote. For, as Madison informed the Convention, "the freeholders of the country would be the safest depositories of republican liberty" (quoted in Keyssar, 22).

Ultimately, the Convention chose not to impose a national standard for voting. Although most delegates probably agreed with Elbridge Gerry of Massachusetts that "Democracy" was the "worst ... of all political evils," they understood the practical difficulties that ratifying the Constitution would entail (quoted in Keyssar, 23). Provisions likely to anger the states were problematic. As Oliver Ellsworth of Connecticut explained, "the right of suffrage was a tender point, and strongly guarded by most of the state constitutions. The people will not readily subscribe to the national Constitution, if it should subject them to be disfranchised" (Elliot, 385). The Convention, rather, compromised on the issue of a national franchise, allowing the individual states to determine who could vote in federal elections by linking the federal franchise to that of the states. Where a state permitted someone to vote for the "most numerous Branch of the state legislature," that voter automatically could also vote in elections for federal office (U.S. Constitution, Art. 1, sec. 2).

Of course, in allowing the states as then structured to determine voter qualifications, the Constitution, in effect, limited who could vote federally. Yet, more significant than its immediate restrictive impact, the decision not to impose national voting standards laid the groundwork for an ongoing struggle over the determination of who could vote; a struggle in which the national government lacked any power, outside of amending the Constitution, by which to determine eligibility in federal elections. In a very real sense, national citizenship had been disassociated from the act of voting (for example, women were citizens but still could not vote). As our concept of national citizenship evolved over time, this separation would prove to be a troubling legacy as a growing democratic impulse collided with the limits imposed by federalism—the idea that power is shared between national and state governments and that some issues are the sole concern of the states.

From the Constitution to the Civil War

The seventy years following the ratification of the Constitution transformed the new nation in ways impossible to contemplate even a few years earlier. From its start as a largely rural, postcolonial, third-rate republic hugging the eastern seaboard, the United States remade itself into a mercantile and industrial powerhouse dominating an entire continent. Fueled by a mix of land purchases, annexations, and military conquests, the nation quickly tripled in size to include the Great Plains, Florida, Texas, and the West Coast from Washington to California. Improvements in transportation technology, in turn, allowed people not only to move into these new lands but to exploit the land's resources and transport the results to market. Rapid population growth (from 4 million inhabitants in 1790 to more than 31 million in 1860) further fueled the need for expansion. The result was a massive shift in population westward. Before 1810, only one in seven Americans lived west of the Appalachian Mountains; by 1840 it was one out of every three; 1860 would see this number grow ever closer to one out of every two.

This movement westward, and the various forces promoting this shift, led to many unforeseen consequences. The most damaging was a growing regional split as to lifestyles, labor methods, and political culture among North, South, and West that ultimately would lead to the Civil War. A similar consequence (though one that took longer to make itself felt) was the growing flood of migrants moving to the cities and small industrial towns of the North, bringing attendant change in lifestyle and political, social, and economic needs and requirements. Yet for our purposes, the primary outcome of this movement west was a growing pressure toward popular democracy—at least for white males.

As new states were added to the nation, each needed to hold a constitutional convention to lay out its blueprint for government. Meanwhile, economic, social, and political changes in those states already in the Union led to calls for new conventions to revise or replace what many argued were outmoded and even obsolete constitutions. An explosion in constitution-writing inevitably followed. Between 1790 and 1860 most of the thirty-one states held at least one constitutional convention; many held more than one. Each dealt with the numerous problems associated with social, political, and economic change. Yet foremost in every convention debate were the linked problems of representation (the apportionment of power in the form of legislative seats) and franchise (who could vote). Who should have political power in the state? How should we choose them? These were the underlying questions of most debates in the conventions. One by one, the answer these conventions arrived at was that political power should rest in the hands of most, if not quite all, white males.

First, property qualifications to vote were abandoned. From the 1790s onward, established states dropped their property requirements for white males to vote. More important, no new state joining the Union after 1790 imposed property qualifications on white males to exercise their franchise. By 1855, only three states had any property qualifications left on the books, and each had ways that native-born white males could circumvent these limits. Next came tax-paying requirements that, by 1830, were found in twelve states; between 1830 and 1855, however, six of those states repealed these limits, while the other six lowered their minimal poll tax requirements to the point of irrelevancy. Most states also liberalized their residency requirements for the vote. Some even extended the franchise to aliens. Concurrent changes in the definitions of the words *resident, citizen,* and *white* further liberalized the voting process.

This shift toward universal (white) manhood suffrage had multiple sources. Ongoing economic and demographic transformations along the eastern seaboard resulted in large urban populations, which in turn produced an expanding body of laborers and small shopkeepers who could not meet the property requirements to vote. In some states, the shift toward tenant farming meant that large numbers of farmers were excluded from the polls. Immigration added still more males to the ranks of those denied the vote. Even residents of the new western states would have had trouble proving property ownership and hence getting the vote in a limited franchise system, given the long time lag in gaining title to land. Competition among states for residents, in turn, heightened the tensions created by demographic and economic change. Citizens are a resource, just like land or timber. In the land-rich but people-poor West, migrants meant wealth and development. In the East, people in the cities and towns meant enough hands to supply workers for new industries. The result was a strong competition among states for residents. In this contest, the right to vote was a strong inducement. Extending the right to vote to all white males was a way that western states could induce immigrants to settle there. As one delegate to the 1848 Illinois constitutional convention asked: "[I]s it our policy, as a state burdened with debt and sparsely settled, to restrict the right to suffrage, and thus prevent immigration to our soil?" His answer, and that of the convention, was no (quoted in Keyssar, 38). Meanwhile, easing state rules on residency or property holding gave eastern residents a reason for not leaving.

Social tensions added still more reasons for states to expand the franchise. Given the relative weakness of the national military during most of this period, the primary source of protection within the states came from the militias. The militia rolls, in turn, were usually based on the voting lists. Exclude poor whites males, and the pool of potential defenders of the community was severely limited. Nor could one simply add poor whites to the militia rolls without extending the franchise. Although technically possible, it was politically dangerous. As Reverend Joseph Richardson asked in the 1820 Massachusetts constitutional convention, what would the "ardor" of disenfranchised soldiers be like "when called upon to defend their country?" Not very much, was his answer. Aside from being a dangerous oversight, it also was morally wrong to deny one who served the community a say in that community's governance. These arguments carried extra weight in the South, where fear of black slave uprisings enhanced the need for a strong militia. As one delegate to the 1831–1832 Virginia constitutional convention made clear, the slave-holding states were "fast approaching a crisis . . . a time when freemen will be needed—when every man must be at his post." Would it not be wise then, he asked, "to call together every last free white human being and unite them in the same common interest and Government?" (all quoted in Keyssar, 38).

At root, however, the shift toward universal (white) manhood suffrage was cultural in nature—cultural with an inevitable shift into the political realm. Between 1800 and 1860 the United States underwent a momentous transformation in the very definition of the concept "American." Whereas elite leaders such as George Washington or John Adams had represented the essence of what it meant to be an

American in the eighteenth century, by the 1830s a new standard of "American-ness" was in place: the Common Man. This is not to say that dominant leaders like Washington or Adams did not exist in the new era. Far from it. Inequality and class differences remained as strong in the early nineteenth century as they had been in the late eighteenth. What had changed was the political and cultural market-place in which such leaders had to sell their wares. By the 1840s the average American, with all his numerous faults (greed, materialism, violence, selfishness, self-importance, insecurity) defined the nature of U.S. society. The United States was no longer a place where gen-teel aristocrats or merchant princes set the cultural standards of the day. Instead, it displayed a robust, if crude, national culture of ambi-tion and forcefulness. Everyone (at least all white males) wanted and expected to rise in society. Old limits on behavior and occupation were abandoned; new barriers were vigorously assaulted. That most Americans never actually succeeded in their efforts had little impact on the cultural force of their dreams. Like him or not, the Common Man in Jacksonian America had to be reckoned with.

It was here that culture merged with politics. Capture and harness the energy released by this vibrant culture, and politicians had an enormous pool of energetic voters to rush them into office. Whereas established politicians had little reason to reach out to this new type of American, those out of power did. To do this, however, the new politicians needed to get this mass of humanity the vote. The needs and objectives of partisan politics thus melded with cultural trends to promote universal suffrage. For with every white American male increasingly freed to vote, the power of the new Democratic Party (created by its founders to tap into this cultural energy) expanded—power that they used to extend the franchise further.

The ongoing shift in U.S. culture, in turn, made this expansion eas-ier. By the 1820s, long-held beliefs against extensive voting were under constant attack. What had once seemed obvious now felt archaic and unreasonable. The link between property ownership and citizenship suddenly seemed weak to such people. "Regard for coun-try did not depend upon property," argued J. T. Austin of Boston in 1820, "but upon institutions, laws, habits and associations." The nonfreeholders of Richmond agreed with this view in 1829. "To ascribe to a landed possession, moral or intellectual endowments," they noted, "would truly be regarded as ludicrous, were it not for the gravity with which the proposition is maintained, and still more for the grave consequences that flow from it." For, as a delegate to the 1845 Louisiana constitutional convention made clear, "if a man can *think* without property, he can *vote* without property." (all quoted in Keyssar, 43, 50).

The result was that, by the Civil War, most white males could vote. The only restrictions on white male voting were new bans imposed by many states on felons, paupers, and the mentally incompetent, along with the continuing limits that some states enacted against voting by migrants (noncitizens, recent arrivals to the state). The general assumption was that so long as a white male retained legal independence (was not a pauper), obeyed the rules of society (was not a felon), was mentally competent, and was a local resident (or citizen in some states), he could vote.

When we look at the remainder of society, however, the picture remained bleak. In fact, existing limits on blacks and women not only were maintained, but were generally increased after 1790. Not a single state granted women the vote during the first half of the nineteenth century. Where women had been able to vote by legislative oversight, as with New Jersey's unintended grant of the vote to property-owning single women, such laws were repealed. The situation was even worse for African Americans. Most early state constitutions, in the South as well as the North, had lacked any explicit restrictions on free black voting. This began to change in the early nineteenth century. In 1820, New Jersey, Maryland, and Connecticut expressly limited the vote to whites. The next year, New York, while removing property qualifications for white males, imposed them (along with residency requirements) for blacks—in the process disenfranchising most of the state's African American residents. North Carolina's 1835 convention added the word *white* to its requirement to achieve the same result. Meanwhile, every state entering the Union after 1819 included explicit bans on black voting in their constitutions. In fact, by the eve of the Civil War, only Maine, Vermont, New Hampshire, Massachusetts, and Rhode Island (which together held only 4 percent of the nation's black population) permitted African Americans to vote.

From the Civil War to World War I

Such was the situation as the nation moved from the Civil War through the remainder of the nineteenth century and into the early years of the twentieth. As with the first half of the nineteenth century, the second half was a time of intense, even wrenching, change. Political events, such as the Civil War and the Reconstruction that followed, quickly merged with structural changes, such as massive increases in population, immigration, and industrial production, to shake the nation's social, political, and economic foundations. The nation's cities, which as late as 1860 housed only one in six Americans, by 1900 were home to one out of every three. The gross national product increased from a mere $7 billion in 1860 to some $35 billion in 1900. The national labor force grew from around 13 million in 1860 to over 19 million by century's end. Then there were the 30 to 40 million new immigrants settling in this country—most of whom were Catholics or Jews from Southern and Eastern Europe lacking the ability to speak English and never having lived in an urban environment.

Changes such as these were profoundly wrenching, and most U.S. institutions were affected by such shifts. Yet, as related to voting, the effects of these changes were less extreme than those of the first sixty years of the century had been. For one thing, by 1860 most white males had the vote. This meant that any increase in access to the polls would have to enfranchise women, aliens (immigrants), or African Americans—all groups facing significant resistance to any expansion of their civil rights. Not that efforts to open the franchise to these groups were abandoned. The fight to extend the vote continued unchecked following the Civil War. Most male immigrants, whatever their origin, grasped the right to vote as soon as they qualified for citizenship; and for a time, even black males shared this right. Yet, by the eve of World War I, the general trend in voting rights was downward, retreating from vote expansion toward explicit vote denial and implicit vote dilution. Despite the best efforts of numerous groups and individuals—not to mention two constitutional amendments directly relating to the issue of civil rights and the right to vote—as the United States entered the new century, those on the political or social margins of public life were still excluded from the franchise.

As regarded women, the method by which they were denied the vote was depressingly simple. Despite years of ever increasing pressure from suffrage groups, the men who ran this nation were simply unreceptive to the equal rights arguments of women reformers. When reformers pointed out the inconsistency of granting the vote to former male slaves, yet denying women the same right (after all, if all men were created equal, as the founding documents proclaimed, even black men, should not all women, and especially white women, be granted the same rights?), the politicians and the courts simply did nothing. When later in the century, similar arguments were made regarding undesirable immigrants, the initial response was the same. Inaction was the only strategy that the opponents of female suffrage needed if they wished to keep women from the polls. Although arguments posing women as the counterweight to dangerous immigrant men would, for a time, prove fruitful, on the eve of World War I only seven states had granted full voting rights to women and only a handful more permitted women to vote for school boards or in municipal elections.

Immigrants and other groups defined as undesirable faced a different sort of voting discrimination. As the shift in women's suffrage arguments noted earlier shows, many in the country viewed the millions of foreigners coming to our shores as a threat. As Carrie Chapman Catt, leader of the National American Woman Suffrage Association would argue around the turn of the century:

> Today there has arisen in America a class of men not intelligent, not patriotic, not moral, nor yet not pedigreed. In causes and conventions, it is they who nominate officials, at the polls through corrupt means, it is they who elect them and by bribery, is it they who secure the passage of many a legislative measure. (quoted in Keyssar, 198)

Immigrant voters were viewed by many as irresponsible, prone to voter fraud and the selling of their vote. All the ills and problems of big city "boss rule" were placed at the feet of immigrant voters. Worse yet, even where they did not sell their vote to the bosses, it was widely believed that immigrants were likely to be dangerous radicals, supporting unions, socialism, and even communism.

Yet as white males, immigrant men could vote, given existing state law. This meant that efforts to minimize the allegedly negative impact of such nonnative voters had to take the form of vote dilution, rather than vote denial (short of implementing hard-to-justify limits for white males who already had the vote). Vote dilution occurs when those in the majority systematically use voting rules, procedures, or practices to diminish the ability of a particular subgroup to vote for candidates of its choice. Put simply, vote dilution takes place when those in charge make it so difficult to vote, or make the voting process so complicated, that certain voters find that their vote has no meaning—and thus are effectively disenfranchised. This is exactly what happened to immigrants in the late nineteenth and early twentieth centuries. Faced with a concerned native electorate, state legislatures rewrote election statutes, updating such procedures as "the timing of elections, the location of polling places, the hours that polls would be open, the configuration of ballots, and the counting of votes" (Keyssar, 127). Other changes included legislative districting that undervalued the votes of urban voters, poll taxes that kept poor voters from the polls, literacy tests that kept immigrants from acquiring the citizenship they needed to vote, and strict rules requiring preregistration for voting. Most intrusive were municipal reforms that effectively transferred power from immigrant majorities toward more affluent native elites. Although in some cases the reforms were legitimate efforts to organize or clean up the election process (for by the early twentieth century, politics had become a corrupt and often venal enterprise), in most cases the changes made had the principal (or only) purpose to limit either the vote, or the impact of the vote, of immigrants. The result was a persistent undervaluation of the potential votes of city-dwelling immigrants in all but the largest of U.S. cities.

Offensive as such limits were, they were mild when compared to the South's efforts to deny African Americans the electoral fruits of the Union's victory in the Civil War. With the end of the Civil War, hope dawned for the nation's millions of African Americans. The Emancipation Proclamation, initially adopted as a war measure but seen by the end of the war as an enduring shift in race relations, effectively freed southern black slaves. This shift was made permanent with adoption of the Thirteenth Amendment in 1865. The requirement that "neither slavery nor involuntary servitude . . . shall exist within the United States," in turn, was understood by the Amendment's Republican authors and most Northerners and Westerners to mean that newly freed blacks would acquire all aspects of freedom, including citizenship and the right to vote. Unfortunately, the South's white inhabitants were not inclined to comply with that meaning. Regaining power soon after the war's end under Presidential Reconstruction, officials and legislatures of the former Confederate states adopted harsh laws, known as Black Codes, aimed at depriving the newly freed slaves of all of the substance of freedom. This included the vote.

Given the South's refusal to accept the command of the Thirteenth Amendment, congressional Republicans soon wrested control over Reconstruction away from the president and quickly proposed the Fourteenth Amendment (ratified in 1868). Aimed squarely at the Black Codes, the Fourteenth Amendment defined national citizenship, upheld a citizen's rights to due process under the law, and prohibited public discriminations that undermined the "privileges or immunities of citizens of the United States." One of those privileges and immunities was the right to vote. Congressional Republicans hoped that by merging the votes of black freedmen with white southern unionists, southern blacks would soon acquire the means to protect themselves from discrimination by electing candidates of their choice into public office. Yet for this to happen, they had to ensure blacks an effective franchise. This proved to be a difficult task. Despite two constitutional amendments and the Civil Rights Act of 1866, the South still refused to abide by the law, attacking blacks' right to vote with public discrimination wherever possible and private intimidation in all cases.

Frustrated with the lack of black electoral success, Congress responded with a third constitutional amendment aimed explicitly at the right to vote (the Fifteenth). This time Congress was serious. Black males had the right to vote, the amendment starkly declared, and no state had the right to deny them that vote: "The right of citizens of the United States to vote shall not be denied or abridged by the United States or by any State on account of race, color, or previous condition of servitude." Combined with the equal protection clause of the Fourteenth Amendment, the law's intent could not be made much clearer, or so congressional Republicans believed. Congress soon followed up the Fifteenth Amendment with the Civil Rights Enforcement Act of 1870 forbidding state elections officials from enforcing discriminatory state election laws or from using violence, intimidation, bribery, or force to interfere with voting. This was soon joined by the Ku Klux Klan Act in 1871, which made it a federal crime for individuals, as well as government officials, to deprive a person of citizenship rights, equal protection of the laws, and/or privileges and immunities—including the right to vote. U.S. attorneys across the South responded quickly to the new laws, bringing federal criminal indictments aimed at upholding black rights to an open franchise. By the end of 1871, the federal government had initiated 1,193 criminal enforcement cases, bringing 271 to trial.

There were even a number of victories at court, leading one North Carolina federal judge to tell his wife, "we have broken up the Ku Klux" (Kaczorowski, 94).

Sadly, this renewed effort to uphold black voting rights soon waned. By 1873, faced with the need to cut the federal budget in increasingly hard economic times and concerned over fading support for Reconstruction by a northern population turning increasingly inward in their interests, the Grant administration put a halt to vigorous prosecution of southern race-based discrimination. That same year the Supreme Court handed down its decision in the *Slaughterhouse Cases*. Though not explicitly concerned with issues of race (the case had to do with state regulations of slaughterhouses in New Orleans), the case had profound consequences for civil rights—and for voting. In his majority opinion, Justice Samuel F. Miller ruled that the Fourteenth Amendment should be limited to its original purpose of guaranteeing the privileges and immunities of former black slaves. Unfortunately, in doing this, Miller identified some privileges and immunities as national and some as local—and thus he severed national citizenship from state citizenship. Worse yet, in defining exactly which privileges and immunities were national and which local, Miller placed the civil rights most important to everyday life, including those protecting voting rights, in the state category. The result "consigned [blacks] to the ingenuities, subterfuges, and legal chicane of white Democrats already returning to power in the South" by means of the sort of intimidations and frauds that the two enforcement acts were supposed to halt (Hyman and Wiecek, 478). One year later, a federal judge in Texas held that no federal rights were infringed when a mob of whites attacked a black man for testifying in court against them. Two years after that, a unanimous Supreme Court in *United States v. Cruikshank* ruled that murder, even the mass murder of more than 100 blacks in a race riot, did not deprive the injured of their federally protected civil rights. Murder, the high Court declared, was a state matter best handled in the state courts. *United States v. Reese*, handed down the same year (1876), produced a similar restrictive result. A final blow came with the so-called Compromise of 1877, in which the Democrats and Republicans cut a deal in settling the contested 1876 presidential election allowing the Republican candidate, Rutherford B. Hayes, to win the presidency but granting the southern-dominated Democrats an end to Reconstruction. No longer would the national government concern itself with the South's handling of race relations; combined with the Supreme Court's limiting of the Civil Rights Amendments in *Slaughterhouse* and *Cruikshank,* this agreement effectively abandoned blacks to the not-so-gentle mercies of southern whites. Before long Jim Crow segregation, race violence, and other denials of equal rights to African Americans were the norm in the South.

In terms of black voting rights, the end of Reconstruction and the subsequent abandonment of southern blacks produced a sharp retreat toward vote denial. Free to act as they wished, southern state governments adopted a series of practices and procedures (described in detail in chapter 2) explicitly aimed at denying blacks the vote. Combining unofficial intimidation and violence with official impediments to black voting, the result was the near total disenfranchisement of southern black males by the turn of the century. Where once southern blacks had served as party chairpersons and had been able to elect black members to Congress, they were now politically voiceless. So circumstances would remain for almost the next 100 years.

The Twentieth Century

The last two thirds of the twentieth century began on a high note as regarded voting rights. After over half a century of organized effort, women won the right to vote by constitutional amendment. Ratified in 1920, the Nineteenth Amendment stated that "the right of citizens of the United States to vote shall not be denied or abridged . . . on account of sex." No longer could women be barred from the polls solely on account of their gender. The numerical majority (women) finally had a voice in the governing process.

The victory of women's suffrage in 1920 would not have been possible without two shifts in strategy by those demanding the vote. The first shift grew out of the interaction between political strategy and institutional and constitutional contexts. The increasingly obvious failure of the state-by-state approach to reform dictated the need for a new political strategy. Despite five decades of effort, by the turn of the century the cause of women's suffrage had stalled. Although by 1900 twenty-eight states granted women some voting rights (mostly the limited right to vote for school boards), and four states had granted the complete franchise, most other states (among them the most populous, such as New York) refused to extend the franchise to women. The problem was not just male opposition to a female franchise. Although sexism clearly had its part in the suffrage move-ment's difficulties, structural impediments also played a significant role. Many states had elaborate, complex, and multilayered amend-ment processes for their state constitutions. Changing these constitu-tions was both costly and time-consuming. Add in the ongoing opposition of many men to change, and state constitution-based structural impediments made changing state franchise law difficult to achieve at best, near impossible at worst. Amending the national Constitution, on the other hand, was comparatively simple. All Arti-cle V requires for an amendment is a two-thirds vote of both houses of Congress, followed by ratification by simple majorities in the state legislatures of three-fourths of the states. To be sure, obtaining the support of three-fourths of the states was not an easy task, but given that by 1918 thirteen states had joined the original four in recogniz-ing a woman's right to vote in all elections, and thirteen others now permitted women to vote for president, a three-fourths vote was not out of reach, even with the deep-seated opposition of some states. Convince a dozen or so states to vote yes, and women nationwide would have the vote.

The second shift was organizational and ideological. Before the early twentieth century, the suffrage movement was largely elitist in both its membership and its message. The shift toward a conserva-tive, anti-immigrant tone to suffrage's message in the late 1800s brought immediate successes, but in the long term posed serious lim-itations. By stressing the idea that some people were not good enough to vote, women reformers played into the hands of those who sought to limit the voting of all unwanted groups—women as well as undesirable men. The lack of success in the early years of the twentieth century was the result. This view also alienated the suffrage movement from potential allies and supporters in the wider working-class and reform communities. Only by changing its restrictive mes-sage could the suffrage movement become a truly mass movement and gain the force necessary to shift entrenched political powers and gain the vote. Turning to working-class women and the reformist Progressive movement, supporters of the vote for women now stressed the link between social reform and female suffrage; in doing so they effectively expanded their movement into a mass movement, gained allies in various reform parties, and even, in time, political bosses (who could read the writing on the wall), and thus gained the clout necessary to get not only Congress to act, but three-fourths of the states as well. Add in the propaganda value of women's war efforts in World War I, the suffragists' claim that enfranchising women would break the corrupting power of the liquor industry, and the Nineteenth Amendment was the result.

Approved by Congress on May 19, 1919, the Nineteenth Amendment was swiftly adopted by the states, gaining the necessary thirty-sixth vote when Tennessee ratified the Amendment by a one-vote majority on August 18, 1920. One week later the secretary of state certified the vote and the Nineteenth Amendment went into affect. Ironically, women gained the vote just as the nation as a whole began a century-long decline in voter turnout. Despite a near-doubling of the electorate around 1920, women voters caused few changes in the outcomes of elections; the same parties largely elected the same candidates after the Nineteenth Amendment as before. Although the issues these candidates and parties were forced to contend with no doubt changed as a result of hundreds of thousands of new female voters, the overall impact was evolutionary, not revolutionary. Women had the vote, but it would take a couple more generations before their presence in the electorate was used to force significant change in government and society.

It took African Americans even longer to achieve their electoral goals, and with less immediate success and fewer easily won victories. Stymied by the late nineteenth century on the political front by the full implementation of Jim Crow segregation, blacks turned to the federal courts to gain access to the polls and other basic civil rights. Sadly, the Supreme Court proved unwilling to help. In 1896's *Plessy v. Ferguson,* the high Court granted constitutional legitimacy to segregation by invoking the new constitutional doctrine of "separate but equal." Although not involving voting rights, the Court's decision in *Plessy* cast a pall on all efforts to defend black civil rights from public attack, including the eroding right to vote. Not until the 1920s would black civil rights groups make serious, organized efforts to combat racism and segregation. Once again, these efforts concentrated largely on the remedies provided by the federal courts. Despite fifty years of negative Supreme Court doctrine, civil rights groups still saw the courts as their best hope for change.

In terms of voting, the renewed effort to tear down the limits of segregation and racism focused first on the all-white primaries common across the South. One of the most successful ways that southern whites kept black votes from having any real meaning, all-white primaries worked by excluding blacks from the only election that really mattered in the one-party South, the Democratic Party primary. Given that the Democratic nominee always won the election in the South, the all-white primary made voting in the general election a largely meaningless act. It also made the Democratic primary the prime forum for making one's electoral choices known. Barred by either party rules or state law from this primary, even where they somehow managed to register to vote, blacks were unable to help select the Democratic Party candidates for office and thus to help choose the leaders of state government.

Organized under the leadership of the National Association for the Advancement of Colored People (NAACP), but driven by local members of the affected communities, efforts to throw out the all-white primary first mobilized in Texas. The fight lasted twenty years, most of that time filled with failures and outright refusals by the courts to hear the African American community's cries for help. But finally, in the 1940s, the Supreme Court responded. Ruling in *Smith v. Allwright,* the high Court held racial limits on voting in primaries unconstitutional. If a black met the qualifications to register to vote in the general election, he or she should be allowed to vote in the primaries as well, the justices ruled. The all-white primary was dead in Texas. Soon it was gone across the South.

Of course, the decision to allow blacks to vote in primary elections was founded on their ability to register to vote in the first place. Southern segregationists quickly responded to the Supreme Court's rulings by toughening the already daunting rules keeping blacks from registering to vote. Combined with informal violence and intimidation, these efforts kept most blacks from the polls and brought still another twenty-year fight by African Americans to gain the vote. Carried out both in the federal courts and the court of public opinion, this struggle to overcome limits to black registration built steam throughout the fifties and early sixties. The Supreme Court's 1954 decision striking down school segregation in *Brown v. Board of Education* helped. So too did passage of federal Civil Rights Acts in 1957, 1960, and especially 1964. There were even some key victories in southern federal district courts in Alabama, Louisiana, and South Carolina. Still, as late as 1962, only a small percentage of southern blacks were registered to vote. In Mississippi, the number stood at only 1.98 percent; other states' numbers were higher, but not by much.

Frustrated by this state of affairs, the Southern Christian Leadership Conference (SCLC) under the leadership of Rev. Martin Luther King Jr. contemplated more direct forms of action on voting rights. They understood that new laws were necessary if real change were to come to the South. The problem was how to get cautious politicians to act. President Lyndon B. Johnson, in common with most white national political leaders at this time, viewed black voting rights from a largely legal perspective. The idea was to do away with arbitrary barriers keeping blacks from registering, and then to allow them to use this access to gain political power through the polls. From such power, the president argued, "many other breakthroughs would follow, and they would follow as a consequence of the blacks man's own legitimate power as an American citizen, not as a gift from the white man" (quoted in Lawson 1976, 300). Yet until southern intransigence both in Congress and the region was overcome, President Johnson did not plan on introducing any new voting rights legislation.

In an effort to rectify this situation, a frustrated SCLC took the risky step of organizing a 1965 voting registration drive in Selma, Alabama, in the hope that the expected violent response to the march by local white officials would increase public pressure for a voting rights act with real teeth in it. Successful in their hopes for a public spectacle (under the leadership of racist Selma sheriff, Jim Clark, the state police used what was recognized as unjustified violence against the protesters, including mass arrests and frequent beatings of demonstrators), they were also successful in putting pressure on Congress and the president to act in these matters. In March 1965, President Johnson called on Congress to pass a new voting rights act in sweeping terms:

> Every device of which human ingenuity is capable has been used to deny the black citizen his right to vote. It is wrong—deadly wrong—to deny any of your fellow Americans the right to vote in this country. . . . The black American's actions and protests, his courage to risk safety and even to risk his life, have awakened the conscience of this nation. [There must be] no delay, no hesitation, no compromise with our purpose. (quoted in Ball et al., 47)

Johnson signed the resulting Voting Rights Act (VRA) into law in August 1965; its enactment would change the character of voting rights forever.

Totaling nineteen sections, the 1965 act was a mix of permanent rule changes regulating the voting process nationwide and temporary special provisions designed to attack specific racial injustices in the South. Before the 1980s, it would be the temporary provisions (found primarily in sections 4 through 9 and renewed and amended in 1970, 1975, and 1982) that had the greatest impact on black voting rights. Thereafter, it would be the permanent section 2 that carried the weight of change. In each case, the act placed authority to protect black voting rights directly in the hands of the executive branch. Federal authorities implemented this objective in three ways.

The first way was by the creation of what was called a triggering formula in section 4 that imposed federal executive authority over any state that employed such voter limiting devices as literacy tests to determine voter qualifications, and where, as of November 1, 1964, less than 50 percent of voting-age residents were registered. Those states that failed this test (between 1965 and 1975, this group included six southern states and part of a seventh) automatically fell under the jurisdiction of the act's other requirements.

Next came a direct assault on the tools of vote denial then in use across the South. Also found in section 4, this part of the VRA abolished the most significant barriers to black voting: literacy tests, "good moral character" and/or "understanding" exams, and the requirement for a registered voter to "vouch" for a potential voter. Extended for another five years by Congress in 1970, this prohibition was made permanent in 1975, at which time an additional triggering formula added states, such as Texas, that discriminated against language-minorities groups (Hispanics, Asian Americans and Native Americans).

Last, sections 5 through 9 expanded the federal government's power and authority to implement these and other reforms. Most important in this regard was section 5, which attempted to check the seemingly endless cycle by which southern states replaced one discriminatory law with another every time the old requirements were either suspended or declared unconstitutional. To achieve this end, all state voting statutes and procedures in place as of November 1, 1964, were frozen pending federal approval for any proposed changes. This meant that any state or county covered by section 4's triggering formula that sought to modify its voting laws had to "preclear" these changes by submitting the proposed revision to the Justice Department and proving that the planned changes did "not have the purpose and . . . [would] not have the effect of denying or abridging the right to vote on account of race or color." All changes not precleared by the Justice Department (which had sixty days to object) were legally barred from implementation. Alternatively, a state could file for a declaratory judgment with the U.S. District Court for the District of Columbia; a positive response by this court served the same purpopse as preclearance by the Justice Department.

Of lesser importance than section 5, but still significant in terms of promoting change, sections 6 and 7 granted the attorney general jurisdiction to appoint federal voting examiners to certify that legally qualified voters were free to register. Section 8 permitted the attorney general to assign, as needed, federal observers to oversee the actual voting process in those areas covered by the triggering formula. Section 9 laid out the procedures for challenging the voter lists drawn up by federal examiners. Other sections defined the terms *vote* or *voting* for purposes of the act (section 14), set out criminal penalties for violating the act (section 12), prohibited voter fraud and outlawed any action "under color of the law" from preventing qualified voters from voting or having their votes fairly counted (section 11), and "suggested" to the attorney general that he bring suit challenging the poll taxes still in use in four states (section 10). Finally, section 2 prohibited discrimination in voting based on race or color, the only one of the permanent sections to have any real impact on voting rights litigation (at least after being amended in 1982 to emphasize that proof of an intent to discriminate was not necessary to initiate reform, merely proof of discriminatory effect).

Expressly designed to attack the perceived sources of almost 100 years of delay and obstructionism to voting rights reform, the nineteen sections of the 1965 act imposed a completely new enforcement methodology for voting rights violations. No longer could intransigent southern officials cheat qualified black voters from their franchise unhindered and without negative consequences. The right to vote was now a national right, enforced by national authorities. The Fifteenth Amendment's promise that "the right of citizens . . . to vote . . . not be denied or abridged" was finally to be met.

Of course, as was the norm in voting rights matters, fulfilling this promise proved more difficult than its making had been. On the positive side, Justice Department lawyers quickly, and successfully, challenged in the courts such blatant methods of vote denial as poll taxes and literacy tests; clear cases of voter fraud by election officials were also quickly terminated. By the end of the 1960s, voter registration rolls swelled with new African American voters—voters who now applied their franchise with near total freedom.

However, when it came to more subtle forms of vote denial and especially of vote dilution, change came more slowly. In 1962's *Baker v. Carr* and 1964's *Reynolds v. Sims,* the Supreme Court had ruled that diluting an individual's vote through excessively malapportioned districting (wherein legislative districts had vastly different numbers of voters yet still elected the same number of representatives) was unconstitutional. "[A]n individual's right to vote for state legislators is unconstitutionally impaired when its weight is, in a substantial fashion, diluted when compared with votes of other citizens living in other parts of the state," declared the justices (*Baker v. Carr,* 268). In its place, the high Court mandated that legislative districts be organized to serve roughly equal populations. Only then could each person's vote be truly equivalent in its impact. The new standard was "one person, one vote," and any legislative districting that perpetuated imbalance no longer would be permitted (*Reynolds v. Sims,* 535). The problem was that many forms of race-based vote dilution and denial did not conflict with the one-person-one-vote requirement. Forcing voters to vote for a full slate of candidates, or to provide a majority vote to elect a particular candidate—both common forms of race-based vote dilution—in no way lessened the comparable effect that every individual's vote had on the election. Considered one-on-one, under such regimes black votes had an equal chance to influence an election's outcome as compared to white votes. Even race-conscious gerrymandering specifically designed to submerge concentrated black communities into white majorities did not conflict explicitly with *Baker* if the districts so created were of equal size.

Responding to these dilemmas, the Supreme Court in 1969's *Allen v. State Board of Elections* ruled that section 5 of the Voting Rights Act encompassed vote dilution as well as vote denial discriminations. Invoking the one-person-one-vote requirement of *Reynolds v. Sims,* the Court concluded that

> the right to vote can be affected by a dilution of voting power as well as by an absolute prohibition on casting a ballot. . . . Voters who are members of a racial minority might well be in the majority in one district, but in a decided minority in the county as was whole. This

type of change could therefore nullify their ability to elect the candidate of their choice just as would prohibiting them from voting.

With this point in mind, the Court rejected all efforts to read section 5 narrowly: "The Voting Rights Act was aimed at the subtle, as well as . . . obvious, state regulations which have the effect of denying citizens their right to vote because of their race," Chief Justice Earl Warren proclaimed. (*Allen v. State Board of Elections*, 556–560, 569). All efforts to dilute the voting strength of minorities were thus constitutionally prohibited.

Allen proved to be an important step in the fight against race-based vote dilution. First, in ruling that vote dilution was covered by section 5 preclearance requirements, the Court freed the Justice Department to prohibit future shifts to at-large elections and other methods of vote dilution. More significantly, the *Allen* decision was a call to arms for the federal courts to attack existing vote dilution laws and procedures. Drawing on standards laid out by the justices in 1973's *White v. Regester*, and further helped out by Congress's 1982 revision of section 2 of the VRA to include vote dilution under its provisions (including an explicit provision for the negative effects of racial vote dilution to serve as proof of wrongdoing), the door opened to literally hundreds of vote dilution suits. Whereas determining the existence of discriminatory effect was never an easy task, by the end of the 1980s the result was a near total reorganization of southern political forms.

Across the South, at-large election systems were replaced with a system of calculated safe minority electoral districts (so called minority-majority districts) organized in rough proportion to the percentage of minority voters within the district. Black officeholding in the South quickly exploded. Numbering fewer than a hundred in 1965, black elected officials in the seven southern states originally targeted by the VRA totaled some 3,265 in 1989—9.8 percent of all elected officials in these states. Similar, if untabulated, gains were made in other states and by non–African American minorities as well. To be sure, increases in minority officeholding did not necessarily alter the material condition of the lives of minorities in the United States. Still, given that as late as 1944 only about 3 percent of southern blacks were even registered to vote, and none had held elected office in and of itself. this rise in southern black officeholding was truly extraordinary—a reconstruction of southern political power structures so profound that its outcome was nothing less than a quiet revolution in southern politics.

Of course, the story did not end here. As is normally the case when it comes to issues of race and rights in this country, the rise of minority-majority districts generated a backlash. Problems soon arose over the drawing of minority-majority districts. Federal judges might intone that the "Voting Right Act does not extend race-based political entitlements to blacks or other minorities and does not secure the right of proportional representation," but in practice this rule was often effectively ignored as judges set about the task of fashioning remedies to racial vote dilution (*Wesley v. Collins,* 802). Experience argued that, for minority voters to elect the candidates of their choice, they needed districts incorporating at least 65 percent minority voters—or, at least, something approaching 65 percent. Anything less, and the court would merely "supplant a plan which denies minorities the opportunity to elect candidates with another one which does the same thing" (Parker 1984, 112). Yet to arrive at this magic 65 percent number, the states were forced to draw extremely convoluted district boundary lines with results that often were—in the words of Justice Sandra Day O'Connor in 1993's *Shaw v. Reno*— "bizarre," "irregular," and "egregious" in form. The district under attack in *Shaw,* for instance, was

> approximately 160 miles long and, for much of its length, no wider than the I-85 corridor. It winds in snake-like fashion through tobacco country, financial centers, and manufacturing areas "until it gobbles in enough enclaves of black neighborhoods." (*Shaw v. Reno,* 509 U.S. 630–631)

Although many were willing to pay the price of irregularity to achieve the goal of minority representation, five of the justices in the *Shaw* case were not; writing for this majority, Justice O'Connor argued that where district lines were drawn *solely* on account of race, even if intended to help minorities gain representation in government, such districts were unconstitutional. Proof of intent, in turn, could be determined (at least in some cases) by the shape of the district. Where district lines lacked regularity and cohesion, Justice O'Connor argued, such districts were suspect as to the intent behind their construction. Where it could then be proven that the purpose behind the strange shape was to gather enough minorities to construct a minority-majority district (in large part by the existence of these large numbers of minority voters), such efforts were illegal.

The impact of *Shaw v. Reno* was electric. By upholding a challenge to a minority-majority district, the high Court threatened the entire enforcement structure built up under the Voting Rights Act. If race-conscious districting was not allowed, and yet districts of at least 65 percent minority voters were necessary to elect minority candidates, then twenty years of African American electoral gains were at risk. Although the *Shaw* decision, along with others that followed, did not explicitly outlaw race-based districting, as the nation moves into the twenty-first century, the issue of minority representation remains an open and contested question.

Conclusion

We come full circle now to the 2000 election and the case of *Bush v. Gore.* As the mess in Florida shows, for all the gains made in extending the vote to every American (and whatever else one can say about the history of voting in this country, the franchise today is available to most citizens), the legacy of vote denial and dilution remains strong. The Constitution left control of the election process in the hands of the states. Local and racial politics, in turn, led the states to limit in numerous ways the availability of the vote. Although constitutional amendments, Supreme Court rulings, and congressional statutes have attempted to regain this power for the national government, the basic power to control (and hence limit) the election process remains in local hands. When it comes to voting, federalism remains the controlling doctrine. Yet the countervailing right of all citizens to the franchise challenges this localism. For how can we be an effective democracy if some of the people are not allowed to vote? Tensions and confusion are the ongoing result.

This is the dilemma facing the nation today. As noted earlier, the Florida election controversy did not just happen. The underlying source of the crisis rested upon more than 200 years of ambivalent feelings about popular democracy and the vote. How we choose to settle this quandary is important. The tension between what we need (for people to vote) and what we achieve (people either not voting or being kept from voting) in the operation of the franchise defines the effectiveness of our political system. Are we a democratic nation? Are we willing to treat all Americans equally in the exercise of their right to vote? Does the Constitution demand equal protection for all voters in the use of their franchise? Should it? Just how are we to define this equality? Such questions lie at the heart of our sense of nationhood (not to mention the conflict over who got to be president in 2000), and such are the questions that we as a people must answer if we hope to live up to our national ideals of a democratic government under the rule of law. In a very real sense, it is not just the right to vote that is "on trial," but our very nature as a people and a nation. As the 2000 election shows, the jury is still out.

References and Further Reading

Adams, Charles Francis, *The Works of John Adams, Second President of the United States,* vol. 9 (Boston: Little, Brown, 1856).

Adams, Willi Paul, *The First American Constitutions: Republican Ideology and the Making of the State Constitutions in the Revolutionary Era* (Chapel Hill: University of North Carolina Press, 1980).

Argersinger, Peter H., "The Value of the Vote: Political Representation in the Gilded Age," *Journal of American History* 76 (June, 1989): 59–90.

Ball, Howard, Dale Urane, and Thomas P. Lauth, *Compromised Compliance: Implementation of the 1965 Voting Rights Act* (Westport, CT: Greenwood, 1982).

Belknap, Michal R., *Federal Law and Southern Order: Racial Violence and Constitutional Conflict in the Post-Brown South* (Athens: University of Georgia Press, 1987).

Benedict, Michael Les, *A Compromise of Principle: Congressional Republicans and Reconstruction, 1836–1869* (New York: W. W. Norton, 1974).

Bernstein, Richard B., *Amending America: If We Love the Constitution So Much, Why Do We Keep Trying to Change It?* (New York: Times Books, 1993).

Carter, Dan T., *When the War Was Over: The Failure of Self-Reconstruction in the South, 1865–1867* (Baton Rouge: Louisiana University Press, 1985).

Chute, Marchette Gaylord, *The First Liberty: A History of the Right to Vote in America, 1619–1850* (New York: Dutton, 1969).

Cogan, Jacob K., "Note: The Look Within: Property, Capacity, and Suffrage in Nineteenth-Century America," *Yale Law Journal* 107 (November, 1997): 473–498.

Davidson, Chandler, "Minority Vote Dilution: An Overview," in Chandler Davidson, ed., *Minority Vote Dilution* (Washington, DC: Howard University Press, 1984) 1–23.

———, "The Voting Rights Act: A Brief History," in Bernard Grofman and Chandler Davidson, eds., *Controversies in Minority Voting: The Voting Rights Act in Perspective* (Washington, DC: The Brookings Institution, 1992): 7–51.

Davidson, Chandler, and Bernard Grofman, eds., *Quiet Revolution in the South: The Impact of the Voting Rights Act, 1965–1990* (Princeton: Princeton University Press, 1994).

Derfner, Armand, "Racial Discrimination and the Right to Vote," *Vanderbilt Law Review* 26(1973): 523–584.

DuBois, Ellen C., *Feminism and Suffrage: The Emergence of an Independent Women's Movement in America* (Ithica, NY: Cornell University Press, 1978).

———, "Outgrowing the Compact of the Fathers: Equal Rights, Women Suffrage, and the United States Constitution, 1820–1876," *Journal of American History* 74 (1987): 836–862.

Farrand, Max, ed., *The Records of the Federal Convention of 1787* (New Haven: Yale University Press, 1966).

Flexner, Eleanor, *Century of Struggle: The Women's Rights Movement in the United States,* rev. ed. (Cambridge: Belknap Press of Harvard University Press, 1975).

Foner, Eric, *Reconstruction: America's Unfinished Revolution, 1863–1877* (New York: Harper & Row, 1988).

Gillette, William, *The Right to Vote: Politics and the Passage of the Fifteenth Amendment* (Baltimore: Johns Hopkins Press, 1965).

Green, Fletcher M., *Constitutional Development in the South Atlantic States, 1776–1860: A Study in the Evolution of Democracy* (Chapel Hill: University of North Carolina Press, 1930).

Guinier, Lani, *The Tyranny of the Majority: Fundamental Fairness in Representative Democracy* (New York: Free Press, 1994).

Hamilton, Alexander, James Madison, and John Jay, *The Federalist Papers* (New York: New American Library of World Literature, 1961).

Hamilton, Charles V., *The Bench and the Ballot: Southern Federal Judges and Black Voters* (New York: Oxford University Press, 1973).

Hays, Samuel P., "The Politics of Reform in Municipal Government in the Progressive Era," reprinted in Barton J. Bernstein and Allen J. Matusow, *Twentieth Century America: Recent Interpretations* (New York: Harcourt, Brace & World, Inc., 1969): 34–58.

Hyman, Harold M., and William M. Wiecek, *Equal Justice Under Law: Constitutional Development, 1835–1875* (New York: Harper & Row, 1982).

Johnson, Lyndon Baines, *The Vantage Point* (New York: Holt, Rinehart, and Winston, 1971).

Kaczorowski, Robert J., *The Politics of Judicial Interpretation: The Federal Courts, Department of Justice and Civil Rights, 1866–1876* (Dobbs Ferry, NY: Oceana Publications, 1985).

Keyssar, Alexander, *The Right to Vote: The Contested History of Democracy in the United States* (New York: Basic Books, 2000).

Kousser, J. Morgan, *The Shaping of Southern Politics, Suffrage, and the Establishment of the One-Party South* (New Haven: Yale University Press, 1974).

———, *Colorblind Injustice: Minority Voting Rights and the Undoing of the Second Reconstruction* (Chapel Hill: University of North Carolina Press, 1999).

Lawson, Stephen F., *Black Ballots: Voting Rights in the South, 1944–1969* (Lanham, MD: Lexington Books, 1976).

———, *In Pursuit of Power: Southern Blacks and Electoral Politics, 1965–1982* (New York: Columbia University Press, 1985).

Meyers, Marvin, *The Jacksonian Persuasion: Politics and Belief* (Stanford: Stanford University Press, 1957).

Montejano, David, *Anglos and Mexicans in the Making of Texas, 1836–1987* (Austin: University of Texas Press, 1987).

Parker, Frank R., "Racial Gerrymandering and Legislative Reapportionment," in Chandler Davidson, ed., *Minority Vote Dilution* (Washington, DC: Howard University Press, 1984): 85–117.

———, *Black Votes Count: Political Empowerment in Mississippi after 1965* (Chapel Hill: University of North Carolina Press, 1990).

Perman, Michael, *Struggle for Mastery: Disenfranchisement in the South, 1888–1908* (Chapel Hill: University of North Carolina Press, 2001).

Pessen, Edward, *Jacksonian America: Society, Personality, and Politics* (Homewood, IL: The Dorsey Press, 1969).

Rakove, Jack N., *Original Meanings: Politics and Ideas in the Making of the Constitution* (New York: A. A. Knopf, 1996).

Steinfeld, Robert J., "Property and Suffrage in the Early American Republic," *Stanford Law Review* 41 (January 1989): 335–376.

Williamson, Chilton, *American Suffrage: From Property to Democracy, 1760–1860* (Princeton: Princeton University Press, 1960).

Wood, Gordon S., *The Creation of the American Republic, 1776–1787* (Chapel Hill: University of North Carolina Press, 1969).

2
Historical Background

Vote Denial: Democracy's Dark Secret

"Don't Vote." For most of the nearly 400 years we have been casting votes in the United States, the message has been the same: "Unless you are rich, white, and male, keep away—we do not want you, or those like you, to vote." More than just a message of exclusion, this demand has been backed up with action. From the early 1600s, when a desperate London Company began to permit landowning Virginia planters (but only planters) to vote for a legislative assembly, to the present day with our near universal adult suffrage, we have excluded people from voting on account of their sex, race, social status, place of birth, legal condition, and lack of wealth. Literacy tests, poll taxes, violence, and other intimidations have all been used at one time or another to limit the voting population. So have education standards, property holding requirements, and so-called moral standing provisions.

The drive toward vote denial of unwanted groups and individuals has been the backbeat to popular democracy's refrain of inclusion. When in 1776 Thomas Jefferson wrote "all men are created equal," he and those who adopted the Declaration of Independence added a mental asterisk excluding women, blacks, members of Indian tribes, and the poor. When in 1863 Abraham Lincoln spoke of "government of the people, by the people, and for the people," listeners attached an implied footnote excluding as many from "the people who governed us" as it included. The dirty little secret of U.S. political life is that vote denial and its cousin, vote dilution, have been a part of our political landscape from the beginning—and in the eyes of some, they remain healthy today.

Of course, reality is not as dark as the preceding paragraph would imply. As chapter 1 makes clear, despite numerous inconsistencies and delays experienced in expanding the franchise, today most adult Americans do have the vote. Although problems still exist, they have become exceptions to the rule, not the rule itself. It may have taken a while, but the promise of U.S. democracy has largely been met.

Yet we still must acknowledge the existence and the importance of vote denial. All too often, the definition of those who could not vote (and why they were not allowed to vote) was as important in shaping the record of U.S. self-government as any listing of those who *could* vote. In exclusion lies the means to create inclusion; for only by creating and defining a "they" were we able to define the group "us." This more limited sense of inclusion came at a very high cost, however. In a real sense, the entire structure of our local and national community was built on the existence of extensive and long-standing vote denial. Ironically, the rise of democracy in this country has been based, in large part, on the on-going exclusion of many among us.

The path to the more noble side of American life accordingly must begin with an examination of its darker side. Only by examining and understanding the actions, explanations, and justifications of those who would limit the franchise can we better understand our changing conception of nationhood and thus of our vision of who we are—and who we should be—as a people. How is it that with Jefferson's immortal words ringing in their ears, he and the other founding fathers felt justified in excluding women, blacks, and the poor from a voice in the governing process? How can one explain our first writing—and then ignoring—the explicitly inclusive Civil Rights Amendments? What does the abrupt shift on a woman's right to vote say about the developing character of American life in the twentieth century? Why is it that, in the year 2000, blacks still saw clear examples of intimidation and fraud in the actions of election officials, government officers, and the police—examples so weighty that they effectively negated the impact of their votes (or even their attempts to vote)? The answers to such questions, as is often the case, lie in our better understanding of the motives, means, and forces by which the vote has been limited—for only then can we comprehend the process and meaning of its ultimate expansion.

The drive to exclude unwanted or distrusted groups from the franchise was not a monolithic effort. There was no master plan for vote denial. Different groups were excluded at different times for many different reasons. Just as the right to vote ebbed and flowed over time, so too did its denial and the justifications made for its denial. Often the inclusion of one group came at the expense of another; in some cases, the justification for excluding group *A* resulted in the inclusion of group *B;* in others, *A*'s exclusion served to facilitate *B*'s exclusion. Generally, however, the process of vote denial can be broken down into five categories of exclusion: class, status, gender, ethnicity, and race.

Class

Of all the various groups who at some point were denied the vote, the exclusion of white males because of their lack of property ownership might be the most curious and difficult for us to understand today. Whereas other voting prohibitions rightly or wrongly excluded groups who were clearly different from those drafting the limits—felons, African Americans, women—limits based on property qualifications banned people who were quite similar in form and disposition to those who could vote. By definition, those excluded for not owning enough property were all male, white, and otherwise free of legal limitations (or else they would have been excluded for other reasons than being propertyless). This reality made class status (variations as to wealth and position) the sole basis for excluding these men. It is this class-based conflict that we find so difficult to understand and accept.

Class, however, can be a very strong source of contrast. Although it is, and has been, the generally accepted belief of most Americans that class doesn't matter in American society, this has not always been the case. Class divisions between the rich and poor are almost inevitable in a society that emphasizes individual initiative and then allows those who practice such initiative to enjoy the fruits of their success. Or, at least, such has been the case for most of U.S. history. From the time of our earliest settlements, it has been the unwritten rule that economic success leads to social prestige; social prestige, in turn, brings political power to those whom society aggrandizes. Political power, of course, then makes it easier for those who have it to expand their economic opportunities, which leads to more success; and so the cycle continues largely unchecked.

The flip side of this state of affairs, of course, is that those who fail economically almost inevitably fail socially and hence politically too. Even where the poor have the vote, they normally gain little benefit from it. Today, as was the case yesterday, most of those who govern are personally wealthy and effectively serve the interests of others who have wealth. Yet more significantly for our purposes here, even while Americans have denied class distinctions as a general concept, most have recognized and accepted the *results* of class differences. Whereas being poor made these males no less white or free, and hence "worthwhile" members of society, it did make them different in the eyes of the rich and powerful who dominated U.S. society and politics. The poor and the rich simply lived different lives, and this schism made each group different from the other in terms of experience, perceptions, and attainments—or so the rich and powerful argued when it was socially and politically acceptable to do so.

This was especially the case early in our nation's history, before and immediately following the American Revolution. Class divisions were seen as exemplifying substantive social, political, and intellectual differences. Although all men might be innately equal in the eyes of God, so the argument went, differences in education, background, and experience all separated the poor from the rich—and to the poor's disadvantage. Foremost on the list of differences was the dependent status that a lack of property imposed on those unlucky enough—or improvident enough—not to have acquired it.

Most colonial Americans, drawing on both the traditions of the common law and the ideological perspectives of republicanism, drew a sharp line of demarcation between those who were independent and those who were dependent. Dependency meant not controlling the forces that shaped one's life; it meant, "an obligation to conform to the will . . . of that superior person . . . upon which the inferior depends," to quote James Wilson in 1774 (quoted in Wood, 56); ultimately it meant having to take actions and abide by the will of others simply to survive. Such need, it was felt, robbed a man of his ability to think and act as a rational human being. For without the resources to support yourself, by definition either you were dependent on others to exist (and hence forced to act as they decreed) or you were dead. It was just common sense, so the argument went, that with the exception of those few who chose death, people facing this reality were unlikely to be strong willed, rational, and thoughtful people. As John Adams explained:

Such is the frailty of the human heart that very few men who have no property, have any judgment of their own. . . . [They are] to all intents and purposes as much dependent upon others, who will please to feed, clothe, and employ them, as women are upon their husbands, or children on their parents.

Dependent people, Adams concluded, inevitably "talk and vote as they are directed by some man of property, who has attached their minds to his interest" (Adams, 376–377).

This idea, that dependent people did as they were told or paid severe penalties, permeated eighteenth century social and political thought. So too the corollary that only those who had independence could be trusted with a voice in government. In the seventeenth century, Henry Ireton had argued in England that "if there be anything at all that is the foundation of liberty, it is this, that those who shall choose the law-maker shall be men freed from dependence upon others" (quoted in Keyssar, 5). Most politically active Americans agreed. Committed to a view of elective government as the people's defender against the tyranny of inherited and unrestrained power (the King, nobles, appointed governors), colonial Americans simply could not conceive of a circumstance in which personal independence and economic security were not the foundation of effective popular government. How else could the people who chose our leaders—not to mention those who were elected our leaders—be trusted with the defense of our liberty? Dare we trust the hungry or the needy not to sell their votes to the highest bidder?

The answer was, of course, that we could not. Let private greed or economic need dictate politics, rather than disinterested concern for the common good, and free government was doomed. Personal independence, in turn, largely depended on property ownership, in particular the ownership of land. Only those who owned "real" property (for instance, land), had the resources to ignore their own personal needs and act for the good of the community as a whole—to say no to the inducements of fear, want, and greed, and hence to defend the people's rights at whatever the personal cost. In a comment often cited by Americans following its publication in the 1760s, Sir William Blackstone argued in his *Commentaries on the Laws of England* that:

[t]he true reason of requiring any qualification, with regard to property, in voters, is to exclude such persons as are in so mean a

situation that they are esteemed to have no will of their own. If these persons had votes, they would be tempted to dispose of them under some undue influence or other. This would give a great, an artful, or a wealthy man, a larger share in elections than is consistent with general liberty.

The problem with letting the propertyless vote, Blackstone explained, was at root a practical one: "If it were probable that every man would give his vote freely and without influence of any kind, then, upon the true theory and genuine principles of liberty, every member of the community, however poor, should have a vote in electing those delegates, to whose charge is committed the disposal of his property, his liberty and his life." Sad experience had shown that this was not the case:

> Since [such independence of action] can hardly be expected in persons of indigent fortunes, or such as are under the immediate dominion of others, all popular states have been obliged to establish certain qualifications; whereby some, who are suspected to have no will of their own, are excluded from voting, in order to set other individuals, whose wills may be supposed independent, more thoroughly upon a level with each other. (Blackstone, vol. 1, 165)

Those without property, in other words, intrinsically lacked the deep and abiding stake in the security and growth of the community so necessary for popular government to work. Such people simply could not be trusted with the power of the franchise. Those who owned property, on the other hand, were the foundation of good and safe government. "Freeholders [landowners] are the strength of this province not the freemen," noted the upper house of Maryland's legislature before the Revolution: "It is their persons, purses and stocks [which] must bear the burden of government, and not the freemen who can easily abandon us" (quoted in Williamson, 6). As it was the landowners who paid most of the taxes, should then they not be granted the primary say in how those taxes were to be spent?

Guided by such views, colonial governments from New Hampshire to Georgia implemented specific voting limits based on property ownership. As early as 1715, Connecticut required voters to own land worth 40 shillings per year, or personal property valued at £40, before they were allowed to the polls. New Hampshire, in a law adopted in 1727, grounded its franchise on landownership worth £50 or more—to which they added the requirement that the land in question had to be located within the district in which the voter voted. Georgia, meanwhile, demanded 50 acres of land, whatever its value might be, to exercise the franchise. North Carolina also had explicit land acreage requirements (50 acres), whereas New York went with a minimum land value approach (lands or tenements worth £40). Virginia, in a 1762 law later updated by a 1776 constitutional provision, demanded 50 acres of unimproved land to vote or, alternatively, 25 acres if the land was improved and had a house on it. South Carolina linked landownership with taxpaying: to vote one had to own 100 acres of unimproved land, or an active plantation, or a town house valued at £60 pounds and then had to have paid taxes on this land; alternatively, payment of 10 shillings per year taxes was sufficient by itself to warrant voting. The remaining states allowed voters to substitute a specific amount of personal property in place of landownership to gain access to the polls: Massachusetts demanded an annual income of 40 shillings; Maryland and Pennsylvania called for land or personal property worth £50, while Delaware set its limit at £40; New Jersey also demanded £50 worth of personal property, but added the requirement that voters had to own some amount of land, however small.

So events stood as the coming of the Revolution and its message of inherent rights called these wealth-based limits into question. If having a say in one's government was the foundation of liberty, as the Declaration of Independence and the general ideology of the Revolution argued, then should not voting be a right available to all? To many, the answer was a resounding yes. As the residents of the rural town of Richmond, Massachusetts, noted in 1780, "excluding persons from a share in representation for want of pecuniary qualifications is an infringement on the natural rights of the subject." For, as voters in the town of Greenwich, Connecticut, argued, it was "the right of the people to elect their own delegates" (both quoted in Keyssar, 12).

Yet convincing as such arguments might have been in the abstract, in many prominent Americans the values and fears that first produced property qualifications remained strong. Long-standing concerns over the need for independence to vote, linked with fears over the unexpected consequences of allowing the poor to vote, counseled against expanding the franchise. It all came down to trust: how could we trust those who had not the financial foundation to make choices for the good of the community? Dare we take the chance given the lessons of the past? Surely some measure of independence was necessary when fulfilling the important task of naming those who would be our leaders. Even the needs of revolutionary government had not changed this principle. Or had it?

As a result of such concerns, though most states decreased their property requirements in the 1770s and 1780s, only Vermont (an independent republic until it gained statehood in 1791) permitted voting by all white males regardless of class. Each of the other thirteen states retained some sort of property or taxpaying limit on voting. Georgia, for instance, reduced its property qualifications from 50 acres of land to ownership of either personal or real property valued at £10, Maryland lowered its property requirement from £50 to £30. North Carolina did away with all property qualifications for those voting for the lower house (opening the vote to all taxpayers) while retaining the 50 acre limit for its senate. New Hampshire in 1784 granted access to all who could pay a poll tax, as did Pennsylvania in 1776 and again in 1790. Similar changes were made by each of the other states.

Only with the arrival of the nineteenth century did wealth-based limits begin to wane. For one thing, as noted in chapter 1, states entering the union after 1790 abandoned all property-holding qualifications for voting. Land-rich but people-poor, these states had few good reasons to limit the vote, and many reasons not to. If it meant attracting settlers, then granting all white males the vote was an obvious and easy choice for frontier states to make. Consequently, no state entering the union after 1790 imposed broad-based property qualifications for voting; most extended the vote to all white male taxpayers and many to any free white male. Soon, under pressure to hold onto residents moving in ever increasing numbers to the western states, those states retaining property qualifications did away with their limits. Georgia opened its franchise to taxpaying white male voters in 1789 and to all white males including nontaxpayers in 1798. Delaware eliminated property requirements in 1792 but retained taxpaying rules until 1831. In South Carolina, the corresponding dates were 1778 and 1810. Maryland dropped all property qualifications in 1801 for state office and, in 1810, for all types of elections. New York followed suit, opening its vote to all white males in 1821 and offering the right to vote to black males as long as they were able to meet explicit, prohibitive wealth requirements. Meanwhile Massachusetts revoked its property qualifications that same year but kept a small poll tax that would remain on the books until 1863. Even New Jersey, Virginia, and North Carolina, which held out longer than most, opened up their balloting to all white males in 1844, 1850, and 1854 respectively.

By the end of the Civil War, class-based exclusions were mostly a thing of the past. Although some states retained taxpaying requirements to vote, the majority were of minimal cost and kept few white males from the polls; most were repealed by century's end. The only exception was in the South, where property-based prohibitions in the form of poll taxes grew both in number and extent. However, unlike earlier forms of property voting limits, these exclusions were aimed not at the poor as a class, but rather at African Americans or Mexican Americans as racial and ethnic minorities. In fact, where poor males faced limits on their voting rights following the Civil War, the motivation behind such limits lay not in their class grouping but elsewhere—usually the negative legal status and/or ethnic background of the poor voter in question.

Status

By midcentury, though voting qualifications based on property ownership were largely gone, the exclusionary intent of such qualifications remained strong. The American habit of defining inclusion by exclusion did not abate. Even as they argued for a working-class franchise, reformers held resolutely to the underlying values that promoted refusing allegedly undeserving white males the vote in the first place; they just disagreed with the prevailing definition of who was undeserving. Conservatives, in turn, gave ground grudgingly on allowing any poor white males the vote. The idea that all voters needed minimum qualifications to vote properly—and that poor people might not possess those qualifications—thus continued largely unchecked.

Yet for all the vigor with which such concerns continued to prompt debate and even action, changing cultural and political realities no longer supported outright bans on voting by the poor. The United States of the early nineteenth century was a vastly different place from the postcolonial nation of the late 1790s and early 1800s. A new market society was taking shape, one in which property was not the stable force it once had been. As legal historian Morton J. Horwitz describes the shift:

> [as] the spirit of economic development began to take hold of American society in the early years of the nineteenth century . . . . the idea of property underwent a fundamental transformation—from static agrarian conception entitling an owner to undisturbed enjoyment, to a dynamic, instrumental, and more abstract view of property that emphasized the newly paramount virtues of productive use and development. (Horwitz, 31)

In an age of industry and innovation, property, prized now for its malleability and efficacy, no longer connoted the range of innate qualities that had made it synonymous with virtue and independence. "Regard for country did not depend upon property," argued J. T. Austin of Boston in 1820, "but upon institutions, laws, habits and associations" (quoted in Keyssar, 43). "Were it not for the gravity with which the proposition is maintained, and still more, for the grave consequences flowing from it," explained Richmond's nonfreeholders in 1829, the ascription "to a landed possession, [of] moral or intellectual endowments, would truly be regarded as ludicrous." Property, these landless men made clear, "no more proves him who has it, wiser or better, than it proves him taller or stronger, than him who has it not" (quoted in Cogan, 482).

At first little more than the whisper of a few discontented landless men, the argument that fitness to vote had nothing to do with class ranking had become by the mid-decades of the nineteenth century, like a firebell in the night loudly demanding that it be heard. "Does not the adventurous mechanic, who . . . turns himself with steady industry to the pursuits of the occupation in which he has been bred, give sufficient 'evidence of permanent common interest with, and attachment to the community'[?]" asked Virginia State Senator William Munford in 1801 (quoted in Cogan, 482). His answer, and that of a growing number of men, was a resounding yes. Given this conclusion, the next contention, that such men should be allowed to vote, came naturally. "If a man can *think* without property," argued a delegate to Louisiana's 1845 constitutional convention, "he can *vote* without property" (quoted in Keyssar, 50).

Yet how to integrate these views with the still strong anxiety over unqualified voters? Even those who pushed for an expanded franchise for white males still worried about incompetent voters. Most did not dispute that property ownership conferred some degree of personal independence on a man. They also accepted the truism that genuinely dependent people should not be permitted to vote, even under a broadened suffrage. At Virginia's 1830 constitutional convention, for example, reformers pushing for an end to property qualifications for the working poor, argued:

> It has been said . . . that we derive a rule from the law of nature and the Bill of Rights, in relation to suffrage, that is in its terms universal, and that we ourselves abandon it, and thereby prove its fallacy: the females, including one half of the population, are disfranchised in one fell swoop; minors, convicts, paupers, slaves, &c., which together, compose a large majority of every community . . . . For this argument, I have a short answer; it will not do to test any rule by extreme cases. I presume it cannot be necessary for me to assign a reason for the exception . . . [because after all], *in the foregoing exceptions we are all agreed.* (quoted in Steinfeld, 356—emphasis added)

A more refined explanation of why some of the poor were so unfit to vote—and by implication, a more accurate delineation of why they could not be trusted at the polls—was needed. It was at this point that both reformers and conservatives turned to the concept of status—limits of character as embodied in practical or legal relationships of dependence like that of a wife to her husband or a slave to his master—as the source of dependency and thus disqualification from the vote. Dependence, reformers argued, arose from personal status, not class membership. The hard-working poor—laborers, craftsmen, tenant farmers—deserved the vote. If a man had strong character and public spiritedness, if he were hard working and loyal, such a man was *not* dependent, even if he worked for another or farmed a tract of land not his own. Yet "those on whom the same natural law has pronounced judgment of disability, or those who have forfeited it by crime or profligacy. . . ." were rightly kept from the ballot box (quoted in Steinfeld, 358). "When a man is so bowed down with misfortune [as to no longer support himself], . . . he voluntarily surrenders his rights," explained reformers in New Jersey's 1844 constitutional convention. "He parts with his liberty—he loses his control of his children and he labors for others [or sits in the poorhouse]. . . . Can we regard [such men] as free agents? As qualified to vote? No, sir! No, Sir" (quoted in Steinfeld, 362).

Hidden within the large class of deserving poor white males, in other words, was a smaller subset of undeserving men: paupers, the mentally incompetent, criminals, and the illiterate. Each was, by definition, a dependent man—controlled, distrusted, and limited in the choices he could make as affected the course of his life. At the least, those with such status were made vulnerable to manipulation and control; at its worst, it deprived them of the reason and thoughtfulness upon which responsible voting depended. It was a legal status of dependency, therefore, and not merely the absence of property, that made men untrustworthy in general and demanded that these particular men be denied the vote.

By the early nineteenth century, copious precedents argued this point, especially as regarded paupers (and by association, the mentally incompetent). By law, paupers in the early nineteenth century lacked control over their persons and actions. Paupers could not contract in their own name, nor did they control the use of their own labor. In 1833, for instance, the Massachusetts Supreme Judicial Court ruled that "the rights and duties of towns and paupers are correlative. While the town supports the pauper, the pauper is bound to labor for the town." Only when the "support becomes unnecessary," that is to say, the man was no longer a pauper, did "the right to control the labor cease" (*Wilson v. Brooks,* 343). Unable to support themselves and their families, paupers were believed to have abandoned any right to a public voice. For, as the aforementioned delegate in New Jersey's constitutional convention in 1844 had noted, entering the poor house meant that one voluntarily gave up one's personal freedom of movement; thus surrendering one's civil rights inevitably followed. Josiah Quincy of Massachusetts agreed with this view, noting how "the theory of our constitution, . . . is that extreme poverty—that is pauperism—is inconsistent with independence" (quoted in Keyssar, 61). Among those rights surrendered was the right to vote. For, as Maine's Supreme Judicial Court explained: "paupers are excepted [from the vote] because they are dependent upon and under the care and protection of others, and necessarily feel that they cannot exercise their judgment or express their opinions with any independence" (*Advisory Opinion,* 498).

Galvanized by such views, fifteen states instituted explicit bans on paupers' voting by 1865, most joined with similar limits on "idiots and insane persons." Tellingly, many of these states excluded paupers and mental incompetents at the same time that they permitted the poor, as a class, to vote; others imposed the ban even after they had already granted the poor the vote. Delaware, for instance, had granted the poor the vote in 1792 (though it kept a poll tax that excluded many poor men from voting) yet chose to exclude paupers in 1831, arguing that "paupers who live on the public funds, and who were under the directions of others, who might control their wills, ought not to be permitted to vote." When New Jersey instituted white manhood suffrage in 1844, it too purposefully excluded paupers because they were not "free agents" (both quoted in Steinfeld, 362). Maine, which never had a property requirement for voting, excluded paupers in its first constitution in 1820, as did West Virginia in 1861. Virginia, which would not terminate property requirements until 1850, nonetheless added an additional limit on paupers in 1830.

The process did not stop with the coming of the Civil War. In the ensuing fifty years, an additional seven states either updated their exclusions or excluded paupers from the polls for the first time. Among them were Arkansas and Texas, which barred paupers for the first time in 1874 and 1876. Other states, such as Massachusetts, Louisiana, and New Hampshire, granted destitute discharged Civil War veterans the vote while keeping their bans on other paupers. Several states—such as California in 1849, Connecticut in 1879, and Missouri in 1875—allowed paupers a general right to vote, but not in the counties or districts in which they were housed (in poor houses); this had the effect of denying such men the vote, in practice if not in theory. Thus the process proceeded state by state.

A similar path was followed in regard to felons. Before the Civil War, twenty-five state constitutions instituted bans on felons voting. Here too, long-held legal traditions (in this case going back to English and even Roman legal sources) called for the disenfranchisement of those convicted of "infamous crimes" (crimes that precluded a felon from serving as a witness in a legal proceeding). Criminals, according to this view, forfeited their rights to independence, and hence the vote, by their acts against the community. How could we trust those who had attacked the peace of society to show the sort of self-control necessary in exercising the franchise? Should we even try?

For these twenty-five states, the answer was a clamorous no. As both social deviants and ongoing threats to society, felons did not deserve a voice in government; their status as felons proved their unfitness for the vote. Still, variations did exist. Sometimes felony bans were limited to specific crimes. Missouri in 1820 excluded only those convicted of electoral bribery; Connecticut in 1818 imposed voting bans only on those guilty of major felonies such as fraud. Other states chose to include "all high crimes and misdemeanors" (Illinois 1818 Constitution) in their felony exclusions. Felony prohibitions also varied in duration: Missouri's lasted for ten years; Minnesota's until the felon had his civil rights restored; New York's until the felon was pardoned; Maryland banned those convicted of bribery at elections "forever."

Following the Civil War, the number of prohibitions on felons voting increased. Most unforgiving were those in the South, where detailed lists of offenses felt likely to be charged against blacks were purposely banned; yet the South was far from alone in denying criminals the vote. In fact, by the early twentieth century, all forty-eight states applied some sort of voting proscription for criminal activity. Many included all convicted felons (though debates as to the proper definition of a felony produced functional variations between the states). Most left the date of redemption undetermined. Widely popular and often adopted with little debate, modern felony exclusions received support from both state courts (most of which agreed with Alabama's Supreme Court in 1884 that such bans "preserve the purity of the ballot box" [*Washington v. State,* 582]) and the U.S. Supreme Court in 1890 (in *Davis v. Beason*). In most states, felony exclusions continue in force to this day, widely seen as a legitimate retribution for past acts and essential deterrence against future wrongs.

Such was not necessarily the case with the last status exclusion on the list: rules denying the vote to those unable to read. Different in scope and method from pauper and felony bans (which both focus on more discrete and uniform populations than literacy rules), reading requirements still had the same general intent of excluding those deemed unfit by nature of their personal status (in this case as an illiterate) to vote. The uneducated, the argument went, lacked the intelligence, knowledge, and/or mental capacity necessary to be a proper voter. In fact, to some, the status of illiteracy demonstrated, "for all practical purposes," the sort of dependency and "mental incapacity" that demanded voting bans on paupers, mental incompetents, and felons (quoted in Keyssar, 143). "Persons wholly destitute of education," argued Samuel Jones, "do not possess sufficient intelligence to enable them to exercise the right of suffrage beneficially to the public" (quoted in Keyssar, 66). At the least, not being able to read placed such voters at a serious—and to some, dangerous—disadvantage. As a delegate to Michigan's 1907 constitutional convention explained, "it is of the highest importance that any man who is called upon to perform the function of voting should be not only intelligent but also be able to find out for himself what the real questions before the public are" (quoted in Keyssar, 143). Sadly, the lack of education fostering illiteracy argued against such skills.

Like rules prohibiting felons from voting, literacy requirements were most common, and most harsh, in the South, where by the early twentieth century they were the cornerstone of black disenfranchisement. The earliest application of literacy tests, however, arose in the North (Connecticut in 1855, Massachusetts in 1857) where growing concern about large immigrant populations led some to propose skill-based status limits as a way of keeping immigrant voters from the polls. In all, thirteen states outside the South adopted some sort of literacy test between 1860 and the 1920s. In 1896, indeed, Senator Henry Cabot Lodge led an unsuccessful effort in Congress to exclude any adult immigrant who could not read forty words in any language. Most state laws, however, went even further, demanding that voters "be able to read the Constitution in the English Language and write his or her name" (to quote California's 1911 state constitution). A few had more general reading or writing requirements. In some states, such as Massachusetts in 1889, rules demanded that anyone not voting within the last four years had to take the literacy test. Most states, North and South, also included exceptions to their literacy rules. Afraid that too extensive an application of illiteracy bans might keep "fit," if still illiterate, voters from the polls, almost all the states also provided waivers for those "who cannot read or write because of physical disability" (1892 Massachusetts Constitution), or grandfather clauses permitting those already voting to retain that right.

Well established by the turn of the twentieth century, literacy tests were frighteningly effective at keeping unwanted voters from the polls. In New York, for instance, of the 472,000 who took the English language literacy test between 1923 and 1929, 55,000 failed (a 15 percent failure rate). Uncounted thousands more simply chose not to attempt a test they were sure to fail. In the South, literacy tests (albeit backed by other forms of vote denial) were even more successful at keeping unwanted voters from the polls. By the mid-twentieth century black registration rates were at less than 3 percent; voting rates were even lower.

Highly controversial, literacy tests exposed the underlying illogic—and intolerance—behind status-based vote denials. For if a lack of education made a citizen unfit to vote, then why would a record of prior voting change this fact? More important, if the lack of an education did *not* disqualify some voters, why should its presence disqualify *any* voters? The same difficulty could be raised for poverty limits that excepted veterans or felony limits that exempted some forms of crime but not others. Clearly the goals behind these limitations were focused on something more than "an educated electorate." It was the illiteracy of *specific* voters—in particular ethnic males in the North and blacks in the South—that sparked such rules. Sadly, as we shall see, literacy rules were just one of many attacks on ethnic and black voting. In any case, literacy limits died out in the North and West by the 1930s. They would remain in place in the South, however, until the 1960s, when the Voting Rights Act of 1965 finally gave the federal government the authority to force recalcitrant states from continuing the practice.

Gender

When it came to the vote, women were different. As noted in chapter 1, the actual process by which women were denied the vote was a simple one. All that politically dominant males had to do to keep women from voting was *do nothing*. The ban on women voting was both long-standing and absolute. Women, the traditional argument went, were by definition dependent persons unfit to exercise the franchise. Economically dependent on men, women lacked the independence necessary for participation in the political process. By law, married women in the eighteenth century could not own property in their own name. In fact, under the traditional common law rule of *femme covert,* a married woman had no separate legal existence from her husband—so how could she have the necessary personal independence to vote? Even single women were deemed to be dependent, under the control of their fathers, brothers, or other male family members. Suffrage, as John R. Cooke explained to the 1829 Virginia constitutional convention, implied wholly masculine traits such as "free-agency and intelligence; free-agency, because it consists in election or choice between different men and different measures; and intelligence, because on a judicious choice depends the very safety and existence of the community." Women, who lacked these masculine traits, therefore had a natural "incapacity to exercise political power" (quoted in Cogan, 486). Nor was it felt that women needed the vote; women were deemed to have a virtual say in public life through the person of fathers, husbands, brothers, or other relatives.

Given such widely held views, it was not surprising that women were not granted the vote in the eighteenth century, nor that things failed to improve in the first decades of the nineteenth. Whereas some states, such as Kentucky, in 1838 debated a female franchise, and a couple of states allowed unmarried women without fathers or brothers to vote in local elections, the general trend was to deny women the vote. In fact, the general trend was not even to discuss the issue of allowing women access to the polls. Never having had the right to vote, women could not point to explicit laws or rules keeping them from voting. This is where gender-based vote denial diverged from most other categories of vote denial. Class-, status-, and race-based denial required expansive legislation and court rulings to exclude such groups from voting; those who opposed a female vote needed only to do nothing.

Passive does not mean effortless or immobile, however. Over time, as the women's suffrage movement organized and pushed more strongly for women's right to vote, it became increasingly difficult for those opposed to women's suffrage to maintain their objections and defend the ban on women voting. Even where the commitment to exclusion remained intense, the need to protect against women's suffrage dictated an ever more active defense of gender-based bans. Thus, although the end result continued to be inaction on the part of legislators, the energy necessary to maintain this inaction grew ever greater over time.

Still, whatever the energy needed to hold fast and ignore arguments supporting a female franchise, the outcome was that women still could not vote. Even those pushing for suffrage expansion elsewhere stood fast on the issue of women voting. In the mid-nineteenth century, for instance, supporters of universal white manhood suffrage claimed a woman's mind was "more fit for the sphere in which [God] intended her to act, [and so He] had made her weak and timid, in comparison with man, and had thus placed her under his control, as well as under his protection" (quoted in Cogan, 486). Women, they argued, lacked the necessary qualities to vote (qualities that, by the way, poor white males did have). Even abolitionists, from whose ranks the modern women's movement would arise, proved tepid in their support for women's suffrage. As the Civil War began, male abolition leaders such as Wendell Phillips cautioned against linking women's and blacks' civil rights: "One question at a time," Phillips advised, "this hour belongs to the Negro" (quoted in Keyssar, 177). At the war's end, Republican Party leaders also abandoned women even as they fought to expand the right of black males to vote. A critical blow against giving women the vote was struck with the adoption of the Fifteenth Amendment with its explicit defense of black voting—and its equally explicit disregard of women's voting rights.

Although such defeats only strengthened the commitment of the women's movement to secure the vote, it also points out the difficulties that women's suffrage faced. Even in what was perhaps the greatest period of rights expansion in U.S. history, it was still the general consensus among men to dismiss the question of voting rights of women. The same forces impelling Republican support of black voting actually hindered support for white women receiving the same entitlement. Women did not seem threatened by their status in society; nor did their inclusion offer the party the political advantages that black voting in the South did. As the *New York Times* argued in March 1869, "we do not concur with those who predict that the question of Suffrage for women will speedily demand public action or engross public attention . . ." (*New York Times,* 8 March, 1869).

Undeterred, women's suffrage leaders kept pushing. Turning the domestic argument on its head, women argued that given the innate characteristics of domesticity—ethics, piety, stability—the presence of women at the polls would elevate the political process. "In so far as motherhood had given to women a distinctive ethical development," Reverend Anna Garlin Spencer of Rhode Island argued in 1898,

> it is that of sympathetic personal insight respecting the needs of the weak and helpless, and of quick-witted, flexible adjustment of means to ends in the physical, mental and moral training of the undeveloped. And thus . . . has motherhood fitted women to give a service to the modern State which men can not altogether duplicate. . . . The earth is ready, the time is ripe, for the authoritative expression of the feminine as well as the masculine [in government]. (Norton, 257)

Generally male society ignored these arguments in the same way it had ignored all others in favor of women voting, including comparable arguments that native-born white women could counteract the presence of undesirable immigrant and black voters.

Over time, however, such arguments proved persuasive, leading a few states to begin granting women the vote (at least for some offices, such as school boards). Still, the general tone in male society was antisuffrage. Many men feared that granting women the vote would somehow undermine traditional gender roles. Pennsylvania politician W. H. Smith attacked women's voting because "the family . . . would be utterly destroyed," if women could vote. California constitutional convention delegate Mr. Caples agreed, noting in 1879 how woman suffrage "proceed[ed] upon the hypothesis that men and women are all the same." Such views, he argued, would abolish "all distinctions between men and women." This, in turn, "attack[ed] the integrity of the family, it attack[ed] the eternal degrees of God Almighty; it denie[d] and repudiate[d] the obligations of motherhood" (quoted in Keyssar, 192).

These were arguments with which most men agreed. Interestingly (at least to modern ears), they were also arguments that many women found convincing. Emily P. Bissell in 1909, for instance, described suffrage as "a reform against nature" and a "threat to the family" (Bissell, 141–143). Fifteen years earlier Heloise Jamison had made a similar point, describing the ballot as "a hindrance" to women applying their real power and "influence"—in the home and through the family (Jamison, 4). Alice Duffield Goodwin, author of the 1903 book, *Anti-Suffrage: Ten Good Reasons,* asserted that the vote would make "inroads upon feminine vitality . . . [by adding] political duties . . . to those bound upon our shoulders first by nature, second by a highly developed civilization" (quoted in Stalcup, 145). As a result, despite the greater logic behind prosuffrage arguments (in 1869 Wyoming granted women the vote with no resulting calamities), the fight for women's suffrage went on and on and on. Even in the twentieth century, as the move toward what became the Nineteenth Amendment gathered momentum, opposition to female suffrage remained strong.

No matter what the time or place, the basic reality in getting women the vote remained that opponents needed only to do nothing to keep women from the polls. The decision to grant women the vote, in turn, rested on social changes both within the women's movement and U.S. society as a whole. As noted in chapter 1, women's suffrage only became a reality when reformers reached out to all women and stressed the link between social reform and female suffrage; in particular, the women's movement turned to working-class women, many of them immigrants, and the reformist Progressive movement for help. In doing so they effectively expanded their movement into a mass movement, gained allies in various reform parties, and thus gained the clout necessary to get not only Congress to act but three-fourths of the states as well.

Female suffrage, in other words, originated not in the rejection of ethnic voting but its expansion. Ironically, the decision to allow women the vote rested on the failure of another category of vote denial, the effort to keep ethnic (and racial) voters from the ballot box—denial efforts that, even more ironically, women reformers themselves had advanced before the twentieth century.

Ethnicity and Race

We move now to the last and greatest category of vote denial: racial and ethnic exclusions. Voting limits based on place of origin or race—what we today would call ethnic and racial identities—cover a wide range of groups and approaches to vote denial. From the vote dilution efforts faced by poor European immigrants to the complete denial of all voting rights suffered by African Americans in the South, ethnic and racial prejudice has led inevitably to voting bans of one sort or another. Every state in the nation has placed specific bars or bans on ethnic or racial voting in their state constitutions and statute books. Even the national government, at least as it related to Asians, Native Americans, immigrants, and blacks, was not immune to such tendencies. The trend against racial and ethnic voting was both long standing and extreme. As with other types of vote denial, the motivation behind ethnic and racial voting bans lay in fear and intolerance in the dominant society. Unlike the groups discussed so far, these people were profoundly different. Immigrants from the poor classes of Europe, especially those coming from southern or eastern Europe after 1890, while technically whites from the same place of origin as most native-born Americans, spoke different languages, practiced different and often unpopular religions, and were generally peasants unfamiliar with the urban lifestyles they would find in the United States. Such people simply did not fit into dominant conceptions of what it meant to be an American. Indians, Asians, Hispanics, and especially African Americans were even more offensive to this perspective. As people of color, such groups were seen as direct threats to the social order—threats so great as to demand extreme action. Put simply, both the new classes of immigrants and the various types of people of color scared the dominant classes of U.S. society, their presence within the body politic challenging long and deeply held prejudices. As is so often the case, fear quickly generated attempts at exclusion.

With immigrants, voting exclusions took the form of vote dilution. After all, these people, strange as they were, were white—which meant that established racial bans were not applicable. Nor, after the mid-nineteenth century, were property exclusions available to keep such people from the polls. Though, as we have seen, status limits such as those imposed on illiteracy could be applied to immigrant voters, the numbers affected by such bans were dwarfed by the size of the total ethnic voting population. In any case, as currently written, state law gave such immigrants (before 1920, male immigrants) the right to vote.

Still, the thought of allowing uneducated former peasants to choose our leaders concerned many native-born Americans. Allow immigrants the vote, argued Charles Francis Adams in 1869 and the result would be "government of ignorance and vice" (quoted in Keyssar, 123). Historian Francis Parkman agreed, explaining in an 1878 *North American Review* article how

> a New England village of the olden times—that is to say, of some forty years ago—would have been safely and well governed by the votes of every man in it; but now, that the village has grown into a populous city, with its factories and workshops, its acres of tenement-houses, and thousands and ten thousands of restless workmen, foreigners for the most part, to whom liberty means license and politics means plunder, to whom the public good is nothing and their own most trivial interests everything, who love the country for what they can get out of it, and whose ears are open to the promptings of every rascally agitator, the case is completely changed, and universal suffrage becomes a questionable blessing.

Immigrants, the argument went, lacked any real understanding of U.S. social forms and traditions. Rather than viewing their vote as a civic duty, they sold it to the highest bidder or, worse yet, used it to attack their social betters. "Liberty" might have been "the watchword of our fathers," wrote Parkman in his 1878 article, but today, "in their hearts, the masses of the nation cherish desires not only different from it, but inconsistent with it. They want equality more than they want liberty" (Parkman, 7). Others were more blunt: "Communism and social chaos are the only possible finality of such a tendency" (quoted in Keyssar, 123).

Over time, as both the number and variety of immigrants coming to this nation grew, so too did concern over their negative impacts on good government. In the 1890s, *Nation* editor Edward Godkin spoke for many when he lamented the negative influences of assumedly ignorant immigrant voters on New York politics. By the early twentieth century, immigrant voting was likened to "licensed mobocracy ... nothing less than 'organized anarchy,' pure and simple." By the era of World War I, critics were equating immigrant voters with "the improvident, the ignorant, the vicious, the stupid, the lazy, the drunken [and] the dirty" (quoted in Keyssar, 123).

It is telling that laws permitting noncitizens to vote (adopted in many states between 1850 and 1889) were terminated soon after the flood of eastern and southern European immigrants arrived around the turn of the century. It was also at this time that Congress began to narrow the window through which immigrants could enter this country. Aimed directly at the flood of new immigrants from southern and eastern Europe, as well as from Asia, Congress in 1882 disallowed entrance to felons, "lunatics," "idiots," and those likely to become public charges. Over time this list of unwanted characteristics grew to include contract laborers, the ill, professional beggars, and especially anarchists (the common view was that most anarchists were immigrants). In the early twentieth century, Congress went even further, rewriting the citizenship laws to require literacy, long-term residency, and proof of fitness before immigrants could be naturalized as citizens. In 1924, Congress closed the door on nearly all immigration.

Even though denying noncitizens the vote, along with limiting the total number of new immigrants, did much to exclude unwanted ethnic voters, such measures did not go far enough to counteract the impact that the large numbers of immigrants who could vote had on the outcomes of elections. This fact spurred those concerned with the negative electoral impacts of ethnic voters to find some way to limit the "damage" that such voters could inflict—either by hindering them from entering a polling booth they had every right to go into, or by minimizing the impact of their votes on the election's outcome. By the last few decades of the nineteenth century, this is exactly what some states did, adopting a number of vote dilution techniques to minimize both the number of ethnic voters and the likelihood that such voters could elect candidates of their choice.

We have already discussed in this regard literacy tests and citizenship rules. Both proved effective at lowering the ethnic voting population. New York alone denied 55,000 immigrant voters the right to vote for failing that state's literacy test between 1923 and 1929. Other states adopting literacy tests showed similar declines. As to citizenship rules, many states went beyond merely excluding noncitizens from the franchise. Twelve states, for instance, required naturalized citizens to show naturalization papers to election officials before registering or, in some cases, voting. Given that many ethnic immigrants no longer had their papers, or were unfamiliar with such rules and thus failed to bring their papers when seeking to vote, this requirement had the effect of keeping out many otherwise qualified voters. Other states imposed strict deadlines for naturalization before a new citizen could even register to vote. California, for example, required in its 1879 constitution that naturalization take place at least ninety days before the election; Colorado set the deadline at four months in 1876; New York originally set its limit at ten days in 1846 but kept increasing the time limit until by 1894 it stood at ninety days. A variant of the naturalization time limit required noncitizens seeking to vote (in those declining number of states in which they still could) to declare their intent to vote well before the election was held. Thus Missouri, in 1870, demanded immigrants seeking the vote declare their intent to become citizens (and thus to vote) "not less than one year nor more than five years before he offers to vote" (1870 Missouri constitution). North Dakota imposed a similar time restriction in 1889; Texas settled on six months in 1896.

Registration rules also could be used to limit unwanted voters in other ways. By the start of World War I, most states had formal registration rules for voting. Most required that voters register before election day. Adopted as a reform of what had been a chaotic voting process, especially in large cities dominated by machine politics, the rules were uncomplicated in concept: fail to register properly and the state had valid grounds to deny you a ballot. In practice, however, things were not this simple. The problem with registration rules lay in their implementation and utilization. Many states, most of them northern with large immigrant urban populations, wrote their registration laws to make registering for the vote as difficult as possible. In Chicago, for instance, an 1885 law created a board of election commissioners, appointed by the county courts, who supervised a small army of election judges and clerks whose main job was to register voters every four years. (In the late 1890s, this requirement was increased to every two years.) However, under the law, registration could only take place (in person at local polling places), on the Tuesday of either the third or fourth week before an election. The election judges, in turn, would use the remaining time before the election to confirm the actual residency and citizenship of the voter, compiling in the process a "suspect list" of improperly registered voters. Those placed on the list had one day, the Tuesday two weeks before the election, to return to the polling place and defend their right to vote. The burden of proving that they were legal voters rested with the voters themselves. Any voter still on the suspect list on the day of the election—or never placed on the registration list in the first place—was denied the vote. The result of such complicated procedures, not surprisingly, was that many otherwise qualified voters were excluded. Similar procedures were implemented in New Jersey, California, and Pennsylvania, among other states.

Yet the most effective means of protecting against ethnic voting were changes in the manner of electing local government officials. In the nineteenth century, the norm for organizing elections was the single-member district. At the city level, this meant that each ward or district was represented by an alderman or commissioner whose primary function was to represent the needs of the residents of his ward or district within city government. As historian Samuel P. Hays notes,

> City councilmen were local leaders. They spoke for their local areas, the economic interests of their inhabitants, their residential concerns, their educational, recreational and religious interests . . . . They rolled logs in the city council to provide streets, sewers, and other public works for their local areas. They defended the community's cultural practices, its distinctive languages or national customs, it liberal attitude toward liquor, and its saloons and dance halls which served as centers of community life. . . . In short, [they] spoke for their

constituencies, inevitably their own wards which had elected them, rather than for other sections or groups of the city. (Hays, 43)

In fact, city government under such a system was little more than an alliance of these neighborhoods, most of which could be divided as well by ethnic origins. Break the power of these locally grounded city leaders and you undermined the political clout of their ethnic constituents.

This is exactly what upper-class, mostly native-born reformers did soon after the turn of the century. Their method was the at-large election, under which city leaders no longer were voted on ward by ward, with each ethnic neighborhood electing its own representative, but rather by the city's entire voting population as a whole. Although not denying any individual voter a voice in city government, at-large elections thus effectively undermined the voice immigrant communities had in local government. For whereas an ethnic group might constitute the majority within a ward or two, spread out among the entire city population, it was a distinct minority. Thus, whereas in the past ethnic voters might have been able to elect one or two members of their own community as alderman, now it was difficult, if not impossible, to do so. Only those with citywide connections (of which well-off businessmen and civic leaders were the most common) had the resources and presence to garner votes from across the city. At the least, it meant that those immigrant candidates who were elected no longer had the close ties to their local communities that they had once had; by necessity, such officials had to service a city-wide constituency.

The result was a diminution of the voice that ethnic voters had in shaping the direction of city government. Combined with another vote-dilution technique, a commission-style government (in which real authority in city government was placed in the hands of experts, each responsible for one component of public service such as police or sanitation) at-large elections consolidated power in the hands of fewer and fewer leaders. Although citizens still voted, the influence that their votes had on actual government activities grew weaker and weaker. This is the definition of vote dilution: lessening the impact of the voting process on governing. Even though reform efforts of this sort were not successful in the larger, more heterogeneous cities—too many ethnic voters allowed the urban machines to retain control with minimal changes—in midsized and especially small cities, elite groups were able to exert their influence, take control, and undermine the impact of immigrant voting. The era of the expert had arrived, and the losers in this change were the poor and ethnic voters who no longer could change their world with their votes.

Offensive as such vote dilution schemes were, the exclusions placed on people of color were worse. Groups such as Native Americans, Asians, Hispanics and blacks scared most native-born, white Americans. In the eyes of many, these groups were outsiders whose presence in the body politic threatened the stability of U.S. society and culture. Give them the vote, the argument went, and everything that native-born, white Americans held dear would be lost. Native Americans were called savages; Asians and Mexican Americans were deemed depraved classes; Africans Americans were viewed as simply less than fully human. Collectively, these groups were—in the words of North Carolina's Hinton Helper in 1855—"befouled with all the social vices, with no knowledge or appreciation of free institutions or constitutional liberty," holders of "heathenish souls and heathenish propensities." Grant such people a voice in the governing of this nation, Helper concluded, and "be prepared to bid farewell to republicanism" (quoted in Takaki, 101).

Native Americans had always been considered strangers to the Constitution. In the nation's formative years, American Indian tribes were viewed as sovereign nations. By definition, this made Indians noncitizens lacking all rights to the vote. Yet, technicalities aside, the reality of Indian-white interaction was much more complex. By the early nineteenth century, Indians east of the Mississippi River were seen by some as a population fit for assimilation (with an eventual total inclusion into American life and society) and by others as barbarous savages deserving of nothing more than isolation and even destruction. Combined, these two objectives—isolation and assimilation—shaped U.S. policy toward Native Americans for the next two hundred years.

Thomas Jefferson, for example, encouraged the assimilation of Indian tribes into American society, especially the tribes of what was then the southwest (today's southeast region), who were thought of as more civilized. A number of tribes, including the Cherokee, Seminoles, and the Creek took him up on this offer and began to integrate white lifestyles into tribal ways. They did not, however, abandon their separate identities as sovereign peoples. This fact, along with tribal control of large sections of land in what were becoming developed states, soon caused problems. By the 1830s, many were calling for these so-called savages to be relocated west of the Mississippi River. As a separate people they did not belong in the middle of the nation. Move them to new lands to live their own lives, went the cry. This would not only open up new opportunities for white Americans (the primary reason for removal) but it also would save the Native Americans from extermination by a more dominant European-American culture. Responding to such calls, President Andrew Jackson negotiated several treaties removing Indian tribes westward to the "Indian Country" (Oklahoma).

The removal agreements were highly controversial (there was some question as to the validity of the Indian "chiefs" who signed the treaties and thus of the treaties themselves), but nevertheless they were backed up by the force of the U.S. Army. Many Indians died on the long road westward to their new home; more died once they got to the undeveloped lands given them in Oklahoma; all suffered privations and want. The Cherokee, giving voice to the effects of removal, called their forced relocation "The Trail of Tears."

Yet, tragic as this event was for those involved, it was the legal response to relocation efforts that proved most significant in the long term, especially in terms of Native Americans' right to vote. Contesting efforts to take away their lands (in this case by Georgia with the support of the federal government), the Cherokee brought suit in 1830 before the Supreme Court to save their homes. As foreign nations having signed formal treaties with the United States, they argued that the individual states lacked all authority over them; the United States, in turn, was limited to only its agreed-upon powers as laid out by said treaties. All efforts at removal were thus improper and should be stopped. Georgia responded that Indian tribes were "subject nations," subservient to both state and federal controls. Ruling for the high Court, Chief Justice John Marshall agreed in part with both sides, splitting the difference between these opposing views. He declared the Indian tribes "domestic dependent nations," subject to the control and authority of the U.S. government in the same way that a "ward" was subject "to his guardian." The federal government, therefore, had a duty to protect and support Native Americans—a duty, incidentally not shared by the states.

Even though none of this denied that Indians were "a distinct political society separated from others" and capable of "managing its own affairs," as Chief Justice Marshall held, as subsequently interpreted this dependent status doomed Indians to the near total dominance of the national government in running their lives (*Cherokee Nation v. Georgia*, 16–17). The result was the rise of the reservation system, begun in the 1850s, under which Native American tribes were forced off their traditional lands and onto small reservations run by the Bureau of Indian Affairs.

By the late nineteenth century, the reservation system was complete. The isolation of Indians from white society was near total. So too, unfortunately, were the devastating effects of life on the reservations: hunger, disease, and hopelessness all plagued Indians on the reservations; poverty was widespread and seemed to inevitably lead to high rates of alcoholism and drug abuse. Worse yet, Indians were powerless to change their situation. As members of "separate" nations—albeit "dependent" ones—Indians were not citizens of the United States and hence had no political voice in the government controlling every aspect of their lives. Having been born within the geographical confines of the United States, it would have seemed that Indians came under the Fourteenth Amendment's ruling that "all persons born or naturalized in the United States, and subject to the jurisdiction thereof, are citizens of the United States." Even so, Congress and the courts created an exception for Indians from this constitutional command. Indians who retained their ties with their tribes, the Senate Judiciary Committee held in 1870, did not come under the jurisdiction of the United States and thus could not be citizens. One year later, Judge Deady of the District Court of Oregon seconded this view, holding that, as Indian tribes were "independent political communities," their members were not fully covered by U.S. legal jurisdiction—including the right to citizenship based on place of birth (*McKay v. Campbell*, 166). Nor did assimilating into white society automatically grant Indians the rights of citizenship. In a later case, Judge Deady explained that

> an Indian cannot make himself a citizen of the United States without the consent and cooperation of the government. The fact that he has abandoned his nomadic life or tribal relations, and adopted the habits and manners of civilized people, may be a good reason why he should be made a citizen . . . , but does not of itself make him one. To be a citizen of the United States is a political privilege which no one, not born to, can assume without its consent in some form. (*United States v. Osborne*, quoted in *Elk v. Wilkins*, 109)

This, in turn, was a view that the Supreme Court found persuasive. In the 1884 case of *Elk v. Wilkins,* the Court concluded that the Fourteenth Amendment did not include Indians, even those who had assimilated into white society. Merely severing one's ties to the tribe of one's birth by "fully and completely surrender[ing]" to the "jurisdiction of the United States," was not enough for a Native American to claim citizenship, the Court ruled. The choice was not theirs to make. Without explicit action on the part of Congress or the president, Indians were not citizens and as such, lacked all citizenship rights—especially the right to vote—a ban made even more explicit by state laws prohibiting Indian voting in fifteen states.

In the years that followed, the Supreme Court's denial of citizenship to Indians began to unravel. Nothing in *Elk v. Wilkins* prohibited the government from *naturalizing* Indians as citizens. In fact, Judge Deady's ruling in *United States v. Osborne* hinted at the standards the government could apply in allowing Indians the privilege of citizenship. Yet, the first and most important step was for individual Indians to sever their ties to tribal life. Only by abandoning their tribes could they prove their intent to act in the manner required of them in order to justify the granting of citizenship with all of its attendant rights, including the right to vote. In 1887, Congress encouraged this assimilation process with the passage of the General Allotment (or Dawes) Act, which broke up a number of reservations and parceled the land among the individual tribe members. The idea was that by becoming landowners and farmers, the Indians would adopt "the habits of civilized life," and thus be fit for citizenship. In fact, the Act granted citizenship to those individuals who accepted allotments and thus exhibited these "habits of civilized life" (23 USCS § 331). Over the years, the number of Indians granted full citizenship rights was expanded by other congressional acts (for example, in 1901 and after World War I). Yet as a group, Native Americans still remained strangers to the constitutional realm. Not until 1924, with passage of the Indian Enfranchisement Act, did all Native Americans—assimilated or not—receive full citizenship rights and vote for the first time in an election.

Like Native Americans, Asian Americans also faced vote denial based on the refusal to grant citizenship—in this case by naturalization. Distrusted as outsiders, reviled for their racial differences, and feared as labor competition, Asians in the United States faced attacks that, if anything, were stronger and more explicit than those aimed at

Indians—if only because the Asian community was a growing community. A 1790 federal law still on the books in the nineteenth century when the first large numbers of Asians, the Chinese, arrived on the West Coast, limited naturalization to whites only. Court rulings and legislative enactments, in turn, defined Asian immigrants as "colored." In 1854, for instance, in *People v. Hall,* the California Supreme Court held that "Indian, Negro, Black, and White" were "generic terms, designating races" for legal purposes—and as the Court saw things, Asians fell into the "people not white" category. Six years later, California added Asians to the list of those who should be placed in segregated schools. Like blacks and Indians, Asians were too different and dangerous to be allowed in the same schools as white children. As the state superintendent of schools explained in 1859, "the great mass of our citizens will not associate on terms of equality with these inferior races; nor will they consent that their children do so." On the national scene, former New York Governor Horatio Seymour drew a direct analogy between Asians and Indians, asking why, if we could drive the Indians to the brink of destruction, we could not "keep away another form of barbarism which has no rights here." President Rutherford B. Hayes argued that "the present Chinese invasion [was] pernicious and should be discouraged. Our experience in dealing with weaker races—the Negroes and Indians . . .—is not encouraging . . . . I would consider with favor any suitable measures to discourage the Chinese from coming to our shores" (all quoted in Takaki, 102–103). Even the U.S. Supreme Court joined in, upholding laws exempting Asians from naturalization in 1922 despite the fact that the plaintiff in this case, Takao Ozawa (an American-educated Japanese immigrant), was "well qualified by character and education for citizenship." Asians, Justice Sutherland explained for the majority, were "clearly of a race [that] is not Caucasian and therefore belongs entirely outside the zone" of legal inclusion—at least pending a change in the laws (*Ozawa v. United States,* 189, 198).

In terms of voting rights, the unwillingness to grant Asians citizenship, or even, in the case of the Chinese, to allow continuing immigration, made it easy to deny Asians the vote. Noncitizens were by definition nonvoters; deny Asians citizenship and you deny them the vote. Yet for some states, vote denial by citizenship exclusions did not go far enough. What about those of Chinese or Japanese ancestry born within the confines of the United States? Would they not be citizens under the Fourteenth Amendment? Although the numbers at stake were at first quite small, they concerned nativist westerners nonetheless. It was with this concern in mind, in fact, that every western state except Nevada refused to ratify the Fifteenth Amendment and its explicit ban on race-based vote exclusions. It was to head off Chinese voting following ratification of that amendment that led California to specify in its 1879 constitution that "no native of China . . . shall ever exercise the privileges of an elector in this state" (California Constitution of 1879). Nor was California alone in its concerns. Oregon had already placed a similar provision in its 1857 constitution, and Idaho followed suit in 1889. These exclusions would remain on the books until World War II finally led the government to open the door to Asian immigration and the courts began to invalidate state laws denying Asians the vote.

Efforts to keep Mexican Americans from the polls took a somewhat different path to vote denial. Long considered citizens of the southwestern states in which they lived, Mexican Americans could not simply be kept from the vote by blanket rejections as non-Americans. Too numerous by the nineteenth century to ignore, even if one excluded more recent migrants from citizenship status, Mexican Americans were an established element of life in the Southwest. In some areas of the region, they made up the majority of the population. Hispanics were also classified as whites by law, which made keeping them from the polls a more difficult proposition than was the case for Indians or Asians. (Until 1930 the U.S. Census classified Mexican Americans under the category of *white*, despite the considerable Indian heritage of most Mexican Americans). Limits on Hispanic voting were thus a much more difficult problem, on a par with the South's dilemmas regarding African American disenfranchisement (to be discussed later). Not surprisingly, then, the forms of Mexican American vote denial looked a lot like those being applied at the same time to southern blacks.

Most popular were poll taxes. First adopted in Texas in 1902, poll taxes were deemed the only way to keep "the flood gates for illegal voting" from opening up. The vast majority of Mexican Americans in Texas were poor. Even a minimal poll tax, which the 1902 law required, was often beyond their means. Yet, to make matters worse, one year later the new Terrell Election Law required that these taxes be paid between October and February of the year *before* an election. The expectation was that poor Mexican Americans either would fail to pay for an event so far in advance they could not see the utility of it, or they would lose the tax receipts before the election came around. In either case, as the bill's author noted, the act effectively eliminated "the thriftless, idle and semi-vagrant element" from the franchise (quoted in Davidson 1990, 21). Fifteen years later, concerned both by the ability of some Hispanics to pay the poll tax and the potential of Mexican immigrants to become naturalized citizens and thus to vote, the Texas legislature shifted gears and prohibited the use of interpreters at the voting polls. The assumption was that poorly educated Mexican Americans would be unable to read the ballot without help and thus effectively could no longer vote. At the same time, and for similar reasons, the legislature also banned election officials from providing help to any naturalized citizens of less than twenty-one years' residence. If none of these tactics worked, there was always the all-white democratic primary, initiated in 1903. For although Mexican Americans were officially classified as white, enforcement of the election laws was left in the hands of local election officials whose outlook toward the racial status of Mexicans differed from that of the national government.

Whatever the case, the outcome in Texas and the other southwestern states—each of which passed similar laws hindering or limiting the right of Hispanics to vote—was profound. By the middle years of the century, few Hispanics in the Southwest voted. Those who did generally did so only so long as they voted for whom the local county boss told them to vote. As one scholar puts it: Mexican Americans were "offered . . . a choice between disfranchisement and a manipulated vote" (Brischetto, 236). Oppose the will of the Anglo majority, and Hispanic voters faced "protests and threats from Anglo-Americans" as "constant reminders of a fragile franchise" (Montejano, 39).

We continue now to the last, and most blatant, category of vote denial efforts—the disenfranchisement of African Americans. Of all the examples of voter exclusion based on race or ethnicity, the worst by far was that imposed by southern whites on southern blacks. As noted in chapter 1, in the years just after the Civil War, hope dawned for the nation's millions of African Americans. The Thirteenth Amendment's requirement that "neither slavery nor involuntary servitude . . . shall exist within the United States," was understood by most Americans to mean that newly freed blacks would acquire all aspects of freedom, including the right to vote. The Fourteenth Amendment's promise of equal protection and its defense of the "privileges or immunities of citizens of the United States" added still more support to newly freed African Americans' right to vote. Then there was the Fifteenth Amendment's declaration that "[t]he right of citizens of the United States to vote shall not be denied or abridged by the United States or by any State on account of race, color, or previous condition of servitude." Combined with the various civil rights and enforcement acts passed by Congress to implement these amendments—not to mention the presence of the U.S. Army empowered to enforce Congressional Reconstruction of the South, including establishing black voting rights—it seemed as if the path to the polls would be a clear and simple one for African Americans.

Events proved otherwise. For a time southern black males did freely exercise their franchise. In 1867 and 1868, blacks across the South allied with white Republicans to elect large numbers of delegates, many of them black, to new state constitutional conventions. These Republican-dominated conventions, in turn, produced extremely liberal constitutions granting full civil rights, including the right to vote, to black Americans. Hundreds of thousands of blacks quickly registered to vote; and in subsequent elections they exercised this right—often voting for black candidates. Ultimately, more than 600 blacks would be elected to office in the state governments organized under the Reconstruction state constitutions, including one black governor (in Louisiana), six lieutenant governors, hundreds of legislators and numerous state treasurers, secretaries of state, and superintendents of education. Many more blacks held local and county offices, including such positions as county supervisor, mayor, sheriff, judge, and justice of the peace.

By the early 1870s, however, things began to fall apart. Most white southerners disliked the entire concept of Reconstruction and opposed the Republican- and black-led governments organized under this process. As early as 1866, white terrorist organizations—the Ku Klux Klan being the best known—organized to oppose all efforts to transform the South's social relations. With the rise of Republican-led government, these groups began a wave of race-based violence and terror that soon spread across the South. Republican Party meetings were broken up. Prominent blacks were attacked and often killed. Before long, even average blacks were assaulted, accused of being impudent toward whites and not knowing their place; in 1870 alone, the death toll was in the hundreds and the number injured even greater. At its worst, white mobs attacked entire groups of blacks, terrorizing most and killing many. In one 1873 incident alone, in Colfax, Louisiana, a white mob attacked and trapped 150 blacks in the county courthouse for three days; before it ended, fifty blacks had been massacred—after they had surrendered under a white flag.

Bad economic times, well-publicized political scandals, and heavy campaigning by Democrats among the region's white voters added to the Republicans' woes. Combined with the chilling effects of violence on black voting, the result was the defeat of the Republican-led forces by the Democrats in all but three southern states by the mid-1870s. When, in 1877, the national Republicans agreed to end Reconstruction in return for the Democrats not contesting the questionable decision granting the Republican candidate, Rutherford B. Hayes, the presidency, the end was near. Soon thereafter, the remaining three Republican governments fell. By the 1880s, political power was firmly in the hands of those opposed to black civil rights.

Yet even here, buffeted by terrorist violence and facing the rise of hostile state governments, blacks still managed to take part in the electoral process—at least for a time. The decline in black electoral access came slowly—even piecemeal—over more than twenty years. As late as the 1890s, many blacks continued to participate in Republican Party politics and the electoral process. In Texas, the Republican Party chairperson through the mid-1890s was black. In 1896, over 130,000 blacks were still registered to vote in Louisiana. Similar numbers were found in other southern states. Many African Americans also continued to run for local and state office. Some even won. Between 1877 and the mid-1890s, fifty black legislators sat in the North Carolina legislature; a similar number served in South Carolina. In Arkansas, forty-seven blacks won seats in the general assembly, and two to the state senate. There was even one black representative who kept his seat in the U.S. House until 1901.

Yet for all such continued electoral success, the general trend after 1877 was toward vote dilution and outright vote denial. Southern white society could not accept the idea of black equality. In their eyes, blacks were not capable of being equal to whites. In 1868, for example, conservative whites from Alabama petitioned Congress against enfranchising blacks. Denouncing the whole idea of letting blacks vote, they warned that blacks were

in the main, ignorant generally, wholly unacquainted with the principles of free Governments, improvident, disinclined to work, credulous yet suspicious, dishonest, untruthful, incapable of self-restrain, and easily impelled . . . into folly and crime . . . how can it be otherwise than that they will bring, to the great injury of themselves as well as of us and our children, blight, crime, ruin and barbarism on this fair land? . . . do not, we implore you, abdicate your own rule over us by transferring us to the blighting, brutalizing and unnatural dominion of an alien and inferior race. (quoted in Keyssar, 93)

With such visions in their heads, how could white southerners *not* fight against the black vote? The answer reached by many whites was that they had no choice. Just give them "free play" to reorder their social and political relations—which by 1877 they finally would get—and southern whites promised to seize every opportunity to go "as far as they dare[d] in restricting colored liberty . . . without actually reestablishing personal servitude" (quoted in Foner, 593). As one southern newspaper promised in 1875, although the Fourteenth and Fifteenth Amendments might "stand forever, . . . we intend . . . to make them dead letters on the statute-book[s]" (quoted in Foner, 590).

That black disenfranchisement took so long was primarily a consequence of just how hard it was to bar those who already had the vote from the polls; at no point did it demonstrate a lack of commitment on the part of southern democrats to deny blacks the vote. Even with the limits imposed on the civil rights amendments by the Supreme Court in the 1870s, 1880s, and 1890s, southern segregationists had to be careful not to run afoul of the Fourteenth and Fifteenth Amendments. Go too far or act too aggressively in limiting black rights, and conservative whites risked a national backlash and federal intervention. Despite the end of Reconstruction, national Republicans still kept a sharp watch on Republican (and hence black) voting patterns in the South. In the mid-1880s, they even attempted to pass a new "Force Bill" imposing federal regulations for elections. Although the bill failed to pass, the specter of a new federal election law made southern white leaders cautious in their attacks on black voting.

Conservative whites also needed time and experience to devise ways to deprive blacks of the vote. The least intrusive approach to vote denial was to depend on intimidation, fraud, and violence to protect southern society from black voting. However, "fraud, trickery, and force had their limitations." Each were "inherently unstable" as a permanent means of race control, "for their effective deployment depended on vigilant local organization." Let one community fail in its efforts, and the entire approach could be threatened (Piven and Cloward, 78–79). The ongoing success of some black candidates in isolated southern districts illustrated the validity of this concern. More was needed. Yet if informal methods were not going to be enough, how much formal government action was called for—and of what sort?

Whites thus began their attack on black suffrage not with its explicit denial, but rather by seeking to dilute the impact of black voting. They did so in a number of inventive ways. Some states passed laws granting the legislature or the governor the power to appoint local government officials who previously had been selected by popular vote. Even where blacks made up the majority of a particular district, what good were majority numbers when there where no offices of meaning to vote for? Such measures thus cost black majorities practical political power. Many southern state legislatures also gerrymandered voting districts to minimize the impact of large black voting populations. Alabama, for instance, divided its black majorities into multiple voting districts so that blacks, no longer a majority in any one district, could always be outvoted by unified white voters. Mississippi took the opposite approach, gathering its blacks into a single district so that their votes could only swing a single election out of the five or six districts contested. In either case, the result was the same: even where blacks voted in large numbers, they were unable to determine the election's outcome so long as white majorities voted as a group. A similar result at the county level was achieved by adopting at-large voting systems in place of the more traditional single-member districts. Denied the power that localized numbers could bring, blacks once again were effectively cut out of the electoral process.

Building on vote dilution schemes, southern officials also adopted rules and procedures making it increasingly difficult for blacks to exercise their voting rights in practice. Hoping to discourage black voters from exercising their franchise, for example, election officials in Georgia, Mississippi, and Louisiana set up polling places in areas inconvenient for blacks. Many were placed at distant locations or in the middle of white sections of the town or county; some were put in businesses owned by known opponents of African American voting. Such situations were intimidating at the least, and often outright dangerous, for those blacks brave enough to attempt to vote. A parallel approach involved limiting the hours when predominantly black polling places were open; a few local officials refused to open these polling places at all. Another popular trick made use of black illiteracy. In 1882, South Carolina implemented what it called the Eight-Box Ballot Law. Under this rule, ballots for individual offices had to be placed in separate ballot boxes. Put your ballot in the wrong box, and it would not be counted. Although the boxes were usually labeled properly, this meant little to illiterate black voters unable to read the labels. As if this were not enough, many election supervisors shifted the boxes around periodically. Countless wrongly placed—and hence uncounted—ballots were the result. A deceptive variant of the eight-box rule included listing candidates alphabetically rather than by office on the ballot. Adopted first by Alabama in the late 1880s, when combined with rules limiting the time available for voters to cast their votes, alphabetically organized ballots made it almost impossible for illiterate or semi-illiterate black voters to pick out the candidates of their choice. Worse yet, the law also made it easy for election officials to throw out "incorrect" black votes since election rules prohibited voting for more than one candidate per office—a result that the alphabetical listing clearly promoted.

More disturbing were laws designed to keep blacks from being listed on the voting rolls, or alternatively, allowing for local officials to purge them from the lists. The most prevalent approach was epitomized by an 1873 Georgia law permitting local election supervisors to close their registration rolls to new applicants *except* during those times when black farmers were too busy to register, such as planting or harvest time. North Carolina and Alabama had similar laws. Some states added the requirement that voters show proof of registration before they could vote or face immediate disqualification. Given the long gap between registering and voting in most southern states, this was a request that many blacks (as well as whites) could not meet. Virginia went one step further, mandating separate registration books for white and black voters; not surprisingly, black registration books regularly came up missing when blacks wished to register or were conveniently lost on voting day. Then there was the increasingly common practice in all the southern states of adding those crimes considered most likely to be committed by blacks—arson, bigamy, and petty theft—to the list of felonies that disqualified the felon from ever voting again. Those felonies thought of as white crimes, on the other hand, such as grand larceny, invoked no such limits.

The most popular and effective means of excluding blacks from the franchise, however, were poll taxes. Many states already had such laws on their books, remnants of the old colonial property-based voting rules. As a result, all they had to do to exclude unwanted voters was make such taxes mandatory and then increase the amount of tax required to vote; raise the total enough, and most blacks would be barred from the vote. This was exactly what Georgia accomplished in 1877 when it not only increased the amount of tax owed to vote but made payment of the tax cumulative before voters were permitted to cast their ballots. As a result, blacks not only had to pay the present year's tax to vote but all the accumulated back taxes imposed by state law—miss one year, and the cumulative and indefinite nature of the poll tax made it near impossible for poor blacks ever to vote again.

Brutally efficient in keeping poor blacks from the polls—one observer described the poll tax as "the most effective bar to Negro suffrage ever devised" (quoted in McDonald, 68)—by the early twentieth century every southern state used some sort of poll tax to deny blacks the vote. Although one unanticipated consequence of the poll tax was the disenfranchisement of many poor whites, this was a price that southern white leaders were willing to pay to keep poor blacks from the voting booth.

Of course, poll taxes did little to hinder blacks who had the resources to pay. As noted earlier, as late as the 1890s many blacks remained on the voting lists. More was needed if conservative whites' dreams of excluding blacks from the vote were to be fully realized. By the early 1890s, southern whites felt confident enough to do more, expanding their attacks on black voting to the next stage: total vote denial based on race. As one delegate to Virginia's 1901 constitutional convention noted, the intent after 1890 was "to disfranchise every Negro that [they] could disfranchise under the Constitution of the United States, and as few white people as possible" (Keyssar, 113). So discriminate they did. Though still operating through the medium of technically race-neutral structures, between 1890 and 1905 governments across the South updated their election laws and revised their constitutions to exclude black voting more fully. The first and most successful of these disenfranchisement plans arose in Mississippi. Written into a new state constitution in 1890, the four-step "Mississippi Plan" included: a $2 poll tax payable before registration; a literacy test in which voters had to read, understand, or interpret any section of the state constitution to the satisfaction of a white (and usually hostile) election official; long-term residency rules demanding two years domicile within the state and one year within the voting district; and permanent disenfranchisement for crimes felt most likely to be committed by blacks.

Extremely popular with local whites, the Mississippi Plan also appealed to whites in the other southern states, each of which soon copied Mississippi's new approach to vote denial. In 1895 South Carolina required all voters to read and explain any section of the state constitution provided by the local voting registrar, as well as meeting a two-year residency requirement. Louisiana added similar literacy requirements to its constitution in 1898, along with a new poll tax and rules denying felons the vote unless pardoned by the governor. Concerned with the potential of these rules to expel poor and illiterate whites from the polls, the state also adopted a grandfather clause which allowed those who had voted before 1867 (when blacks could not vote) or whose fathers and grandfathers had voted then to waive the new requirements. Two years later, North Carolina imposed a poll tax and adopted literacy tests administered by local registrars (who had full discretion as to which parts of the state constitution applicants had to read) as its primary tool of vote denial; the state added a grandfather clause similar to Louisiana's to protect poor white voters. Similar outcomes followed as Alabama in 1901, Virginia in 1902, Texas in 1904, and Georgia in 1908 revised their constitutions.

The results of such efforts were immediate and drastic. By 1900 all forms of voter participation in Mississippi had declined to a mere 17 percent; black turnout stood at less than 9,000 out of a potential 147,000 voting-age blacks. In Louisiana registered black voters declined by 99 percent to just 1,300 in 1904; eight years earlier it had stood at 130,000. Alabama kept only 3,000 registered black voters in 1902, this from a pool of 181,000 voters in 1900. In Georgia, only 4 percent of black males were even registered to vote as of 1910. Texas saw black voting decline to a mere 5,000 votes in 1906. In fact, across the entire region, voter turnout fell from a high of 85 percent of all voters during Reconstruction to less than 50 percent for whites—and single-digit percentages for blacks—in the new century.

By the early 1900s, the fight against black voting was largely complete. Most southern states had revised their constitutions and statutes to exclude blacks (and many poor whites) from the vote by using techniques similar to Mississippi. As of 1915 no southern state was without some sort of vote-denial program. Yet one final step still remained. Even with poll taxes and literacy requirements, felony exclusions and grandfather clauses, some blacks still managed to gain the franchise. If black disenfranchisement were to be made total, if the very meaning of the vote and its denial for blacks were to be separated from that of the party primaries—in particular that of the all-important Democratic Party primary. The last step was what came to be called the all-white primary.

Adopted in every southern state between 1896 and 1915, the all-white Democratic primary was the capstone of the region's race-based disenfranchisement edifice. All-white primaries kept those few blacks who managed to register despite race-neutral exclusions from voting in the one election that meant anything. The reason for this need lay in the vagaries of southern political life. After the late 1880s, the southern Republican Party was powerless. With the vast majority of southern whites voting Democratic and an ever-decreasing number of blacks available to vote Republican, the general election had become a sham. Everyone knew who was going to win the general election: the Democratic candidate. This reality changed the South's political dynamic. If the Democratic candidate was fated to win office, then the real choice of who would hold office was made in the Democratic primary. Exclude blacks from this vote (which the Democratic Party, as a "private" organization, was fully empowered to do if it so chose), and you effectively barred them from any meaningful expression of political choice. Blacks could cast as many votes as they wished in the general elections (if they could, which most could not), but they would be meaningless votes.

For the next forty years, with a few minuscule and irrelevant exceptions, southern blacks were unable to vote in any significant numbers. Merging race-neutral exclusions with the all-white primary was an extraordinarily effective tactic. Registration rates for blacks across the South dropped to just above 2 percent; even those who were registered were unable to vote in the one election that had significance. Frustrated and angry, many blacks tried to fight back. From the 1920s onward, campaigns against African American exclusion from the polls arose in a number of states. Their target was the all-white primary, since rules that excluded registered voters seemed more vulnerable to attack than technically race-neutral statutes and constitutional provisions that indirectly disallowed black voting. Filled more often with defeats than victories, the fight for the vote progressed slowly. Finally, by the 1940s, the tide began to turn. With 1941's *United States v. Classic* and 1944's *Smith v. Allwright,* the all-white primary was finally defeated. Blacks' misgivings that these decisions would actually make a difference was understandable, but they proved misplaced. At liberty to vote in the Democratic primary when the next election rolled around, registered blacks voted with little hindrance. The fight had been won; the all-white primary was really dead.

Victory, however, proved to be a relative concept. Though blacks now could vote in the important Democratic Party primaries, southern state officials quickly responded by implementing (or in some cases, merely intensifying the enforcement of) a wide range of procedural devices aimed at undermining the ability of blacks to vote or, where they could vote, diluting the effectiveness of these votes.

In Alabama, for instance, such time-tested disenfranchisement techniques as the poll tax, literacy tests, long-term residency requirements, and the precondition of gainful employment to vote (all in place by 1900) were updated by such drastic procedures as a 1946 amendment to the state constitution (the Boswell Amendment) limiting registration to only those who, in the view of local registrars, "could 'understand and explain' any article of the federal constitution"—a requirement that few blacks could seem to meet. A subsequent constitutional amendment required the Alabama Supreme Court to create a uniform voter registration form whose content, when written by that court, proved to be so complex and legalistic as to fulfill the same exclusionary result as the Boswell Amendment. Even more extreme was the 1957 gerrymandering of the municipal boundaries of Tuskegee, Alabama, to exclude all but 4 or 5 of the city's 400 or so qualified black voters (but none of the whites) from city elections. Less drastic, but perhaps for this reason more effective, was a 1951 law prohibiting single-shot voting in at-large county elections. In at-large elections, all the candidates run against each other, with the top vote-getters filling the available seats. Single-shot voting occurs when a particular subgroup withholds some of its votes to ensure that their preferred candidate is one of the top vote-getters. Under the 1951 law, all ballots failing to include a full slate of preferences were disqualified, making single-shot voting impossible and thus undermining the ability of blacks to elect even one candidate in an at-large election.

Georgia focused its discriminatory efforts on undermining black voter registration. In 1949, the state legislature passed a "registration and purge" law. Under this statute, any voter who failed to vote in an election at least once in a two year period was automatically expunged from the voter rolls. Further, anyone reregistering following removal from the election lists (or registering for the first time) had to pass the state's existing literacy test or answer ten of thirty questions aimed at proving their "good character" and their "understanding of the duties of citizenship." A 1958 statute increased the difficulty level of the questions while simultaneously expanding the number of required correct answers to twenty out of thirty. Enforcement of the literacy and good-character tests, in turn, was left to the discretion of unsympathetic, and usually hostile, local election officials whose standards were so demanding that even educated blacks had trouble passing these tests; for illiterate blacks, they proved to be an almost insurmountable barrier. As a judge in the Middle District of Georgia explained in 1960, local county registrars commonly "required [black applicants] to read and write a longer and more difficult passage of said Constitution or of the Georgia Constitution" to prove literacy than whites. They also

> [i]n administering tests to applicants . . . tested each of the Negro applicants one at a time outside the hearing and presence of the other applicants. . . . [while] [t]he white applicants, [would be] . . . tested in a group. Each white applicant [would] read aloud Article 2, Section 4, Paragraph 1 of the Constitution of Georgia in the presence of the other applicants. Thus, each applicant, other than the first to read, had the benefit of hearing the paragraph read aloud by another or other applicants before having to read himself. (*United States v. Raines*, 131)

Robert Flanagan, field director of the Georgia office of the NAACP, had a more prosaic description of the intent of the law: the only correct answer to such questions was "white folks ain't going to let blacks folks vote" (McDonald, 72). In 1964, these efforts were replaced by a majority-vote clause to the state election code requiring that candidates receive a majority of the votes cast to win their seat— a requirement specifically designed to undermine the chances that large black pluralities could slip in a candidate in at-large elections.

The result, not surprisingly, was that few Georgia blacks were able to take advantage of their voting rights even fifteen years after the defeat of the all-white primary. In Terrell County, for instance, although 64 percent of the residents were black, only forty-eight blacks had registered to vote by 1958; by 1960 the number had grown to only fifty-three. Similar dismal registration numbers were found in Sumpter County as well: with a black plurality of 44 percent, only 8.2 percent of blacks were registered to vote in the early 1960s.

Mississippi likewise relied most heavily on local county registrars to limit black voting. The Mississippi Plan of 1890 had kept blacks from the polls for over sixty years. Subsequent laws had added a moral-character test to the state's laundry list of effective exclusionary techniques. When the all-white primaries ended, these laws were still in force. Thus, local and state officials quickly turned to the plan's most exclusionary component, the literacy test, to maintain white-only voting. Under this rule, to register to vote, "applicants had to demonstrate their literacy by filling out in their own handwriting and without any assistance a long, complicated voter registration form asking detailed questions regarding occupation and business, residence, and criminal record." Applicants also were required to "copy any section of the Mississippi Constitution chosen by the registrar, write a correct interpretation of that section, and then explain in writing 'your understanding of the duties and obligations of citizenship under a constitutional form of government.'" Any mistake or error in filling out the form automatically disqualified the application. It was at this point that local officials stepped in, ensuring white electoral dominance by the simple expedient of selectively enforcing the literacy requirement. In fact, registrars routinely failed black applicants for such simple mistakes as not signing their name on the correct line of the form. Where literacy failed to bar black voters, registrars would refuse to credit black answers to the moral-character test. Often registrars would fail an applicant for misinterpreting a complicated passage of the state constitution—a passage that, as one commentator notes, "they themselves could not interpret" (Parker, 26–28). As if such restrictive rules were not enough, a 1962 law required the publication of the names of all those taking the registration test in local newspapers; intimidation, reprisals, and outright violence soon followed.

Similar efforts to maintain white electoral dominance spread across the South. North Carolina centralized control over elections, established intricate procedures for voter registration, and granted extensive powers to local registrars to use these complex registration procedures to undermine black voting. South Carolina responded to the court-ordered end of the all-white primary in *Smith v. Allwright* by removing from the statute books all 150 state laws regulating primary elections (in the hope that making the democratic primary a totally "private" affair would solve the constitutional problems condemned in *Smith*). These efforts later were superseded by three measures aimed at diluting black voting strength: the first extended the literacy test to party primaries, the second implemented "full-slate" and "majority-vote" requirements for those same elections, and the third shifted from district to at-large electoral systems in county elections. Texas placed its faith in a poll tax that, though only a small amount of money ($1.75), was still prohibitive for poor black and Hispanic laborers, to whom $1.75 was a day's wages. Virginia allowed a proportionally larger black vote in primaries and general elections than other southern states, but largely because it had faith that the existing system of poll taxes, understanding requirements, and literacy tests would limit the electoral impact of black voting. In 1959, Tennessee, concerned that Memphis's 30.5 percent of black registered voters might elect a black city officials through single-shot voting, substituted a system of designated positions for the existing free-for-all method of electing city commissioners, school board members, and the county's state legislative delegation. Finally, Louisiana used a constitutional interpretation test, along with a system by which any two registered voters could legally challenge the registration of another voter, to purge blacks from the voter rolls.

The results of these exclusionary efforts, though not completely successful in stopping all black registration or voting, were still considerable. As late as 1940, only 3 percent of voting-age southern blacks had been registered to vote (and with the all-white primary, none of them were able to vote in the one election that had practical meaning). Following *Smith v. Allwright,* this situation began to change. In 1956, 25 percent of voting-age blacks were registered to vote; by 1964, this number had increased to 43.3 percent across the South. Raw numbers can be deceiving, however. Most registered black voters lived in the border states or Florida; in the deep south, where the majority of blacks lived, African American voter registration stood at only 22.5 percent as late as 1964, with Mississippi setting the lowest standard at 6.7 percent (itself an increase from a rate of 1.98 percent a mere two years earlier). Worse yet, the application of such vote dilution techniques as voting lists purges, at-large elections, and full-slate and majority-vote requirements—not to mention the ever-present threat of economic reprisals and physical violence against any black trying to vote—meant that, even in those areas where blacks made up a majority of the population, no black candidates were elected to office. Things got so bad that one observer at the time would maintain that "for Negroes in some sections of the South, an attempt to exercise their right of franchise as Americans seemed a greater risk in 1958 than at any time since the outlawing of the white primary in 1944" (quoted in Garrow, 10–11). In fact, it was in those counties where blacks most outnumbered whites that black enfranchisement was at its lowest; the specter of black political power so terrified local whites that it spurred extraordinary efforts to keep blacks from the polls.

A similar pattern followed the passage of the Voting Rights Act of 1965. The act, which in time provided African Americans and other excluded minorities the final key to an effective franchise, angered and terrified most Southerners. Their response, as before, was massive resistance to change. Mississippi, for instance, in direct contradiction of both the intent and objectives of the VRA, amended its state constitution in 1966 to permit the consolidation of adjacent counties as a direct means of undermining black majorities; at the same time, the state legislature revised statute law to permit county supervisors to shift from district to at-large elections and multiplied by ten the number of signatures required to run as an independent candidate. In Louisiana, white officials "actively solicited absentee ballots from whites and set up voting 'substations' to make it easier for whites to case their ballots," while refusing to do the same for black voters (Brown v. Post, 60). One enterprising parish registrar, faced with a black Democratic Party candidate for town marshal, removed that nominee's name from the official list of Democratic Party candidates and then told black voters that they could vote for this candidate by casting a straight Democratic Party ticket vote—an act that denied the nominee those votes. Alabama's registrars took such efforts even further, limiting black electoral success by the simple expedient of ballot-box stuffing: in one election district, for example, the number of white voters in the 1966 election outnumbered those in 1960 by 5,547—this despite a countywide *decline* in white population over this period. Another popular obstruction in Alabama was to extend the term of office of white county officials when threatened by black candidates. In Texas, responding to the demise of the poll tax, the state legislature quickly adopted an equally burdensome annual voter registration requirement, one that demanded that voters reregister every year between November 1 and February 1 for the *next* year's election. As a district court judge noted while overturning this law in 1971, it was "beyond doubt that the . . . Texas voter registration procedures tend to disenfranchise multitudes of Texas citizens otherwise qualified to vote." (*Beare v. Smith,* 1103).

Yet this time, events played out to a different conclusion. Finally, the federal government was serious; the message of the Voting Rights Act was both specific and strong—vote denial based on race or ethnicity was no longer permissible. The days when the South could hide within its splendid isolation and do as it pleased regarding race relations was past. Although the South did not want to hear this message, the constant and vigorous demands by the federal courts and the Justice Department would make them listen. True, these demands would not really start until 1969 and would not carry much weight until the end of the 1970s, but the tide was finally turning. Faced with a constant round of negative court decisions, vehement executive orders, and extensive congressional revisions of the law, recalcitrant southern governments finally backed down in the late 1970s and 1980s, opening the polls to everyone and ending their obstruction of minority voting rights. Race-based and ethnic-based vote denial would finally become a thing of the past—or so it seemed until events in Florida implied that its tenure was not quite finished. Chapter 4 explores this possibility in more detail.

Conclusion

Varied in both nature and scope, the drive to exclude unwanted or distrusted groups from the franchise has ebbed and flowed over time. Currently, vote denial is in full retreat. With the exception of an ongoing (and in the minds of many, questionable) felony exclusion, few of the techniques of vote exclusion discussed above retain force. Women have had the vote since 1920; blacks and other people of color have had a meaningful voice at the polls since the 1960s and 1970s; even the poorest among us, the indigent and homeless, can vote if they register. Although outdated registration or residency rules keep many from the polls—white as well as black, Anglo-Saxon Protestants as well as ethnic minorities—the vast majority of those Americans still denied the vote are excluded because of long-settled age-based limits barring the young from voting (and even here, a constitutional amendment lowered the voting age to eighteen in 1971) or established citizenship requirements that exclude those who are not yet full members of the body politic. Otherwise, if they are willing to meet the procedural requirements to vote, all adult Americans have the franchise.

Yet the legacy of vote denial endures—a constant in American political history. The fact remains that at one time or another, in a few states or all, potential voters have been excluded because of the color of their skin, place of origin, gender, legal status, or lack of wealth. In most cases these exclusions were both deeply seated in the law and of long duration. The list of those unable to vote has been both longer and more far-reaching than any listing of those who could vote. Worse yet, the exclusionary intent behind these efforts still resonates across American life. Even where we have allowed unpopular or distrusted groups the franchise, we put up significant road blocks to their effective use of this right. Convoluted registration rules, intentionally inconvenient polling places, and various vote dilution techniques such as at-large voting, have all undermined the meaning and substantive impact of voting for such groups over the years.

The impact of this dark episode in U.S. history has been considerable. How could it not? As recent events have shown, the memory of vote denial still resonates within the African American community and so too its actual accomplishments. How can we claim to be a truly democratic nation when we have excluded so many from the vote—and for such impoverished reasons? The only logical conclusion we can draw from this dismal picture is that collectively we really did not, and perhaps still do not, want people to vote.

Yet, as is often the case, the darkest picture has within it rays of hope. As undeniable as voter exclusions have been, so too has its opposite reality, vote expansion. As noted, more Americans can vote today than every before. Although the fight against vote denial did not come easily nor quickly, it *did* succeed. The promise of U.S. democracy was not forever foreclosed, merely delayed. Consequently, we can shift our examination of voting rights in the United States to more positive ground—to the proceedings by which vote denial was first assaulted, and then largely (if not finally) defeated through court action.

References and Further Reading

Adams, Charles Francis, *The Works of John Adams, Second President of the United States*, vol. 9 (Boston: Little, Brown, 1856).

Argersinger, Peter H., "The Value of the Vote: Political Representation in the Gilded Age," *Journal of American History* 76 (June, 1989): 59–90.

Belknap, Michal R., *Federal Law and Southern Order: Racial Violence and Constitutional Conflict in the Post-Brown South* (Athens: University of Georgia Press, 1987).

Bissell, Emily P., "A Talk to Women on the Suffrage Question," reprinted in Brenda Stalcup, ed., *The Women's Rights Movement: Opposing Viewpoints* (San Diego: Greenhaven Press, 1996): 140–146.

Blackstone, William, *Commentaries on the Laws of England*, 4 Vols. (New York: Oceana Publications, 1967).

Brischetto, Robert, et al., "Texas," in Chandler Davidson and Bernard Grofman, eds., *Quiet Revolution in the South: The Impact of the Voting Rights Act, 1965–1990* (Princeton: Princeton University Press, 1994): 233–270.

Burton, Orville Vernon, et al., "South Carolina" in Chandler Davidson and Bernard Grofman, eds., *Quiet Revolution in the South: The Impact of the Voting Rights Act, 1965–1990* (Princeton: Princeton University Press, 1994): 191–232.

Carter, Dan T., *When the War Was Over: The Failure of Self-Reconstruction in the South, 1865–1867* (Baton Rouge: Louisiana University Press, 1985).

Chute, Marchette Gaylord, *The First Liberty: A History of the Right to Vote in America, 1619–1850* (New York: Dutton, 1969).

Cogan, Jacob K., "Note: The Look Within: Property, Capacity, and Suffrage in Nineteenth-Century America," *Yale Law Journal* 107(November, 1997): 473–498.

Davidson, Chandler, *Race and Class in Texas Politics* (Princeton: Princeton University Press, 1990).

———, "The Voting Rights Act: A Brief History," in Chandler Davidson and Bernard Grofman, eds., *Controversies in Minority Voting: The Voting Rights Act in Perspective* (Washington, DC.: The Brookings Institution, 1992): 7–51.

———, "The Recent Evolution of Voting Rights Law Affecting Racial and Language Minorities," in Chandler Davidson and Bernard Grofman, eds., *Quiet Revolution in the South: The Impact of the Voting Rights Act, 1965–1990* (Princeton: Princeton University Press, 1994): 21–37.

Davidson, Chandler, and Bernard Grofman, eds., *Quiet Revolution in the South: The Impact of the Voting Rights Act, 1965–1990* (Princeton: Princeton University Press, 1994).

Engstrom, Richard, et al., "Louisiana," in *Quiet Revolution in the South: The Impact of the Voting Rights Act, 1965–1990* (Princeton: Princeton University Press, 1994): 103–135.

Fleming, Walter C., "Politics in the Mainstream: Native Americans as the Invisible Minority," in Wilber C. Rich, ed., *The Politics of Minority Coalitions: Race, Ethnicity, and Shared Uncertainties* (Westport, CT: Praeger, 1996): 233–246.

Foner, Eric, *Reconstruction: America's Unfinished Revolution, 1863–1877* (New York: Harper & Row, 1988).

Franklin, John Hope, and Alfred A. Moss Jr., *From Slavery to Freedom: A History of Negro America* (New York: Alfred A. Knopf, 1988).

Garrow, David J., *Bearing the Cross: Martin Luther King and the Southern Christian Leadership Conference* (New York: Quill, 1986).

Gillette, William, *The Right to Vote: Politics and the Passage of the Fifteenth Amendment* (Baltimore: Johns Hopkins Press, 1965).

Hamilton, Charles V., *The Bench and the Ballot: Southern Federal Judges and Black Voters* (New York: Oxford University Press, 1973).

Hays, Samuel P., "The Politics of Reform in Municipal Government in the Progressive Era," reprinted in Barton J. Bernstein and Allen J. Matusow, *Twentieth Century America: Recent Interpretations* (New York: Harcourt, Brace & World, Inc., 1969): 34–58.

Horwitz, Morton J., *The Transformation of American Law, 1770–1860* (Cambridge: Harvard University Press, 1977).

Jamison, Heloise, "The Wrong of Suffrage," in *American Women's Journal* (May, 1894), reprinted in *Pamphlets Printed and Distributed by the Women's Anti-Suffrage Association of the Third Judicial District of the State of New York* (Littleton, CO: Fred B. Rothman & Co., 1990 [1905]): n. p.

Keech, William R., and Michael P. Sistrom, "North Carolina," in Chandler Davidson and Bernard Grofman, eds., *Quiet Revolution in the South: The Impact of the Voting Rights Act, 1965–1990* (Princeton: Princeton University Press, 1994): 155–190.

Keyssar, Alexander, *The Right to Vote: The Contested History of Democracy in the United States* (New York: Basic Books, 2000).

Kousser, J. Morgan, *The Shaping of Southern Politics, Suffrage, and the Establishment of the One-Party South* (New Haven, Yale University Press, 1974).

———, *Colorblind Injustice: Minority Voting Rights and the Undoing of the Second Reconstruction* (Chapel Hill: University of North Carolina Press, 1999).

Lawson, Stephen F., *In Pursuit of Power: Southern Blacks and Electoral Politics, 1965–1982* (New York: Columbia University Press, 1985).

———, *Black Ballots: Voting Rights in the South, 1944–1969* (Lanham, MD: Lexington Press, 1999 [orig. pub. 1976]).

Levine, Michael, L., *African Americans and Civil Rights: From 1619 to the Present* (Phoenix, AZ: Orox Press, 1996).

McCray, Peyton, et al., "Alabama," in Chandler Davidson and Bernard Grofman, eds., *Quiet Revolution in the South: The Impact of the Voting Rights Act, 1965–1990* (Princeton: Princeton University Press, 1994), 38–66.

McDonald, Laughlin, et al., "Georgia," in Chandler Davidson and Bernard Grofman, eds., *Quiet Revolution in the South: The Impact of the Voting Rights Act, 1965–1990* (Princeton: Princeton University Press, 1994): 67–102.

Montejano, David, *Anglos and Mexicans in the Making of Texas, 1836–1987* (Austin: University of Texas Press, 1987).

Morris, Thomas R., and Neil Bradley, "Virginia," in Chandler Davidson and Bernard Grofman, eds., *Quiet Revolution in the South: The Impact of the Voting Rights Act, 1965–1990* (Princeton: Princeton University Press, 1994): 271–298.

New York Times, 8 March, 1869.

Norton, Mary Beth, ed., *Major Problems in American History: Documents and Essays* (Lexington, MA: D. C. Heath, 1989).

Parker, Frank, *Black Votes Count: Political Empowerment in Mississippi after 1965* (Chapel Hill: University of North Carolina Press, 1990).

Parkman, Francis, "The Failure of Universal Suffrage," *North American Review* 263 (July–August, 1878): 1–21.

Piven, Frances Fox, and Richard A. Cloward, *Why Americans Don't Vote* (New York: Pantheon, 1988).

Porter, Kirk Harold, *A History of Suffrage in the United States* (New York: AMS Press, 1971 [1918]).

Stalcup, Brenda, ed., *The Women's Rights Movement: Opposing Viewpoints* (San Diego: Greenhaven Press, 1996).

Steinfeld, Robert J., "Property and Suffrage in the Early American Republic," *Stanford Law Review* 41 (January 1989): 335–376.

Takaki, Ronald, *Strangers from a Different Shore: A History of Asian Americans* (New York: Penguin Books, 1989).

Williamson, Chilton, *American Suffrage: From Property to Democracy, 1760–1860* (Princeton: Princeton University Press, 1960).

Wolfley, Jeannette, "Jim Crow, Indian Style: The Disenfranchisement of Native Americans," *American Indian Law Review* 16 (1991): 167–202.

Wood, Gordon S., *The Creation of the American Republic, 1776–1787* (New York: W. W. Norton, 1969).

Yarbrough, Tinsley E., *A Passion for Justice: J. Waties Waring and Civil Rights* (New York: Oxford University Press, 1987).

3

Cases

The decision to turn to the courts for help is never an easy choice, nor is it always the best available. Though powerful institutions, courts have serious limitations on both their power and influence. First, judges cannot initiate litigation on their own. They are prisoners of their docket; they must deal with the lawsuits that litigants—individuals, businesses, organizations, or the government—ask them to hear. Judicial rules and precedents, in turn, often restrict the judiciary's ability to hear every matter brought before them. Fail to show a direct link to a constitutional right or federal law, for instance, and the federal courts are generally powerless even to hear your complaint, let alone to act on it. Statutes of limitations and jurisdictional boundaries further limit a court's reach. There are even judicial doctrines that prohibit—or at least counsel against—courts hearing political questions. Worse yet, even when the courts are able to hear a particular matter, additional limits to the judiciary's reach and power often make judges extremely cautious, even conservative, in their approach to ordering change. For one thing, judges do not have the authority to make new law. Although they can, and often do, reinterpret existing laws in ways unintended when they were originally written, this is not the same as creating a new law out of whole cloth. If the original law is antithetical to change, most likely its reinterpretation also will be contrary to the hopes of those seeking social or political modification. More importantly, even if they could make new law on their own initiative, judges lack the ability to enforce their decisions alone. There are no judicial police; judges do not have the power to raise money to pay for reforms by imposing new taxes or fees; they cannot even force people into court without the help of others. In fact, without the help of the other branches of government—and the support of at least some portion of the general public—courts lack the power to force change. As Alexander Hamilton notes in *Federalist #78,* by their very nature courts have "no influence over either the sword or the purse; no direction either of the strength or of the wealth of the society; and can take no active resolution whatever." In fact, Hamilton explains, "[they] may truly be said to have neither FORCE nor WILL, but merely judgment; and must ultimately depend upon the aid of the executive arm even for the efficacy of its judgments" (Hamilton, 465).

Courts, in other words, face many institutional and political constraints on their ability to generate change. Unable to promote reform on their own, they are constrained by their nature as courts of law as to the roles they can serve and the changes they can produce. Without the assistance of forces and factors external to themselves—litigants, social movements, legislative initiatives, and statutes—courts are severely limited institutions in the promotion of change.

Yet, as events of the last fifty years have shown, despite such limitations, courts can still be powerful sources of social and political transformation. School desegregation, affirmative action on the job and in university admissions, and fair housing rules are just some of the revolutionary changes initiated by the judiciary in the last half of the twentieth century. To this list we can add the discovery and protection of a personal right to privacy, the defense of a women's right to choose (or not choose) to have an abortion, and various protections of the rights of the accused from government intervention. In fact, to those coming of age in the last third of the twentieth century, the presence of judges at the center of reform and change—especially as relates to individual and group civil rights—seems both customary and natural. Courts, especially the federal courts, have become the primary forum by which the voiceless in our society—the powerless, the despised, and the forgotten—seek remedies for their wrongs.

Free from the many practical limitations imposed by the political process, courts combine the protection of lifetime or extensive tenure (which allows judges to take socially unpopular but constitutionally necessary actions) with open access for all Americans whose problems fall within their jurisdiction. Whereas other leaders might hide or compromise in the face of political pressure, judges are free—even mandated—to ignore politics and solve complex and difficult dilemmas. Although it is true that judges can do little good without the compliance of the other branches of government, their ability to take the heat and demand unpopular actions actually provides these other branches a shield under which they too can do the right thing despite the political costs (all too often while protesting their innocence and blaming the judges for their actions). As Justice William J. Brennan Jr. noted in 1981, "insulated as they are from political pressures, and charged with the duty of enforcing the Constitution, courts are in the strongest position to insist that unconstitutional conditions be remedied, even at significant financial cost" (*Rhodes v. Chapman*, 359).

In the proper situation and faced with the right issue, then, courts can initiate a wide range of social changes. In fact, as the judiciary's job description is currently understood, judges are actually *required* to take on such difficult tasks. Judge Frank M. Johnson of Alabama explained: "The cornerstone of our American legal system rests on recognition of the Constitution as the supreme law of the land, and the paramount duty of the federal judiciary is to uphold that law. Thus, when a state fails to meet constitutionally mandated requirements," or where the right of a citizen to fair and equal treatment is somehow denied, "it is the solemn duty of the courts to assure compliance with the Constitution" (Johnson, 914–915). What could be more basic than this?

Before the mid-twentieth century, however, such potential power to bring about change meant little. For over 150 years, U.S. judges refused to give the defense of political and social rights a high priority in setting their courts' objectives. Rather, most judges upheld vote denial and other limits on political participation as constitutionally permissible. Only with the rise of the civil rights revolution in the mid-twentieth century—some seventy years after the adoption of the three civil rights amendments—did the federal courts begin to enhance, rather than limit, the rights of all Americans to the franchise. Once started—hesitantly to be sure, with as many contractions early on as there were expansions—judges attacked the problem with energy, becoming in the process some of the most ardent proponents of a universal right to vote. In fact, working both alone and in concert with the other branches of government, federal judges over the last sixty years have initiated a virtual revolution in voting rights—not only expanding the range of those who could vote, but our very conceptions of this right and its meaning to U.S. politics, government, and democracy.

The history of voting rights in the courts thus mirrors the ambivalence and contradictions of voting rights history in general. From the depths of vote denial in the nineteenth century to the near universal suffrage of today, the history of voting rights on trial is a story of inertia followed by a slow, often contrary, but ever quickening shift away from vote denial in favor of vote expansion.

Initially impediments to change, by the mid-twentieth century federal judges were finally struggling with the implications and extents of an expanded vote. Along the way, old forms of vote denial were prohibited and newer forms of vote dilution challenged. Although this was never an easy task, by the 1970s these judges were finally successful in their efforts to expand the reach and meaning of the franchise. Empowered by new legislation and spurred by changing societal shifts, they became the preeminent defenders of the vote—taking the Constitution and election laws farther than ever contemplated and in directions few expected. By the late 1980s a quiet revolution in U.S. politics and government was largely complete—one based on constitutional amendments and new laws to be sure, but implemented largely by litigation in the federal courts. The formerly voiceless and powerless among us—in particular ethnic and racial minorities—finally had a say in the operation of our government by means of the vote.

The impact of this expanded vote is felt to this day. At a minimum, it has meant the construction of an entirely new character for U.S. government and politics. At the most, the revolution in voting rights has transformed the entire nature of U.S. democracy—and with it, the nation's society and life. Though the actions of the U.S. Supreme Court in the late 1990s and in the 2000 election call into question just how extensive the changes in politics and society have been, not to mention how long the judiciary's leadership in these matters will last, they do not lessen the impact or importance of the process by which millions of Americans sought out their rights in the courts, forced compliance with the Constitution and the laws of the land, and won the right to vote.

The Courts Say No to
Expanded Voting Rights

For most of their history, U.S. courts—especially the federal courts—gave the defense of political and social rights a low priority. Unfamiliar and largely unconcerned with the intricacies of such matters, judges simply ignored repressed minorities' demands for protection of political and social rights. As they saw it, such matters were not their concern. In fact, before World War II, most federal judges held a conception of their job that emphasized private, as opposed to public, matters—and few issues were more public than voting rights.

In the context of the nineteenth century's vision of society as merely the collective actions of autonomous individuals, courts were seen "as an adjunct to private ordering," an agency "whose primary function was the resolution of disputes about the fair implications of individual interactions." Judges, in turn, were supposed to be passive players in litigation. Their role was "to decide only those issues identified by the parties," based on evidence supplied by those parties, using rules "established by the appellate courts or, infrequently, the legislature," and providing relief in direct proportion to the substantive violation in contention (the remedy must be in direct proportion to the specific wrong caused by the defendant). Taken to its logical extreme, this traditional conception of adjudication severely limited the role of the trial judge and his court to private—usually economic—matters (Chayes, 1285). Reshaping social and political structures (especially when these changes were being demanded by the disadvantaged in U.S. society, as they usually were), was not in a federal judge's job description.

In fact, not only were these judges unconcerned with such deprivations, they felt they had good reason *not* to get involved. Voting rights cases raised troubling questions. Brought by distrusted, dismissed, and often despised groups, suits of this sort challenged existing social and economic relations; expand the reach of the Fourteenth or Fifteenth Amendment in terms of voting, and by implication you expanded it for a whole range of other civil rights denied to racial or gender minorities. This was a disconcerting result for most federal judges before World War II. By definition, federal judges were the allotted defenders of existing social and economic relationships— appointed by those already in power to uphold the legal status quo, not to change it. In fact, shaped by an appointment process that put the choice of judges in the hands of mostly conservative senators—not to mention as members of the social elite sharing the social biases of their contemporaries—most federal judges were extremely conservative in their social and legal views. On the whole, judges feared the effects of radical change and distrusted the benefits of enhanced rights for the body politic as a whole. Combined with technical and conceptual difficulties, these negative preconceptions made federal judges wary of efforts to expand the franchise. Indeed, they led most federal judges to oppose any attempts to increase the pool of voters to include ethnic, gender, or racial minorities.

To make matters worse, before the 1940s, there was little that federal judges could have done to help the voteless even had they wished to change priorities and work to foster the franchise for every American. As jurists in a limited judicial system, federal judges could only hear matters brought under federal laws or involving constitutional rights; with a few technical exceptions involving diverse state citizenship, state law matters were beyond their authority. Unfortunately, this ban included voting rights. As noted in chapter 1, in an effort to ease the ratification of the Constitution, the founders had severed all control over who can vote from the national government, separating national citizenship from the act of voting. Before ratification of the Fourteenth Amendment in 1868 and the Fifteenth Amendment in 1870, the voting process was regulated entirely by state laws.

Of course, adoption of the Fourteenth and Fifteenth Amendments did not actually change matters noticeably either—at least at first. Although federal judges finally had a constitutional license to explore voting rights, they still had little motivation to do so. Those seeking aid from the judiciary still faced significant hurdles in their efforts to use the federal courts as a mechanism of change. Yet, the opportunity was there; if the voteless could somehow convince a federal judge that laws excluding them from the franchise infringed their constitutional rights, change was possible—unlikely, but possible.

Encouraged—and as they saw it, empowered—by the civil rights amendments, many ethnic-, racial-, and gender-based groups did exactly this in the years following ratification of the civil rights amendments, turning to the federal courts for help in forcing the states to allow them to vote. Each felt that they had a strong case to make. After all, what could be a more fundamental right of citizenship than the right to vote? Did not Congress just add to the Constitution one amendment guaranteeing equal protection and another explicitly upholding the right of formerly excluded African Americans to vote? As citizens born in the geographic confines of the United States, were they not entitled to the full range of privileges and immunities of citizenship—including the right to vote? These voteless groups were convinced that if they could just make their case to the highest courts of the land—and if the judges on those courts would just listen—justice would be achieved and their right to vote finally acknowledged.

Sadly, cogent as such claims were, for over seventy years the hopes of each of these groups were fated to be disappointed by the judicial response to their calls for help. Federal judges might have had the authority to act, but before the 1940s they saw little reason to do so. Asked by excluded groups, "Did not the Fourteenth Amendment cover us too," the federal courts' repeated answer was an echoing "NO."

One of the first groups to argue its case before the federal courts was that of Native Americans. As noted in chapter 2, Indians had been challenging their status within the American nation in the federal courts since the 1830s. By the 1870s the reigning doctrine was that Indians, as domestic dependents, were not citizens and thus could not vote. The Fourteenth Amendment, however, called this understanding into question. There was little doubt that Indians were born within the borders of the United States. By a literal reading of the Fourteenth Amendment, this should have made Indians citizens with all the rights of citizenship, including the right to vote. Although a legitimate argument might have been made for excluding those Indians still living on reservations (as partly sovereign territories, perhaps reservations were not fully a part of the United States, at least for purposes of assigning citizenship), what about those Indians living off the reservation? Far from isolating themselves, these Indians lived and worked in the general population. They bought homes, paid taxes, and even intermarried with whites. Surely these Indians were covered by the Fourteenth Amendment's grant of citizenship.

Yet as early as 1871 the federal courts spurned this claim. The suit was filed by Alexander McKay, born in Oregon of a Canadian father and an Indian mother. At the time of the trial, McKay had lived his entire life in Oregon except for five years when he traveled to New York to attend school. At no time did he reside among his mother's people. Still, when McKay attempted to vote in 1870, he was turned away as a noncitizen. In the eyes of the local election officials, McKay was either British or Indian; in either case, this made him a noncitizen and thus ineligible to vote. McKay objected and brought suit, claiming, among other arguments, that as the child of an American Indian, born within the confines of the United States, he was a citizen by virtue of the Fourteenth Amendment.

Taking the case under advisement, Judge Matthew Deady of the U.S. District Court of Oregon took exception to McKay's reading of the law. As Deady read the precedents, McKay was not a citizen. "Being born a member of 'an independent political community'— the Chinook [Indian Tribe]—[McKay] was not born subject to the jurisdiction of the United States—not born in its allegiance," the judge argued. As such, McKay could not be a citizen without being naturalized first. Yet here too, McKay was out of luck. Unfortunately, "as the law now stands," the judge explained, McKay "cannot be admitted to citizenship, because he is neither a 'white alien' nor a person of 'African nativity or descent.'" Wrong as that may sound, even to the judge, there was nothing to be done about it—for naturalization was "a matter within the exclusive cognizance of congress."

Before concluding, Judge Deady noted his understanding of the scope and impact of his decision. He was "aware that the ruling in this case, would exclude from the privilege of voting quite a number of persons of mixed blood—persons whose fathers were British subjects, and mothers, Indian women—who have heretofore often, if not uniformly been allowed to vote in this state." Yet they did so "by common consent, and under the authority of a vague public opinion that these persons by remaining south of the forty-ninth parallel after the treaty of 1846, could, and thereby did, elect to become American citizens." Sadly, "'public opinion is not any authority on a point of law,'" and it appears in this instance as in others, "'that common consent is sometimes a common error.' The remedy, if any is deemed necessary, is with the legislature, and not the courts" (*McKay v. Campbell*, 166–167).

Sadly, Congress was not interested in acting on this matter. This left Native Americans only the courts in which to fight their exclusion from the polls. The courts, however, remained unwilling to act. A few years later, for instance, Judge Deady again faced the question of Indian citizenship. Here the contention was that assimilating into white society automatically granted to Indians the rights of citizenship. Again the judge disagreed:

> An Indian cannot make himself a citizen of the United States without the consent and cooperation of the government. . . .The fact that he has abandoned his nomadic life or tribal relations, and adopted the habits and manners of civilized people, may be a good reason why he should be made a citizen . . . , but does not of itself make him one. To be a citizen of the United States is a political privilege which no one, not born to, can assume without its consent in some form. (*United States v. Osborne*, quoted in *Elk v. Wilkins*, 109)

Once again, until Congress chose to act and change the laws, Indians—even assimilated Indians—were strangers banned from citizenship and the vote by nature of their birth.

This was a view shared by other judges. In 1884, for instance, in *Elk v. Wilkins* the U.S. Supreme Court refused to extend the privileges and protections of the Fourteenth Amendment to Indians in these matters. The facts of the case mirrored those presented to Judge Deady years before. John Elk, born on an unnamed Indian reservation, had subsequently "severed his tribal relation to the Indian tribes." At the time of the case, he had been residing in Omaha for a number of years and felt that he was a citizen. Yet when he tried to vote, he was denied as a noncitizen.

The question before the Court was simple: was "an Indian, born a member of one of the Indian tribes within the United States, . . . merely by reason of his birth within the United States, and of his afterwards voluntarily separating himself from his tribe and taking up his residency among white citizens, a citizen of the United States, within the meaning of the first section of the Fourteenth Amendment of the Constitution [?]" The majority on the Court felt not. "Indians born within the territorial limits of the United States, members of . . . one of the Indian tribes (an alien, though dependent, power), although in a geographical sense born in the United States," explained Justice Horace Gray, "are no more 'born in the United States and subject to the jurisdiction thereof,' within the meaning of the first section of the Fourteenth Amendment, than the children of subjects of any foreign government born within the domain of that government, or the children born within the United States, of ambassadors or other public ministers of foreign nations."

Nor did moving away from their tribe change this condition. "The alien and dependent condition of the members of the Indian tribes could not be put off at their own will, without the action or assent of the United States," Justice Gray asserted. In fact,

> the question whether any Indian tribes, or any members thereof, have become so far advanced in civilization, that they should be let out of the state of pupilage, and admitted to the privileges and responsibilities of citizenship, is a question to be decided by the nation whose wards they are and whose citizens they seek to become, and not by each Indian for himself.

Until Congress chose to naturalize Elk and other Indians of his condition, there was nothing anyone else could do to change their status; the choice was not theirs, nor the courts', to make (*Elk v. Wilkins,* 99, 100–102, 106–107). As already noted, until the 1920s, Congress was not interested in acting. Hence, until then, the Fourteenth Amendment did not include Indians within its reach.

This was a conclusion that the courts reached just as quickly in regard to women voting. In fact, if anything, judicial opposition to women voting was even stronger than had been the case over Indian citizenship. Women had also taken up the challenge of the Fourteenth Amendment quite early. Throughout the 1860s and 1870s, many women made attempts to force female suffrage on the states by court order. Among them were two relatively unknown sisters in Glastonbury, Connecticut, who, throughout the late 1860s and early 1870s, brought suit and refused to pay taxes on their land until they were granted the right to vote. Another was Susan B. Anthony, leader of the women's rights movement, who was arrested and convicted in 1870 for illegally voting.

Most significant in this regard, however, if only because it reached the Supreme Court, was the challenge of Virginia Minor against the state of Missouri and local election registrar Reese Happersett. In 1872, Minor had attempted to vote for president and been refused by Happersett. Minor sued, claiming that both under the First Amendment (as a limitation on her speech) and the Fourteenth (as a denial of the privileges or immunities of citizenship), Missouri's constitution and election laws violated the U.S. Constitution by excluding women from the vote. The lower courts had disagreed, throwing out

Minor's case without even holding a trial. The Supreme Court was her last hope. It proved a poor one.

Writing for the Court, Chief Justice Morrison Waite noted that, "there is no doubt that women may be citizens. They are persons, and by the fourteenth amendment 'all persons born or naturalized in the United States and subject to the jurisdiction thereof' are expressly declared to be 'citizens of the United States and of the State wherein they reside.'" Yet to say that women are citizens did not mean that they were necessarily empowered to vote. The term "citizen" merely denoted "membership of a nation," identifying those who "owe [the nation] allegiance and [are] entitled to its protection... nothing more." Voting, in fact, was not a "privilege or immunity" granted by the Constitution. At the Constitution's writing, not every male was allowed to vote, and yet they were still citizens; the same was true of women who had been born in the United States. The issue was settled. "For nearly ninety years the people have acted upon the idea that the Constitution, when it conferred citizenship, did not necessarily confer the right of suffrage" the justices concluded. The Court's hands were tied.

> Our province is to decide what the law is, not to declare what it should be.... No argument as to woman's need of suffrage can be considered. We can only act upon her rights as they exist. It is not for us to look at the hardship of withholding. Our duty is at an end if we find it is within the power of a State to withhold.

So far as the nine men who presided over the Supreme Court were concerned, "the Constitution of the United States does not confer the right of suffrage upon anyone, and that the constitutions and laws of the several States which commit that important trust to men alone are not necessarily void" (*Minor v. Happersett,* 165–166, 177–178).

Decisions such as *Elk v. Wilkins* and *Minor v. Happersett* exemplify the tone underlying the judicial response to voting rights suits before the 1940s. Expanding the breadth of those who could vote was not a proper judicial task, as the judges saw things. Despite the Fourteenth Amendment, the constitutional compromise on suffrage remained intact. With the sole exception of African American males, deciding who could vote was a local matter beyond the federal courts' ability to change (and as we shall see, before long judges were even adding black males to this list as well). The range of those told no could, in fact, be substantial.

In 1902 the New York Court of Appeals upheld wealth-based limits, denying a challenge to a state law limiting municipal elections over issuing bonds to taxpayers only. In their eyes, "the proposition that the incurring of such indebtedness shall be sustained only when a majority of the taxable inhabitants shall vote in its favor, seems . . . only to be pre-eminently just." (*Spitzer v. Village of Fulton,* 958). Thirteen years later, the U.S. Supreme Court in *Myers v. Anderson,* while overturning a similar statute in Maryland as racially discriminatory, upheld this same exclusion in the abstract.

In 1904 the high Court affirmed state rules denying recent migrants the vote in *Pope v. Williams,* also out of Maryland. As far as the justices saw things, the statute did "not violate any Federal right of the plaintiff." The Maryland law was "neither an unlawful discrimination . . . nor [did] it deny . . . the equal protection of the laws, nor [was] it repugnant to any fundamental or inalienable right of citizens" (*Pope v. Williams,* 633). Barring evidence of such limitations, there was no reason for the Court to act.

In 1922 a Japanese immigrant, Takao Ozawa, challenged his denial of citizenship and hence the vote. Yet the Supreme Court refused his plea, noting Asians were "clearly of a race [that] is not Caucasian and therefore belongs entirely outside the zone" of legal inclusion—at least pending a change in the laws (*Ozawa v. United States,* 189, 198).

Then there were the litigation efforts by African Americans, excluded from the vote despite the Fifteenth Amendment. Surprisingly slow to start (perhaps because, until the 1890s, many blacks still had access to the polls; or maybe because blacks had other discrimination issues to cope with), the African American community's efforts to gain the vote proved to be the most significant and long-lasting in the end of any attempt by minorities to put voting rights on trial. Lasting over a generation, the legal fight for race-neutral voting soon dominated the voting rights debate. It also provided some of the earliest and hardest fought victories of any minority group seeking the vote through court action. Consequently, our discussion of voting rights in the courts must move on into the twentieth century and the black community's assault on race-based vote denial and the all-white primary.

The Fall of the All-White Primary

By the second decade of the twentieth century, the situation for southern blacks was not a good one. What had once seemed like the road to full inclusion into U.S. society had turned into a complete denial of citizenship and even of personhood. Segregation, legal separation of the races in all aspects of public life, was now the law—and brutal reality—in the South. Empowered by the U.S. Supreme Court's "separate but equal" ruling in 1896's *Plessy v. Ferguson,* the South's twenty-five-year effort to lock out blacks from the public realm was near complete by 1900.

Still, despite these difficulties, blacks continued to turn to the federal courts as their best hope to combat discrimination and segregation (a sign of just how desperate the situation was, given federal judges' distaste for civil rights suits of all sorts). Led by the NAACP, but drawing on deep-seated local concerns and priorities, blacks attacked a wide range of discriminations in the federal courts, losing more often than winning, but gaining just enough victories to encourage continued effort. By the time of *Brown v. Board of Education* in 1954, these efforts would prove increasingly successful as legal campaigns against segregated education, housing, and the large number of race-based lynchings across the South brought about real reforms—or at least the potential for reform.

The same held true for voting rights. Here, the NAACP's target was the all-white primary. As noted in chapter 2, blacks chose to attack the all-white primary mostly because rules that excluded registered voters seemed more vulnerable to attack than technically race-neutral statutes and constitutional provisions that circuitously disallowed black voting. (This was, in fact, an accurate assumption. In *Breedlove v. Suttles,* for example, the Supreme Court in 1937 would unanimously uphold Georgia's poll tax, putting this particular barrier to voting out of reach of reformers until the 1960s. Similar Supreme Court rulings in the 1930s and 1940s would affirm literacy tests and gerrymandered districting as constitutional.)

How these efforts fared in the courts can best be seen through the example of the twenty-five-year fight to break the Texas all-white Democratic Party primary. Not only was the battle against the all-white primary in Texas the first actually to succeed—a major achievement—but the process by which this particular form of segregation was ended is instructive about the process by which court-ordered change operated in these matters. In particular, it shows both the ongoing opposition within the lower federal judiciary to change and the Supreme Court's slow, often ambiguous shift in judicial policy on voting rights matters. The tide was finally about to turn, but the method of its shift was anything but straightforward or comprehensive. Still, it was in Texas that the first steps in the judiciary's attack on vote denial were made.

Whites had effectively excluded blacks from voting in the Texas Democratic primary since the passage of the 1903 Terrell Election Act. The first Texas law to fully regulate primary elections, the Terrell Act granted all qualified voters in the state the right to vote in any party primary as long as they had successfully completed a prescribed "party test." Determining the exact content of this test, however, was left to the individual parties. The act further allowed any "county executive committee of the party holding any primary election" the right to "prescribe additional qualifications" for participating voters (1903 *General Laws of Texas*, 148–152). With no guidelines to limit party action, most Democratic county executive committees quickly adopted party membership qualifications banning blacks from voting in the Democratic primary. Twenty years later, the state legislature made this prohibition official, ordering "that in no event shall a negro be eligible to participate in a Democratic party primary" (1923 *General Laws of Texas*, 74–75). Since the Texas Democratic Party controlled the state government, as well as most local governments in Texas, this ban on participation meant the effective disenfranchisement of Texas blacks. With only Democratic Party candidates standing a serious chance of electoral victory, the real choices about who would govern Texas were made in the Democratic primary; voting in the general election or the Republican primary, in both of which registered blacks were permitted to participate, were meaningless acts.

Angered, Texas blacks challenged the white primary in the courts. The first such effort was made by Houston journalist C. N. Love, who, along with other community leaders, filed suit in state district court on February 5, 1921, against Harris County Democratic Party Chairperson James Griffith and numerous local elections judges. Charging that state laws prohibiting qualified blacks from voting in the Democratic primary violated the Fourteenth and Fifteenth Amendments, the plaintiffs sought an injunction preventing the defendants from disallowing the votes of Houston blacks in the upcoming primary election. The defendants argued that the state law prohibiting blacks from voting in the Democratic primary did not infringe upon the Fifteenth Amendment and that the plaintiffs' complaint, flawed for including arguments to this end, was inadequate to justify court jurisdiction. State District Judge Charles Ashe agreed and ordered the plaintiffs to submit a new complaint minus the offending sections. Love and his fellow plaintiffs refused. The Fifteenth Amendment was the foundation to their case. To remove it would destroy their chances of victory. With no new complaint filed, Judge Ashe ordered Love's case dismissed.

Subsequently appealed to both the Court of Civil Appeals and the Texas Supreme Court, the case was dismissed each time on the grounds that, as the election had already passed, no actual controversy or injury existed; with no real controversy present, equity jurisdiction could not arise and the appeals courts had no case to rule upon. Persisting, Love and his associates brought the case to the United States Supreme Court on a writ of error, charging that the state appellate courts had erred in failing to rule on the case. Justice Oliver Wendell Holmes, writing for the majority, affirmed the state courts' positions, however. As the cause of action had ceased to exist, Holmes wrote, " . . . there was no constitutional obligation to extend the remedy beyond what was prayed." Holmes did, however, hold out a ray of hope to Texas blacks: "If the case [had] stood here as it stood before the court of first instance, it would [have] presented a grave question of constitutional law [that the Court] should be astute to avoid hindrances in the way of taking it up" (*Love v. Griffith*, 45, 32).

Encouraged by Holmes's *dicta* in the *Love* case, El Paso physician Dr. L. A. Nixon, made a second attempt to break the all-white primary in 1924. Nixon had recently been denied the right to vote in the Democratic primary by election judge C. C. Herndon who cited the state's 1923 election law. The U.S. District Court for the Western District of Texas and the Fifth Circuit Court of Appeals both dismissed Nixon's motions for the reasons given in *Love v. Griffith:* the event that Nixon sought to avoid had already occurred, and hence no actual controversy or pending harm existed for the court to prohibit. Nixon then appealed to the U.S. Supreme Court. This time, the outcome was different. Holmes, again writing for the majority, held the 1923 voting rights law an unconstitutional violation of the Fourteenth Amendment. "It seems . . . hard to imagine a more direct and obvious infringement of the Fourteenth Amendment," he wrote. "While states may do a good deal of classifying that is difficult to believe rational, there are limits [to this power], and it is too clear for extended argument that color cannot be made the basis of a statutory classification affecting the right" to vote in a primary election (*Nixon v. Herndon*, 536).

Jubilation with the *Nixon* decision proved short-lived, however. Holmes's opinion dealt only with the explicit prohibition of black voting by the legislature. In response to the *Holmes* ruling, Governor Dan Moody quickly called a special session of the state legislature to amend the primary voting law by deleting provisions explicitly barring black voting. The Democratic Party again would determine voter qualifications. Soon after the amended law was passed (June 7, 1927), the Democratic Party Executive Committee resolved that "All white Democrats who are qualified voters under the Constitutions and laws of Texas . . . and none other, [will] be allowed to participate in the primary elections to be [subsequently] held" (quoted in Hainsworth, 177–178).

Once again barred from voting, a number of prominent black Houstonians, led by James Grigsby and Owen DeWalt, set out to challenge the Texas Democratic Party's ban. In July 1928, they appeared before Judge Joseph C. Hutcheson Jr. of the U.S. District Court for the Southern District Court of Texas, seeking a temporary injunction to bar the Executive Committee of the Harris County Democratic Party from hindering qualified black voter participation in the upcoming primary, in violation of the Fourteenth and Fifteenth Amendments. Primaries existed under authority of the state of Texas, they argued, which made the party's actions "state action" under the Constitution. In line with Holmes's *dicta* in *Nixon*, the plaintiffs contended, the Court could not allow a ban on black voting to continue.

Judge Hutcheson disagreed. The State Executive Committee resolution was "purely party action." Though Texas authorized the Democratic Party to run its primaries, it was still a private, voluntary organization and the party could limit its membership as it chose. The ban on joining the Democratic Party therefore posed no "invasion of [the plaintiffs'] legal rights." As no legal rights were threatened, the judge concluded, no decision on relief need be made. Hutcheson therefore denied the request for a restraining injunction (*Grigsby v. Harris*, 942).

By 1930 Texas blacks were ready to try once again to challenge the white primary. Julius White, a Houston nightclub owner, sued in state court against J. B. "Shorty" Lubbock, Harris County Democratic Party executive committee chairperson, seeking an injunction ordering Lubbock to ignore orders from the State Executive Committee to bar blacks from voting. Concurrent with this suit, C. N. Love turned to the Southern District of Texas for a similar injunction. Citing *Grigsby v. Harris,* both the Texas Court of Civil Appeals and Judge Hutcheson refused the requested writ. As both the state and federal judges saw matters, until the Supreme Court acted against the all-white primary, the law was settled.

Soon after this, a second suit by El Paso's Dr. Nixon, this time against election judge James Condon, resulted in just such a Supreme Court opinion challenging the Texas all-white primary. Justice Benjamin N. Cardozo spoke for the Court. The Texas Democratic Party was not a simple voluntary association in primary elections, wrote Cardozo. Its organization and control of these elections derived directly from a "grant of power" from the state, and hence was a prohibited "state action" under the Fourteenth Amendment as constituted; the all-white primary was unconstitutional. However, as with Holmes's earlier opinion attacking the Texas all-white primary, Cardozo left a loophole through which the Texas Democrats could circumvent the Court's ruling. Cardozo noted that "[w]hatever inherent power a state political party has to determine the content of its membership resides in the state convention." Further, the Justice pointed out, this body had never declared its "will to bar negroes of the state from admission to the party ranks" (*Nixon v. Condon,* 73).

Responding to this decision, Texas Democrats quickly called a state convention that limited participation in the party to "all white citizens." Foiled by this concession and resolution in their efforts to break the all-white primary, Texas blacks turned once more to the Southern District of Texas for relief, hoping that the court's new judge, Thomas M. Kennerly, would prove more open to their arguments than Judge Hutcheson.

In part, this hope was vindicated. Given Justice Cardozo's opinion in the second *Nixon* case, Judge Kennerly ruled that "the powers exercised by the [state Democratic] convention in passing such a resolution [banning black voting] were derived from the state of Texas" and hence prohibited by the Fourteenth Amendment. "Unlike Moses, who refused to be known as the son of Pharaoh's daughter, the Democratic Party in Texas has over a period of twenty-five years, chosen to be known as a child and agency of the state of Texas, abandoning its own inherent powers, and choosing to conduct its affairs under grants of power from the state."

Yet despite this concession to the right of blacks to vote in the Democratic primary, Kennerly ultimately proved no more willing to act than had Judge Hutcheson, dismissing this case on the grounds that his court did not have "jurisdiction to entertain complainant's bill because of the nature of his prayer for relief." In effect, Kennerly explained, the plaintiffs were requesting "a mandamus against respondents to require [the] respondents . . . to allow [blacks] to vote in such primary." Although his court had "jurisdiction of the parties and the subject matter," the judge concluded, "[it had] no jurisdiction to grant [said] mandamus." Unable to provide a remedy, Kennerly was forced, as he put it, to dismiss the case. (*White v. County Democratic Executive Committee of Harris County*, 973).

With their right to vote upheld but unprotected by Kennerly's decision, Texas blacks once again were refused the ballot by election judges in the next Democratic primary. In 1932, Kennerly once more refused to hear the case, citing the past justifications for inaction and the technicality that the plaintiffs' attorneys had given insufficient notice of the case to the defendants.

This pattern continued for the remainder of the 1930s. Cases would be brought before the Texas federal district courts, only to have the judge refuse to order injunctions, citing a number of procedural and occasionally substantive reasons for this opinion. In 1933, for example, Julius White sued the Houston Democratic Party to uphold his right to vote in a primary election for city officials. Kennerly denied his plea on the grounds that, in barring blacks from voting, city Democrats had been acting under an "inherent power of the party." As no state power was involved in city primaries, Kennerly asserted, their conduct was not governed by *Nixon v. Condon* or even by his opinion in *White v. Lubbock* (*White v. Executive Committee of Harris County*, 973). In 1938, Houston blacks tried again, only to have Kennerly refuse to consider the case on the grounds that it offered no new arguments beyond those made in 1933.

Only in the early 1940s did this trend begin to change. Following the Supreme Court's 1941 decision in *United States v. Classic* that Article I, Section 4 of the U.S. Constitution gave Congress the power to regulate primary elections "where the primary is by law made an integral part of the election machinery," Dr. Lonnie Smith sued S. E. Allwright and James E. Luizza, elections judges of the Forty-eighth Precinct, for refusing to allow him to vote in a July 1940 primary in Houston.

Smith's lawyer, NAACP chief counsel Thurgood Marshall, intended a direct attack on the Texas all-white primary. However, few expected Judge Kennerly or the Fifth Circuit to rule in the plaintiff's favor. Nor were they disappointed in their expectations. Despite Marshall's arguments seeking to extend *United States v. Classic* to the Texas situation, neither Kennerly nor the judges of the fifth circuit agreed with this reading of the *Classic* rule to the Texas situation. "In Louisiana," Kennerly noted, "the State Law . . . made the primary 'an integral part of the procedure of choice.' In Texas it has not" ("Memorandum," *Smith v. Allwright*).

Rather, Marshall's arguments were aimed at the U.S. Supreme Court. Ruling in 1944, the Court followed the logic of *Classic* and held that the Texas Democratic Party's control of the state's primary system was evidence that it operated as an "agency of the state" and hence was prohibited by the Constitution from denying any citizen the right to vote on the basis of race alone. That this ban reflected the wishes of Democratic Party members was no valid excuse, the Court ruled: "The party takes its character as a state agency from the duties imposed upon it by state statutes; the duties do not become matters of private law because they are performed by a political party." The Democratic Party's exclusion of blacks, therefore, was a constitutional violation that the courts could not allow. "The fusing by the *Classic* case of the primary and general elections into a single instrumentality for the choice of officers has [created]," the high Court ruled, a definite prohibition as to "the permissibility under the Constitution of excluding Negroes from primaries" (*Smith v. Allwright*, 639).

At first skeptical that *Smith v. Allwright* would have any greater impact than the two *Nixon* cases, Texas blacks soon realized that they had won a major victory. In the summer of 1944, Texas blacks voted in the Democratic primary for the first time without (serious) contest or conflict. The Texas all-white primary had died. Before long, the all-white primary was dead by court order across the South.

Yet significantly, the Texas all-white primary died despite, rather than because of, the actions of the lower levels of the federal judiciary. If anything, the refusal of the lower federal courts to promote this

end, despite a clear, if slowly evolving, shift in Supreme Court attitudes in these matters, delayed the white primary's demise by years.
As late as 1940, enforcing social rules in conflict with community
standards and traditions were still not a part of their job description
as these judges understood it; and although this view was soon to
change, as late as 1950 it still held strong force. The result was a pattern of opposition to expanding the protections of civil rights
matched with token compliance with changing appellate court policies; barring explicit orders, these judges saw little reason to act, and
where such orders existed, they would act only as specifically
required by the Supreme Court, no more.

Of equal significance for lower federal courts' unwillingness to act
in such matters was the Supreme Court's tentative response to their
refusal. The main reason for the Texas district courts' footdragging
was that the Supreme Court itself was unsure where to go in these
matters. This was especially the case in the three decades before 1950,
when the Court sought a coherent policy on civil rights, one that
accorded with the limitations imposed by past precedent (*Plessy v.
Ferguson* and the "separate but equal" doctrine) yet also met the
legitimate demands of African Americans for justice. Clearly the
nineteenth century response to voting rights matters—a complete
refusal to act—was no longer an appropriate response to civil rights
injustices. Yet, what should replace this policy? Unsure how to act,
the Supreme Court took a piecemeal approach to the problem, ruling
narrowly on issues raised by specific civil rights cases. This approach
had the advantage of being easy to defend within both the Court and
U.S. society as a whole. By the early 1940s these narrow rulings had
become a fully formed doctrine in opposition to the unequal application of law for blacks. Yet one unavoidable result of a piecemeal
approach to reform was that it left a lot of conceptual "wiggle room"
for the lower courts—room that these judges willingly accepted and
used.

If radical decisions actually granting blacks their constitutional
right to vote were to come, the drive for change not only had to orig-
inate in the Supreme Court, but it had to be delivered in an unam-
biguous form backed by a commitment to force change. Unfortunately, as we have just seen, when the Supreme Court finally did take
a stand on the question of racism and vote denial, clarity of focus was
not the result. The meanings of these rulings were both vague and
uncertain. Explicit segregation in voting was no longer permitted,

but what this meant for other limits on voting rights was left unclear. Did an end to the all-white primary mean that all forms of vote denial had to go? What about those denials that were (technically) race neutral? The Supreme Court did not say. In fact, with a few minor exceptions, the Supreme Court would not provide clear rulings on the issue as regarded voting rights until the early 1960s. Until then, the issue was squarely in the lower federal courts' hands—and they were unsure how to respond. The result was a wide range of responses to civil rights suits. In consequence, the next twenty years gave blacks fighting for the vote both litigation successes and failures. Although the general trend was slowly moving in the direction of enhanced voting rights, the overall experience would be an uncertain one filled with delay and obstructionism. Change was coming, but it was going to take a few more years to be fully realized.

Victory and Defeat in the Lower Federal Courts

Encouraged by the victory in *Smith v. Allwright*, blacks across the South quickly moved against other exclusionary voting practices in the federal courts—with mixed results. In a surprisingly large number of cases, they were able to convince southern district judges to overturn clear violations of both the letter and spirit of the *Smith* decision. Using both individual case studies and broad statistics, civil rights lawyers educated these judges as to the injustices and gross inequalities present at that time in the South. Court orders requiring the registration and balloting of black voters soon followed.

In 1947, for instance, U.S. District Judge J. Waties Waring declared unconstitutional South Carolina's attempt to rewrite its election laws to "completely renounce control of political parties and [the] primaries held thereunder." Such efforts to divorce party primaries from state authority and thus continue the prohibition on black voting in the Democratic primary, though inventive, were not constitutionally sufficient, he held. Despite the rules change, "the present Democratic Party in South Carolina is acting for and on behalf of the people of South Carolina." This simple reality was the controlling factor in such matters. As Judge Waring explained, "all citizens of this State and Country are entitled to cast a free and untrammeled ballot in our elections ... and if the only material and realistic elections are clothed with the name 'primary,' they are equally entitled to vote there." It was "time for South Carolina to rejoin the Union," he concluded; "time to fall in step with the other states and to adopt the American way of conducting elections" (*Elmore v. Rice*, 521, 528).

Two years later, a three-judge court concluded that Alabama's Boswell Amendment's "understand and explain" requirements did not provide "a reasonable standard" by which local registrars could properly administer their test; as written, the amendment "confer[red], . . . a naked and arbitrary power to give or withhold consent" according to that local official's personal biases. This was wrong. "The board has the power to establish two classes," wrote Judge Clarence H. Mullins for the panel. "Those to whom they consent and those to whom they do not—those who may vote and those who may not. . . . Such arbitrary power, amount[ed] to a denial of equal protection of the law within the meaning of the Fourteenth Amendment to the Constitution." Worse yet, the requirement clearly had been adopted for the sole "purpose of excluding Negro applicants for the franchise." Hence, "while it [was] true that there [was] no mention of race or color in the Boswell Amendment, this does not save it." The amendment was unconstitutional: "we cannot ignore the impact of the Boswell Amendment upon Negro citizens because it avoids mention of race or color," the court concluded. "To do this would be to shut our eyes to what all others than we can see and understand" (*Davis v. Schnell*, 877–878, 881).

In 1950, Southern District of Texas Judge Thomas Kennerly—who a decade earlier had ruled against Smith and affirmed the all-white primary—held the segregated Jaybird Democratic Association (a purportedly self-governing voluntary private club, which put forth a slate of candidates that "nearly always" ran unopposed in the Democratic primaries) to be "a political organization or party" and ruled "that its chief object had always been to deny Negroes any voice or part in the election of county officials." Judge Kennerly therefore ruled the association's racial discriminations invalid and entered judgment accordingly (*Terry v. Adams* [1950], 595). Interestingly, the court of appeals reversed this decision, holding that "there was no constitutional or congressional bar to the admitted discriminatory exclusion of Negroes because Jaybird's primaries were not to any extent state controlled" (*Adams v. Terry*, 600). Appealed to the Supreme Court in 1953, the result shifted again. Justice Hugo L. Black, writing for the majority, agreed with Kennerly and ruled the

Jaybird election the real primary election in Texas; the Court then remanded the case back to his district court to "consider and determine what provisions are essential to afford Negro citizens of the County full protection from such future discriminatory election practices which deprive citizens of voting rights because of their color" (*Terry v. Adams* [1953], 461–463).

In 1959, Eastern District of Louisiana Judge J. Skelly Wright, faced a constitutional challenge to the Civil Rights Act of 1957, which had granted to the Justice Department's Civil Rights Division authority to prosecute voting rights violations. The challenge (a motion to dismiss) arose in response to an attack by the Justice Department on Louisiana's purging law under which any two registered voters could demand the removal of all so-called illegally registered voters. Before 1959, the Citizen's Council of Washington Parish had successfully challenged the status of 85 percent of the parish's black voters, but only .07 percent of white, arguing that they, the black voters, were illegally registered. The Justice Department objected, charging that the Citizen's Council's "profession of high purpose was a fraud designed to [wrongfully] deny Negro citizens of a right to vote." The defendants, members of the Citizen's Council and the local Registrars of Voters, never denied the truth of the allegations. Rather, they argued that, as the Civil Rights Act of 1957 authorized "action against private individuals as well as persons acting under color of law," the statute as written was invalid. Judge Wright rejected this proposition:

> In a democratic society there is no greater offense than illegally depriving a citizen of his right to vote. Such discrimination strikes at the very foundation of constitutional government. This offense is compounded when, as alleged here, it is committed under the guise of enforcing the law. The United States has made the solemn charge that these defendants have committed such an offense. Instead of challenging the constitutionality of the Civil Rights Act of 1957, these defendants should be searching their souls to see if this charge is well founded.

Three months later, Judge Wright did just this, ruling in favor of the plaintiff and issuing an injunction returning 1,377 blacks to the voter rolls (*United States v. McElveen*, 356–360).

In the 1960s, Judge Frank M. Johnson of the Middle District of Alabama ruled twice against the double standard prevalent in Alabama's voter enrollment practices. "The evidence . . . is overwhelmingly to the effect that the State of Alabama, acting through its agents, . . . has deliberately engaged in acts and practices designed to discriminate against qualified Negroes in their efforts to register to vote," the judge noted in the first case, *United States v. Alabama* (1961). Such practices as "providing registration facilities sufficient to handle the registration of all unregistered eligible white persons, but insufficient to handle more than a token number of unregistered eligible Negroes," or "assisting white applicants for registration, but rendering no such assistance to Negro applicants," perpetuated "the disparity between the relative percentages of Negroes and whites registered to vote" (*United States v. Alabama*, 679). The bias could be quite blatant. In the second case, 1962's *United States v. Penton,* Judge Johnson found that "prior to June 1, 1960, the [Montgomery County Voter Registration] Board registered over 96 percent of the white applicants and rejected for registration over 75 percent of the Negro applicants—including 710 Negro applicants who had 12 years or more of formal education." Such practices were simply wrong, he concluded. More important, they constituted a clear "denial of due process of law and an abridgment of privileges and immunities of citizens under the Constitution of the United States." With this in mind, Judge Johnson ordered that the rejected applicants be immediately placed on the voter rolls. More significantly, Johnson forbade the state from continuing such discriminatory practices and demanded that in the future blacks be registered by the exact same standards and rules as whites "at the time [blacks had] applied for and were deprived registration by the defendants." (*United States v. Penton,* 196–197, 200–201).

This last proviso was an important ruling. Before Judge Johnson's decision in *Penton,* the Justice Department was worried that local registrars might "freeze" out the clear intent of a judicial order against future discrimination by "strictly applying the suffrage procedures to both races" in registering new voters. "Since most whites and few blacks were enrolled, crafty officials could [thus] perpetuate the status quo and not technically violate the law" by simply following the exclusionary "letter" of the existing statutes. With this possibility in mind, the Justice Department asked southern federal judges to order that the traditional beneficial application of those rules now be applied to blacks. This meant that adult blacks only had "to meet the criteria, or lack thereof, that whites had during the period of disfranchisement" (Lawson 1999, 268).

To ensure that his decree was enforced, Judge Johnson retained jurisdiction, required county registrars to submit monthly progress reports with the names and dates of applications received during the reporting period (including listing the exact reasons for all applicants rejected), and threatened to appoint federal voter referees if his decree were not followed to the letter.

The victories in these and other cases were genuine. In many instances, the changes demanded were significant in terms of allowing blacks to register to vote (though less so in terms of black access to political power). Yet for all these gains, such cases were atypical of southern federal judges' response to voting rights suits. Instead, delay and obstructionism proved to be much more the norm when blacks turned to the southern district courts for relief following *Smith v. Allwright*. As with other civil rights matters in this time, most southern district judges felt ambivalent about extending the reach of the Supreme Court's voting rights rulings beyond their explicit boundaries. Decades of token compliance with changing appellate court policies had produced a tradition of narrow decisions in civil rights matters. Barring definitive orders, southern district judges saw little reason to act; where such orders existed, they would respond as specifically required by the Supreme Court, but only that far, no more.

This was especially the case with voting rights. Many judges, as avowed segregationists, were opposed to any efforts to extend the black franchise. They agreed (though no doubt in less prosaic terms) with the words of one white cotton ginner when faced with the prospect of black suffrage: "The niggers would take over the county if they could vote in full numbers. They'd stick together and vote blacks into every office in the county. Why you'd have a nigger judge, nigger sheriff, a nigger tax assessor—think what the black SOB's would do to you" (quoted in Lawson 1999, 130). With such visions flashing before their eyes, the judges deemed maintaining the status quo in voting rights by any and all means to be their public duty.

An early example of such extreme resistance by southern district judges to voting rights suits came in a 1945 case filed by William P. Mitchell against the Registrars of Voters of Macon County, Alabama. Mitchell alleged that he had fulfilled all the requirements for registration including "producing two persons to vouch for him as required by the board" and correctly answering "such questions as were asked in proof of his qualifications," but was subsequently denied registration "solely on account of his race, color and previous condition of servitude." He requested $5,000 in personal damages and an injunction against the county registrars. In addition, because such discriminations were "habitual and systematic," Mitchell called on the court to grant class action status to his case for all other persons similarly situated. The defendants responded with a motion to dismiss, questioning both the court's jurisdiction in this matter and the "sufficiency of the complaint as to form." In particular, the defendants denied the corporate nature of the class in question and argued that, as Mitchell had not exhausted the remedies provided by state law, he had no right to seek redress in federal court.

Judge Charles Kennamer of the Middle District of Alabama found these latter arguments more convincing. In regard to the motion for class action, Judge Kennamer suggested that "for the plaintiff Mitchell to be able to prosecute this action as a class action, it must be brought in behalf of other persons similarly situated. And for these other persons to be similarly situated, . . . the 'Class' must be a reality, not a possibility." This was not the case with voter registration. "Registration is an individual matter," observed the judge, "each case . . . considered on its own merits and demerits." Thus, although such categories as "Negro school teachers" related to a "specific, . . . definite, [and] easily recognizable . . . group or class," combining all blacks who "possess all the qualifications to be registered as voters and possess none of the disqualifications of voters" did not. Moving on to the jurisdictional issue, the judge ruled that Mitchell, by not fully utilizing the state's administrative remedies (which in this case would have been "an appeal to the circuit court of Macon County, . . . and from that court to the Supreme Court of Alabama") was now in the wrong court. It was the actions of the board of registrars that Mitchell objected to, Judge Kennamer noted, not the "administrative remedy afforded by the laws of Alabama"; it was thus incumbent upon Mitchell to continue the state administrative remedy process before seeking federal relief. For this reason, the judge approved the motion to dismiss and threw Mitchell's case off his docket (*Mitchell v. Wright*, 581–582, 585).

Angered by this result, Mitchell appealed to the Fifth Circuit, which reversed and remanded. As the appellate judges saw it, the remedy provided by Alabama law in these matters was "of the type of proceeding traditionally considered judicial," not administrative.

Precedent, in turn, made clear that where complaints were made on the "basis of . . . inequality of treatment under color of law," a plaintiff did not have to exhaust state judicial remedies before seeking federal relief. As long as Mitchell had a legitimate cause of action, he had the right to have his case heard by the district court. (*Mitchell v. Wright*, 154 F. 2d 925–927).

When the case returned to his court for a hearing on the merits, Judge Kennamer once again ruled in favor of the defendants. Putting aside for the time Mitchell's request for class action status, the judge reviewed the factual question of whether Mitchell had been illegally denied the right to vote. His answer was no. As he saw it, the rules were clear. If one wished to register to vote in Macon County, one had to produce two individuals to vouch for that individual's residency in the county. Where applicants had been "properly vouched for," the election board "registered Negroes and whites alike." Where they were not vouched for, the board rightly denied registration. The record showed that Mitchell's references had not signed the registration form as required by law; Mitchell was correctly denied registration. As the judge saw it, "racial prejudice or racial discrimination" had nothing to do with the board's actions. That the board's normal registration procedures actively hindered the ability of blacks to register was not an issue for the judge. (Those seeking to vouch for an applicant would arrive to find a crowded room where they would wait only to be told that "it would be necessary for them to come back when they, the Board members, were through taking applications"; of course, those seeking to vouch for a black would never be "informed as to when the Board would be through taking applications," making it nearly impossible, in practice, for blacks to get the necessary references.) As long as the rule formally applied to whites as well as blacks, which it did on paper, the judge was satisfied that racial discrimination was not an issue (*Thornton v. Martin*, 213).

Mitchell appealed once again, only to find that he had actually been certified to vote by the Macon County Registrars of Voters Board in 1943 but had never been informed of this fact. Needless to say, this negated years of unnecessary litigation and disclosed a five-year period in which Mitchell could have voted but did not. A disgusted Mitchell later noted: "It is doubtful whether we won anything from all that drawn out court battle. One Negro was registered" (quoted in Hamilton 1973, 35).

A drawn out court battle, however, was exactly what Kennamer and many other segregationist district judges wanted from these cases. Bothered by the expansion of their court's powers into the realm of voting rights, many district judges welcomed chances to delay or obstruct in these cases. In fact, extending the litigation process as long as possible was a major tactic used to preserve the status quo by segregationist judges seeking to hinder the black franchise (and by segregationist state leaders in all types of civil rights cases).

In this regard, the ongoing efforts of Mississippi District Court Judges Sidney R. Mize, William Harold Cox, and Claude Clayton, each of whom sought to delay and frustrate every effort to expand black voting in Mississippi in the early 1960s, are instructive about just how far some judges would go in resisting black voting.

In August, 1960, the Justice Department requested copies of the Forrest County election and registration records as permitted under Section III of the new Civil Rights Act of 1960. The county registrar refused and in January 1961 the Justice Department brought suit to force compliance with their request. First placed on Judge Sidney R. Mize's docket, the case languished unsettled (in fact, unargued) for over a year as Judge Mize accepted motion after motion by the defendants for more time to file their answers. The case was transferred to Judge Cox in January 1962 following a frustrated Justice Department's decision to go ahead and sue the county registrar for civil rights violations even without the requested records in hand. Judge Cox dismissed the original motion for access to the voting records as moot and once again granted the defendants extra time to prepare their case on the new substantive charges. In March 1962, a clearly impatient Fifth Circuit granted the Justice Department access to the requested records. Of course, this still left the substantive discrimination cases, filed in July 1961, to be tried. Here too, Judge Cox proved unwilling to act expeditiously. As early as September 1961, he had delayed proceedings by ordering the government to make its complaint more specific. Hearings on the government's motion for a temporary injunction to end discriminatory voting practices would not even be held until March 5, 1962, at which point the Justice Department was forced to amend their complaint once again to meet Judge Cox's demands. Thereafter, Judge Cox granted the defendants an additional thirty days to prepare their answer to the newly revised complaint. Another appeal to the Fifth Circuit got the government the temporary injunction they desired, but only two years after the original suit had been filed. Judge Cox, however, would continue to deny any discriminatory intent behind such actions in this case. Thus, despite the appellate decision on the temporary injunction, final action on the case was still pending as of 1965.

At the same time that the Forrest County case languished on Judge Cox's docket, Judge Claude Clayton faced the same opportunities for delay in Bolivar County—with similar results. Filed in October 1961, the case involved a simple request by the Justice Department to view the voting records for Bolivar County. The Justice Department first requested the records in August 1960, but the county registrar refused to grant the Justice Department lawyers access, and the government therefore sought an injunction to force action. It would be a long time in coming. As was the case with Judge Cox, Judge Clayton was in no rush to act. Every time the government lawyers came into court seeking a decision, he granted the defense additional time to construct their reply. By June 1962, the government had had enough, filing a petition for a writ of mandamus (an order from a court to a government official to do his job) with the Fifth Circuit. "Judge Clayton has taken no action of any kind in response to [the government's] requests [for the injunction]," a Justice Department brief argued. "It is in view of this complete frustration that petitioner seeks relief of writ of mandamus as the only available remedy" (quoted in United States Commission on Civil Rights, 53–54). Although Judge Clayton opposed the motion for the writ (he argued that he had acted in this case), it did push him to act, some twenty-eight months after the original request to view the records. The Justice Department could have access to the registrar's records. Yet even here, the judge worked to obstruct the government's aims, limiting the inspection to the records of only those who had been registered, not rejected. The result, needless to say, was a continuation of the pattern of costly delay and obstructionism for years to come. In fact, trial on the merits of the case would not start until July 1964, after which Judge Clayton "held the case under advisement" until January 1965, when he ordered the registrar to apply the same lenient standards in grading blacks' applications that he had used for whites. The judge refused to hold the interpretation test illegal, however.

Fortunately for blacks, most southern district judges were not as steadfast in their antagonism toward black voting as Judges Kennamer, Mize, Cox, or Clayton. Unfortunately, opposition to black voting rights did not always depend on the judge being a rabid segregationist;

in fact, though die-hard segregationist judges were among the worst when it came to denying change, they were not alone in allowing their discomfort with changing the racial status quo to shape their judicial performance. Acceptance of delay and inaction held true even for judges whose opposition to black voting was not so deeply seated. Many judges, considered by civil rights advocates to be "judicial grad-ualists" able to overcome their segregationist views when pushed by higher courts, still were limited by a conception of their court's func-tions that questioned the federal courts' powers to shape these events. The southern federal trial courts' traditional de-emphasis of social reform combined with its institutional embedding in the mores and social currents of the South made change a difficult proposition for most southern district judges. Their discomfort was only exacerbated by ambiguous Supreme Court leadership in these matters. As legal scholar Joseph P. Viteritti notes, "Notwithstanding their profound effect on American political life, [the Supreme Court's Voting Rights decisions before 1965] provided future plaintiffs with rather vague guidelines for litigation. The Court did not specify how equal partici-pation in elections should be achieved and left the job of fashioning relief to the federal district courts" (Viteritti, 205). In some cases it would take years for their evolving attitudes to produce concrete results—years in which federal district judges stood firm in denying, or more likely delaying, black access to the polls. As the Commission on Civil Rights reported in 1963: "case by case proceedings, helpful as they have been in isolated localities, have not provided a prompt or adequate remedy for widespread discriminatory denials of the right to vote" (quoted in Lawson 1999, 299).

Lacking clear Supreme Court precedents promoting action, hin-dered by an inadequate set of legal powers and authorities to act, and faced with extremely hostile public opinion—not to mention the effect of their own segregationist views—most southern district judges refused to force the pace of change in voting rights. Barring explicit appellate court instructions, these judges saw little reason to act; and, as was also the case with the early school cases, even with strong remands, those changes that did come were usually narrow in their application and impact.

Actually, the picture was not quite as grim with voting rights as was the case with other civil rights issues. At least in some voting rights cases, southern district judges were pushing for real change and not just tokenism. More importantly, in those cases where the judge was willing to act, concrete changes were secured; many of the various devices used by local registrars and state legislatures to keep blacks from registering were ultimately abolished by court order. Still, by the mid-1960s, the track record of the courts on voting rights was mixed at best. If action were to come, it first would have to be grounded upon Supreme Court and even congressional action. Luckily, such action was soon forthcoming on both fronts.

The One Person/One Vote Standard

Throughout the 1950s, the Supreme Court spoke with increasing force on the issue of voting rights. In 1949, in *Schnell v. Davis* the Court affirmed a three-judge court's decision that Alabama's "understanding test" arbitrarily excluded blacks from the polls. Four years later, in *Terry v. Adams,* the justices went beyond the surface reality and overruled the Fifth Circuit, declaring the Jaybird primary elections the real primary election in Texas. Meanwhile, in 1960, the Court validated the investigative powers of the Federal Commission on Civil Rights—refusing, as the justices put it, to shut their "eyes to actualities" and allow the good of the commission to be undermined by requiring it to "reveal its sources and subject them to cross-examination." As the commission's procedural rules were authorized by the Civil Rights Act of 1957 and did not, given the purely investigative nature of the commission's function, violate the due process clause of the Fifth Amendment, the justices held that "the narrow risk of unintended harm to the individual is outweighed by the legislative justification for permitting the commission to be the critic and protector of the information given it" (*Hannah v. Larche,* 489).

Yet, powerful as these and similar rulings were, they still suffered the same limitations that hobbled the Court's civil rights rulings in the prior four decades: narrowness of focus and inconsistency in outcomes. Feeling their way, the justices continued to apply a piecemeal approach to the problem of voting rights, ruling narrowly on the issues raised by specific civil rights cases but no further. As the cases we have examined demonstrate, given such "wiggle" room, the ability of lower federal court judges to act as they wished in these matters—or not to act—was substantial.

Worse yet, taken as a whole, the Court's voting rights rulings were often self-contradictory, providing mixed messages to these same lower federal court judges. For every decision upholding or expanding the rights of minorities to the vote, the Court issued decisions permitting the continued limitation of these rights. In *South v. Peters* (1950) the Court upheld a district court's refusal to review Georgia's county election system, even though charges of unfair discrimination had been made. As Justice William O. Douglas noted in dissent,

> Population figures show that there is a heavy Negro population in the large cities [of Georgia]. . . . Yet the County Unit System [of determining who had won a primary election] heavily disenfranchises that urban Negro population. The County Unit System has indeed been called the "last loophole" around our decisions holding that there must be no discrimination because of race in primary as well as in general elections.

Yet the majority ignored these facts. As they saw it, the issue at hand was whether the federal courts had the authority to make such determinations. Their answer was no: "Federal courts consistently refuse to exercise their equity powers in cases posing political issues arising from a state's geographical distribution of electoral strength among its political subdivision," they wrote (*South v. Peters*, 277–278).

Nine years later, the Court again accepted as gospel the proposition that certain political issues were state matters beyond the scope of federal review. At issue was whether a North Carolina law requiring all voters to "be able to read and write any section of the Constitution of North Carolina in the English language" was constitutional in light of the Supreme Court's own decision in *Davis v. Schnell*. In a unanimous decision, the Court answered yes. Whereas Alabama's "understand and explain" requirement had "made clear that a literacy requirement was merely a device to make racial discrimination easy," in North Carolina this was not the case. By making the literacy requirement "applicable" to all races, the North Carolina law met the constitutional threshold (*Lassiter v. Northampton County Board of Elections*, 53–54). Of course, just how one could determine the difference between these two laws—both of which on the surface were applicable to all voters—was not made clear, and that was the problem.

It was this lack of focus and intensity that needed to change if the high Court were to attack the voting rights quandary effectively and force compliance from the lower federal judiciary. Voting rights might be a "political thicket," dangerous ground beyond the proper scope for Court action—to quote the words of Justice Felix Frankfurter in 1946's *Colegrove v. Green*—but if real change were to come, the Court was going to have to enter this thicket and blaze a trail for all to follow.

By 1962 the Court was ready to try. It got its first chance with an appeal from Tennessee. The facts in *Baker v. Carr* were all too common in states across the country—North as well as South. Years earlier, Tennessee's legislature had drawn the state's legislative districts to reflect the then current distribution of population. However, over time, the flow of people into the cities had transformed the population mix. Unchanged since 1901, the way the district lines were drawn meant that the number of people voting for each legislator was sharply unequal. Rural districts with populations one-tenth or even less than those of urban districts still voted for the same number of legislators that they had in 1901; the same was true in the reverse, of course, for the urban districts. This gave voters in rural districts an electoral advantage in terms of the effect of their vote: a smaller number of voters in a rural district had the same impact in terms of relative political power within the legislature as did the much larger number of voters in the urban district. Worse yet, there were more of these small-population rural districts than there were large urban ones. This meant effectively that a small percentage of the state's population (the rural voters) picked those who were in charge of state government.

It was this unequal distribution of electoral clout that the urban voters bringing the suit challenged. They complained that the mass migration of voters into the cities since 1901 had made the current districting unconstitutional and obsolete. They called on the Supreme Court to fix the problem by ordering the state legislature to redistrict more equitably.

These were serious charges. Few denied the factual basis on which they were laid. The real issue before the Court, however, involved much more—and less—than the electoral impact of a 1901 statute. Before they could even speak to the merits of the plaintiff's case, the justices had to decide if they had the power and right even to decide this matter. Sixteen years earlier, in *Colegrove v. Green,* the Court had ruled that the decision over the proper application of state legislative districting rules was beyond the scope of the federal courts. "Courts ought not to enter this political thicket," cautioned Justice Frankfurter for the Court. "The remedy for unfairness in districting is to secure State legislatures that will apportion properly, or to invoke the ample powers of Congress," not to turn to the courts which lacked the authority to enforce the remedies sought. "The Constitution has many commands that are not enforceable by courts because they clearly fall outside the conditions and purposes that circumscribe judicial action," Frankfurter explained—and legislative districting was definitely one of them. Justice Wiley B. Rutledge, in a concurrence, went even further, warning that "the cure sought [court-ordered redistricting] may be worse than the disease" (*Colegrove v. Green,* 555, 566).

Adding to the difficulties facing justices seeking an opportunity to act in these matters, *Colegrove* was but one of a long list of precedents that argued that legislative districting was a political question beyond the scope of judicial review. The same year it decided *Colegrove,* the Court had reaffirmed its understanding of the law in denying review of Georgia's unit system primary (*Cook v. Fortson,* 675). In *South v. Peters* (1950) the Court reiterated this same decision, noting how "federal courts consistently refuse to exercise their equity powers in cases posing political issues arising from a state's geographical distribution of electoral strength among its political subdivisions (*South v. Peters,* 277). Six years later, the Justices dismissed an appeal from the Tennessee Supreme Court posing exactly the same arguments as those made in *Baker* (*Kidd v. McCanless,* 920).

These and similar precedents seemed to tie the justices' hands. Although those justices seeking change did not deny the long list of precedents limiting the power of the Court on legislative districting, they were not so sure that they were applicable in this matter. They believed that despite the obvious political context of the controversy, the case also raised important equal protection issues—and these the Court had full authority to decide. Just two years before, in *Gomillion v. Lightfoot* (1960), the Court had "applied the Fifteenth Amendment to strike down a redrafting of municipal boundaries which effected a discriminatory impairment of voting rights, in the face of . . . a sweeping commitment to state legislatures of the power to draw and redraw such boundaries" (*Baker v. Carr,* 229). As the Court had argued in *Gomillion:*

> Legislative control of municipalities, no less than other state power, lies within the scope of relevant limitations imposed by the United States Constitution.... The opposite conclusion, urged upon us by respondents, would sanction the achievement by a State of any impairment of voting rights whatever so long as it was cloaked in the garb of the realignment of political subdivisions. "It is inconceivable that guaranties embedded in the Constitution of the United States may thus be manipulated out of existence."

Hence, when a "State exercises power wholly within the domain of state interest, it is insulated from federal judicial review. But such insulation is not carried over when state power is used as an instrument for circumventing a federally protected right" (*Gomillion v. Lightfoot,* 344–345, 347). This logic had lifted *Gomillion* "out of the so-called 'political' arena and into the conventional sphere of constitutional litigation" (*Baker v. Carr,* 230). Perhaps it could do the same if adopted in *Baker.*

Although *Baker* did not carry the racial overtones of *Gomillion* (the redistricting in that case was an intentional gerrymander that excluded almost every eligible black voter from the municipal boundaries of Tuskeegee, Alabama), the seven justices in the *Baker* majority did feel the paradigm *Gomillion* created was applicable to the Tennessee case as well. Equal protection claims were not political questions, even though they might somehow involve politics. "The mere fact that the suit seeks protection of a political right," explained Chief Justice Earl Warren for the Court, "does not mean it presents a political question." The issue at hand was the right of individuals and groups to equal protection of the law, nothing more. Political questions had nothing to do with it. "The question here is the consistency of state action with the Federal Constitution. We have no question decided, or to be decided, by a political branch of government coequal with this Court. Nor do we risk embarrassment of our government abroad, or grave disturbance at home if we take issue with Tennessee as to the constitutionality of her action here challenged." Given this fact, "the equal protection claim tendered in this case does not require decision of any political question, ... the presence of a matter affecting state government does not render the case nonjusticiable." If anything, "the complaint's allegations of a denial of equal protection present a justiciable constitutional cause of action upon which appellants are entitled to a trial and a decision" (*Baker v. Carr*, 209, 226, 232, 236). Although the justices made no official comment whether the plaintiffs' claims were likely to win or lose at trial, they felt the plaintiffs had the right to take their chances. They therefore reversed the lower court's decision and remanded the case for trial on the merits.

For a Court that had refused for over 150 years to delve into political questions, *Baker v. Carr* was earth-shaking. Of course, at no point did the majority actually uphold the right of white urban voters in Tennessee to force legislative redistricting. They hinted that it should but did not come out and order it. One year later, though, in *Gray v. Sanders,* the Court began to apply the activist logic behind *Baker,* overturning Georgia's county-unit method of primary elections that gave rural voters a significantly heavier weight than urban voters. Writing for the Court, Justice Douglas asked "how then can one person be given twice or ten times the voting power of another person in a statewide election merely because he lives in a rural area or because he lives in the smallest rural county?" Answering his own question in the negative, he declared that

> once the geographical unit for which a representative is to be chosen is designated, all who participate in the election are to have an equal vote—whatever their race, whatever their sex, whatever their occupation, whatever their income, and wherever their home may be in that geographical unit. . . . The concept of "we the people" under the Constitution visualizes no preferred class of voters but equality among those who meet the basic qualifications. The idea that every voter is equal to every other voter in his State, when he casts his ballot in favor of one of several competing candidates, underlies many of our decisions.

The standard to be applied in such cases, Douglas concluded, was a simple, yet effective one—"one person, one vote" (*Gray v. Sanders,* 379–380, 381). The very next year, the justices took on Georgia's unbalanced congressional districting system, arguing again that "to say that a vote is worth more in one district than in another would . . . run counter to our fundamental ideas of democratic government" (*Wesberry v. Sanders,* 8).

Reynolds v. Sims, the final act in this transformation of the Supreme Court's understanding of voting rights, came out of Alabama in 1964. Like *Baker,* the lawsuit in *Reynolds* challenged malapportioned state legislative districts. In fact, the population imbalance in Alabama was even more egregious than had been the case in Tennessee. In some instances, the population variance was so great that a 41 to 1 discrepancy existed between voting districts (in the state senate, for example, the smallest district had only 15,417 inhabitants while the largest had 634,864). Thus a vote in an underpopulated rural district had forty-one times more impact on the outcome of an election than a similar urban vote. Indeed, by 1964, things were so bad that just one-quarter of the state's voters controlled the selection of a majority of the seats in both the state senate and house of representatives.

A three-judge court from the Middle District of Alabama ruled that state's apportionment schemes unconstitutional, and—to "break the strangle hold" of the rural counties on the legislature—ordered a temporary reapportionment so that it could reapportion itself permanently. It was this declaration of constitutional impairment and proposed remedy that came before the U.S. Supreme Court.

Noting that it was "undeniabl[e] . . . that all qualified voters have a constitutionally protected right to vote and to have their votes counted," Chief Justice Warren, writing for a six justice majority, asserted, "Legislators represent people, not trees or acres. . . . As long as ours is a representative form of government, and our legislatures are those instruments of government elected directly by and directly representative of the people, the right to elect legislators in a free and unimpaired fashion is a bedrock of our political system." To the extent that a citizen's right to vote was "debased," the chief justice continued, "he is that much less a citizen." That an individual lived "here or there" was "not a legitimate reason for overweighting or diluting the efficacy of his vote." Granting one place a greater vote than another was not permissible under the Constitution. "Full and effective participation by all citizens in state government requires, therefore, that each citizen have an equally effective voice in the election of members of his state legislature. Modern and viable state government needs, and the Constitution demands, no less."

Taking all this into account, the Court majority ruled that "the Equal Protection Clause requires both houses of a state legislature to be apportioned on a population basis." The "fundamental goal" and "plain objective" of the Constitution demanded the application of the "easily demonstrable" standard of one person/one vote. Though the Court did acknowledge "that it is a practical impossibility to arrange legislative districts so that each one has an identical number of residents, or citizens, or voters"—thus making "mathematical exactness or precision" a goal, rather than a fixed "constitutional requirement"—they implied strongly that anything less than "an honest and good faith effort" on the part of the state to reach this goal was likely to be constitutionally inadequate. The district court's ruling was correct. Its decision was not only affirmed, it was praised as "an appropriate and well-considered exercise of judicial power" (*Reynolds v. Sims*, 559–560, 563–565, 567, 576–577, 586–587).

Reynolds was a major change. Although one can overstate the importance of this shift in Supreme Court doctrine—and one person/one vote did have its practical limits, as will be discussed below—we should not understate it either. As Alexander Keyssar notes, "by 1965, the Constitution was interpreted to mean that individuals not only had the right to register, cast their ballots, and have their ballots counted, but also that they had the right to have their votes count as much as the votes of other citizens. Votes could not be weighted more heavily in some locales than in others; nor could voting districts be significantly unequal in population." Most important of all, it was now the job of "the federal government" to judge "the legality and legitimacy of federal, state and local electoral arrangements." All this was based, in turn, on a "one person-one vote standard" (Keyssar, 287). Given the Court's past lack of focus and commitment, *Reynolds* signaled a serious shift in policy—symbolically and practically—whose impact would be felt long after the justices who reached these decisions had left the bench. Yet, still more was needed before the final battle over vote denial could begin.

The Voting Rights Act of 1965 and the Attack on Race-Based Vote Denial

Powerful as one person/one vote could be, as both symbol and legal doctrine, it still did not deal directly with the principal forms of vote denial still in force across the country. As promulgated by the Supreme Court, the one person/one vote doctrine only attacked unequal distribution of representation. This was vote dilution, not vote denial. Worse yet, neither *Baker* nor *Reynolds* said anything about race-based vote dilution. Both cases arose from the complaints of urban white voters in their struggle for power with rural whites. Race was not an issue. Hence, although one person/one vote was a powerful symbol of change, as regarded rules and procedures used to deny blacks and other minorities the vote, it had little practical impact.

Still, *Baker* and *Reynolds* did raise the stakes for voting rights. Both cases were major expansions of the national control of the voting process—unprecedented and potentially earth-shattering in their future impact. Never again could state officials get away with denying that voting—and a meaningful vote—was a basic right of citizenship. Yet alone, these decisions were not enough to turn the tide against vote denial. A rallying cry to attack vote denial had been given, but the orders explaining how this attack was to be carried out were still unclear and confusing. This point is where the president and Congress reentered the picture.

For years, the political branches of the national government had been seeking legislative solutions to the voting rights problem—with little success. Enactment of civil rights acts in 1957 and 1960 were a start, solving some of the worst problems by giving the Justice Department the right to bring civil suits in federal district courts to enforce the Fifteenth Amendment (1957 act) and to examine voter registration records in preparation for those suits (1960 act). However, these laws still depended on costly and time-consuming litigation, not to mention a willingness on the part of a judge to act, to further the cause of minority voting rights. The Civil Rights Act of 1964 helped even more, speeding up the ability of three-judge courts to hear voting rights cases, requiring that any literacy test employed be given entirely in writing, demanding that black registration be based upon the same voter qualifications at that applied to whites, and allowing for the temporary appointment of federal voting registrars. Yet even here, the law's continued reliance on litigation without clear standards and guidelines as to who should be allowed to vote meant that it too was not the legislative solution called for. Only with 1965's Voting Rights Act (VRA), spurred by the Supreme Court's rulings in *Baker* and *Reynolds* and by the political pressure generated by the civil rights movement, did Congress and the president provide the statutory breakthrough so needed. This time they got it right, for with the VRA's passage, the character of voting rights litigation changed forever.

Expressly designed to attack the perceived sources of delay in the case-by-case litigation approach—obstructionist southern federal judges and the ability of southern governments to come up with an unending series of inventive new ways to deny blacks the vote—the nineteen sections of the VRA imposed a new enforcement methodology for voting rights. Not only did it outlaw vote denial based on race or color (and later ethnicity) in section 2; it also gave both the executive branch and the courts a powerful new set of tools and objectives for voting rights enforcement. Among them were the power to appoint federal examiners and observers in whatever numbers the president felt necessary, prohibitions on literacy tests and poll taxes, and rules outlawing any action "under color of the law" that prevented qualified voters from voting or having their votes fairly counted.

In terms of the executive branch, however, the most significant part of this tool kit was found in section 5, designed expressly to check the seemingly endless cycle by which southern states replaced one discriminatory law with another every time the old requirements were suspended or declared unconstitutional. To achieve this end, all state voting statutes and procedures in place as of November 1, 1964, were frozen pending federal approval for any proposed changes. This meant that any state or county covered by the act's triggering formula that sought to modify its voting laws first had to "preclear" these changes by submitting the proposed revision to the Justice Department and proving that the planned changes did "not have the purpose and . . . [would] not have the effect of denying or abridging the right to vote on account of race or color" (section 5, VRA of 1965). All changes not precleared by the Justice Department (which had sixty days to object) were legally barred from implementation.

As regarded the courts, the shift in approach was more diffuse. On the one hand, the expansion of the Justice Department's role in voting rights enforcement gave federal judges a powerful ally in forcing change. For while section 5 preclearence sought to bypass the courts, government lawyers still needed to bring suits in the federal courts to fulfill their multifaceted enforcement mission. For example, as written, section 5 affected only new laws or regulations "denying or abridging" black voting rights. Where discriminatory laws already were in place as of November 1, 1964, the Justice Department was powerless on its own to force change. Worse yet, as interpreted by the attorney general and later the Supreme Court, the Justice Department could only deny those changes that significantly *increased* discrimination; where election laws already discriminated against blacks, and where the changes proposed merely maintained this level of discrimination, the department's hands were tied and the changes had to be approved. Meanwhile, many techniques used to deny or dilute black voting were illegal applications of new and old laws, not their creation. This too was beyond the scope of section 5 preclearance. Similarly, section 4's abolition of literacy tests did not have a separate enforcement component. The same held true for section 10's instruction to the attorney general to attack the remaining vestiges of the poll tax. In both cases the Justice Department was going to need federal court help to force change.

Like it or not, the federal courts were a necessary part of enforcing black voting rights. In fact, over the next few years, both Justice Department lawyers and private civil rights attorneys would file hundreds of cases in the federal courts attacking a wide range of voting rights abuses: most initially focused on the ongoing problem of vote denial, but then moved on to enforcement of section 5's preclearance provisions and the troubling problem of vote dilution in local government. This time, with sufficient statutory authority backing action, the results would be much more to the minority community's liking.

Among the first such suits filed by the Justice Department were motions seeking elimination of poll taxes in the four southern states still using them—Texas, Mississippi, Alabama, and Virginia. Taking a similar position in each case, the government argued that poll taxes "as a precondition for voting" were devices "conceived primarily to deprive Negroes of the franchise." With "inadequate and disparate educational opportunity," government lawyers explained, blacks were at an "economic disadvantage." This made "the payment of the . . . tax a heavier burden on the Negro than on whites." Such a racially biased result, in turn, placed the poll tax "in violation of the Equal Protection Clause." It also transgressed the Fifteenth Amendment's right to vote, and, more important, lacked "any adequate state justification" for an exception under the Due Process Clause. In sum, the Justice lawyers declared, the poll tax was "a restraint . . . on the exercise of the fundamental right to vote" and therefore unconstitutional (*United States v. Texas*, 236).

This conclusion was one that the Texas and Alabama district courts found themselves in complete agreement with. Ruling in February and March 1966, three-judge panels in each state declared the poll tax unconstitutional. As these judges saw it, in the 1960s, poll taxes were irrelevant to the voting process and thus unconstitutionally exclusionary in their effects. The courts differed, however, as to which constitutional provisions this exclusion violated. The Texas judges felt that the imposition of an unnecessary tax on the right to vote infringed upon "the concept of liberty as protected by the Due Process Clause," and thus constituted "an invalid charge on the exercise of one of our most precious rights—the right to vote." In their view, however, it did not violate the equal protection clause or the Fifteenth Amendment (*United States v. Texas*, 255). The majority of the Alabama court, on the other hand, largely ignored the due process effects of the tax, but found that, by retaining its original purpose of disenfranchising blacks, the tax violated the Fifteenth Amendment's voting rights protections (*United States v. Alabama*, 96, 104). Interestingly, when the same matter came before the Supreme Court one month later (on an appeal from a private lawsuit filed in the Eastern District of Virginia in 1964), the justices looked to the equal protection clause as authority to overrule the poll tax. Yet whatever the reasoning employed, the final result of these cases was a quick and total end to the poll tax.

The courts responded similarly when the Justice Department sought to enforce section 4's suspension of literacy tests. The moratorium on these tests was not the problem. Section 4 made clear that, for those jurisdictions falling under the VRA's triggering formula, such tests were no longer permissible. A 1967 Supreme Court decision only reinforced this understanding when it ruled that, because unequal southern educational facilities left blacks unprepared to meet literacy requirements, even "fairly" administered tests were discriminatory (*Gaston County v. United States*, 296–297). Rather, the problem centered on whether the VRA now required southern states to provide help to illiterate voters in casting their vote. For years, most southern states had provided assistance to illiterate white voters needing help in filling out the ballot. Following passage of the 1965 Act, however, these states repealed their laws permitting such help. From here on out, illiterate voters were on their own in the voting booth.

Challenged as unfair and discriminatory (once again due to the negative effects that unequal southern educational services had on blacks—in this case, in creating a greater number of black illiterates than white), district courts in Mississippi, Louisiana, Georgia, and Virginia swiftly ordered such practices halted. Most notable in this regard were Mississippi and Louisiana; both faced extensive court orders requiring local voting officials "to provide to each illiterate voter who may request it such reasonable assistance as may be necessary to permit such voter to cast his ballot in accordance with the voter's own decision" (*United States v. Mississippi*, 349). As Circuit Judge John Minor Wisdom explained for the three-judge panel in *United States v. Louisiana:* "Louisiana [has] recognized for 150 years, [that] if an illiterate is entitled to vote, he is entitled to assistance at the polls that will make his vote meaningful. We cannot impute to Congress the self-defeating notion that [by passing the 1965 VRA] an illiterate has the right to pull the lever of a voting machine, but not the right to know for whom he pulls the lever" (*United States v. Louisiana*, 708). This same logic held true in the Northern District of Georgia, where another three-judge panel struck down a Georgia law restricting private citizens (who under state law could help other voters place their votes) to providing voting assistance to no more than one illiterate voter. Previously, such helpers were able to assist up to ten voters per election. This was a number the district court felt reasonable. The court thus invalidated the changed law as "unduly restrictive," and restored the ten-person limit (*Morris v. Fortson*, 540).

Still another popular form of vote denial involved voter fraud by local officials. One of the more common frauds involved absentee ballots. In *Brown v. Post*, Judge Benjamin C. Dawkins of the Western District of Louisiana faced a challenge brought by blacks against local election officials who had supervised a 1966 school board election. The plaintiffs charged that the defendants had solicited absentee ballots from white voters while denying absentee ballots to qualified black voters; the result was that, in a black-majority district, more whites than blacks voted. Defendants countered that whereas they had helped white voters to obtain absentee ballots, they never denied such ballots to blacks. Their intent was never discriminatory; if blacks did not request such ballots, there was nothing the officials could do to change the situation. Their job was overseeing the election process, not helping specific groups elect the candidates of their choice.

Ruling on the merits, Judge Dawkins accepted the defendants' assertions of nondiscriminatory intent, yet nonetheless held the defendants' actions discriminatory in effect. As the judge saw it, when voting officials made special effort to help one race, they had to make equal effort on behalf of the other; any other result, whatever the intent, was "discriminatory in fact" and thus not permitted under the law. He therefore invalidated the election with instructions to the defendants to administer the voting process "in such a manner that will afford equal opportunities to vote to all qualified voters regardless of race or color" (*Brown v. Post*, 62–63).

A second, even more popular, election fraud grew out of white officials' intentional misuse of the nomination and voting process. In Georgia, for instance, local officials intentionally set up their voting stations at sites that were inconvenient for black voters; in early 1972, the Northern District Court required the reallocation of polling places to sites that were more convenient to local blacks. The same thing happened in Wilcox County, Alabama, which located its voting precincts in private businesses owned by whites; worse yet, voting in these precincts was carried out in the open and absentee ballots were not given out until the day of the election. Ultimately, all three practices were enjoined by a 1973 consent decree worked out in the Southern District of Alabama. In 1968, facing a somewhat different fraud, the previously described case of the enterprising parish registrar who did not inform voters that in casting a straight Democratic Party ticket vote they were not voting for their desired nominee (*United States v. Post*), the Western District of Louisiana declared the election null and void. One year later, the same court faced the same defendants, this time charged with improperly removing black voters from the registration rolls so close to the 1970 election that the challenged voters were unable to contest their removal and thus were not able to vote in the election. Once again, the court invalidated the results and called for new elections.

Perhaps the most extreme efforts to deny blacks the vote involved racially motivated election "reforms" affecting terms and duties of office. When blacks seemed likely to win elected office, one of the more common responses was for southern states to extend the terms of office for incumbents. In Alabama, for instance, the state legislature in 1965 had increased the terms of county commissioners in Bollock County from four to six years. That change sparked two separate cases consolidated for hearing before a three-judge court, which declared this term extension invalid, not because the law was intentionally discriminatory (the defendants convinced the majority that this was not the case) but because given the long "history of discrimination against Negroes in Bullock County, ... the effect" was discriminatory. "Under such circumstances, to freeze elective officials into office [was], in effect, to freeze Negroes out of the electorate," Judge Rives ruled for the court, declaring the freeze-out a violation of the Fifteenth Amendment. It also violated section 5 of the Voting Rights Act, because Alabama at no time sought preclearance of this change from the Justice Department, nor a declaratory judgment from the D.C. district court. Given these facts, the court invalidated those parts of the state's election law pertaining to "County Commissioner Terms" (*Sellers v. Trussell*, 915).

Common across the South at the time of the Voting Rights Act's passage in 1965, strategies aimed at denying blacks the vote were effectively negated by Justice Department actions and federal court decisions over the next five to ten years. Whatever the judge's feelings toward extending the vote to blacks, the clear intent of Congress in writing the 1965 VRA (matched with the excessive and usually offensive nature of southern vote denial efforts) was to make such decisions relatively easy for the judge. Like it or not, convinced of the discriminatory intent of white officials or not, the law's meaning was clear—states could not bar someone from voting based on race, color, or, after 1975, language-minority status. By the mid-1970s, race-based vote denial was rapidly becoming a thing of the past.

So too with other types of vote denial. Though in the last decades of the twentieth century southern blacks were the preeminent target of vote denial and dilution, they were not the only victims. Longstanding rules denying paupers and the illiterate the vote, along with convoluted residency and registration requirements that denied mostly urban ethnics a place at the polls, still kept tens of thousands from exercising their voting rights. Largely excluded from the VRA's most potent provisions (which only covered southern states), these groups still benefited from Supreme Court rulings that spurred change. In *Harper v. Virginia Board of Elections* (1966), for instance, the Supreme Court took aim at the poll tax, declaring that "a State violates the Equal Protection Clause of the Fourteenth Amendment whenever it makes the affluence of the voter or payment of any fee an electoral standard." One's wealth or ability to pay a tax, as Justice Douglas wrote for the majority, had "no relation to voting qualifications; the right to vote is too precious, too fundamental to be so burdened or conditioned." This ruling was explosive in its results.

Despite *Harper's* exclusive focus on poll taxes, those eight states still imposing voting bans on paupers—including Delaware, Massachusetts, Rhode Island, and Texas—saw the constitutional writing on the wall and quickly revised their statutes and state constitutions to abide by the new rule. As Justice Douglas wrote, wealth was no longer "germane to one's ability to participate intelligently in the electoral process" (*Harper v. Virginia Board of Elections*, 669). Four years later, the Court took more direct action, excluding rules that limited municipal voting on bond issues to property owners only. As the Court explained in *City of Phoenix v. Koldziejski*, taxpaying but non-property-owning citizens had just as much interest as property owners did in whether to issue bonds that their tax money would be used to pay off. Statutes such as the Arizona law thus violated the equal protection rights of non-property-owning taxpayers. That same year, similar explosive results ensued when the Supreme Court upheld the VRA's suspension of literacy tests in *Oregon v. Mitchell.* Arguing that, as minority groups had a long history of inferior education, literacy tests were inherently biased and hence unconstitutional, the Court invalidated all remaining literacy tests nationwide. Of even greater impact, *Oregon v. Mitchell* also raised questions about long-term registration rules still in force in many states. Oregon required registration one year before voting in a statewide election and ninety days for local elections. This time frame, the Court declared, was an irrational delay whose only intent could be to keep voters from the polls (which it largely was). The Court therefore upheld a 1970 Voting Rights Act provision that barred the states from denying any qualified voter from voting for president on account of state-imposed registration limits and that restricted the states to a thirty-day registration limit on absentee voting (again only in presidential elections). This, the justices felt, was a reasonable time limit to allow for efficient processing of absentee ballot applications. Two years later, the Court imposed a similar time limit on *state* elections.

By the mid-1970s, the only nonracial exclusions untouched by the federal courts were felony bans and well-established limits based on age and citizenship. Vote denial was largely a thing of the past. The fight to expand access to the polls was over. All bets were off, however, when the issue moved from *denying* minorities the vote to *diluting the effect* of their vote. What good was a right to vote if it did no appreciable good? This was the dilemma facing the nation once race-based and other forms of vote denial were eradicated. Merely getting excluded groups the vote was not enough. If the meaning and purpose of having the vote were to be sustained, then vote dilution techniques had to go. The campaign against vote dilution was the next battle in the fight for an expanded vote. As was normal in these matters, it was not going to be an easy task.

Vote Dilution, Redistricting, and the Shift from At-Large Elections to Single-Member Districts

The problem with vote dilution was conceptual. As noted, *Baker* and *Reynolds* ruled that diluting an individual's vote through excessively malapportioned districting was unconstitutional. "[A]n individual's right to vote for state legislators is unconstitutionally impaired when its weight is, in a substantial fashion, diluted when compared with votes of other citizens living in other parts of the state," declared the justices. In its place, the Court mandated that legislative districts be organized to serve roughly "equal" populations. Only then could each person's vote be truly equivalent in its impact. The new standard was "one person, one vote," and any legislative districting that per-petuated imbalance would no longer be permitted (*Baker v. Carr,* 268; *Reynolds v. Sims,* 587). The Voting Rights Act, in turn, provided an enforcement mechanism to ensure continuing vote equality through section 5's preclearance provisions.

The difficulty was that guaranteeing each *individual's* vote rough-ly the same "weight" did not address the problem of *racially* moti-vated vote dilution. For one thing, the most common form of race-based vote dilution, at-large elections, did not conflict with the one person/one vote requirement. As structured, at-large voting actually came very close to the abstract ideal behind one person/one vote—every voter in a particular jurisdiction voted for or against every can-didate running. How could one's vote be made any more equal to another person's vote than this? Nor did other types of vote dilu-tion—majority-vote requirements or prohibitions on single-shot voting, for example—challenge the logic behind *Reynolds's* propor-tional vote requirement; forcing voters to vote for a full slate of can-didates, or to provide a majority vote to elect a particular candidate, in no way lessened the comparable effect that every individual's vote had on the election. Considered one-on-one, black votes had equal chance to influence the election's outcome as compared to white votes under such regimes. Even race-conscious gerrymandering specifically designed to submerge concentrated black communities into white majorities did not explicitly conflict with *Baker* if the districts so created were of equal size. Why then were blacks able to elect so few candidates, even where they made up a large part of a district's population, in at-large elections across the South?

The answer, of course, lies in the collective, as opposed to individual, nature of raced-based discriminations. By their nature, at-large elections are designed to undermine the ability of minority-groups to elect the candidates of their choice by submerging their votes into a larger number of majority group votes. This had been the case at the turn of the century when at-large election systems first entered the political scene, and it remained the case in the 1960s and beyond. Most contemporary shifts to at-large elections by southern states were, in fact, explicit in their exclusionary intentions. As one Mississippi state senator explained following his state's move to at-large county elections in 1966, Mississippi shifted to at-large elections explicitly *because* they protected "a white board and preserve[d] our way of doing business" (Parker 1990, 54).

So long as the white majority was willing to vote as a group (and given southern fears of black political power, this was a likely outcome), they could keep minority candidates out of office indefinitely by using an at-large electoral system. Yet proving this discriminatory effect (let alone proving the intent behind such efforts) was difficult. Unlike vote denial, vote dilution is a subtle process. Not all at-large election systems are discriminatory in their effects. Nor is the majority-vote requirement always inequitable; after all, the Constitution itself requires a majority vote of the electoral college to elect the president. What makes one election method dilutionary, and another not, depends on a unique mixture of local history, evolving social trends, and political results. As the Fifth Circuit noted in 1979, "the resolution of a voting dilution claim requires close analysis of unusually complex factual patterns. . . . Perhaps in no other area of the law is as much specificity in reasoning and fact finding required" (*Cross v. Baxter*, 875).

This was the predicament facing both litigants and judges when they confronted vote dilution suits beginning in the late 1960s: determining which elections involved legitimate policy choices, and which illegal discriminations, was an extremely difficult, time consuming, and fact-based proposition. How much minority exclusion from political office was needed before lawful choices became constitutional violations? To what extent did the intent of the framers of these systems matter? Or, was merely proving that the system's effect was discriminatory enough? More important, what were the proper standards of proof in such cases? What facts were conclusive?

These were difficult questions to answer. For years the Supreme Court would struggle with them, unable to construct consistent and conclusive answers despite their best efforts. Soon after the Voting Rights Act's passage in late 1965, for instance, the Court *rejected* claims that Georgia's multimember state senatorial districts unconstitutionally diluted black votes. Plaintiffs had argued that Georgia's multimember district system permitted majority white voters spread across the district to defeat the election of minority black candidates who could have won if the countywide district had been broken up into single-member districts—an assertion that the three-judge district court panel originally hearing the case had agreed with. Not so, said the justices, who saw such claims as "highly hypothetical assertion[s], ... that ... ignore[d] the practical realities of representation in a multi-member constituency." The Court did concede, however, that even though such districts were not inherently unconstitutional, they might, in the right circumstances, be "designedly or otherwise [operated] to minimize or cancel out the voting strength of racial or political elements of the voting population." Just what those right circumstances were, however, was left unsaid (*Fortson v. Dorsey,* 437–438, 439).

Four years later, in *Allen v. State Board of Elections* (challenging Virginia's and Mississippi's election law reforms, including the shift to at-large county elections following passage of the VRA of 1965), the Court seemingly found those right circumstances, holding that section 5 of the Voting Rights Act encompassed vote dilution as well as vote denial discriminations. Invoking the one person/one vote requirement of *Reynolds v. Sims,* the Court concluded:

the right to vote can be affected by a dilution of voting power as well as by an absolute prohibition on casting a ballot.... Voters who are members of a racial minority might well be in the majority in one district, but in a decided minority in the county as was whole. This type of change could therefore nullify their ability to elect the candidate of their choice just as would prohibiting them from voting.

With this in mind, the Court rejected all efforts to read section 5 narrowly: "the Voting Rights Act was aimed at the subtle, as well as . . . obvious, state regulations which have the effect of denying citizens their right to vote because of their race." Laws seeking to dilute the voting strength of minorities were not constitutionally permissible, Chief Justice Warren proclaimed (*Allen v. State Board of Elections,* 565–566, 569).

Allen proved to be an important step in the fight against race-based vote dilution. First, in ruling that vote dilution was covered by section 5 preclearance requirements, the Court freed the Justice Department to prohibit current and future shifts to at-large elections. In the next few years, the Justice Department objected to 88 vote dilution changes. By 1989, it had refused some 2,335 proposed changes, most for diluting minority voting strength. More significantly, the *Allen* decision solidified the position that, in some cases at least, at-large election systems could be unconstitutionally exclusionary in their effect. This included judging preexisting vote dilution efforts (adopted before November 1964) that were beyond the scope of section 5.

What *Allen* did not do, however, was provide easily applied standards by which to judge whether past adoptions of at-large vote methods were legitimate or illegitimate election schemes. Whereas the justices found reasons in *Allen* to declare Mississippi's and Virginia's actions improper, they declined to explain by what means they had come to this conclusion. Yet, without adequate standards to judge the validity of minority claims of vote dilution, lower federal court judges were left once again to their own judgments of right and wrong, acceptable and unacceptable, in judging these matters.

It would not be until 1973's *White v. Regester* that the Supreme Court provided standards and a test for proving vote dilution. Even then, the standards were still less than completely helpful. Growing out of Texas's longstanding denial of political power to blacks and Mexican Americans, *White* generated a trial record cataloging many and varied economic, social, educational, and political discriminations that combined to dilute minority voting strength. Swayed by the sheer bulk of discriminations—including such factors as the long history of state-sanctioned discrimination against blacks and Mexican Americans in Texas, the small number of blacks and Mexican Americans elected to office, and the existence of majority-vote and numbered-place rules designed to maintain white electoral dominance—the Supreme Court ruled that, viewed in the "totality of the circumstances," these factors were more than adequate to prove the existence of unconstitutional discriminations. In sum, Texas blacks and Mexican Americans "had less opportunity than did other residents in the district to participate in the political processes and to elect legislators of their choice." Hence, although multimember districts were still not unconstitutional per se, and disproportionate representation was not by itself evidence of a discriminatory intent, they could be determinative when viewed in the context of other "intensely local" factors (*White v. Regester*, 766–769).

Finally, both litigants and trial judges had a standard they could apply to vote dilution cases. Over the next few years, dozens of separate cases challenging vote dilution were filed in district courts across the South, the numbers mounting every year. This flood of cases only grew following Congress's 1982 revision of section 2 of the Voting Rights Act to include vote dilution under its provisions (including an explicit provision that the negative "effects" of racial vote dilution could serve as proof of wrongdoing), all opening the door to literally hundreds of vote dilution suits. The assault on race-based vote dilution was at hand.

In 1972, Judge Benjamin Dawkins heard a lawsuit brought by the black citizens of Ferriday, Louisiana, arguing that the existing at-large voting system (which required that "any candidate who receives a mere plurality must stand for election in a second primary"), combined with Louisiana's "anti-single shot" or "full slate" voting rules ("which in at-large elections forces the voter to cast ballots for candidates whom he does not support as well as for candidates he supports"), "effectively excluded the black community from participation in the political process of electing Aldermen in a reliable and meaningful manner." In fact, they explained, despite a 3 to 2 black majority within the city, only "one black [had ever] been elected to serve on the [city commission] board." The judge's response was to declare at-large elections in Louisiana unconstitutional as then constituted (*Wallace v. House*, 1196).

Three years later, blacks successfully challenged at-large municipal voting in towns and cities across Mississippi. Observing that the 1962 law imposing at-large municipal voting was written by a legislator who urged its passage by asserting that "this is needed to maintain our southern way of life," the three-judge court concluded that "the case at bar [was] entirely consistent with the racially discriminatory motive attributed to its sponsor." They continued:

> Considering the paucity of registered black voters in Mississippi in 1962, a requirement for at-large elections for all municipal posts would certainly tend to forestall the possibility that black aldermen might in some instances win election. Moreover, the Act's requirement that a successful candidate would have to receive a majority of the votes cast, and not a plurality, as was the case prior to the 1962 Act, is indicative of an intent to thwart the election of minority candidates to the office of alderman. Finally, the expenses and other burdens attendant upon mounting a city-wide campaign for office are calculated to deter blacks from seeking aldermanic posts against white contenders.

The judges therefore struck down Mississippi's election law under the Fourteenth and Fifteenth Amendments "as a purposeful device conceived and operated to further racial discrimination in the voting process" (*Stewart v. Waller*, 214).

That same year, Judge Newell Edenfield of the Northern District of Georgia ruled that Fulton County's at-large elections system, though not intentionally discriminatory, had the effect of "grossly minimiz[ing] the possibility of blacks fully participating in their county government and particularly in the election of county commissioners of their choice." He therefore declared unconstitutional the law implementing at-large elections and imposed a new means of selecting candidates for the next election (*Pitts v. Busbee*, 40–41).

In 1981 the District Court of the District of Columbia refused to accept a new election scheme in Port Arthur, Texas, as "the implementation of any of the voting schemes presented would most probably have the effect of abridging the electoral rights of Port Arthur's minority communities." An order to devise a plan that did not dilute minority votes, or else face one imposed by the court, soon followed (*City of Port Arthur v. United States* 991).

In 1984, Judge James Fox of the Eastern District of North Carolina imposed a preliminary injunction halting voting under Halifax County's at-large voting system; the judge held that the plaintiffs had "met their burden of showing they will suffer irreparable injury without the requested relief" (*Johnson v. Halifax Co.*, 171). Soon after, a consent decree produced a more acceptable election system.

The list of court orders attacking at-large elections as unacceptable dilutions of minority voting power, and hence unconstitutional, could go on and on. In Louisiana, of the twenty-seven suits challenging at-large and multimember districts filed before 1989, only nine did not end in a changed voting system, whether by court order, consent decree, or out-of-court settlement. In Georgia, forty-one cities had their elections methods challenged in court between 1974 and 1989, forty cases resulting in some sort of change. At the county level, the equivalent numbers were fifty-seven and fifty-three—and three of those unchanged were still pending decision in 1989. All told, between 1982 and 1989, "nearly 65 percent of all changes from at-large elections" across the South, were the result of litigation or settlements resulting from litigation in the federal courts—with another 10 percent arising from "voluntary" changes made under the "threat of litigation" (Davidson and Grofman, 385).

Yet, as important as these judgments overturning vote diluting election systems were—and given the many years of inaction in these matters until then, the mere choice to act was very important—the truly revolutionary part of the federal bench's response to vote dilution lay not in the decision to order change, but in the remedies imposed. Given the traditional unwillingness of southern political leaders to act in these matters, the determination to force change was usually an easy one to make—at least, once the judge had decided to act at all. The more difficult problem lay in how to change the system to end vote dilution. For unlike vote denial where the remedy was simple (let minorities vote), vote dilution cases posed the difficult challenge of constructing remedies that would solve the problems without limiting other individual rights.

The *White* majority never explained exactly how they had determined that, in this instance, the "totality of the circumstances" demanded court action, yet why in earlier cases action was not necessary. How did one establish when the "totality of the circumstances" mandated action, and when it did not? In *Zimmer v. McKeithen*, the Fifth Circuit simplified the district judges' job by reorganizing the *White* standards into a more useful set of four primary and four enhancing tests to determine illegal discriminations. (Among the criteria were the inability of minorities to have "access . . . [to] the process of slating candidates," legislative unresponsiveness "to their particularized interests," "a tenuous state policy [in]... preference for multi-member or at-large districting," and the existence of past discriminations that precluded "the effective participation [by minorities] in the election system.") But, just as in *White*, the *Zimmer* tests still did not specify at what point violations of the prescribed factors demanded action. Rather, like the Supreme Court in *White*, the Fifth Circuit fell back on a preponderance of the evidence standard: "The fact of dilution is established," the court ruled, "upon proof of the existence of an aggregate of these factors" (*Zimmer v. McKeithen*, 1305). More significantly, both *White* and *Zimmer* ignored the issue of remedies: once the determination had been made, by whatever means chosen, how was the district judge to fix the problem? What remedies were available and appropriate in such situations?

The problem was not an easy one to solve. Orders to state or local officials to produce race-neutral plans were not realistic solutions in this context. Politicians knew where their minority populations could be found. It was for this very reason that they had turned to at-large elections, racial gerrymanders, and majority-vote requirements in the first place: to undercut the electoral strength of these minorities. Race-conscious remedies were going to have to be used for the district courts to solve these problems, but how such remedies would fit under *Baker*'s one person/one vote requirement remained unclear and problematic.

It was at this point that the courts turned to single-member districts and proportional representation—to the use of what have come to be called majority-minority districts—as the only workable solution to race-based vote dilution. As noted, the Supreme Court began its consideration of vote dilution by adopting a remedy for *individual* vote dilution—one person/one vote—that, abstractly applied, actually permitted race-based dilution. The justices had chosen this mathematical approach both for its neutrality and for its simplicity of application: where individual vote dilution existed, one merely shifted district boundaries until each district had the same number of voters. With racial vote dilution, this simple mathematical formula did not work. Race-based dilution was a group problem, not individual. This fact required viewing the evidence of vote dilution in terms of its effects on the whole of the minority community, and, even more so, creating solutions that undiluted the effects of the entire minority group's voting. Race-based vote dilution cases, in other words, demanded a group-based approach.

Yet, once judges began to view voting rights issues in terms of competing group interests (and given the collective nature of substantive vote dilution, this was an inevitable result), the application of group-based remedies that purposefully divided up access to political power among the various segments of society based on group identification and proportional numbers was sure to follow. As voting rights scholar Lani Guinier notes, "judicial preference for easy-to-apply, judicially manageable racial vote dilution standards prompted the search for quantifiable and uniform measures of empowerment." Given that dilution was the "submergence of minority votes in a racially polarized electorate," the courts "needed a mechanism for distinguishing that phenomenon from undilution." They found this mechanism, in turn, by recognizing and reacting to the group nature of voting rights in a racially polarized society. "If whites refused to vote for black candidates, and whites were in the majority, then political market failure existed." Their answer to this failure: change the market by helping more blacks to get elected. "Black electoral success, which apparently defined undilution, [thus] became the . . . metaphor for equal political opportunity." Yet once "the right to a meaningful voice through voting" was transformed into the "right of minorities" to elect "'representatives of choice,'" the objective in vote-dilution litigation quickly centered on finding ways "to elect black representatives in rough proportion to their presence in the population" (Guinier, 51–53).

Applied to specific voting rights cases, this approach meant creating an electoral system that assured that blacks (and other minorities) whose votes had been diluted now could elect public officials in numbers that more accurately reflected their proportion of the district's population. In practical terms, meeting this objective meant "subdivid[ing] larger, heterogeneous electorates into smaller, homogeneous, majority-black districts where black voters could elect candidates of their choice to the governing body" (Guinier, 51–53). Federal judges at all levels might intone that the "Voting Rights Act does not extend race-based political entitlements to blacks or other minorities and does not secure the right of proportional representation," but in practice this rule was often effectively ignored as judges set about the task of fashioning remedies to racial vote dilution (*Wesley v. Collins*, 802).

As early as 1976, the Fifth Circuit noted that while "redistricting plans must not divide along racial lines, geographic or proportional,"

they must also "be prepared honestly on nonracial and rational criteria that, *when tested against proportional norms,* deny to no group
equal access to political process or fair chance to realize its full voting
potential, even one based on irrelevant criterion of race" (*Kirksey v.
Board of Supervisors of Hinds County,* 536—emphasis added). Quo-
tas were not to be permitted, in other words, but neither were electoral systems that "cancel out or minimize the voting strength of
racial groups" defined in terms of proportionality (*Pitts v. Busbee,*
35).

So how does one tell if the voting strength of a particular group is
canceled or minimized without exploring the gap between black voting strength and the number of elected black officials? The answer
was that one could not; there was no rational way to do so. As the
Eleventh Circuit explained to district judges in 1984,

> the absence of minority elected officials *may be considered as an
> indicium* of violation of section 2 of Voting Rights Act prohibiting any
> voting practice imposed in a manner which results in denial of the
> right to vote on account of race, and an at-large system will violate the
> statute if it results in a denial of equal participation. (*United States v.
> Marengo County Commission,* 1546—emphasis added)

Like it or not, the undeniable standard in vote dilution cases was the
percentage of minority representation compared to minority population in the district; barring other factors, that minorities did not elect
representatives in rough equality to their numbers was effective
proof of vote dilution.

Once the district judge had determined that vote dilution had
occurred, the move to creating majority-black districts—to predeter-
mining the relative weight of a group's vote in terms of who was likely to be elected—was almost a certainty. Supreme Court rulings
made single-member districts the "preferred" remedy "absent
unusual circumstances" in vote dilution cases (*East Carroll Parish
School Board v. Marshall,* 639). Practical experience argued that for
minority voters to elect the candidates of their choice, they needed
districts incorporating at least 65 percent minority voters—or, at
least, something approaching 65 percent. Anything less, and the
court would merely "supplant a plan which denies minorities the
opportunity to elect candidates with another one which does the
same thing" (Parker 1984, 112). Thus, influenced by both evolving

legal doctrine and the practical considerations, federal judges increasingly demanded the inclusion of minority-majority districts in rough proportion to the minorities' total population when constructing these new single-member districts—with incendiary results.

In Alabama, for example, 42 of the state's 48 cities of 6,000 or larger shifted from at-large elections to single-member or mixed at-large/single-member district plans by 1990. Of this number, 27 switched as a result of district court litigation, while most of the rest did so in response to Justice Department objections and the fear of facing expensive lawsuits that the cities were likely to lose. Most of these new single-member district plans, in turn, included black-majority districts as a necessary component of combating racial vote dilution. In one 1990 case, the district judge even accepted a majority-black district that was noncontiguous to create the second black-majority district needed to reflect more accurately the population of that community. As Judge Myron Thompson of the Middle District of Alabama noted, "In the case of Louisville, no single-member scheme can be devised under current population conditions that will meet all [the normal voting rights] concerns—that it consist of only contiguous districts, that it comply with the requirement of one-person-one-vote, and that it enable blacks within the town to elect candidates of their choice in at least two districts." Given these facts, the "town's proposed solution" of a "non-contiguous" district was "appropriate and, indeed, necessary" (*Dillard v. Town of Louisville*, 1548–1549). The result, given decisions such as *Dillard*, was that by 1990 "black office-holding in Alabama approached the level of proportional representation" (McCray, 54–55).

In Arkansas, a three-judge panel struck down a 1989 state reapportionment plan (which had included five black-majority districts) as not proportional enough. Finding that voting in the state was "markedly polarized by race," the court argued that, as currently constructed, state legislative district lines made "it very difficult [for blacks] to elect more than six black legislators, out of a total in both houses of 135 members." Given that blacks made up "about 16 per cent" of the state's population, this was not enough to meet section 2's nonexclusionary requirements. "We find," ruled the court, "that a total of 16 such districts . . . could have been created" given state populations and residential patterns. The judges did not require "the creation of any particular number of majority-black districts," but they did note "a sort of presumption that any plan adopted should contain that number of majority-black districts." Instructions to return in ninety days with a constitutional plan, or else, quickly followed (*Jeffers v. Clinton*, 198, 218).

Mississippi's blacks had a much harder time combating vote dilution schemes, in particular racial gerrymandering that lasted well into the 1980s for congressional, state legislative, and even county districts. Not only did state officials vigorously defend white electoral dominance (often with the help of the Reagan administration), but Mississippi federal judges proved, as usual, unreceptive to black cries for judicial help. Yet even here, changes came. By 1990, most at-large elections were ended either by court injunctions (twenty-nine) or consent decrees (twenty-seven) ordering the creation of single-member or mixed districts. Similarly, in *Jordan v. Winter*, the Northern District of Mississippi implemented an "interim redistricting plan" in place of a state plan that had unconstitutionally diluted black voting strength by splitting black populations among multiple congressional districts. Drawing on Mississippi's long history of discrimination, the court found that blacks held "less than ten percent of all elective offices in Mississippi, though they constitute 35 percent of the state's population and a majority of the population of 22 counties." Under the state plan, this trend was not likely to change, the court concluded. This was not acceptable. Hence, the judges' interim plan was designed to "create a rural Delta-River area district with a black voting age population majority, . . . containing voters with similar interests . . . and comply[ing] with the legislative goal of achieving high impact districts without splintering cohesive black populations" (*Jordan v. Winter*, 812). The result, not incidentally, was the creation of a black-majority Second Congressional District and the election of Mississippi's first black representative since Reconstruction.

Meanwhile in Louisiana, where 12 out of 27 cities moved away from at-large systems in response to litigation (with an additional three "coerced" by threats of lawsuits), blacks soon made up 11 percent of all elected officials in the state, some 500 in total; most of these newly elected officials, in turn, were from the newly created minority-majority districts. At the state level, this meant that 24 black representatives (22.0 percent) and 8 black senators (20.5 percent) served in the state house by 1990, each from newly created districts found in predominantly black parishes. The same result followed when it came to congressional districting. Ruling in the 1983 case of *Major v. Treen*, an Eastern District of Louisiana three-judge panel held the state's 1981 redistricting plan unconstitutional. (In its effort to split the mostly black Orleans parish in two, the legislature's plan so contorted the boundary lines of the new Second Congressional District that it resembled nothing so much as a duck). Disregarding arguments that these changes were merely the result of a color-blind effort to protect incumbent positions, the court ruled that:

> The protection of existing relationships among incumbents and their constituents, and the benefits accruing to the state from the seniority its delegation may have achieved in Congress, are pragmatic considerations which often figure prominently in the drawing of congressional districts. These considerations are not talismanic, however, and may not serve to protect incumbents by imposing an electoral scheme which splinters a geographically concentrated black populace within a racially polarized parish, thus minimizing the black citizenry's electoral participation.

An order for the state to fix the problem and construct a black-majority district (or face a redistricting plan imposed by the court) followed (*Major v. Treen*, 356).

So events progressed across the South once again, only now in support of minority electoral rights, not their denial or dilution. In Georgia, 84 separate challenges to at-large voting in counties or cities with populations over 10,000 were compelled as a result of district court judgments or consent decrees worked out under district court supervision. Most called for single-member districts with a proportional number of these districts serving black-majority populations. "Invariably," to quote one group of commentators, the result was an "increase in the number of black elected officials" (McDonald, 78). North Carolina had 49 cities or counties change to pure single-member or mixed district plans, 29 induced by lawsuits and two more by threat of legal action. The effect here was just as significant as in Georgia: in jurisdictions made up of 50 percent or more minority population, black representation stood at 46.8 percent; even in cities or counties with only 30 to 50 percent black residents, minority officials were still elected at a rate of almost 40 percent. Similar percentages held for those districts using mixed at-large/single-member district plans. Following the same pattern, South Carolina's district court forced 41 cities and counties to shift from at-large voting by

1989; subsequent black election rates shot up from 25 to 45.5 percent. In Texas, district court litigation (or fear of litigation) increased minority officeholding in some 52 cities from 11 percent under at-large voting to 29 percent with pure or mixed district voting—a shift that moved minorities from "under-represent[ation] by a factor of three . . . [to being] almost proportionally represented" in a 15-year period. (Brischetto, 246, 256). Virginia, meanwhile, had "nine counties create black-majority districts for the first time . . . , and six towns chang[e] from at-large to mixed electoral plans" in response to litigation under the Voting Rights Act. These new black-majority districts, in turn, became the primary source of black electoral gains in the 1980s, as the election of new black officials in those cities arose "as a result of the creation of black-majority districts where none had previously existed" (Morris and Bradley, 288, 290).

Similar gains were made outside the South as well. In 1979, the District Court of Connecticut held that "where there is an indication of racial bias, scrutiny of apportionment of elective state bodies [should be] particularly strict, and even generally acceptable apportionment procedures may be invalid in such circumstances" (*Baker v. Regional High School Dist. No. 5*, 319).

Five years later, a three-judge court in Indiana ruled that a 1980–1981 redistricting of the legislature that had used "multi-member districts" to stack or split "concentrations of black Democratic voters so that their elective power would be minimized" produced an illegal apportionment scheme whose primary effect "was to dilute the votes of those who are aligned with the Democratic Party." This included the state's black voters, who voted almost exclusively Democratic. The court was thus "drawn to the conclusion that in the 1981–82 reapportionment of the Indiana legislative districts, political gerrymandering did occur and as such violated the plaintiffs' rights to equal protection." They therefore ordered that, although past elections would be allowed to stand, no additional elections should be held under this law (*Bandemer v. Davis*, 1419, 1495).

In 1985, black and Hispanic voters in New York challenged the state's primary runoff law (requiring a second round of voting if no candidate won a majority vote in the primary, and which applied only to the City of New York, and then only to the three citywide offices of mayor, city council, and comptroller). Their contention, to which the judge hearing the case agreed, was that "the operation of the run-off statute was intended to . . . make it more difficult for a

Black or Hispanic candidate to emerge as the party nominee." An order to change the system to allow victory on a plurality of the votes soon ensued (*Butts v. City of New York*, 1529).

In 1990's *Garza v. County of Los Angeles* Hispanic voters charged that the Los Angeles County Board of Supervisors had adopted a 1981 redistricting plan that impaired Hispanics' chances to gain representation on the board. Taking note of "the explosive and continuous growth of the Los Angeles County Hispanic community, . . . the steady decline of the County's non-Hispanic white population," and the "long and painful history of discrimination against Hispanics in this County," the judge ruled "that the Los Angeles County Board of Supervisors knew that by adopting the 1981 redistricting plan, they were further impairing the ability of Hispanics to gain representation on the Board"—an action for which "no legal justification," including "the protection of" an incumbent's job, was justified (*Garza v. County of Los Angeles*, 1304).

Slow to start, and often hesitant and contradictory in its expansion, voting rights litigation in the federal courts nonetheless proved to be among the most significant and successful of the post-1950s civil rights reform efforts. Judges finally had both the tools and the motivation they needed to force radical changes in social and political reforms. It was an opportunity of which both the voting rights bar and judges took full advantage. Brought by minority plaintiffs and their specialized voting rights lawyers who increasingly trusted that federal judges would answer their cry for help, litigation in the federal courts ultimately proved a major forum for change. As voting rights scholars Chandler Davidson and Bernard Grofman note with regard to the South (but increasingly true also for the nation as a whole), "from 1982 to 1989 . . . . nearly 65 percent of all changes from at-large elections in . . . [the South] can be attributed to litigation or to settlements resulting from litigation." Add in the roughly 10 percent of "voluntary" changes undertaken under the "threat of litigation," and the percentage of federal court mediated voting rights changes grows to almost "80 percent" (Davidson and Grofman, 385).

The result of this litigation, in turn, was a near-total reconstruction of U.S. political forms. As Davidson and Grofman explain, "hundreds of southern cities, counties, and other kinds of jurisdictions shifted from at-large elections in the 1980s. . . . [with] remarkable gains in [minority] officeholding" the inevitable effect. Numbering less than a hundred in 1965, black elected officials in the seven southern states originally targeted by the Voting Rights Act tallied some 3,265 in 1989—9.8 percent of all elected officials in these states (Davidson and Grofman, 383). Similar, if untabulated, gains were made by blacks in other states and by non-African American minorities as well. Although increases in minority officeholding did not necessarily "alter the material condition of the lives of America's subjugated minorities" (Guinier, 54), given the extent of the change in terms of both officeholding and political power across the nation, this shift was truly extraordinary—a reconstruction of political power structures so profound that its outcome was nothing less than a quiet revolution in U.S. politics.

The Conservative Reaction to Expanded Voting Rights

By the early 1990s, the quiet revolution was largely complete. With the exception of felony exclusions, age-based limits, and citizenship requirements, vote denial was no more. Even the more diffuse forms of vote denial, registration rules and property-based exclusions for taxing districts, were abandoned. The victory against vote dilution was also nearly complete, organized around the concept of proportional representation through majority-minority districts. Racial and ethnic minorities across the country were electing group members to positions of power in numbers nearly proportional to their percentages within the population. It had been a long hard fight, but victory was finally a reality.

Or so it seemed. As should be all too familiar by now in our discussion of voting rights in the United States, no voting rights victory is without its contradictions and counterreactions. The application of race-conscious districting to combat group-based vote dilution was no exception.

For years, a growing segment within the governing elite of this country—politicians, political action groups, and especially conservative judges—worried about the justifications and implications of the federal courts' anti–vote dilution efforts. As early as 1962, in his dissent to *Baker v. Carr*, Justice Felix Frankfurter had warned that "such a massive repudiation of the experience of our whole past in asserting destructively novel judicial power . . . may well impair the Court's position as the ultimate organ of 'the supreme Law of the

Land' in that vast range of legal problems, often strongly entangled in popular feeling, on which this Court must pronounce." The Court's authority, Frankfurter explained, "possessed of neither the purse nor the sword—ultimately rests on sustained public confidence in its moral sanction." Such feelings needed to be "nourished by the Court's complete detachment, in fact and in appearance, from political entanglements and by abstention from injecting itself into the clash of political forces in political settlements." Yet the majority's opinion, ignoring years of precedents, was proposing to enforce a "hypothetical claim resting on abstract assumptions . . . [as the] basis for affording illusory relief for a particular evil." This was a mistake. Not only did it go well beyond the powers granted to the courts by the Constitution; it set up an unmanageable situation in which the justices' "private views of political wisdom would [become the] measure of the Constitution." Apportionment, Justice Frankfurter concluded, was too complex a process to be standardized within a simple numerical formula. Yet the lack of such a unifying methodology doomed the endeavor to inevitable failure. "To promulgate jurisdiction in the abstract is meaningless . . . as devoid of reality as 'a brooding omnipresence in the sky,' for it conveys no intimation what relief, if any, [the courts are] capable of affording." Without a consistent remedy to offer, the courts were likely to do more harm than good by their actions. As Justice John Marshall Harlan added in his dissent in *Baker*, "lack of standards by which to decide such cases as this, is relevant not only to the question of 'justiciability,' but also, and perhaps more fundamentally, to the determination whether any cognizable constitutional claim has been asserted in this case" (*Baker v. Carr*, 266–268, 301, 337).

Two years later, in a dissent to *Lucas v. Forty-Fourth General Assembly of Colorado*, a companion case to 1964's *Reynolds v. Sims*, Justice Potter Stewart took up the questions of manageability and intent. Objecting to the *Reynolds* one person/one vote solution to the effective remedy problem—which Justice Stewart described as "the uncritical, simplistic, and heavy-handed application of eighth-grade arithmetic"—Stewart argued that redistricting based solely on population was an improper reading of the Constitution, incorrect "as a simple matter of fact." Worse yet, it showed an arrogance of over-confidence on the part of the Court that boded badly for the future. The Court's "draconian pronouncement," Justice Stewart argued, which makes unconstitutional the legislatures of most of the 50 States, finds no support in the words of the Constitution, in any prior decision of this Court, or in the 175-year political history of our Federal Union. With all respect, I am convinced these decisions mark a long step backward into that unhappy era when a majority of the members of this Court were thought by many to have convinced themselves and each other that the demands of the Constitution were to be measured not by what it says, but by their own notions of wise political theory. (*Lucas v. Forty-Fourth General Assembly of Colorado*, 747–748, 750)

In the years that followed, Justices Harlan and Stewart would continue their vocal opposition to the one person/one vote concept, arguing (to quote Justice Stewart) that legislative apportionment was "too subtle and complicated a business to be resolved as a matter of constitutional law in terms of sixth-grade arithmetic" (*Avery v. Midland County*, 510). In *Swann v. Adams* (1967), they commented how the evolving doctrine of mathematical equality in legislative districting turned the judicial doctrine of the presumed constitutionality of state laws on its head, forcing *defendants* to prove that any population variances did not have "invidious purpose or effect" (*Swann v. Adams*, 447–448). Even Justice Byron R. White, who generally supported vote dilution litigation, warned that the Court's reach for a manageable solution in legislative districting had led it to "a confusion of priorities" (*Kirkpatrick v. Preisler*, 555).

Similar concerns surfaced when the issue shifted to race-based vote dilution. Whereas all the justices supported the general intent of the VRA and the federal courts' ongoing efforts to attack the remains of race-based vote denial and even dilution, some questioned the extensive and intrusive reach this enforcement effort was increasingly demanding. In 1969's *Allen v. Board of Elections*, Justice Harlan expressed reservations about the extension of section 5 preclearance to include "all those laws that could arguably have an impact on Negro voting power, even though the manner in which the election is conducted remains unchanged." As he read the VRA, this was much too wide an interpretation of Congress's intent. Section 5 was written primarily to enforce section 4's suspension of all literacy tests and similar devices. Yet in *Allen*, the majority was permitting "the tail to wag the dog." As now construed, section 5 "require[d] a revolutionary innovation in U.S. government that goes far beyond that which was accomplished by [section] 4." This was an improper reading of the statute:

> The fourth section of the [VRA] had the profoundly important purpose of permitting the Negro people to gain access to the voting booths of the South once and for all. But the action taken by Congress in § 4 proceeded on the premise that once Negroes had gained free access to the ballot box, state governments would then be suitably responsive to their voice, and federal intervention would not be justified. In moving against "tests and devices" in § 4, Congress moved only against those techniques that prevented Negroes from voting at all. Congress did not attempt to restructure state governments.

Troubling as it might be, vote dilution—such as that imposed by at-large voting systems—was beyond the proper scope of the VRA, Harlan concluded. To force preclearence beyond its proper scope was not only to grant the federal courts a power they did not rightly have, but to empower one segment of the population (southern blacks) with protections they did not need, nor properly have claim to, as the law was currently written (*Allen v. Board of Elections*, 584–586).

These and similar concerns continued to surface in the years that followed. Despite the victory of an anti–vote dilution reading of the VRA and the Constitution—or perhaps because of it—many judges grew increasingly worried over trends in voting rights litigation. They particularly fretted over what they saw as a growing bias in the application of anti–vote dilution standards. As noted above, following the Court's unanimous 1973 opinion in *White v. Regester* that at-large election systems could be unconstitutional—and especially after its reinterpretation by the Fifth Circuit in *Zimmer v. McKeithen* to emphasize the unconstitutionality of election systems that simply *operated* to minimize minority voting power, whatever the intent—district courts across the South overturned large numbers of local election structures. Both the scope and direction of this trend bothered a number of the justices. In 1978, four justices criticized the *Zimmer* analysis as an "amorphous theory" (*Wise v. Lipscomb*, 549). The next year, in *United Jewish Organizations v. Carey*, a legislative districting case from New York, a highly divided Supreme Court carried out a dialogue of concurring opinions that hinted at a growing movement on the Court toward applying some sort of "intent" stan-

dard in vote dilution cases to rein in the excesses in vote dilution litigation (that is to say, requiring that plaintiffs show not only the *presence* of discrimination in the voting structures of a state, but also the
discriminatory *intent* behind these improper voting structures). In
1980, these concerns coalesced in the majority opinion in *City of
Mobile v. Bolden,* demanding that a "plaintiff must prove that the
disputed plan was 'conceived or operated as [a] purposeful device to
further racial discrimination'" (*City of Mobile v. Bolden,* 66).

Congress's 1982 revision of the VRA reversed the *Mobile v. Bold-
en* intent requirement, replacing it with a "disparate impact" standard
similar to that created by *Zimmer.* (If the effects were discriminatory
in their impact, treating minorities differently from whites, then the
voting structure was constitutionally unacceptable whatever the
original intent in creating the voting structure.) Yet the trend within
the Supreme Court remained one of continued discomfort with too
extensive an application of race-conscious judicial remedies—in particular the growing shift toward majority-minority districting. In
1986 the Court hinted at this continuing discomfort in *Thornburg v.
Gingles.* Though technically in line with the 1982 revision of the
VRA, *Thornburg* imposed a new standard in vote dilution cases, one
demanding that "the minority group . . . demonstrate that it is sufficiently large and geographically compact to constitute a majority in
a single-member district." Failing this test, "as would be the case in a
substantially integrated district," the Court reasoned that "the multi-
member form of the district cannot be responsible for minority voters' inability to elect its candidates." If race was not the cause of electoral failure, then race-conscious districting was obviously not the
proper remedy (*Thornburg v. Gingles,* 50).

The peak of the Supreme Court's attack on race-conscious districting came in 1993. The case was *Shaw v. Reno.* Brought in
response to North Carolina's congressional redistricting efforts following the 1990 census, the plaintiffs in *Shaw* challenged the entire
structure of minority-majority districting. As they saw it, minority-
majority districting was nothing more than racial gerrymandering;
one imposed in favor of blacks instead of whites this time—but
racial gerrymandering nonetheless. In particular, plaintiffs—white
voters in a new black-majority congressional district created at the
urging of the Justice Department—complained that the new district
was created expressly to give blacks a secure second congressional
district. This was in violation of the Fourteenth Amendment's equal

protection clause. As evidence of their contention, they pointed to the new district's shape, which wandered across the north central region of North Carolina, linking together minority communities with land bridges no wider than the interstate highway that connected them.

Opening her opinion for a five-justice majority with a review of the long history of vote denial and dilution in the country, Justice Sandra Day O'Connor then examined the North Carolina district in light of this long and sad history. What she found appalled her. "It is unsettling," she wrote, "how closely the North Carolina plan resembles the most egregious racial gerrymanders of the past." The district under attack, she noted, was

> approximately 160 miles long and, for much of its length, no wider than the I-85 corridor. It winds in snake-like fashion through tobacco country, financial centers, and manufacturing areas "until it gobbles in enough enclaves of black neighborhoods."

The result was simply too "bizarre," "irregular," and "egregious" in form to pass constitutional muster:

> Reapportionment is one area in which appearances do matter. A reapportionment plan that includes in one district individuals who belong to the same race, but who are otherwise widely separated by geographical and political boundaries, and who may have little in common with one another but the color of their skin, bears an uncomfortable resemblance to political apartheid. It reinforces the perception that members of the same racial group—regardless of their age, education, economic status, or the community in which they live—think alike, share the same political interests, and will prefer the same candidates at the polls. . . . By perpetuating such notions, a racial gerrymander may exacerbate the very patterns of racial bloc voting that majority-minority districting is sometimes said to counteract.

In fact, wrote O'Connor, in some "exceptional cases, a reapportionment plan may be so highly irregular that, on its face, it rationally cannot be understood as anything other than an effort to 'segregate . . . voters' on the basis of race."

For these reasons, the majority in *Shaw* concluded that "a plaintiff challenging a reapportionment statute under the Equal Protection

Clause may state a claim by alleging that the legislation, though race neutral on its face, rationally cannot be understood as anything other than an effort to separate voters into different districts on the basis of race, and that the separation lacks sufficient justification." Where a state "concentrated a dispersed minority population in a single district, disregarding traditional districting principles such as compactness, contiguity, and respect for political subdivisions," a red flag of warning demanded a close examination to ensure that race was not the only determinant in creating the district. As Justice O'Connor explained in conclusion:

> Racial classifications of any sort pose the risk of lasting harm to our society. They reinforce the belief, held by too many for too much of our history, that individuals should be judged by the color of their skin. Racial classifications with respect to voting carry particular dangers. Racial gerrymandering, even for remedial purposes, may balkanize us into competing racial factions; it threatens to carry us further from the goal of a political system in which race no longer matters—a goal that the Fourteenth and Fifteenth Amendments embody, and to which the Nation continues to aspire. It is for these reasons that race-based districting by our state legislatures demands close judicial scrutiny. (*Shaw v. Reno*, 630–632, 640–641, 647, 649)

Although the five justices in the majority did not comment on the justification for the oddly shaped North Carolina district (merely remanding it back to the district court with instructions to explore the facts in this particular situation, although, ironically, the lower court upheld the district as properly formed), *Shaw v. Reno* effectively imposed a new and complex standard in voting rights litigation, one that made the defense of minority-majority districts more difficult. The new standard in voting rights was race-neutral remedies judged—at least in the case of legislative districting—as much by aesthetics as by a close examination of the realities in race relations and political action. Race-based districting—and by implication, all forms of race-conscious remedies—were called into question as an appropriate response to discrimination and exclusion from power. Subsequent rulings by the Supreme Court against majority-minority districting in cases such as *Miller v. Johnson* (1995), *United States v. Hays* (1995), *Bush v. Vera* (1996), and *Reno v. Bossier Parish School*

Board (1997) only intensified this trend. In the process, almost thirty years of litigation against race-based vote denial—not to mention the solutions these cases had generated—were suddenly in jeopardy of constitutional irrelevancy.

Conclusion

Thus the debate on the nature of voting rights in the courts came full circle as the twentieth century came to an end. Who should have the right to vote and how should we choose them? Should such matters as class or race matter in distribution of the vote? If yes, then how could we implement this impact? If not, then how could we organize the election process to be class- or race-neutral when U.S. society was neither? The questions did not change. As *Shaw v. Reno* makes clear, neither did the answers. In 1800, 1900, or 2000, the dilemma was still the same: how to resolve the tension between what we needed (for people to vote) and what we achieved (that we have made voting a very difficult proposition for large numbers of Americans). Although the general trend was in favor of vote expansion—even at the cost of the principle of majority rule or race-neutral remedies—as late as the 1990s we still had not yet committed fully to the idea that the popular conception of democracy clearly manifests: that *democracy* means a system in which everybody votes and that those votes have real meaning and impact.

Still, despite the discrepancies, exceptions, and paradoxes—not to mention the negative effects of ongoing racial, ethnic, class, and gender tensions still bubbling up within the wider society—the result of voting rights litigation is nothing less than a revolution in U.S. democracy and government. Vote denial is gone; so too are most forms of vote dilution. No longer is the act of voting a closely held privilege of the few; today the vote is a clearly articulated and assumed right of national citizenship. Considering that U.S. courts started this process in the mid-nineteenth century with a blanket refusal to view voting rights as even a legitimate matter of judicial concern let alone a foundation of U.S. citizenship, that we are debating the guidelines not of vote inclusion but of actual power sharing, is extraordinary. It is a truly momentous conversion whose impact should be felt for years to come.

References and Further Reading

Alt, James E., "The Impact of the Voting Rights Act on Black and White Voter Registration in the South," in Chandler Davidson and Bernard Grofman, eds. *Quiet Revolution in the South: The Impact of the Voting Rights Act, 1965–1990* (Princeton: Princeton University Press, 1994): 351–377.

Basch, Norma, "Reconstructing Female Citizenship: *Minor v. Happersett*," in Donald Nieman, ed., *The Constitution, Law and American Life: Critical Aspects of the Nineteenth-Century Experience,* (Athens: University of Georgia Press, 1992): 52–66.

Binion, Gayle, "The Implementation of Section 5 of the 1965 Voting Rights Act: A Retrospective on the Role of Courts," *Western Political Quarterly* 32(1979): 154–173.

Blacksher, James U., and Larry T. Menefee, "From *Reynolds v. Sims* to *City of Mobile v. Bolden:* Have the White Suburbs Commandeered the Fifteenth Amendment?" *Hastings Law Journal* 34(Sept., 1982): 1–64.

Brischetto, Robert, et al., "Texas," in Chandler Davidson and Bernard Grofman, eds. *Quiet Revolution in the South: The Impact of the Voting Rights Act, 1965–1990* (Princeton: Princeton University Press, 1994): 233–270.

Burton, Orville Vernon, et al., "South Carolina" in Chandler Davidson and Bernard Grofman, eds. *Quiet Revolution in the South: The Impact of the Voting Rights Act, 1965–1990* (Princeton: Princeton University Press, 1994): 191–232.

Chayes, Abram, "The Role of the Judge in Public Law Litigation," *Harvard Law Review* 89 (May 1976): 1281–1316.

Davidson, Chandler, "Negro Politics and the Rise of the Civil Rights Movement in Houston, Texas," (Ph.D. Dissertation, Princeton University, 1968).

———, *Race and Class in Texas Politics* (Princeton: Princeton University Press, 1990).

———, "The Voting Rights Act: A Brief History," in Chandler Davidson and Bernard Grofman, eds. *Controversies in Minority Voting: The Voting Rights Act in Perspective* (Washington, DC: The Brookings Institution, 1992): 7–51.

———, "The Recent Evolution of Voting Rights Law Affecting Racial and Language Minorities," in Chandler Davidson and Bernard Grofman, eds. *Quiet Revolution in the South: The Impact of the Voting Rights Act, 1965–1990* (Princeton: Princeton University Press, 1994): 21–37.

Davidson, Chandler, and Bernard Grofman, "The Voting Rights Act and the Second Reconstruction," in Chandler Davidson and Bernard Grofman, eds. *Quiet Revolution in the South: The Impact of the Voting Rights Act, 1965–1990* (Princeton: Princeton University Press, 1994): 378–388.

———, eds. *Quiet Revolution in the South: The Impact of the Voting Rights Act, 1965–1990* (Princeton: Princeton University Press, 1994).

Engstrom, Richard, et al., "Louisiana," in Chandler Davidson and Bernard Grofman, eds., *Quiet Revolution in the South: The Impact of the Voting Rights Act, 1965–1990* (Princeton: Princeton University Press, 1994): 103–135.

Guinier, Lani, *The Tyranny of the Majority: Fundamental Fairness in Representative Democracy* (New York: Free Press, 1994).

Hainsworth, Robert, "The Negro and the Texas Primaries," *Journal of Negro History* 18 (October, 1933): 426–450.

Hamilton, Alexander, James Madison, and John Jay, *The Federalist Papers* (New York: New American Library of World Literature, 1961).

Hamilton, Charles V., *The Bench and the Ballot: Southern Federal Judges and Black Voters* (New York: Oxford University Press, 1973).

Hine, Darlene Clark, *Black Victory: The Rise and Fall of the White Primary in Texas* (Millwood, New York: KTO Press, 1979).

Johnson, Frank M., Jr., "The Role of the Federal Courts in Institutional Litigation," *Alabama Law Review* 32(Winter, 1981): 271–279.

Keech, William R., and Michael P. Sistrom, "North Carolina," in Chandler Davidson and Bernard Grofman, eds., *Quiet Revolution in the South: The Impact of the Voting Rights Act, 1965–1990* (Princeton: Princeton University Press, 1994): 155–190.

Kerber, Linda, *No Constitutional Right to be Ladies: Women and the Obligations of Citizenship* (New York: Hill and Wang, 1998).

Keyssar, Alexander, *The Right to Vote: The Contested History of Democracy in the United States* (New York: Basic Books, 2000).

Kousser, J. Morgan, *The Shaping of Southern Politics, Suffrage, and the Establishment of the One-Party South* (New Haven: Yale University Press, 1974).

———, *Colorblind Injustice: Minority Voting Rights and the Undoing of the Second Reconstruction* (Chapel Hill: University of North Carolina Press, 1999).

Lawson, Stephen F., *In Pursuit of Power: Southern Blacks and Electoral Politics, 1965–1982* (New York: Columbia University Press, 1985).

———, *Black Ballots: Voting Rights in the South, 1944–1969* (Lanham, MD: Lexington Press, 1999 [orig. pub. 1976]).

McCarty, L. Thorne, and Russell B. Stevenson, "The Voting Rights Act of 1965: An Evaluation," *Harvard Civil Rights-Civil Liberties Law Review* 2(Spring, 1968): 375–413.

McCray, Peyton, et al., "Alabama," in Chandler Davidson and Bernard Grofman, eds., *Quiet Revolution in the South: The Impact of the Voting*

Rights Act, 1965–1990 (Princeton: Princeton University Press, 1994): 38–66.

McDonald, Laughlin, et al., "Georgia," in Chandler Davidson and Bernard Grofman, eds., *Quiet Revolution in the South: The Impact of the Voting Rights Act, 1965–1990* (Princeton: Princeton University Press, 1994): 67–102.

Morris, Thomas R., and Neil Bradley, "Virginia," in Chandler Davidson and Bernard Grofman, eds., *Quiet Revolution in the South: The Impact of the Voting Rights Act, 1965–1990* (Princeton: Princeton University Press, 1994): 271–298.

Norton, Mary Beth, ed., *Major Problems in American History: Documents and Essays* (Lexington, MA: D. C. Heath, 1989).

Parker, Frank R., "Racial Gerrymandering and Legislative Reapportionment," in Chandler Davidson, ed., *Minority Vote Dilution* (Washington, DC: Howard University Press, 1984): 85–117.

———, *Black Votes Count: Political Empowerment in Mississippi after 1965* (Chapel Hill: University of North Carolina Press, 1990).

Phillips, Barbara Y., "Reconsidering *Reynolds v. Sims:* The Relevance of Its Basic Standard of Equality to Other Vote Dilution Claims," *Howard Law Journal* 38(Summer, 1995): 561–585.

Piven, Frances Fox, and Richard A. Cloward, *Why Americans Don't Vote* (New York: Pantheon, 1988).

Porter, Kirk Harold, *A History of Suffrage in the United States* (New York: AMS Press, 1971 [1918]).

SoRelle, James, "The Darker Side of 'Heaven'," (Ph. D. Dissertation, Kent State University, 1980).

Stern, Gerald E., "Judge William Harold Cox and the Right to Vote in Clarke County, Mississippi," in Leon Freidman, ed., *Southern Justice* (Cleveland: Meridian Books, 1965): 165–186.

Takaki, Ronald, *Strangers from a Different Shore: A History of Asian Americans* (New York: Penguin Books, 1989).

Tushnet, Mark V., *The NAACP's Legal Strategy against Segregated Education, 1925–1950* (Chapel Hill: University of North Carolina Press, 1987).

United States Commission on Civil Rights, *Voting in Mississippi* (Washington, DC: Government Printing Office, 1965).

Viteritti, Joseph P., "Unapportioned Justice: Local Elections, Social Science, and the Evolution of the Voting Rights Act," *Cornell Journal of Law and Public Policy* 4 (Fall 1994): 199–271.

Wolfley, Jeannette, "Jim Crow, Indian Style: The Disenfranchisement of Native Americans," *American Indian Law Review* 16(1991): 167–202.

4
Impact and Legacy

Equal Protection or Equal Effect?
Voting Rights in the Twenty-first Century

As noted in chapter 1, the long and convoluted history of voting rights litigation opens an informative window onto the entire course of vote expansion in the United States—the negatives as well as the positives, the ambiguities and contradictions as well as the ultimate triumphs (followed, seeming inevitably, by counterreactions and renewed debate and conflict). Viewed entire, the story of voting rights on trial is not a pretty story; but then, the history of voting rights in the United States is not a pretty story either. It is, however, an extremely important and enlightening story, one whose lessons we ignore at our own risk.

What is most telling in exploring the federal courts' struggle with the issue of the right to vote is the process by which opposition and obstruction—both within the court system and the nation as a whole—was overcome. Merely declaring a right was not enough. This was obvious when Thomas Jefferson wrote that "all men are created equal" and the states did not even include "all men" among those who could vote; and it remains obvious today as we struggle to find race-neutral answers to race-based problems. For voting rights to be real rather than symbolic, they must be enforced. Further, enforcement of voting rights must cope with the contradictions within U.S. society and democracy—the tensions between localism and

161

centralization; the drive to exclude even while we include—and yet, at the same time, to find, despite such conflicts, a middle ground of mutual respect and acceptance lest the nation fall apart.

Within the federal courts, as in U.S. society as a whole, this process took time. Frustrating as it was for the disenfranchised, it needed time. Judges had to be educated as to the evils and wrongs of vote denial; those who could not learn had to be replaced by judges who could learn; and those who could had to be forced to assume leadership roles and push the envelope. New doctrines and understandings as to the roles and functions of the judiciary needed to be devised, as did new enforcement methodologies to implement these doctrines. No one knew how far the courts would have to go in their attempt to ensure a real vote for everyone. In fact, few would have willingly gone as far as the courts ultimately did, had they known where it was going to end. As Yale law professor Owen Fiss said of Judge Frank M. Johnson, in words applicable to almost every judge facing these dilemmas, "[Judge] Johnson didn't begin where he wound up. I think it was just a kind of education that he got sitting on the bench trying to do his job, being confronted with outright and open defiance time and time again." If he was creative in working out original seeming solutions, "he was creative under the force of circumstance, . . . he was responding to the necessities of the situation, and [he] improvised and innovated" as necessary (quoted in Bass, 90).

This same mix of inventiveness and complexity in the face of defiance shaped vote expansion in Congress, in various parts of the executive branch, and within the states. Like the courts, they too needed to learn important lessons and try out new approaches to protect and enhance the voting rights of all Americans. Like the courts, they fought the process, giving ground slowly—in fact, often holding out for decades—but giving ground nonetheless. Like the courts, once they found reason to act, they did so with increasing speed and force.

Combined with the federal courts' actions, the result has been nothing less than a revolution in U.S. democracy and government. It's not just that women, blacks, Hispanics, and the poor can now vote—though that change is stunning. Yet even more important is the impact of such voting on U.S. politics and society. As Chief Justice Earl Warren noted in *Reynolds v. Sims,* "the right to vote freely for the candidate of one's choice is of the essence of a democratic society, and any restrictions on that right strike at the heart of representative government" (*Reynolds v. Sims,* 555). By allowing the dispossessed the vote—and in giving that vote meaning by attacking vote dilution—we have given these groups a true voice in the shaping of our nation's government and society. Politicians have to listen to groups whom they formerly ignored. Even if this attention lasts only for the short interval before an election, it still is more attention than such groups had been given in the past. More importantly, the means by which we have attacked vote denial and dilution (majority-minority districting, one person/one vote) have resulted in significant and concrete gains for minorities in terms of actual political power. Though serious problems still exist, and real power-sharing among the races and genders is not yet a complete reality, U.S. democracy is healthier today than it has ever been.

Yet just how secure the place at the table of democracy is for those formerly excluded remains an open question. Ending the twentieth century with as controversial a decision as *Shaw v. Reno,* the Supreme Court now calls into question the durability of the method chosen to ensure equal access to the franchise for all Americans, especially minorities long denied a fair voice in government. What are our priorities in voting rights? Is it to be vote expansion? Or perhaps we are moving toward some sort of renewed belief in vote restriction? Is some middle ground possible?

These questions lie at the heart of voting rights' future. Both vote expansion and vote limitation are, if properly constituted, legitimate goals for government to promote. Ensuring the rights of all Americans to equal protection of the law (even at the expense of limiting access to the polls) is no less essential to the future of democracy than expanding the range of those who can vote. Ideally, we should expect—in fact demand—both from our political system. Yet can we? In practice, each is often exclusive of the other. The problem is that, to ensure that the votes of those who had long been excluded have meaning, the remedies applied must take into account the very differences that led in the first place to the original exclusion of these groups. Experience shows that the only effective way to combat *group*-specific denials and dilutions is *group*-specific remedies, yet the result of such ethnic-, gender-, class-, and race-conscious remedies is to give unequal weight to some voters' votes—in the opposite direction to similar machinations in the past, but unequal nonetheless. So, which is more important to democracy's survival in the United States: that everyone vote and that his or her vote have practical and real impact (equal effect), or that everyone's vote be treated in as equitable a manner as possible (equal protection)?

Then there is the ongoing issue of federalism and the vote. As originally written into the Constitution, voting was a distinctly local phenomenon. The states chose who could vote in national as well as local elections, writing the rules and organizing the procedures by which we vote. The states, in turn, often distributed the actual decision making about elections to local officials in counties and towns, further decentralizing the voting process. Yet by its nature such a decentralized election oversight system entails the sorts of dissimilar voting standards and procedures that lead almost inevitably to vote denial and dilution. What standards and methodologies are proper in enforcing equality and power-sharing? Is the tradition of local autonomy more or less important than creating a voting system in which everyone can vote? Put another way, whose constitutional rights should be empowered: the individual's or the state's?

Finally, there are the problems posed by voter turnouts of 50 percent or less in most presidential elections (and even lower for state and local balloting). Despite the massive increase in voter access to the polls, the number of Americans choosing to vote has declined over the years to dangerously low levels. What good does voter inclusion do when, despite open access to the polls, so many of us feel alienated and excluded from the governing process? Does the right to vote even matter anymore? Perhaps the lesson here is that the fight against vote denial and dilution is not yet complete. Perhaps the next stage in the ongoing struggle over voting rights lies in expanding the *meaning*—in terms of process, accessibility, and impact—of the vote. Yet how do we do this?

Clearly, when it comes to voting rights, the future is not set, nor assured. Significant questions and dilemmas remain. Challenges abound. The very meaning of democracy and popular government rests on the answers we choose in these matters. Today and in the years to come, the fight over voting rights goes on.

The Election the Judges Resolved: *Bush v. Gore* and the Debate over the Nationalization of Voting in America

All of the above takes us back to the extraordinary events of the 2000 presidential election and its place in the evolving story of U.S.

democracy. It is hard to overstate the importance of the 2000 election controversy and of the resulting court battles between George W. Bush and Al Gore. Whereas courts had been ruling with increasing significance on voting rights for over eighty years, it was only with the 2000 election controversy that the foundational issues of vote inclusion—equal protection versus equal impact, localism versus national rights, and the negative effects of increasing voter dissatisfaction with the political process—came into focus with painful clarity. The 2000 election litigation is one of those major turning points that shapes public debate for a generation or even more. *Bush v. Gore* ranks with *Minor v. Happersett, Smith v. Allwright, Reynolds v. Sims,* and *Shaw v. Reno* as defining moments in the fight over the meaning and form of U.S. government. In fact, in terms of its long-term impact on both the nation and the Court itself, *Bush v. Gore* might even rank along side some of the Supreme Court's most famous—and infamous—rulings: *Marbury v. Madison* (judicial review), *Dred Scott v. Sandford* (slavery), *Slaughterhouse* (the meaning of the Fourteenth Amendment), *Plessy v. Ferguson* (segregation), *Brown v. Board of Education* (desegregation), and *Roe v. Wade* (abortion). For better or worse, in 2000 the future of U.S. voting rights passed through Florida with its butterfly ballots, hanging chads, and intimations of voter fraud and intimidation. The right to vote in the United States will never be the same again.

In examining the 2000 election, and especially its litigation aftermath, it is useful to start by understanding the multiple levels on which this unique situation unfolded. The 2000 election controversy raised political, social, legal, and constitutional questions essential to the health of the U.S. body politic. Politically, the Florida mess not only posed the question of who would be the forty-third president of the United States—it challenged the political structures by which we had organized politics in this country for over 200 years—for if so many votes could be thrown out uncounted in Florida, how legitimate could *any* election using similar voting technologies and procedures be? Socially, it exposed the still deep racial and ethnic divides that separate us. Almost 200 years of vote denial and dilution had left their mark on the psyche of this nation's minorities, creating expectations of exclusion that the events of the 2000 election seemed to bear out; yet, so long as such feelings of alienation remain, the fight for minorities' full inclusion into U.S. society remained incomplete. Last, and for our purposes, most important, the litigation that grew out of the Florida election controversy raised important yet difficult legal and constitutional questions whose answers will shape the voting rights debate for years to come.

It is to these legal and constitutional questions that we must turn, keeping in mind at all times, however, the presence and importance of the political and social dimensions of this matter. For, as we shall see, it is only in light of more than 200 years of vote denial—not to mention the all-important question of who got to be the next president of the United States—that the answers arrived at in *Bush v. Gore* make any sense in terms of the motivations and actions of the players in this drama. Racial tensions and political preference were key to shaping the answers we arrived at. However, it is in the legal and constitutional realm that its impact will be longest felt.

As described in chapter 1, the election difficulty in Florida began with balloting so evenly divided that the normal election machinery proved inadequate to the job. Undertrained voluntary election staffs, outdated voting technology, and local autonomy over the election process all conspired to derail the normal election process in Florida. The problem was not just Florida's inability to determine a winner, but also its failure even to agree upon the proper standards to use in determining who had won; and, inasmuch as victory in Florida meant victory nationwide, no one was willing to back down and accept defeat. A combination of partisan politics, technological inadequacies, and procedural confusion thus merged with the long history of vote denial and dilution to produce what can only be described as a constitutional train wreck. This is where the courts came into the picture.

The courts became involved in attempts to settle the election mess almost from the start of the controversy. As early as Saturday, November 11—just four days after the election—George W. Bush asked the U.S. District Court for the Southern District of Florida to block manual recounts. Two days later, that court refused, leading Bush to file an immediate appeal with the Eleventh Circuit Court of Appeals (which would rule against Bush in December). Meanwhile, on November 14, Judge Terry Lewis of Florida's Leon County Circuit Court (Florida law gave the power to hear all election matters to the Tallahassee-based Leon County courts) heard motions challenging the recount deadline as set by Florida's Secretary of State, Katherine Harris. Applying a literal reading of the state statutes, Harris had set a November 14 deadline for submission of all county vote totals.

On November 9, the Democrats had requested hand recounts in Volusia, Palm Beach, Broward, and Miami-Dade counties. In most cases, these hand recounts were not going to be completed by November 14. The request was for a few more days—and in some cases, hours—in which to finish the hand recounts. Judge Lewis, however, upheld the deadline, ruling it a mandatory requirement— although he did allow the Secretary of State, using her discretion, to accept amended late returns. The next day, Secretary Harris, applying this discretion, refused petitions from all four counties for permission to amend their vote totals returns based on hand recounts. One day later, the Democrats appealed her decision to Judge Lewis (requesting a contempt order compelling Harris to accept the amended returns), which Judge Lewis denied. Meanwhile, on November 16, an earlier petition by the election boards of Palm Beach and Broward Counties to the Florida Supreme Court challenging the time limits on hand recounts resulted in a 7–0 ruling that both counties could continue their recounts.

So events progressed for the next thrity-three days, court case following court case, appeal following appeal. In all, some fifteen separate lawsuits and appeals were filed in various state and federal courts by the candidates and their parties. Many were argued and reargued many times, as each side fought for a resolution that brought them victory. In the end, Florida trial courts issued four rulings, the Florida Supreme Court nine different judicial pronouncements, and the U.S. Supreme Court handed down one stay of lower-court proceedings and two substantive judgments, the last of which ended the election debate.

A complete discussion of the ins and outs of this litigation is beyond the scope of this book. It is enough here to note the willingness—in fact, the eagerness—of each side to seek judicial resolution whenever they looked likely to lose the political debate and thus the election. Both sides might proclaim their commitment to a political settlement to the dispute, attacking the other side as "the first to go to the courts," but the reality was that each turned to the courts whenever they felt it was in their best interests to do so. Every issue that could be forged in legal terms was so forged; even when the questions were not legal in nature, they were reworked into legal terms. The courts were on the hot seat, and like it or not, they were the ones who had to find a solution. In consequence, final resolution of this matter was going to rest on the usually technical issues that concern courts of law—and on the controversial legal and constitutional perspectives, values, and approaches of the Florida and federal benches.

Both sets of judges, state and federal, took this job seriously. They all understood the complex and disputed nature of the issues raised by the election; they also all shared, most likely, a growing appreciation of Justice Felix Frankfurter's depiction of voting rights as a "political thicket." In fact, the first response of almost every court when faced with these questions was a refusal to act. In the end, however, events and the needs of the political system forced the courts to act. No matter what, the job was theirs.

Taking the lead in this process were two supreme courts—Florida's and the nation's. It was in these courts of last resort that the law's meaning and reach would be set. Each court took a very different approach to settling the issues raised by the election controversy. In fact, for our purposes, one of the most interesting aspects of the legal battles fought over the 2000 election was the completely opposite readings of the law by each set of jurists.

When faced with conflicting statutory provisions in Florida's election law, for example, a majority of the judges of the Florida supreme court emphasized voter inclusion as the primary objective in constructing their rulings. Drawing both on statutory law and Florida's constitution, they ruled that: "This Court has repeatedly held . . . that so long as the voter's intent may be discerned from the ballot, [said] vote constitutes a 'legal vote' that should be counted." They ruled this way, the judges explained, not only because this was the standard imposed by Florida statute, but because it was "only by examining the contested ballots" that "a meaningful and final determination in this election contest [could] be made." Voter empowerment was the supreme objective in determining judicial action in these matters; "notwithstanding" such other legitimate concerns as "time constraints" or the need to produce a clear winner, "we must do everything required by law to ensure that legal votes that have not been counted are included in the final election results." To this end, the Florida supreme court remanded the case to the circuit court "to immediately tabulate by hand the approximate 9,000 [remaining] . . . ballots, which the counting machine registered as non-votes, but which have never been manually reviewed, and for other relief that may thereafter appear appropriate" (*Gore v. Harris*, 1261–1262).

A majority of the U.S. Supreme Court saw things differently. Although empowering voters was a laudable goal in the abstract, seven justices held, a lack of concrete and uniform standards as to what was, and was not, a proper vote raised serious constitutional problems. The Florida court's objective in applying the "intent of the voter" as the primary ingredient of a proper vote was "unobjectionable as an abstract proposition and a starting principle." However, "in the absence of specific standards to ensure its equal application," this standard was functionally meaningless. The Florida supreme court's order, the justices explained, "did not specify who would recount the ballots." This omission forced "the county canvassing boards ... to pull together *ad hoc* teams comprised of judges from various Circuits who had no previous training in handling and interpreting ballots." Even worse, "the standards for accepting or rejecting contested ballots [under this system] might vary not only from county to county but indeed within a single county from one recount team to another." Such failings were constitutionally unacceptable: "When a court orders a statewide remedy, there must be at least some assurance that the rudimentary requirements of equal treatment and fundamental fairness are satisfied." They were also unnecessary. Granted, "in some cases the general command to ascertain intent is not susceptible to much further refinement." In this instance, however,

the question is not whether to believe a witness but how to interpret the marks or holes or scratches on an inanimate object, a piece of cardboard or paper which, it is said, might not have registered as a vote during the machine count. The factfinder confronts a thing, not a person. The search for intent can be confined by specific rules designed to ensure uniform treatment.

The deficiency of such uniform rules in Florida, the justices concluded, meant that the "recount mechanisms implemented in response to the decisions of the Florida Supreme Court [did] not satisfy the minimum requirement for non-arbitrary treatment of voters necessary to secure the fundamental right." Lacking necessary procedural "safeguards," the contest provisions were simply "not well calculated to sustain the confidence that all citizens must have in the outcome of elections." As such, they were in direct violation of the equal protection clause of the Constitution (*Bush v. Gore*, 530, 531–532).

It did not automatically follow, however, that the recounts had to end. All seven justices in the majority agreed that a proper recount demanded more detailed standards. But that was all they agreed upon. In the normal course of events, a ruling such as *Bush v. Gore* customarily would be followed by an order remanding the matter back to the lower court for "further proceedings not inconsistent with this opinion." In fact, two members of the majority, Justices Stephen Breyer and David H. Souter, argued strongly for just such a remand. Justice Breyer felt the Court should "remand this case with instructions that . . . would permit the Florida Supreme Court to require recounting all undercounted votes in Florida, . . . in accordance with a single-uniform substandard." Justice Souter, in turn, found "no justification for denying the State the opportunity to try to count all disputed ballots." Give the Florida courts a chance "to do their best to get that job done," he concluded (*Bush v. Gore*, 533, 546, 551).

The other five justices in the majority disagreed. The time for recounts had run out. "Upon due consideration of the difficulties identified to this point," the majority opinion declared,

> it is obvious that the recount cannot be conducted in compliance with the requirements of equal protection and due process without substantial additional work. It would require not only the adoption (after opportunity for argument) of adequate statewide standards for determining what is a legal vote, and practicable procedures to implement them, but also orderly judicial review of any disputed matters that might arise.

Recounting votes in a constitutional matter was going to take time—something the presidential election process could not afford to spare. As the majority explained, the Florida supreme court had emphasized in its earlier decisions the Florida legislature's intention to have its electors "'participate fully in the federal electoral process,' as provided [for by federal laws requiring] that any controversy or contest that is designed to lead to a conclusive selection of electors be completed by December 12." Unfortunately, as Chief Justice William H. Rehnquist noted in his concurrence (quoting from the dissent in *Gore v. Harris*), "that date is upon us, and . . . . I respectfully submit this [recount] cannot be completed without taking Florida's presidential electors outside the safe harbor provision, creating the very real possibility of disenfranchising those nearly 6 million voters who are able to correctly cast their ballots on election day." Given these facts, these five justices felt that they had no option but "to reverse the judgment of the Supreme Court of Florida ordering a recount to proceed." The election was over; George W. Bush was the winner (*Bush v. Gore*, 532–533).

Obviously, this was a result that many found hard to swallow. The four justices in dissent were particularly harsh in their objections. As just noted, Justices Breyer and Souter complained that the majority was implementing the wrong remedy. "Of course, the selection of the President is of fundamental national importance," Justice Breyer wrote. "But that importance is political, not legal." For this reason alone, "this Court should resist the temptation unnecessarily to resolve tangential legal disputes, where doing so threatens to determine the outcome of the election. . . . However awkward or difficult it may be for Congress to resolve difficult electoral disputes, Congress, being a political body, expresses the people's will far more accurately than does an unelected Court. And the people's will is what elections are about." Justice Souter was even more blunt in his conclusions: "If this Court had allowed the State to follow the course indicated by the opinions of its own Supreme Court, it is entirely possible that there would ultimately have been no issue requiring our review, and political tension could have worked itself out in the Congress following the procedure provided in 3 U.S.C. § 15." Sadly it did not. Having wrongly taken up the case, the "resolution by the majority" was producing "another erroneous decision" (*Bush v. Gore*, 555, 542).

Justice John Paul Stevens, objecting to the whole of the majorities' rulings, voiced even stronger objections. He complained that "the Constitution assigns to the States the primary responsibility for determining the manner of selecting the Presidential electors"; "when questions about the meaning of state laws, including election laws" arose in the past, it was the Court's "settled practice to accept the opinions of the highest courts of the States as providing the final answers." This was decidedly not the case here. The federal questions raised by this case were "not substantial." Nor were there any reasons "to think that the guidance provided to the factfinders, . . . by the "intent of the voter" standard [was] any less sufficient—or [would] lead to results any less uniform—than, for example, the 'beyond a reasonable doubt' standard employed everyday by ordinary citizens in courtrooms across this country." Underlying the entire assault on the Florida election procedures, Justice Stevens argued, was "an unstated lack of confidence in the impartiality and capacity of the state judges who would make the critical decisions if the vote count were to proceed." This was a troubling view, one "only lend[ing] credence to the most cynical appraisal of the work of judges throughout the land." Time will one day "heal the wound to that confidence that will be inflicted by today's decision," Justice Stevens concluded. Yet, "one thing, . . . is certain. Although we may never know with complete certainty the identity of the winner of this year's Presidential election, the identity of the loser is perfectly clear. It is the Nation's confidence in the judge as an impartial guardian of the rule of law" (*Bush v. Gore,* 539, 540–541, 542).

Most angry was Justice Ruth Bader Ginsburg. Taking the majority to task, Ginsburg complained how "the extraordinary setting of this case has obscured the ordinary principle that dictates its proper resolution: Federal courts defer to state high courts' interpretations of their state's own law." This simple principle lay at "the core of federalism, on which all agree," and the majority's holding that it was not operative here was troublesome. In fact, the five justices in the majority normally were among the strongest supporters of state authority under federalism. This role reversal frustrated Justice Ginsburg. "Were the other members of this Court as mindful as they generally are of our system of dual sovereignty," she charged, "they would affirm the judgment of the Florida Supreme Court." That they did not do this—and in fact, for as limited a reason as "time will not permit an 'orderly judicial review of any disputed matters that might arise'"—was improper. "No one has doubted the good faith and diligence with which Florida election officials, attorneys for all sides of this controversy, and the courts of law have performed their duties." Yet, the Court has adopted a conclusion that "is a prophecy the Court's own judgment will not allow to be tested." Such untested prophecies, she concluded, "should not decide the Presidency of the United States." Lacking all respect for the majority's logic, and perhaps distrusting their motives, Justice Ginsburg broke tradition and ended her views bluntly: "I dissent" (*Bush v. Gore,* 549–550).

Explosive in its content and results alike, *Bush v. Gore* seemed destined to provoke an unending controversy about what it meant and what significance it would have for the constitutional dimension of voting rights. In particular, the result of this case raised questions pivotal to the future not just of voting rights, but of the judicial and political processes in general: What should the objective be in regulating the voting process, empowering voters or protecting the integrity and equality of the voting process? Who should make these decisions, state or federal officials? Were these even matters susceptible to judicial resolution? Once acted upon, would the American people accept the process applied, and the solutions arrived at, in settling these matters?

Of the four, the last two questions are the most speculative in nature. Justices Ginsburg, Breyer, and Stevens each argued that the specter of federal judges picking the next president threatened the integrity of the Supreme Court and the entire judicial process. It was also just plain wrong. As Justice Breyer eloquently argued:

> Those who caution judicial restraint in resolving political disputes have described the quintessential case for that restraint as a case marked, among other things, by the "strangeness of the issue," its "intractability to principled resolution," its "sheer momentousness, . . . which tends to unbalance judicial judgment," and "the inner vulnerability, the self-doubt of an institution which is electorally irresponsible and has no earth to draw strength from." . . . Those characteristics mark this case.

To take such conclusive action in so highly politicized a matter, especially by a split 5–4 vote, thus ran the unnecessary risk "of undermining the public's confidence in the Court itself":

> That confidence is a public treasure. It has been built slowly over many years, some of which were marked by a Civil War and the tragedy of segregation. It is a vitally necessary ingredient of any successful effort to protect basic liberty and, indeed, the rule of law itself. We run no risk of returning to the days when a President (responding to this Court's efforts to protect the Cherokee Indians) might have said, "John Marshall has made his decision; now let him enforce it!" . . . . But we do risk a self-inflicted wound—a wound that may harm not just the Court, but the Nation.

"In order to bring this agonizingly long election process to a definitive conclusion," Breyer concluded, the Court had overstepped the proper bounds of its authority and should retreat from this drift immediately. For, as "Justice Brandeis once said of the Court, 'The most important thing we do is not doing.'" Sadly, this was not the case here. "What it does today, the Court should have left undone" (*Bush v. Gore*, 557–558).

The majority, on the other hand, argued that it was the Florida supreme court's inadequate "contest provision[s]," and not its own ruling, that were "not well calculated to sustain the confidence that all citizens must have in the outcome of elections." As Chief Justice Rehnquist noted in his concurrence:

> This inquiry does not imply a disrespect for state courts but rather a respect for the constitutionally prescribed role of state legislatures. To attach definitive weight to the pronouncement of a state court, when the very question at issue is whether the court has actually departed from the statutory meaning, would be to abdicate our responsibility to enforce the explicit requirements of Article II.

Whereas the majority justices on the Florida Supreme Court and the dissenting justices of the U.S. Supreme Court had seen the need to count every vote as the foundation of public acceptance, the majority of the U.S. Supreme Court asserted the need for technical accuracy and for practical finality. Anything less and the Court would be ignoring its duty as the nation's court of last resort. As the per curiam decision noted in conclusion:

> None are more conscious of the vital limits on judicial authority than are the members of this Court, and none stand more in admiration of the Constitution's design to leave the selection of the President to the people, through their legislatures, and to the political sphere. When contending parties invoke the process of the courts, however, it becomes our unsought responsibility to resolve the federal and constitutional issues the judicial system has been forced to confront. (*Bush v. Gore*, 532, 535, 533)

Only time will tell who was correct. The decision raised passionate debate within the legal, political and scholarly communities as well as within the general public. The decision has had both its defenders and its detractors. The political implications of the ruling—over who got to be president; over what that president would do on the job; over whom he might appoint to the very Court picking him—were staggering. Many who agreed with the ultimate outcome still were troubled by the process by which this outcome was reached. Others felt that there should never have been a debate over recounts in the first place and spared the Court any censure for its difficult decision. In truth, although everyone has an opinion, even months later, confusion and uncertainty still reign supreme.

The same can be said for the more technical debate over which set of judges should have ruled in these matters. Whereas most Americans do not understand the intricacies of federalism (nor likely wish to understand it) when it is reworked as a question of state rights versus federal power, most are split in their views about which court should have ruled in this matter—a split based largely on their support for or opposition to the decisions reached. Republicans pointed to Florida statutes and complained that a partisan, pro-Democratic Florida Supreme Court was rewriting the election laws in an effort to "steal the election." Viewed in this light, it was necessary for the federal courts to step in and save the nation from an out-of-control court. As Chief Justice Renhquist pointed out in his concurrence, presidential elections are different:

In any election but a Presidential election, the Florida Supreme Court can give as little or as much deference to Florida's executives as it chooses, so far as Article II is concerned, and this Court will have no cause to question the court's actions. But, with respect to a Presidential election, the court must be both mindful of the legislature's role under Article II in choosing the manner of appointing electors and deferential to those bodies expressly empowered by the legislature to carry out its constitutional mandate. (*Bush v. Gore*, 534)

Democrats responded to such arguments by waving in the conservative majority's face the Supreme Court's traditional concerns with empowering state courts under federalism (the idea that some matters are truly matters of state interest alone). If cooperative federalism was a legitimate goal in other matters, they asked, should it not be the case here as well? As Justice Ginsburg noted in her dissent:

This Court more than occasionally affirms statutory, and even constitutional, interpretations with which it disagrees.... And not uncommonly, we let stand state-court interpretations of federal law with which we might disagree.... In deferring to state courts on matters of state law, we appropriately recognize that this Court acts as an "'outsider' lacking the common exposure to local law which comes from sitting in the jurisdiction." . . . [Hence,] notwithstanding our authority to decide issues of state law underlying federal claims, we have . . . afford[ed] state high courts an opportunity to inform us on matters of their own State's law because such restraint "helps build a cooperative judicial federalism."

When ruling in such matters, Justice Ginsburg concluded, "the Court [normally] adheres to the view that there is 'no intrinsic reason why the fact that a man is a federal judge should make him more competent, or conscientious, or learned with respect to [federal law] than his neighbor in the state courthouse'" (*Bush v. Gore*, 546). This case with its mix of state and federal law, the four justices in dissent contended, should be no different. Numerous Gore supporters and political and legal commentators agreed.

Even when we move into the realm of constitutional doctrine, the meaning of *Bush v. Gore* remains unclear—and highly polarized. The equal protection and due process justifications cited by the majority invite two opposed readings of their constitutional and political implications—one liberal and the other conservative. On the one hand, taking the equal protection arguments of *Bush v. Gore* at face value opens up whole new vistas for the expansion of vote inclusion. If the Florida recount was invalid because differing election technologies and effective local control of the election process produced inconsistent and imbalanced standards for the definition of a proper vote, then by implication all such differences in the ways we collect and count votes are similarly improper. This means, again by implication, that those local authorities using less accurate voting technologies could demand—as a matter of equal protection and due process—that the states provide them with equal methods of placing and counting their vote. Anything less would be a denial of equal protection. Given that, at least in Florida, the less accurate voting technology was used mostly in urban districts with large minority populations, the power to demand equal treatment from election officials potentially could transform the voting electorate. (In fact, after the election, the Florida legislature did adopt uniform statewide voting standards and technologies.) At the least, it imposes a renewed duty on the states to see to it that all voters are given an equal chance to make known their political choices and wishes. Viewed in this light,

Bush v. Gore might just be the most expansive voting rights ruling since *Reynolds v. Sims.*

Unfortunately, the odds of this expansive shift in policy actually happening are slim. As already noted, in his concurrence, Chief Justice Rehnquist took pains to stress the uniqueness of the situation underlying *Bush v. Gore.* He began by noting how "we deal here not with an ordinary election, but with an election for the President of the United States." This basic fact made this election contest different from all others. "In ordinary cases," Chief Justice Rehnquist explained, "the distribution of powers among the branches of a State's government raises no questions of federal constitutional law, subject [only] to the requirement that the government be republican in character." However, "there are a few exceptional cases in which the Constitution imposes a duty or confers a power on a particular branch of a State's government. This is one of them" (*Bush v. Gore,* 534). Even more to the point, the majority opinion explicitly ignored the potential constitutional problems posed by the use of disparate voting technologies in different counties or states. All they said on the topic was that "the question before the Court is *not* whether local entities, in the exercise of their expertise, may develop different systems for implementing elections." Rather, they explained, this case raised the "*special* instance of a statewide recount under the authority of a single state judicial officer" (*Bush v. Gore,* 532—emphasis added). Thus, although nothing in the ruling prohibits future application of equal protection logic to expand the rights of all citizens to demand equal voting technologies and standards, it does show a clear reluctance on the part of at least five of the justices to do so.

A much more likely doctrinal shift would be for the Court to extend the equal protection logic of *Bush v. Gore* beyond the issue of vote counting to the more contentious aspects of suffrage, in particular race-specific legislative districting. After all, if a lack of standards for what is a proper vote is at odds with equal protection, should not the more egregious forms of unequal treatment in the voting process, such as race-conscious districting, which intentionally seeks to treat various groups differently, be impermissible under the law too? Such views are in line with the Court's 1993 ruling in *Shaw v. Reno.* In fact, they are in line with the general trend of their rulings in voting rights matters for over a decade.

Applying the majority's approach in *Bush v. Gore* to the sorts of race-conscious districting challenged in *Shaw,* in turn, calls into question the legitimacy of any form of race-conscious remedies in this country. If, as the majority noted in their opinion (quoting *Reynolds v. Sims*) "the right of suffrage can be denied by a debasement or dilution of the weight of a citizen's vote just as effectively as by wholly prohibiting the free exercise of the franchise," then applying different standards to different groups in creating legislative districts is by definition an even more prejudicial form of unequal treatment than using disparate standards in vote counting. This being the case, the logic of *Bush v. Gore* demands an end to this practice (*Bush v. Gore*, 530). Even the uniqueness of *Bush v. Gore* is unlikely to impede the Court's adoption of such logic. After all, race-conscious districting for its own sake is already constitutionally impermissible—all that *Bush v. Gore* provides is extra incentive for the Court to apply this logic ever wider and with greater force.

Should the U.S. Supreme Court chose to travel this road—and as with all aspects of *Bush v. Gore's* impact, only time will tell—it promises a new age for voting rights in the United States. Like it or not, the application of group-specific remedies to group-based problems has been the primary means employed to combat vote dilution and denial. Although a return to the days of widespread vote denial is unlikely, given the still potent presence of class, race, and gender conflict in U.S. society, the potential for renewed vote dilution is strong. So long as we choose to define ourselves largely by who we are not—and to do this not only as an entire people, but in terms of the subgroups that make up the *genus* American—the tendency will endure to exclude those who are different from the process by which we choose our leaders. If race-conscious remedies to vote dilution are no longer permitted, some other method will have to come to the fore. Just what that method will be, however, remains to be seen.

Conclusion

A more complete discussion of the range and impact of these and similar debates as to the future of voting rights is beyond the scope of this book. Even if it were within its scope, the ongoing nature of these debates makes reaching any valid conclusions difficult. Beyond noting the interest, anger, frustration, and confusion of a large segment of the nation's voters over these matters, any historical verdict we reach must be so tentative in nature as to undermine its usefulness. Still, regarding the convictions of the U.S. public, its legal community, and its judiciary as to the meaning and lessons learned from the 2000 election mess—not to mention the long and convoluted history of voting rights in the United States—one general conclusion is possible: in the long run, what matters most are not our current attitudes, but the Supreme Court's future actions. As legal scholar Michael Klarman notes in an article analyzing *Bush v. Gore*, "roughly half the nation probably will believe for the indefinite future that the Supreme Court stole a presidential election from their candidate." The other half, needless to say, will accept the opposite view as gospel. Yet in time, these feelings will shift from "constant irritant" to "unhappy memory" (Klarman, 52). The only things likely to reawaken these more intense feelings are further controversial rulings by the Supreme Court (especially on the issue of voting rights) or controversial appointments by President George W. Bush to the Supreme Court.

Whether one approves or disapproves of the specter of five Supreme Court justices picking the next president of the United States, the decision was made. Once George W. Bush was sworn in as our forty-third president, there was no going back. It is the future of voting rights that matters now. As is so often the case in the history of voting in the United States, we find ourselves at the cusp of a new era in the ongoing evolution of democracy and participatory government. Will the march toward including more and more Americans in the voting and governing processes continue its drawn-out journey toward universal suffrage and equal participation in governance? Or will our concerns with equality and equal treatment roll back the gains of the last hundred years? Can a new methodology of voter inclusion be applied that meets both objectives? Does such a methodology even exist? As is so often true in history as a whole, only time will tell.

So what is one to make of the strange career of voting rights in the United States? From a distance, what we see seems to be a triumphal story of ever greater inclusion, expansion, and empowerment leading to a present of near universal suffrage; viewed by its details, the story seems more a horror tale of denials, exclusions, and omissions. The reality is obviously somewhere in the middle. The truth is that we have expanded the range of those who can vote—and enhanced the meaning and power of that vote—to levels unimaginable when this country was formed. Yet also true is the long list of the many ways that we have kept people from voicing their opinions and commitments in the public realm and the all too slow path by which these limits were abolished.

Yet whatever the conflicts or difficulties, the contradictions or confusions, the hopes and disappointments associated with voting rights, one simple set of facts remains constant: every two years we vote for one-third of the Senate and the entire House of Representatives, and every four years we vote in the process that chooses the president of the United States. The same choices at even shorter intervals exist in state and local politics as well. We may fight over the outer limits of who should vote. We may stress equal protection or equal access at different times and in different ways. We may take up or discard different methods of vote inclusion. We might even choose—as today we seem to do in ever-larger numbers—not to vote and hence to abandon our right to the franchise. Yet, with all these nuances and complications, the process of voting goes on.

For better or worse, voting is the primary way that we as a people affect the shape, direction, and development of our government and society. Who should have this power, and how we should use it, are questions that spark debates that never will end—and never can end. The struggle over the vote is intrinsic to the ongoing evolution of democracy in the United States. Our willingness to search for answers, to debate priorities, and to make hard choices is vital to democracy's future—both in our own country and throughout the world. So long as we are willing to debate who can vote and how, and so long as our answers allow most of us to vote, democracy in the United States remains strong. For where the right to vote exists, the possibility of change exists, and change is essential to a living democracy.

References and Further Reading

Bass, Jack, *Taming the Storm: The Life and Times of Judge Frank M. John-son, Jr., and the South's Fight over Civil Rights* (New York: Doubleday, 1993).

Berry, Mary Frances, "Diluting the Vote: The Irony of *Bush v. Gore,*" *Journal of American History* 88 (September 2001): 436–443.

Dershowitz, Alan M., *Supreme Injustice: How the High Court Hijacked Election 2000* (Oxford: Oxford University Press, 2001).

Dionne, E. J., and William Kristol, eds., Bush v. Gore: *The Court Cases and the Commentary* (Washington, DC: Brookings Institution Press, 2001).

Greenfield, Jeff, *"Oh Waiter! One Order of Crow!": Inside the Strangest Presidential Election Finish in American History* (New York: G. Putnam and Sons, 2001).

Keyssar, Alexander, *The Right to Vote: The Contested History of Democracy in the United States* (New York: Basic Books, 2000).

Klarman, Michael J., *"Bush v. Gore* through the Lens of Constitutional History," (Unpublished manuscript, January 30, 2001).

Posner, Richard A., *Breaking the Deadlock: The 2000 Election, the Constitution, and the Courts* (Princeton: Princton University Press, 2001).

Pressley, Sue Anne, and Thomas B. Edsall, "Florida Lawmakers Approve Elections System Overhaul," *Washington Post,* May 5, 2001, p. A1.

Part Two

Documents

Foundations: The Constitution of the United States (1787)

The foundation for all voting rights in this country rests in the Constitution of the United States and eight of twenty-seven amendments made over a 200-year period. Some of these provisions deal with the highly technical process by which we choose our government officials. (For example, Articles I and II, Amendment XII and XVII). Others are more basic statements of individual rights and constitutional objectives. These include the Civil Rights Amendments, (XIII, XIV, and XV) as well as those amendments granting women and eighteen year olds the vote (XIX and XXVI). Finally there is Amendment XXIV, which outlaws one of the most effective methods of vote denial, poll taxes. As you read these provisions, note the ongoing struggle with the problems posed by voting rights as we have sought to answer such basic questions as: Who could and should vote in this country? How should we organize our voting to maximize (or perhaps to minimize) the will of the electorate? And how should we combat efforts to deny or dilute the vote of some groups?

Article I

Section 2. The House of Representatives shall be composed of members chosen every second year by the people of the several states, and the electors in each state shall have the qualifications requisite for electors of the most numerous branch of the state legislature.

. . .

Section 4. The times, places and manner of holding elections for Senators and Representatives, shall be prescribed in each state by the legislature thereof; but the Congress may at any time by law make or alter such regulations, except as to the places of choosing Senators.

The Congress shall assemble at least once in every year, and such meeting shall be on the first Monday in December, unless they shall by law appoint a different day.

Section 5. Each House shall be the judge of the elections, returns and qualifications of its own members, and a majority of each shall constitute a quorum to do business; but a smaller number may adjourn from day to day, and may be authorized to compel the attendance of absent members, in such manner, and under such penalties as each House may provide.

. . .

Article II

Section 1. The executive power shall be vested in a President of the United States of America. He shall hold his office during the term of four years, and, together with the Vice President, chosen for the same term, be elected, as follows:

Each state shall appoint, in such manner as the Legislature thereof may direct, a number of electors, equal to the whole number of Senators and Representatives to which the State may be entitled in the Congress: but no Senator or Representative, or person holding an office of trust or profit under the United States, shall be appointed an elector.

The electors shall meet in their respective states, and vote by ballot for two persons, of whom one at least shall not be an inhabitant of the same state with themselves. And they shall make a list of all the persons voted for, and of the number of votes for each; which list they shall sign and certify, and transmit sealed to the seat of the government of the United States, directed to the President of the Senate. The President of the Senate shall, in the presence of the Senate and House of Representatives, open all the certificates, and the votes shall then be counted. The person having the greatest number of votes shall be the President, if such number be a majority of the whole number of electors appointed; and if there be more than one who have such majority, and have an equal number of votes, then the House of Representatives shall immediately choose by ballot one of them for President; and if no person have a majority, then from the five highest on the list the said House shall in like manner choose the President. But in choosing the President, the votes shall be taken by States, the representation from each state having one vote; A quorum for this purpose shall consist of a member or members from two thirds of the states, and a majority of all the states shall be necessary to a choice. In every case, after the choice of the President, the person having the greatest number of votes of the electors shall be the Vice President. But if there should remain two or more who have equal votes, the Senate shall choose from them by ballot the Vice President.

The Congress may determine the time of choosing the electors, and the day on which they shall give their votes; which day shall be the same throughout the United States.

. . .

Amendment XII (1804)

The electors shall meet in their respective states and vote by ballot for President and Vice-President, one of whom, at least, shall not be an inhabitant of the same state with themselves; they shall name in their ballots the person voted for as President, and in distinct ballots the person voted for as Vice-President, and they shall make distinct lists of all persons voted for as President, and of all persons voted for as Vice-President, and of the number of votes for each, which lists they shall sign and certify, and transmit sealed to the seat of the government of the United States, directed to the President of the Senate;—The President of the Senate shall, in the presence of the Senate and House of Representatives, open all the certificates and the votes shall then be counted;—the person having the greatest number of votes for President, shall be the President, if such number be a majority of the whole number of electors appointed; and if no person have such majority, then from the persons having the highest numbers not exceeding three on the list of those voted for as President, the House of Representatives shall choose immediately, by ballot, the President. But in choosing the President, the votes shall be taken by states, the representation from each state having one vote; a quorum for this purpose shall consist of a member or members from two-thirds of the states, and a majority of all the states shall be necessary to a choice. And if the House of Representatives shall not choose a President whenever the right of choice shall devolve upon them, before the fourth day of March next following, then the Vice-President shall act as President, as in the case of the death or other constitutional disability of the President. The person having the greatest number of votes as Vice-President, shall be the Vice-President, if such number be a majority of the whole number of electors appointed, and if no person have a majority, then from the two highest numbers on the list, the Senate shall choose the Vice-President; a quorum for the purpose shall consist of two-thirds of the whole number of Senators, and a majority of the whole number shall be necessary to a choice. But no person constitutionally ineligible to the office of President shall be eligible to that of Vice-President of the United States.

Amendment XIII (1865)

Section 1. Neither slavery nor involuntary servitude, except as a punishment for crime whereof the party shall have been duly convicted, shall exist within the United States, or any place subject to their jurisdiction.

Section 2. Congress shall have power to enforce this article by appropriate legislation.

Amendment XIV (1868)

Section 1. All persons born or naturalized in the United States, and subject to the jurisdiction thereof, are citizens of the United States and of the state wherein they reside. No state shall make or enforce any law which shall abridge the privileges or immunities of citizens of the United States; nor shall any state deprive any person of life, liberty, or property, without due process of law; nor deny to any person within its jurisdiction the equal protection of the laws.

Section 2. Representatives shall be apportioned among the several states according to their respective numbers, counting the whole number of persons in each state, excluding Indians not taxed. But when the right to vote at any election for the choice of electors for President and Vice President of the United States, Representatives in Congress, the executive and judicial officers of a state, or the members of the legislature thereof, is denied to any of the male inhabitants of such state, being twenty-one years of age, and citizens of the United States, or in any way abridged, except for participation in rebellion, or other crime, the basis of representation therein shall be reduced in the proportion which the number of such male citizens shall bear to the whole number of male citizens twenty-one years of age in such state.

Section 3. No person shall be a Senator or Representative in Congress, or elector of President and Vice President, or hold any office, civil or military, under the United States, or under any state, who, having previously taken an oath, as a member of Congress, or as an officer of the United States, or as a member of any state legislature, or as an executive or judicial officer of any state, to support the Constitution of the United States, shall have engaged in insurrection or rebellion against the same, or given aid or comfort to the enemies thereof. But Congress may by a vote of two-thirds of each House, remove such disability.

Section 4. The validity of the public debt of the United States, authorized by law, including debts incurred for payment of pensions and bounties for services in suppressing insurrection or rebellion, shall not be questioned. But neither the United States nor any state shall assume or pay any debt or obligation incurred in aid of insurrection or rebellion against the United States, or any claim for the loss or emancipation of any slave; but all such debts, obligations and claims shall be held illegal and void.

Section 5. The Congress shall have power to enforce, by appropriate legislation, the provisions of this article.

Amendment XV (1870)

Section 1. The right of citizens of the United States to vote shall not be denied or abridged by the United States or by any state on account of race, color, or previous condition of servitude.

Section 2. The Congress shall have power to enforce this article by appropriate legislation.

Amendment XVII (1913)

The Senate of the United States shall be composed of two Senators from each state, elected by the people thereof, for six years; and each Senator shall have one vote. The electors in each state shall have the qualifications requisite for electors of the most numerous branch of the state legislatures.

When vacancies happen in the representation of any state in the Senate, the executive authority of such state shall issue writs of election to fill such vacancies: Provided, that the legislature of any state may empower the executive thereof to make temporary appointments until the people fill the vacancies by election as the legislature may direct.

This amendment shall not be so construed as to affect the election or term of any Senator chosen before it becomes valid as part of the Constitution.

Amendment XIX (1920)

The right of citizens of the United States to vote shall not be denied or abridged by the United States or by any state on account of sex.

Congress shall have power to enforce this article by appropriate legislation.

Amendment XXIV (1964)

Section 1. The right of citizens of the United States to vote in any primary or other election for President or Vice President, for electors for President or Vice President, or for Senator or Representative in Congress, shall not be denied or abridged by the United States or any state by reason of failure to pay any poll tax or other tax.

Section 2. The Congress shall have power to enforce this article by appropriate legislation.

Amendment XXVI (1971)

Section 1. The right of citizens of the United States, who are 18 years of age or older, to vote, shall not be denied or abridged by the United States or any state on account of age.

Section 2. The Congress shall have the power to enforce this article by appropriate legislation.

The Courts Say No to Expanded Voting Rights: *Elk v. Wilkins* and *Minor v. Happersett*

Voting rights was not a matter for judicial concern for the first seventy years under the constitution. As originally written, voting was a local matter under state law. This excluded the federal courts—not to mention the protections of the Bill of Rights—from affecting the issue of voting rights. Only with passage of the Civil Rights Amendments, in particular Amendments XIV and XV, did voting become a legitimate concern of the national courts. The federal courts, however, were not interested in the job of expanding the voting rights of those excluded from the franchise by reason of their race, class, gender, or ethnicity. Federal judges did not see this task as properly their func-

tion, and further, were troubled by the potentially negative effects of an expanded franchise. Consequently, for the next sixty some years, in case after case involving a wide range of excluded groups, federal judges refused to extend the protections of the civil rights amendments to minorities seeking the vote.

The two cases excerpted here exemplify the negative attitudes of the federal bench during this period. Elk v. Wilkins *concerns the efforts of a Native American, born in the United States and living within white society, to gain citizenship and with it the right to vote.* Minor v. Happersett *concerns the same questions as regards a woman's right to vote. In reading these cases, note the similarity of argument and logic between these two cases. Why do you think this might be the case? Do you see any differences in how the justices dealt with each group's claims?*

Elk v. Wilkins

Supreme Court of the United States
112 U.S. 94
November, 1884
Opinion by JUSTICE GRAY:
The plaintiff, in support of his action, relies on the first clause of the first section of the Fourteenth Article of Amendment of the Constitution of the United States, by which "all persons born or naturalized in the United States, and subject to the jurisdiction thereof, are citizens of the United States and of the State wherein they reside;" and on the Fifteenth Article of Amendment, which provides that "the right of citizens of the United States to vote shall not be denied or abridged by the United States or by any State on account of race, color, or previous condition of servitude." . . . .

The question then is, whether an Indian, born a member of one of the Indian tribes within the United States, is, merely by reason of his birth within the United States, and of his afterwards voluntarily separating himself from his tribe and taking up his residency among white citizens, a citizen of the United States, within the meaning of the first section of the Fourteenth Amendment of the Constitution.

Under the Constitution of the United States, as originally established, "Indians not taxed" were excluded from the persons according to whose numbers representatives and direct taxes were apportioned among the several States; . . . . The Indian tribes, being within the territorial limits of the United States, were not, strictly speaking, foreign States; but they were alien nations, distinct political communities, with whom the United States might and habitually did deal, as they thought fit, either through treaties made by the President and Senate, or through acts of Congress in the ordinary forms of legislation. The members of those tribes owed immediate allegiance to their several tribes, and were not part of the people of the United States. They were in a dependent condition, a state of pupilage, resembling that of a ward to his guardian.... General acts of Congress did not apply to Indians, unless so expressed as to clearly manifest an intention to include them....

The alien and dependent condition of the members of the Indian tribes could not be put off at their own will, without the action or assent of the United States. They were never deemed citizens of the United States, except under explicit provisions of treaty of statute to that effect, either declaring a certain tribe, or such members of it as chose to remain behind on the removal of the tribe westward, to be citizens, or authorizing individuals of particular tribes to become citizens on application to a court of the United States for naturalization, and satisfactory proof of fitness for civilized life....

Indians born within the territorial limits of the United States, members of, and owing immediate allegiance to, one of the Indian tribes (an alien, though dependent, power), although in a geographical sense born in the United States, are no more "born in the United States and subject to the jurisdiction thereof," within the meaning of the first section of the Fourteenth Amendment, than the children of subjects of any foreign government born within the domain of that government, or the children born within the United States, of ambassadors or other public ministers of foreign nations....

National legislation has tended more and more towards the education and civilization of the Indians, and fitting them to be citizens. But the question whether any Indian tribes, or any members thereof, have become so far advanced in civilization, that they should be let out of the state of pupilage, and admitted to the privileges and responsibilities of citizenship, is a question to be decided by the nation whose wards they are and whose citizens they seek to become, and not by each Indian for himself.

There is nothing in the statutes or decisions, referred to by counsel, to control the conclusion to which we have been brought by a consideration of the language of the Fourteenth Amendment, and of the condition of the Indians at the time of its proposal and ratification....

The law upon the question before us has been well stated by Judge Deady in the District Court of the United States for the District of Oregon. In giving judgment against the plaintiff in a case resembling the case at bar, . . . he said: "But an Indian cannot make himself a citizen of the United States without the consent and cooperation of the government. The fact that he has abandoned his nomadic life or tribal relations, and adopted the habits and manners of civilized people, may be a good reason why he should be made a citizen of the United States, but does not of itself make him one. To be a citizen of the United States is a political privilege which no one, not born to, can assume without its consent in some form. The Indians in Oregon, not being born subject to the jurisdiction of the United States, were not born citizens thereof, and I am not aware of any law or treaty by which any of them have been made so since." . . .

The plaintiff, not being a citizen of the United States under the Fourteenth Amendment of the Constitution, has been deprived of no right secured by the Fifteenth Amendment, and cannot maintain this action.

JUDGMENT AFFIRMED.

Minor v. Happersett

Supreme Court of the United States
  88 U.S. 162
  October, 1874
  Opinion by CHIEF JUSTICE WAITE:
  The question is presented in this case, whether, since the adoption of the fourteenth amendment, a woman, who is a citizen of the United States and of the State of Missouri, is a voter in that State, notwithstanding the provision of the constitution and laws of the State, which confine the right of suffrage to men alone. . . .

It is contended that the provisions of the constitution and laws of the State of Missouri which confine the right of suffrage and registration therefore to men, are in violation of the Constitution of the United States, and therefore void. The argument is, that as a woman, born or naturalized in the United States and subject to the jurisdiction thereof, is a citizen of the United States and of the State in which she resides, she has the right of suffrage as one of the privileges and immunities of her citizenship, which the State cannot by its laws or constitution abridge.

There is no doubt that women may be citizens. They are persons, and by the fourteenth amendment "all persons born or naturalized in the United States and subject to the jurisdiction thereof" are expressly declared to be "citizens of the United States and of the State wherein they reside." But, in our opinion, it did not need this amendment to give them that position. . . . There cannot be a nation without a people. The very idea of a political community, such as a nation is, implies an association of persons for the promotion of their general welfare. Each one of the persons associated becomes a member of the nation formed by the association. He owes it allegiance and is entitled to its protection. Allegiance and protection are, in this connection, reciprocal obligations. The one is a compensation for the other; allegiance for protection and protection for allegiance.

For convenience it has been found necessary to give a name to this membership. The object is to designate by a title the person and the relation he bears to the nation. . . . Citizen is now more commonly employed, . . . as it has been considered better suited to the description of one living under a republican government, ... When used in this sense it is understood as conveying the idea of membership of a nation, and nothing more. . . .

Looking at the Constitution itself we find that it was ordained and established by "the people of the United States," and then going further back, we find that these were the people of the several States that had before dissolved the political bands which connected them with Great Britain, and assumed a separate and equal station among the powers of the earth, and that had by Articles of Confederation and Perpetual Union. . . .

Whoever, then, was one of the people of either of these States when the Constitution of the United States was adopted, became ipso facto a citizen—a member of the nation created by its adoption. He was one of the persons associating together to form the nation, and was, consequently, one of its original citizens. As to this there has never been a doubt. Disputes have arisen as to whether or not certain persons or certain classes of persons were part of the people at the time, but never as to their citizenship if they were . . . .

[I]f more is necessary to show that women have always been considered as citizens the same as men, abundant proof is to be found in the legislative and judicial history of the country. . . . Under [the Constitution] it has been uniformly held that . . . citizenship [is] necessary to give the courts of the United States jurisdiction . . . . If found not to exist the case must be dismissed. Notwithstanding this the records of the courts are full of cases in which the jurisdiction depends upon the citizenship of women, and not one can be found, we think, in which objection was made on that account.... On the contrary, her right to citizenship has been in all cases assumed. The only question has been whether, in the particular case under consideration, she had availed herself of the right....

Other proof of like character might be found, but certainly more cannot be necessary to establish the fact that sex has never been made one of the elements of citizenship in the United States. In this respect men have never had an advantage over women. The same laws precisely apply to both. The fourteenth amendment did not affect the citizenship of women any more than it did of men. In this particular, therefore, the rights of Mrs. Minor do not depend upon the amendment. She has always been a citizen from her birth, and entitled to all the privileges and immunities of citizenship. The amendment prohibited the State, of which she is a citizen, from abridging any of her privileges and immunities as a citizen of the United States; but it did not confer citizenship on her. That she had before its adoption.

If the right of suffrage is one of the necessary privileges of a citizen of the United States, then the constitution and laws of Missouri confining it to men are in violation of the Constitution of the United States, as amended, and consequently void. The direct question is, therefore, presented whether all citizens are necessarily voters.

The Constitution does not define the privileges and immunities of citizens. For that definition we must look elsewhere. In this case we need not determine what they are, but only whether suffrage is necessarily one of them.

It certainly is nowhere made so in express terms. The United States has no voters in the States of its own creation. The elective officers of the United States are all elected directly or indirectly by State voters.... The power of the State in this particular is certainly supreme until Congress acts.

The [Fourteenth] amendment did not add to the privileges and immunities of a citizen. It simply furnished an additional guaranty for the protection of such as he already had. No new voters were necessarily made by it. Indirectly it may have had that effect, because it may have increased the number of citizens entitled to suffrage under the constitution and laws of the States, but it operates for this purpose, if at all, through the States and the State laws, and not directly upon the citizen.

It is clear, therefore, we think, that the Constitution has not added the right of suffrage to the privileges and immunities of citizenship as they existed at the time it was adopted. This makes it proper to inquire whether suffrage was coextensive with the citizenship of the States at the time of its adoption. If it was, then it may with force be argued that suffrage was one of the rights which belonged to citizenship, and in the enjoyment of which every citizen must be protected. But if it was not, the contrary may with propriety be assumed.

When the Federal Constitution was adopted, all the States, with the exception of Rhode Island and Connecticut, had constitutions of their own. . . . Upon an examination of those constitutions we find that in no State were all citizens permitted to vote. Each State determined for itself who should have that power. . . .

In this condition of the law in respect to suffrage in the several States it cannot for a moment be doubted that if it had been intended to make all citizens of the United States voters, the framers of the Constitution would not have left it to implication. So important a change in the condition of citizenship as it actually existed, if intended, would have been expressly declared.

. . .

Certainly, if the courts can consider any question settled, this is one. For nearly ninety years the people have acted upon the idea that the Constitution, when it conferred citizenship, did not necessarily confer the right of suffrage. If uniform practice long continued can settle the construction of so important an instrument as the Constitution of the United States confessedly is, most certainly it has been done here. Our province is to decide what the law is, not to declare what it should be.

We have given this case the careful consideration its importance demands. If the law is wrong, it ought to be changed; but the power for that is not with us. The arguments addressed to us bearing upon such a view of the subject may perhaps be sufficient to induce those having the power, to make the alteration, but they ought not to be permitted to influence our judgment in determining the present rights of the parties now litigating before us. No argument as to woman's need of suffrage can be considered. We can only act upon her rights as they exist. It is not for us to look at the hardship of withholding. Our duty is at an end if we find it is within the power of a State to withhold.

Being unanimously of the opinion that the Constitution of the United States does not confer the right of suffrage upon any one, and that the constitutions and laws of the several States which commit that important trust to men alone are not necessarily void, we AFFIRM THE JUDGMENT.

The Fall of the All–White Primary: *Smith v. Allwright*

By the middle decades of the twentieth century, the status of minority voting rights was bleak. While women had gained the vote through constitutional amendment, other minorities were still excluded from the vote. This was about to change. A two generation fight for enhanced voting rights was starting, and the first step was to end the all-white primaries that prohibited blacks from voting in the only elections of any significance in the South, the Democratic primary.

The centerpiece of the all-white primary's demise was Smith v. Allwright. *The culmination of twenty-five years of political and legal effort,* Smith *effectively ended the all-white primary not only in Texas, but across the South as a whole. In reading, note the effort by the majority to explain why, after sixty years of saying no, the courts were suddenly willing to enhance minority voting rights. Note also, however, the concurrent effort to narrow the meaning, and hence reach, of this decision. In particular, note the interplay between Justice Reed for the majority and Justice Roberts in dissent on the law's proper reach in such matters.*

Smith v. Allwright

Supreme Court of the United States
321 U.S. 649
April 3, 1944
MR. JUSTICE REED delivered the opinion of the Court.

This writ of certiorari brings here for review . . . the refusal of respondents, election and associate election judges . . . , to give petitioner a ballot or to permit him to cast a ballot in the primary election of July 27, 1940, for the nomination of Democratic candidates for the United States Senate and House of Representatives, and Governor and other state officers. The refusal is alleged to have been solely because of the race and color of the proposed voter. . . .

Texas is free to conduct her elections and limit her electorate as she may deem wise, save only as her action may be affected by the prohibitions of the United States Constitution or in conflict with powers delegated to and exercised by the National Government. The Fourteenth Amendment forbids a State from making or enforcing any law which abridges the privileges or immunities of citizens of the United States and the Fifteenth Amendment specifically interdicts any denial or abridgement by a State of the right of citizens to vote on account of color. Respondents . . . defended on the ground that the Democratic party of Texas is a voluntary organization with members banded together for the purpose of selecting individuals of the group representing the common political beliefs as candidates in the general election. As such a voluntary organization, it was claimed, the Democratic party is free to select its own membership and limit to whites participation in the party primary. Such action, the [Respondent's] answer asserted, does not violate the Fourteenth, Fifteenth or Seventeenth Amendment as officers of government cannot be chosen at primaries and the Amendments are applicable only to general elections where governmental officers are actually elected. Primaries, it is said, are political party affairs, handled by party, not governmental, officers. . . .

The right of a Negro to vote in the Texas primary has been considered heretofore by this Court. The first case was *Nixon v. Herndon* . . . . At that time, 1924, the Texas statute, . . . declared "in no event shall a Negro be eligible to participate in a Democratic Party primary election in the State of Texas." Nixon was refused the right to vote in a Democratic primary and brought a suit for damages against the election officers . . . . It was urged to this Court that the denial of the franchise to Nixon violated his Constitutional rights under the Fourteenth and Fifteenth Amendments. Without consideration of the Fifteenth, this Court held that the action of Texas in denying the ballot to Negroes by statute was in violation of the equal protection clause of the Fourteenth Amendment and reversed the dismissal of the suit.

The legislature of Texas reenacted the article but gave the State Executive Committee of a party the power to prescribe the qualifications of its members for voting or other participation. . . . The State Executive Committee of the Democratic party adopted a resolution that white Democrats and none other might participate in the primaries of that party. Nixon was refused again the privilege of voting in a primary and again brought suit for damages . . . . This Court again reversed the dismissal of the suit for the reason that the Committee action was deemed to be state action and invalid as discriminatory under the Fourteenth Amendment. The test was said to be whether the Committee operated as representative of the State in the discharge of the State's authority. . . . The question of the inherent power of a political party in Texas "without restraint by any law to determine its own membership" was left open. . . .

In *Grovey v. Townsend*, . . . this Court had before it another suit for damages for the refusal in a primary of a county clerk, a Texas officer with only public functions to perform, to furnish petitioner, a Negro, an absentee ballot. The refusal was solely on the ground of race. This case differed from *Nixon v. Condon*, . . . in that a state convention of the Democratic party had passed the resolution of May 24, 1932, [excluding blacks]. It was decided that the determination by the state convention of the membership of the Democratic party made a significant change from a determination by the Executive Committee. The former was party action, voluntary in character. The latter, . . . was action by authority of the State. The managers of the primary election were therefore declared not to be state officials in such sense that their action was state action. . . . This Court went on to announce that to deny a vote in a primary was a mere refusal of party membership with which "the State need have no concern," . . . while for a State to deny a vote in a general election on the ground of race or color violated the Constitution. . . .

Since *Grovey v. Townsend* and prior to the present suit, no case from Texas involving primary elections has been before this Court. We did decide, however, *United States v. Classic* . . . . We there held that § 4 of Article I of the Constitution authorized Congress to regulate primary as well as general elections, . . ."where the primary is by law made an integral part of the election machinery." . . . The *Nixon* Cases were decided under the equal protection clause of the Fourteenth Amendment without a determination of the status of the primary as a part of the electoral process. The exclusion of Negroes from the primaries by action of the State was held invalid under that Amendment. The fusing by the *Classic* case of the primary and general elections into a single instrumentality for choice of officers has a definite bearing on the permissibility under the Constitution of excluding Negroes from primaries. . . . When *Grovey v. Townsend* was written, the Court looked upon the denial of a vote in a primary as a mere refusal by a party of party membership. . . . As the Louisiana statutes for holding primaries are similar to those of Texas, our ruling in *Classic* as to the unitary character of the electoral process calls for a reexamination as to whether or not the exclusion of Negroes from a Texas party primary was state action.

. . .

We think that this statutory system for the selection of party nominees for inclusion on the general election ballot makes the party which is required to follow these legislative directions an agency of the State in so far as it determines the participants in a primary election. The party takes its character as a state agency from the duties imposed upon it by state statutes; the duties do not become matters of private law because they are performed by a political party. . . . When primaries become a part of the machinery for choosing officials, state and national, as they have here, the same tests to determine the character of discrimination or abridgement should be applied to the primary as are applied to the general election. If the State requires a certain electoral procedure, prescribes a general election ballot made up of party nominees so chosen and limits the choice of the electorate in general elections for state offices, practically speaking, to those whose names appear on such a ballot, it endorses, adopts and enforces the discrimination against Negroes, practiced by a party entrusted by Texas law with the determination of the qualifications of participants in the primary. This is state action within the meaning of the Fifteenth Amendment. . . .

The United States is a constitutional democracy. Its organic law grants to all citizens a right to participate in the choice of elected officials without restriction by any State because of race. This grant to the people of the opportunity for choice is not to be nullified by a State through casting its electoral process in a form which permits a private organization to practice racial discrimination in the election. Constitutional rights would be of little value if they could be thus indirectly denied. . . .

The privilege of membership in a party may be, as this Court said in *Grovey v. Townsend,* . . . no concern of a State. But when, as here, that privilege is also the essential qualification for voting in a primary to select nominees for a general election, the State makes the action of the party the action of the State. In reaching this conclusion we are not unmindful of the desirability of continuity of decision in constitutional questions. However, when convinced of former error, this Court has never felt constrained to follow precedent. In constitutional questions, where correction depends upon amendment and not upon legislative action this Court throughout its history has freely exercised its power to reexamine the basis of its constitutional decisions. This has long been accepted practice, and this practice has continued to this day. This is particularly true when the decision believed erroneous is the application of a constitutional principle rather than an interpretation of the Constitution to extract the principle itself. Here we are applying, contrary to the recent decision in *Grovey v. Townsend,* the well-established principle of the Fifteenth Amendment, forbidding the abridgement by a State of a citizen's right to vote. *Grovey v. Townsend* is overruled.

JUDGMENT REVERSED.

MR. JUSTICE ROBERTS, Dissenting.

. . . I have expressed my views [elsewhere] with respect to the present policy of the court freely to disregard and to overrule considered decisions and the rules of law announced in them. This tendency, it seems to me, indicates an intolerance for what those who have composed this court in the past have conscientiously and deliberately concluded, and involves an assumption that knowledge and wisdom reside in us which was denied to our predecessors. I shall not repeat what I there said for I consider it fully applicable to the instant decision, which but points the moral anew.

. . .

The reason for my concern is that the instant decision, overruling that announced about nine years ago, tends to bring adjudications of this tribunal into the same class as a restricted railroad ticket, good for this day and train only. I have no assurance, in view of current decisions, that the opinion announced today may not shortly be repudiated and overruled by justices who deem they have new light on the subject. . . .

It is suggested that *Grovey v. Townsend* was overruled *sub silentio* in *United States v. Classic.* . . . If so, the situation is even worse than that exhibited by the outright repudiation of an earlier decision, for it is the fact that, in the *Classic* case, *Grovey v. Townsend* was distinguished in brief and argument by the Government without suggestion that it was wrongly decided, and was relied on by the appellees, not as a controlling decision, but by way of analogy. . . .

I do not stop to call attention to the material differences between the primary election laws of Louisiana under consideration in the

Classic case and those of Texas which are here drawn in question. These differences were spelled out in detail in the Government's brief in the *Classic* case . . . . It is enough to say that the Louisiana statutes required the primary to be conducted by state officials and made it a state election, whereas, under the Texas statute, the primary is a party election conducted at the expense of members of the party and by officials chosen by the party. If this court's opinion in the *Classic* case discloses its method of overruling earlier decisions, I can only protest that, in fairness, it should rather have adopted the open and frank way of saying what it was doing than, after the event, characterize its past action as overruling *Grovey v. Townsend* though those less sapient never realized the fact.

It is regrettable that in an era marked by doubt and confusion, an era whose greatest need is steadfastness of thought and purpose, this court, which has been looked to as exhibiting consistency in adjudication, and a steadiness which would hold the balance even in the face of temporary ebbs and flows of opinion, should now itself become the breeder of fresh doubt and confusion in the public mind as to the stability of our institutions.

Victory and Defeat in the Lower Federal Courts: *Terry v. Adams*

Despite the demise of the all-white primary in 1944, the transition toward universal suffrage was a slow one. Confusion as to the Smith *decision's meaning—both legally and practically—abounded. The federal courts, in consequence, struggled with the problem of enforcing minority voting rights in a political and social system still strongly opposed to any expansion of the franchise to the African American community. Hence, while blacks won some important victories in district courts across the South, they also suffered many significant defeats.*

The three decisions excerpted here, each regarding the same case out of Texas, show the federal courts' struggles with the question of how far to take the Smith *doctrine. Despite arising from the same state as* Smith *—in fact, despite its raising essentially the same issues as* Smith *—the judges ruling in* Terry v. Adams *came to wildly different conclusions, and pushed for different results, based on very different understandings of the law. In reading these decisions note the differing reasoning adopted by the judges. Where some saw state action,*

*others did not. So too for the range of permissible remedies available
to the courts. What factors might explain these differences? What
issues are raised in the opinions that hint at each judge's perspectives
in these matters? The judges ruling in favor of the Jaybird primary
were not extreme segregationists opposed to any equal rights for
blacks, and yet they still ruled in favor of a system they acknowledged
was purposefully exclusionary. Why? What factors were controlling
the pace and direction of change in these matters?*

Terry v. Adams

U.S. District Court for the Southern District of Texas 90 F. Supp. 595
    May 1, 1950
    Opinion by JUDGE THOMAS M. KENNERLY:
    This is a suit by John Terry, et al., citizens and residents of Fort
Bend County, . . . against A. J. Adams, et al., also residents and citizens
of Fort Bend County . . . . Defendants are sued individually and as
representatives of the governing body of the Jaybird Democratic
Association of Fort Bend County commonly known, and described
by Plaintiffs, as the Jaybird Party.

Such Association is a political organization or party. About April,
May, or June of each election year, it holds a primary election or elections . . . determine to what persons such Association will give its
endorsement for County and Precinct Officers in Fort Bend County to
be voted on in the Democratic Primaries to be held the following July
and August. No Negro is allowed to vote in such Jaybird Primary.
Plaintiffs, "who are Negroes and qualified voters in such County, bring
this suit for themselves and others similarly situated seeking a Decree
declaring that they are legally entitled to vote in such Jaybird Primary," . . . and enjoining Defendants from refusing to allow them to
vote. . . . Defendants have filed a Motion to Dismiss and have Answered,
and this is a hearing on such Motion and a trial on the merits.

. . .

The Jaybird . . . Primaries are held . . . each election year to elect or
select the persons who are to and will receive the endorsement of the
Association for County and Precinct Officers in Fort Bend County, to
be voted on at the Democratic Primary . . . in July and August following. Such Jaybird . . . Primaries are held and conducted . . . [in] substantially the same way as such Democratic Primaries are held and

conducted under the Laws of Texas. Except that . . . the Executive Committee of such Association does not certify the successful candidates. Such successful candidates must file their own applications for a place on the ballot used in such Democratic Primaries. . . .

There is no other organization in Fort Bend County similar to such Association, and generally the persons endorsed in the Jaybird Primary are the only persons whose names appear on the ballot at the Democratic Primaries. And such persons are almost invariably . . . nominated at such Democratic Primaries and their names appear as Democratic Nominees on the official ballot at the General Election in November. The Democratic Nominees are almost invariably elected at such General Election. In other words, an endorsement at the Jaybird Primary generally means an election at the General Election in November. A majority of the white voters in Fort Bend County vote in the Jaybird Primaries, and generally abide by and support in the Democratic Primaries the persons endorsed by the Jaybird Primaries, although such Association has no way of requiring them to do so.

It is perfectly plain that the main and primary object of such Association has been from the beginning of its organization and still is to aid and enable the white voters of Fort Bend County to select and elect the County and Precinct officers of Fort Bend County and to deny the Negro voters any voice or part therein.

. . .

Defendants contend that such Association is a self-governing voluntary association or club, and not a political party nor a creature or agency of the State of Texas. They also contend that there is no law of Texas regulating it, and that it has the legal and inherent right to prescribe who shall be its members and who shall vote in its primaries, and to exclude negroes from its membership and from voting in its primaries. Defendants cite and stand upon *Drake v. Executive Committee,* . . . decided by this Court in 1933. In that case, it was held that there was no law of Texas which regulated or controlled the Democratic Party of the City of Houston nor its Executive Committee in the matter of holding Primary Elections in Houston for nominating City Officers. And that such party in Houston and its Committee had the inherent right to say who should vote in such City Primaries.

But Counsel overlooked some recent cases in which the Law is held to be to the contrary. In the State of South Carolina, after the decision of the Supreme Court in *Smith v. Allwright,* . . . the Legislature of that State repealed all primary election laws regulating political parties, yet in *Rice v. Elmore,* . . . it was held that Negroes were legally entitled to vote in the Democratic primaries of South Carolina held and controlled by the Democratic Party. . . .

But I do not agree with Defendants' contention that such Association is not a political party, nor that it is not regulated by the Laws of Texas, nor that it is not an agency of the State. Such Association is a political party and comes clearly within the terms of Article 3163, Vernon's Texas Civil Statutes which regulates it and makes it an agency of the State. All that is said by this Court in *White v. Executive Committee,* . . . which Defendants also cite, is applicable here. Such Association cannot avoid the effect of Article 3163 by holding its primaries on a date different from the date fixed by such Article, nor by different methods.

. . .

My conclusion is:

That Plaintiffs are entitled to Judgment, declaring that Plaintiffs and those similarly situated and for whom Plaintiffs sue, are legally entitled to vote in the Jaybird Primary and/or Primaries held by such Association and specifically those to be held May 6, 1950, and June 3, 1950.

Adams v. Terry

U.S. Court of Appeals Fifth Circuit
    193 F.2d 600
    January 11, 1952
    Opinion by JUDGE JOSEPH C. HUTCHESON:
    Brought March 16, 1950, as a class action against defendants, sued individually and as members of the Jaybird Party, the suit was for a declaratory judgment as to the rights of plaintiffs and their class to vote in primaries of the Jaybird Party, scheduled for May 6, and June 3, 1950, and for an injunction protecting those rights.

. . .

The district judge found: that the main and primary purpose of the organization is to enable the white voters of Fort Bend County to select and elect the county and precinct officers of Fort Bend County and to deny the negro voters any voice or part therein; and that, though the association does not conform to a single requirement of Art. 3163 [the Texas law regulating political parties], it is a political party coming clearly within the terms of that article. . . .

Defendants are here insisting that in so ruling and adjudging, the district court erred, in that he mistakenly applied to the undisputed facts of this case, principles applied in decisions dealing with entirely different facts and situations. They point out that the election dealt with here is not one of the steps in "a two step election machinery for that state," as was the case in the cases the district judge relied on. . . . So pointing, appellants insist that the decision in this case is a complete departure from, indeed is in direct contravention of . . . the settled course of decision culminating in *Collins v. Hardyman,* . . . that it was not against individual, but against state, action that the Fourteenth and Fifteenth Amendments . . . were, and are, directed.

We agree with defendants, and shall briefly set forth our reasons for doing so.

. . .

Because the principle controlling this case has already been clearly stated and correctly applied in the cases cited by the district judge . . . it will not be necessary for us to extend this opinion by an elaborate discussion of that principle. It will be sufficient, . . . to show that in the decision below a clear and good principle has been misapplied and thereby run into the ground.

This principle is that no forms of device, through the use of which negroes are, because they are negroes, prevented from voting at an election, which is in effect a part and parcel of state election machinery, may be effectively employed. All such forms will be penetrated and the illegal devices will be exposed and stricken down. In *Rice v. Elmore,* . . . the controlling facts are precisely stated thus: "The use of the Democratic primary in connection with the general election in South Carolina provides, . . . a two step election machinery for that state; and the denial to the Negro of the right to participate in the primary denies him all effective voice in the government of his country."

[Conversely], the Jaybird Democratic Association does not in any way or manner operate as a part or parcel of, or in liaison with, state political or elective machinery. In short, it is not a part of the two step arrangement, the Democratic primary and the general election, so as to make its action state action.

It is true that in the main, though there have been, and are, exceptions, the indorsement of the Jaybird primary does usually mean that the winner of that indorsement will have no opposition in the Democratic primary. This is not, however, because of any provision of state law or any agreement or arrangement with the Democratic party having the effect of state action. It is because, and only because there is a consensus of opinion in the country that the indorsement should be regarded as decisive.

No claim is made, or could be made, that anybody, including any of the plaintiffs, is misled, by collusion of state authorities, or of managers, or officers of the State Democratic Party, with these defendants, into believing that the advisory vote taken by the white voters of Fort Bend County has any legal or binding effect whatever. Indeed, while the form and pattern of an election has been followed, nothing more in substance has occurred here than if, in precinct by precinct, neighborhood by neighborhood, or by straw ballot in a newspaper, the white voters of Fort Bend County had indicated their choice for the offices to be filled and had made that choice publicly known.

If, upon the overall facts, the question for our decision were whether, from the standpoint of good neighborliness and good government in the changed and changing climate of opinion in this state, there is any point in clinging, under the greatly different conditions now prevailing, to this outworn and outmoded shadow boxing, these mock elections, we should be constrained to declare that it seems to us that the white voters of Fort Bend County are vainly holding to the husks of a respected tradition long after the ripe grain has fallen.

But this is not our question. What and all that is for decision here is whether the complained of action is action under color of state law, depriving plaintiffs of rights accorded them by the invoked constitutional and statutory provisions. To answer that question in the affirmative and to hold that it is, would be, we think, to go directly contrary to the long line of cases beginning with the *In re Civil Rights Cases,* . . . and ending with *Collins v. Hardyman.* . . .

The judgment is reversed and the cause is remanded for further and not inconsistent proceedings.

Terry v. Adams

Supreme Court of the United States
   345 U.S. 461
   May 4, 1953
   Opinion By JUSTICE BLACK:
   In *Smith v. Allwright,* . . . we held that rules of the Democratic Party of Texas excluding Negroes from voting in the party's primaries

violated the Fifteenth Amendment. While no state law directed such exclusion, our decision pointed out that many party activities were subject to considerable statutory control. This case raises questions concerning the constitutional power of a Texas county political organization ... to exclude Negroes from its primaries on racial grounds. ...

It is apparent that Jaybird activities follow a plan purposefully designed to exclude Negroes from voting and at the same time to escape the Fifteenth Amendment's command that the right of citizens to vote shall neither be denied nor abridged on account of race. ...

It is significant that precisely the same qualifications as those prescribed by Texas entitling electors to vote at county-operated primaries are adopted as the sole qualifications entitling electors to vote at the county-wide Jaybird primaries with a single proviso—Negroes are excluded. Everyone concedes that such a proviso in the county-operated primaries would be unconstitutional. The Jaybird Party thus brings into being and holds precisely the kind of election that the Fifteenth Amendment seeks to prevent. When it produces the equivalent of the prohibited election, the damage has been done.

For a state to permit such a duplication of its election processes is to permit a flagrant abuse of those processes to defeat the purposes of the Fifteenth Amendment. The use of the county-operated primary to ratify the result of the prohibited election merely compounds the offense. It violates the Fifteenth Amendment for a state, by such circumvention, to permit within its borders the use of any device that produces an equivalent of the prohibited election.

The only election that has counted in this Texas county for more than fifty years has been that held by the Jaybirds from which Negroes were excluded. The Democratic primary and the general election have become no more than the perfunctory ratifiers of the choice that has already been made in Jaybird elections from which Negroes have been excluded. It is immaterial that the state does not control that part of this elective process which it leaves for the Jaybirds to manage. The Jaybird primary has become an integral part, indeed the only effective part, of the elective process that determines who shall rule and govern in the county. The effect of the whole procedure, Jaybird primary plus Democratic primary plus general election, is to do precisely that which the Fifteenth Amendment forbids—strip Negroes of every vestige of influence in selecting the officials who control the local county matters that intimately touch the daily lives of citizens.

We reverse the Court of Appeals' judgment reversing that of the District Court. We affirm the District Court's holding that the combined Jaybird-Democratic-general election machinery has deprived these petitioners of their right to vote on account of their race and color. The case is remanded to the District Court to enter such orders and decrees as are necessary and .... In exercising this jurisdiction, the Court is left free to hold hearings to consider and determine what provisions are essential to afford Negro citizens of Fort Bend County full protection from future discriminatory Jaybird-Democratic-general election practices which deprive citizens of voting rights because of their color.

Reversed and remanded.

MR. JUSTICE FRANKFURTER, In Concurrence.

This case is for me by no means free of difficulty. Whenever the law draws a line between permissive and forbidden conduct cases are bound to arise which are not obviously on one side or the other. These dubious situations disclose the limited utility of the figure of speech, "a line," in the law. Drawing a "line" is necessarily exercising a judgment, however confined the conscientious judgment may be within the bounds of constitutional and statutory provisions, the course of decisions, and the presuppositions of the judicial process. If "line" is in the main a fruitful tool for dividing the sheep from the goats, it must not be forgotten that since the "line" is figurative the place of this or that case in relation to it cannot be ascertained externally but is a matter of the mind.

Close analysis of what it is that the Fifteenth Amendment prohibits must be made before it can be determined what the relevant line is in the situation presented by this case. The Fifteenth Amendment, not the Fourteenth, outlawed discrimination on the basis of race or color with respect to the right to vote..... The command against such denial or abridgment is directed to the United States and to the individual States. Therefore, violation of this Amendment and the enactments passed in enforcement of it must involve the United States or a State. In this case the conduct that is assailed pertains to the election of local Texas officials. To find a denial or abridgment of the guaranteed voting right to colored citizens of Texas solely because they are colored, one must find that the State has had a hand in it.

The State, in these situations, must mean not private citizens but those clothed with the authority and the influence which official position affords. The application of the prohibition of the Fifteenth Amendment to "any State" is translated by legal jargon to read "State action." This phrase gives rise to a false direction in that it implies some impressive machinery or deliberative conduct normally associated with what orators call a sovereign state. The vital requirement is State responsibility—that somewhere, somehow, to some extent, there be an infusion of conduct by officials, panoplied with State power, into any scheme by which colored citizens are denied voting rights merely because they are colored.

. . .

Whether the Association is a political party regulated by Texas and thus subject to a duty of nondiscrimination, or is, as it claims, clearly not a party within the meaning of that legislation, failing as it does to attempt to comply with a number of the State requirements, . . . is a question of State law not to be answered in the first instance by a federal court. We do not know what the Texas Supreme Court would say. . . . But even if the Jaybird Association is a political party, it is one that must be devised by the Texas courts. For the same reason, we cannot say that the Jaybird primary is a "primary" within the meaning of Texas law and so regulated by Texas law that *Smith v. Allwright* would apply.

But assuming, as I think we must, that the Jaybird Association is not a political party holding a State-regulated primary, we should nonetheless decide this case against respondents on the ground that in the precise situation before us the State authority has come into play.

The State of Texas has entered into a comprehensive scheme of regulation of political primaries, including procedures by which election officials shall be chosen. The county election officials are thus clothed with the authority of the State to secure observance of the State's interest in "fair methods and a fair expression" of preferences in the selection of nominees. . . . If the Jaybird Association, although not a political party, is a device to defeat the law of Texas regulating primaries, and if the electoral officials, clothed with State power in the county, share in that subversion, they cannot divest themselves of the State authority and help as participants in the scheme. Unlawful administration of a State statute fair on its face may be shown "by extrinsic evidence showing a discriminatory design to favor one individual or class over another not to be inferred from the action itself"; here, the county election officials aid in this subversion of the State's official scheme of which they are trustees, by helping as participants in the scheme.

. . .

The exclusion of the Negroes from meaningful participation in the only primary scheme set up by the State was not an accidental, unsought consequence of the exercise of civic rights by voters to make their common viewpoint count. It was the design, the very purpose of this arrangement that the Jaybird primary in May exclude Negro participation in July. That it was the action in part of the election officials charged by Texas law with the fair administration of the primaries, brings it within the reach of the law. The officials made themselves party to means whereby the machinery with which they are entrusted does not discharge the functions for which it was designed.

It does not follow, however, that the relief granted below was proper. Since the vice of this situation is not that the Jaybird primary itself is the primary discriminatorily conducted under State law but is that the determination there made becomes, in fact, the determination in the Democratic primary by virtue of the participation and acquiescence of State authorities, a federal court cannot require that petitioners be allowed to vote in the Jaybird primary. The evil here is that the State, through the action and abdication of those whom it has clothed with authority, has permitted white voters to go through a procedure which predetermines the legally devised primary. To say that should be allowed to vote in the Jaybird primary would be to say that the State is under a duty to see to it that Negroes may vote in that primary. We cannot tell the State that it must participate in and regulate this primary; we cannot tell the State what machinery it will use. But a court of equity can free the lawful political agency from the combination that subverts its capacity to function. What must be done is that this county be rid of the means by which the unlawful "usage," . . . in this case asserts itself.

MR. JUSTICE MINTON, Dissenting.

I am not concerned in the least as to what happens to the Jaybirds or their unworthy scheme. I am concerned about what this Court says is state action within the meaning of the Fifteenth Amendment to the Constitution. For, after all, this Court has power to redress a wrong under that Amendment only if the wrong is done by the State. That has been the holding of this Court since the earliest cases. . . .

As I understand MR. JUSTICE BLACK'S opinion, he would have this Court redress the wrong even if it was individual action alone. I can understand that praiseworthy position, but it seems to me it is not in accord with the Constitution. State action must be shown.

MR. JUSTICE FRANKFURTER recognizes that it must be state action but he seems to think it is enough to constitute state action if a state official participates in the Jaybird primary. That I cannot follow. For it seems clear to me that everything done by a person who is an official is not done officially and as a representative of the State. However, I find nothing in this record that shows the state or county officials participating in the Jaybird primary.

. . . Surely white or colored members of any political faith or economic belief may hold caucuses. It is only when the State by action of its legislative bodies or action of some of its officials in their official capacity cooperates with such political party or gives it direction in its activities that the Federal Constitution may come into play. A political organization not using state machinery or depending upon state law to authorize what it does could not be within the ban of the Fifteenth Amendment. . . . The Jaybird Association did not attempt to conform or in any way to comply with the statutes of Texas covering primaries. No action of any legislative or quasi-legislative body or of any state official or agency ever in any manner denied the vote to Negroes, even in the Jaybird primaries.

So it seems to me clear there is no state action, and the Jaybird Democratic Association is in no sense a part of the Democratic Party. If it is a political organization, it has made no attempt to use the State, or the State to use it, to carry on its poll.

Smith v. Allwright, . . . is in no manner controlling. In that case, the State had set up the machinery for the Democratic Party to conduct its primary. The State of Texas made the Democratic Party its agent for the conducting of a Democratic primary. Of course, the Democratic Party could not run that primary, set up under the auspices of the State, in a manner to exclude citizens of Texas there from because of their race. . . .

This case does not hold that a group of Democrats, white, black, male, female, native-born or foreign, economic royalists or working-men, may not caucus or conduct a straw vote. What the Jaybird Association did here was to conduct as individuals, separate and apart from the Democratic Party or the State, a straw vote as to who should receive the Association's endorsement for county and precinct offices.

It has been successful in seeing that those who receive its endorsement are nominated and elected. That is true of concerted action by any group. In numbers there is strength. In organization there is effectiveness. Often a small minority of stockholders control a corporation. Indeed, it is almost an axiom of corporate management that a small, cohesive group may control, especially in the larger corporations where the holdings are widely diffused.

I do not understand that concerted action of individuals which is successful somehow becomes state action. . . .

In the instant case, the State of Texas has provided for elections and primaries. This is separate and apart and wholly unrelated to the Jaybird Association's activities. Its activities are confined to one County where a group of citizens have appointed themselves the censors of those who would run for public offices. Apparently so far they have succeeded in convincing the voters of this County in most instances that their supported candidates should win. This seems to differ very little from situations common in many other places far north of the Mason-Dixon line, such as areas where a candidate must obtain the approval of a religious group. . . . The propriety of these practices is something the courts sensibly have left to the good or bad judgment of the electorate. It must be recognized that elections and other public business are influenced by all sorts of pressures from carefully organized groups. We have pressure from labor unions, from the National Association of Manufacturers, from the Silver Shirts, from the National Association for the Advancement of Colored People, from the Ku Klux Klan and others. Far from the activities of these groups being properly labeled as state action, under either the Fourteenth or the Fifteenth Amendment, they are to be considered as attempts to influence or obtain state action.

The courts do not normally pass upon these pressure groups, whether their causes are good or bad, highly successful or only so-so. It is difficult for me to see how this Jaybird Association is anything but such a pressure group. Apparently it is believed in by enough people in Fort Bend County to obtain a majority of the votes for its approved candidates. This differs little from the situation in many parts of the "Bible Belt" where a church stamp of approval or that of the Anti-Saloon League must be put on any candidate who does not want to lose the election.

The State of Texas in its elections and primaries takes no cognizance of this Jaybird Association. The State treats its decisions apparently with the same disdain as it would the approval or condemnation of judicial candidates by a bar association poll of its members.

In this case the majority have found that this pressure group's work does constitute state action. The basis of this conclusion is rather difficult to ascertain. Apparently it derives mainly from a dislike of the goals of the Jaybird Association. I share that dislike. I fail to see how it makes state action.

I would affirm.

The One Person/One Vote Standard: *Reynolds v. Sims*

Throughout the 1950s, the Supreme Court had begun to speak with increasing force on voting rights. Yet this growing commitment to enhanced minority voting rights lacked focus and intensity. If the federal courts were to effectively attack the voting rights dilemma, this needed to change. In 1962's Baker v. Carr the Court was ready to try, ruling that the constitutionality of imbalanced legislative districts—as a matter of equal protection of the law—was a legitimate issue for federal adjudication. One year later, in Gray v. Sanders, the Court overturned Georgia's county-unit method of primary elections, which gave rural voters a significantly heavier weight than that of urban voters. Finally, 1964s Reynolds v. Sims held that "the Equal Protection Clause requires both houses of a state legislature to be apportioned on a population basis." The new standard when it came to counting the votes of citizen was one person/one vote, and any variation from that standard was most likely "constitutionally inadequate." The result of this new constitutional reasoning, though not immediately apparent, was electric. When matched with legislative initiatives that arrived in 1965, these and subsequent rulings laid the groundwork for a total revolution in voting rights—not to mention political power—affecting us to the present day.

Most representative of this one person/one vote revolution was the Supreme Court's ruling in Reynolds v. Sims. It was here that the court laid down the gauntlet and made numerical equality the constitutional standard in voting rights matters. As you read Chief Justice Warren's opinion, note the Court's growing concerns with vote dilution—rules and procedures that rob a vote of its meaning and impact. Having the right to vote was in itself not enough; for a vote to be meaningful, it also had to have impact on government policy and pro-

*cess. Yet how could the courts determine when vote dilution was tak-
ing place? And once they found it, how could they legitimately correct
the problem? Did the courts even have the power to act in these matters, and if so, to what extent?*

Reynolds v. Sims

> Supreme Court of the United States
> 377 U.S. 533
> June 15, 1964
> Opinion By MR. CHIEF JUSTICE WARREN
> Involved in these cases are an appeal . . . from a decision of the Fed-
> eral District Court for the Middle District of Alabama holding invalid,
> under the Equal Protection Clause of the Federal Constitution, the
> existing and two legislatively proposed plans for the apportionment of
> seats in the two houses of the Alabama Legislature, and ordering into
> effect a temporary reapportionment plan comprised of parts of the
> proposed but judicially disapproved measures.
>
> . . .
>
> ## II
> Undeniably the Constitution of the United States protects the right of
> all qualified citizens to vote, in state as well as in federal elections. A
> consistent line of decisions by this Court in cases involving attempts
> to deny or restrict the right of suffrage has made this indelibly
> clear. . . . In *Mosley* the Court stated that it is "as equally unquestion-
> able that the right to have one's vote counted is as open to protec-
> tion . . . as the right to put a ballot in a box." . . . . In *Classic,* [the Court
> noted that] "obviously included within the right to choose, secured by
> the Constitution, is the right of qualified voters within a state to cast
> their ballots and have them counted . . . ." [In fact], history has seen a
> continuing expansion of the scope of the right of suffrage in this coun-
> try. The right to vote freely for the candidate of one's choice is of the
> essence of a democratic society, and any restrictions on that right
> strike at the heart of representative government. And the right of suf-
> frage can be denied by a debasement or dilution of the weight of a cit-
> izen's vote just as effectively as by wholly prohibiting the free exercise
> of the franchise.
>
> In *Gray v. Sanders,* . . . we held that the Georgia county unit system,
> applicable in statewide primary elections, was unconstitutional since it

resulted in a dilution of the weight of the votes of certain Georgia voters merely because of where they resided. After indicating that the Fifteenth and Nineteenth Amendments prohibit a State from overweighting or diluting votes on the basis of race or sex, we stated: How then can one person be given twice or ten times the voting power of another person in a statewide election merely because he lives in a rural area or because he lives in the smallest rural county? Once the geographical unit for which a representative is to be chosen is designated, all who participate in the election are to have an equal vote—whatever their race, whatever their sex, whatever their occupation, whatever their income, and wherever their home may be in that geographical unit. This is required by the Equal Protection Clause of the Fourteenth Amendment. The concept of "we the people" under the Constitution visualizes no preferred class of voters but equality among those who meet the basic qualifications. The idea that every voter is equal to every other voter in his State, when he casts his ballot in favor of one of several competing candidates, underlies many of our decisions.

Continuing, we stated that "there is no indication in the Constitution that homesite or occupation affords a permissible basis for distinguishing between qualified voters within the State." And, finally, we concluded: "The conception of political equality from the Declaration of Independence, to Lincoln's Gettysburg Address, to the Fifteenth, Seventeenth, and Nineteenth Amendments can mean only one thing—one person, one vote." . . .

In *Wesberry v. Sanders,* . . . decided earlier this Term, ... we decided that an apportionment of congressional seats which "contracts the value of some votes and expands that of others" is unconstitutional, since "the Federal Constitution intends that when qualified voters elect members of Congress each vote be given as much weight as any other vote . . . ." We concluded that the constitutional prescription for election of members of the House of Representatives "by the People," construed in its historical context, "means that as nearly as is practicable one man's vote in a congressional election is to be worth as much as another's." . . .

We found further, in *Wesberry,* that "our Constitution's plain objective" was that "of making equal representation for equal numbers of people the fundamental goal . . . ." We concluded by stating:

No right is more precious in a free country than that of having a voice in the election of those who make the laws under which, as good citizens, we must live. Other rights, even the most basic, are illusory if the right to vote is undermined. Our Constitution leaves no room for classification of people in a way that unnecessarily abridges this right.

. . .

III

A predominant consideration in determining whether a State's legislative apportionment scheme constitutes an invidious discrimination violative of rights asserted under the Equal Protection Clause is that the rights allegedly impaired are individual and personal in nature. . . .

Legislators represent people, not trees or acres. Legislators are elected by voters, not farms or cities or economic interests. As long as ours is a representative form of government, and our legislatures are those instruments of government elected directly by and directly representative of the people, the right to elect legislators in a free and unimpaired fashion is a bedrock of our political system. It could hardly be gainsaid that a constitutional claim had been asserted by an allegation that certain otherwise qualified voters had been entirely prohibited from voting for members of their state legislature. And, if a State should provide that the votes of citizens in one part of the State should be given two times, or five times, or 10 times the weight of votes of citizens in another part of the State, it could hardly be contended that the right to vote of those residing in the disfavored areas had not been effectively diluted. It would appear extraordinary to suggest that a State could be constitutionally permitted to enact a law providing that certain of the State's voters could vote two, five, or 10 times for their legislative representatives, while voters living elsewhere could vote only once. And it is inconceivable that a state law to the effect that in counting votes for legislators, the votes of citizens in one part of the State would be multiplied by two, five, or 10, while the votes of persons in another area would be counted only at face value, could be constitutionally sustainable. Of course, the effect of state legislative districting schemes which give the same number of representatives to unequal numbers of constituents is identical. Overweighting and overvaluation of the votes of those living here has the certain effect of dilution and undervaluation of the votes of those living there. The resulting discrimination against those individual voters living in disfavored areas is easily demonstrable mathematically. Their right to vote is simply not the same right to vote as that of those living in a favored part of the State. Two, five, or 10 of them must vote before the effect of their voting is equivalent to that of their favored neighbor. Weighting the votes of citizens differently, by any method or means, merely because of where they happen to reside, hardly seems justifiable. One must be ever aware that the Constitution forbids "sophisticated as well as simple-minded modes of discrimination." As we stated in *Wesberry v. Sanders*, . . .

We do not believe that the Framers of the Constitution intended to permit the same vote-diluting discrimination to be accomplished through the device of districts containing widely varied numbers of inhabitants. To say that a vote is worth more in one district than in another would . . . run counter to our fundamental ideas of democratic government.

. . . Representative government is in essence self-government through the medium of elected representatives of the people, and each and every citizen has an inalienable right to full and effective participation in the political processes of his State's legislative bodies. Most citizens can achieve this participation only as qualified voters through the election of legislators to represent them. Full and effective participation by all citizens in state government requires, therefore, that each citizen have an equally effective voice in the election of members of his state legislature. Modern and viable state government needs, and the Constitution demands, no less.

Logically, in a society ostensibly grounded on representative government, it would seem reasonable that a majority of the people of a State could elect a majority of that State's legislators. To conclude differently, and to sanction minority control of state legislative bodies, would appear to deny majority rights in a way that far surpasses any possible denial of minority rights that might otherwise be thought to result. Since legislatures are responsible for enacting laws by which all citizens are to be governed, they should be bodies which are collectively responsive to the popular will. And the concept of equal protection has been traditionally viewed as requiring the uniform treatment of persons standing in the same relation to the governmental action questioned or challenged. With respect to the allocation of legislative representation, all voters, as citizens of a State, stand in the same relation regardless of where they live. . . . Since the achieving of fair and effective representation for all citizens is concededly the basic aim of legislative apportionment, we conclude that the Equal Protection Clause guarantees the opportunity for equal participation by all voters in the election of state legislators. Diluting the weight of votes because of place of residence impairs basic constitutional rights under the Fourteenth Amendment just as much as invidious discriminations based upon factors such as race . . . or economic status. . . . Our constitutional system amply provides for the protection of minorities by means other than giving them majority control of state legislatures. And the democratic ideals of equality and majority rule, which have served this Nation so well in the past, are hardly of any less significance for the present and the future.

We are told that the matter of apportioning representation in a state legislature is a complex and many-faceted one. We are advised that States can rationally consider factors other than population in apportioning legislative representation. We are admonished not to restrict the power of the States to impose differing views as to political philosophy on their citizens. We are cautioned about the dangers of entering into political thickets and mathematical quagmires. Our answer is this: a denial of constitutionally protected rights demands judicial protection; our oath and our office require no less of us. As stated in *Gomillion v. Lightfoot*, . . .

When a State exercises power wholly within the domain of state interest, it is insulated from federal judicial review. But such insulation is not carried over when state power is used as an instrument for circumventing a federally protected right.

To the extent that a citizen's right to vote is debased, he is that much less a citizen. The fact that an individual lives here or there is not a legitimate reason for overweighting or diluting the efficacy of his vote. The complexions of societies and civilizations change, often with amazing rapidity. A nation once primarily rural in character becomes predominantly urban. Representation schemes once fair and equitable become archaic and outdated. But the basic principle of representative government remains, and must remain, unchanged—the weight of a citizen's vote cannot be made to depend on where he lives. Population is, of necessity, the starting point for consideration and the controlling criterion for judgment in legislative apportionment controversies. A citizen, a qualified voter, is no more nor no less so because he lives in the city or on the farm. This is the clear and strong command of our Constitution's Equal Protection Clause. This is an essential part of the concept of a government of laws and not men. This is at the heart of Lincoln's vision of "government of the people, by the people, [and] for the people." The Equal Protection Clause demands no less than substantially equal state legislative representation for all citizens, of all places as well as of all races.

IV

We hold that, as a basic constitutional standard, the Equal Protection Clause requires that the seats in both houses of a bicameral state legislature must be apportioned on a population basis. Simply stated, an individual's right to vote for state legislators is unconstitutionally impaired when its weight is in a substantial fashion diluted when compared with votes of citizens living in other parts of the State. . . .

Legislative apportionment in Alabama is signally illustrative and symptomatic of the seriousness of this problem in a number of the States. At the time this litigation was commenced, there had been no reapportionment of seats in the Alabama Legislature for over 60 years. Legislative inaction, coupled with the unavailability of any political or judicial remedy, had resulted, with the passage of years, in the perpetuated scheme becoming little more than an irrational anachronism. Consistent failure by the Alabama Legislature to comply with state constitutional requirements as to the frequency of reapportionment and the bases of legislative representation resulted in a minority strangle hold on the State Legislature. Inequality of representation in one house added to the inequality in the other.

. . .

VI

By holding that as a federal constitutional requisite both houses of a state legislature must be apportioned on a population basis, we mean that the Equal Protection Clause requires that a State make an honest and good faith effort to construct districts, in both houses of its legislature, as nearly of equal population as is practicable. We realize that it is a practical impossibility to arrange legislative districts so that each one has an identical number of residents, or citizens, or voters. Mathematical exactness or precision is hardly a workable constitutional requirement.

In *Wesberry v. Sanders*, . . . the Court stated that congressional representation must be based on population as nearly as is practicable. In implementing the basic constitutional principle of representative government as enunciated by the Court in *Wesberry*—equality of population among districts—some distinctions may well be made between congressional and state legislative representation. Since, almost invariably, there is a significantly larger number of seats in state legislative bodies to be distributed within a State than congressional seats, it may be feasible to use political subdivision lines to a greater extent in establishing state legislative districts than in congressional districting while still affording adequate representation to all parts of the State. To do so would be constitutionally valid, so long as the resulting apportionment was one based substantially on population and the equal-population principle was not diluted in any significant way. Somewhat more flexibility may therefore be constitutionally permissible with respect to state legislative apportionment than in congressional districting. Lower courts can and assuredly will work out more concrete and specific standards for evaluating state legislative apportionment schemes in the context of actual litigation. For the present, we deem it expedient not to attempt to spell out any precise constitutional tests. What is marginally permissible in one State may be unsatisfactory in another, depending on the particular circumstances of the case. Developing a body of doctrine on a case-by-case basis appears to us to provide the most satisfactory means of arriving at detailed constitutional requirements in the area of state legislative apportionment.

. . .

X

We do not consider here the difficult question of the proper remedial devices which federal courts should utilize in state legislative apportionment cases. Remedial techniques in this new and developing area of the law will probably often differ with the circumstances of the challenged apportionment and a variety of local conditions. It is enough to say now that, once a State's legislative apportionment scheme has been found to be unconstitutional, it would be the unusual case in which a court would be justified in not taking appropriate action to insure that no further elections are conducted under the invalid plan. However, under certain circumstances, such as where an impending election is imminent and a State's election machinery is already in progress, equitable considerations might justify a court in withholding the granting of immediately effective relief in a legislative apportionment case, even though the existing apportionment scheme was found invalid. In awarding or withholding immediate relief, a court is entitled to and should consider the proximity of a forthcoming election and the mechanics and complexities of state election laws, and should act and rely upon general equitable principles. With respect to the timing of relief, a court can reasonably endeavor to avoid a disruption of the election process which might result from requiring precipitate changes that could make unreasonable or embarrassing demands on a State in adjusting to the requirements of the court's decree. As stated by MR. JUSTICE DOUGLAS, concurring in *Baker v. Carr*, "any relief accorded can be fashioned in the light of well-known principles of equity."

It is so ordered.

Voting Rights Act of 1965

Though the Supreme Court's decisions in Baker v. Carr *and* Reynolds v. Sims *were major expansions in the judicial fight for enhanced voting rights, in themselves they were not enough to turn the tide against vote denial and dilution. Both were simply too deeply entrenched in the procedures and laws of the day to be dealt with by judicial fiat alone. Before the courts could fully act to advance minority voting rights, Congress had to provide judges with a more complete "tool kit" of rules and powers. This was provided by 1965's Voting Rights Act, passed on August 6, 1965.*

Expressly designed to attack the perceived sources of delay in the case-by-case litigation approach, the nineteen sections of the VRA imposed a completely new enforcement methodology for voting rights violations. Not only did it outlaw vote denial based on race or color (and later ethnicity) in section 2, it also gave both the executive branch and the courts a powerful new set of tools and objectives for voting rights enforcement. Among them were the power to appoint federal examiners and observers in whatever numbers the president felt necessary, prohibitions on literacy tests and poll taxes, and rules outlawing any action "under color of the law" that prevented qualified voters from voting or having their votes fairly counted.

As you read the excerpt from the VRA of 1965 below, note the various ways Congress sought to combat the vote denial problem. Note also the different levels of government officials empowered by the act. Why do you think that Congress shared out authority for enforcement among the executive and judicial branches? Which branch do you

think that Congress intended to carry the primary enforcement bur-
den here? Why?

42 U.S. C. § 1973

79 U.S. Statutes At Large, 437
AN ACT To enforce the fifteenth amendment to the Constitution
of the United States, and for other purposes. . . .

Section 2
No voting qualification or prerequisite to voting, or standard,
practice, or procedure shall be imposed or applied by any State or
political subdivision to deny or abridge the right of any citizen of the
United States to vote on account of race or color.

Section 3
(a) Whenever the Attorney General institutes a proceeding under any
statute to enforce the guarantees of the fifteenth amendment . . . the
court shall authorize the appointment of Federal examiners by the
United States Civil Service Commission . . . to enforce the guarantees
of the fifteenth amendment. . . . Provided, that the court need not
authorize the appointment of examiners if any incidents of denial or
abridgement of the right to vote on account of race or color (1) have
been few in number and have been promptly and effectively corrected
by State or local action, (2) the continuing effect of such incidents has
been eliminated, and (3) there is no reasonable probability of their
recurrence in the future.
   (b) If . . . the court finds that a test or device has been used for the
purpose or with the effect of denying or abridging the right of any citizen of the United States to vote on account of race or color, it shall
suspend the use of tests and devices . . . as the court shall determine is
appropriate and for such period as it deems necessary.
   (c) If . . . the court finds that violations of the fifteenth amendment
justifying equitable relief have occurred . . . , the court, in addition to
such relief as it may grant, shall retain jurisdiction for such period as it
may deem appropriate and during such period no voting qualification
or prerequisite to voting, or standard, practice, or procedure with
respect to voting different from that in force or effect at the time the
proceeding was commenced shall be enforced unless and until the

court finds that such qualification, [etc] . . . does not have the purpose [nor] . . . the effect of denying or abridging the right to vote on account of race or color. . . .

Section 4

(a) To assure that the right of citizens of the United States to vote is not denied or abridged on account of race or color, no citizen shall be denied the right to vote in any Federal, State, or local election because of his failure to comply with any test or device in any State with respect to which the determinations have been made under subsection (b) . . . unless the United States District Court for the District of Columbia in an action for a declaratory judgment . . . has determined that no such test or device has been used during the five years preceding the filing of the action for the purpose or with the effect of denying or abridging the right to vote on account of race or color.
. . .

(b) The provisions of subsection (a) shall apply in any State or in any political subdivision of a state which (1) the Attorney General determines maintained on November 1, 1964, any test or device, and with respect to which (2) the Director of the Census determines that less than 50 percentum of the persons of voting age residing therein were registered on November 1, 1964, or that less than 50 percentum of such persons voted in the presidential election of November 1964. A determination or certification of the Attorney General or of the Director of the Census under this section or under section 6 or section 13 shall not be reviewable in any court and shall be effective upon publication in the Federal Register.

(c) The phrase "test or device" shall mean any requirement that a person as a prerequisite for voting or registration for voting (1) demonstrate the ability to read, write, understand, or interpret any matter, (2) demonstrate any educational achievement or his knowledge of any particular subject, (3) possess good moral character, or (4) prove his qualifications by the voucher of registered voters or members of any other class.

(d) For purposes of this section no State or political subdivision shall be determined to have engaged in the use of tests or devices for the purpose or with the effect of denying or abridging the right to vote on account of race or color if (1) incidents of such use have been few in number and have been promptly and effectively corrected by State or local action, (2) the continuing effect of such incidents has been eliminated, and (3) there is no reasonable probability of their recurrence in the future.

(e) ... (2) No person who demonstrates that he has successfully completed the sixth primary grade ... in which the predominant classroom language was other than English, shall be denied the right to vote in any Federal, State, or local election because of his inability to read, write, understand, or interpret any matter in the English language. ...

Section 5
Whenever a state ... with respect to which the prohibitions set forth in section 4(a) are in effect shall enact or seek to administer any voting qualification or prerequisite to voting, or standard, practice, or procedure with respect to voting different from that in force or effect on November 1, 1964, such State or subdivision may institute an action in the United States District Court for the District of Columbia for a declaratory judgment that such qualification, prerequisite, standard, practice, or procedure does not have the purpose and will not have the effect of denying or abridging the right to vote on account of race or color, and unless and until the court enters such judgment no person shall be denied the right to vote for failure to comply with such qualification, [etc] ... : Provided, That such qualification, prerequisite, standard, practice, or procedure may be enforced without such proceeding if the qualification, prerequisite, standard, practice, or procedure has been submitted ... to the Attorney General and the Attorney General has not interposed an objection within sixty days after such submission ...

Section 6
Whenever (a) a court has authorized the appointment of examiners ... or ... the Attorney General certifies with respect to any political subdivision named ... that (1) he has received complaints in writing from twenty or more residents of such political subdivision alleging that they have been denied the right to vote under color of law on account of race or color, and that he believes such complaints to be meritorious, or (2) that, in his judgment (considering, among other factors, whether the ratio of nonwhite persons to white persons registered to vote within such subdivision appears to him to be reasonably attributable to violations of the fifteenth amendment or whether substantial evidence exists that bona fide efforts are being

made within such subdivision to comply with the fifteenth amendment), the appointment of examiners is otherwise necessary to enforce the guarantees of the fifteenth amendment, the Civil Service Commission shall appoint as many examiners for such subdivision as it may deem appropriate to prepare and maintain lists of persons eligible to vote in Federal, State, and local elections. . . .

Section 7

(a) The examiners . . . shall, at such places as the Civil Service Commission shall by regulation designate, examine applicants concerning their qualifications for voting. . . .

(b) Any person whom the examiner finds . . . to have the qualifications prescribed by State law not inconsistent with the Constitution and laws of the United States shall promptly be placed on a list of eligible voters. . . . Any person whose name appears on the examiner's list shall be entitled and allowed to vote in the election district of his residence unless and until the appropriate election officials shall have been notified that such person has been removed . . . . Provided, That no person shall be entitled to vote in any election by virtue of this Act unless his name shall have been certified and transmitted on such a list to the offices of the appropriate election officials at least forty-five days prior to such election.

. . .

Section 8

Whenever an examiner is serving under this Act in any political subdivision, the Civil Service Commission may assign, at the request of the Attorney General, one or more persons, who may be officers of the United States, (1) to enter and attend at any place for holding an election in such subdivision for the purpose of observing whether persons who are entitled to vote are being permitted to vote, and (2) to enter and attend at any place for tabulating the votes cast at any election held in such subdivision for the purpose of observing whether votes cast by persons entitled to vote are being properly tabulated. . . .

Section 9

(a) Any challenge to a listing on an eligibility list prepared by an examiner shall be heard and determined by a hearing officer appointed by and responsible to the Civil Service Commission and under such rules as the Commission shall by regulation prescribe. . . .

Such challenge shall be determined within fifteen days after it has been filed. . . . Any person listed shall be entitled and allowed to vote pending final determination by the hearing officer and by the court . . .

Section 10

(a) The Congress finds that the requirement of the payment of a poll tax as a precondition to voting (i) precludes persons of limited means from voting or imposes unreasonable financial hardship upon such persons as a precondition to their exercise of the franchise, (ii) does not bear a reasonable relationship to any legitimate State interest in the conduct of elections, and (iii) in some areas has the purpose or effect of denying persons the right to vote because of race or color. Upon the basis of these findings, Congress declares that the constitutional right of citizens to vote is denied or abridged in some areas by the requirement of the payment of a poll tax as a precondition to voting.

(b) In the exercise of the powers of Congress under section 5 of the fourteenth amendment and section 2 of the fifteenth amendment, the Attorney General is authorized and directed to institute forthwith in the name of the United States such actions, including actions against States or political subdivisions, for declaratory judgment or injunctive relief against the enforcement of any requirement of the payment of a poll tax as a precondition to voting, or substitute therefor enacted after November 1, 1964, as will be necessary to implement the declaration of subsection (a) and the purposes of this section.

(c) The district courts of the United States shall have jurisdiction of such actions which shall be heard and determined by a court of three judges . . . and any appeal shall lie to the Supreme Court. It shall be the duty of the judges designated to hear the case to assign the case for hearing at the earliest practicable date, to participate in the hearing and determination thereof, and to cause the case to be in every way expedited.

(d) During the pendency of such actions, and thereafter if the courts, notwithstanding this action by the Congress, should declare the requirement of the payment of a poll tax to be constitutional, no citizen of the United States who is a resident of a State . . . shall be denied the right to vote for failure to pay a poll tax if he tenders payment of such tax for the current year to an examiner or to the appropriate State or local official at least forty-five days prior to election, whether or not such tender would be timely or adequate under State law. . . .

Section 11

(a) No person acting under color of law shall fail or refuse to permit any person to vote who is entitled to vote under any provision of this Act or is otherwise qualified to vote, or willfully fail or refuse to tabulate, count, and report such person's vote.

(b) No person, whether acting under color of law or otherwise, shall intimidate, threaten, or coerce, or attempt to intimidate, threaten, or coerce any person for voting or attempting to vote, or intimidate, threaten, or coerce, or attempt to intimidate, threaten, or coerce any person for urging or aiding any person to vote or attempt to vote, or intimidate, threaten, or coerce any person for exercising any powers or duties under section 3(a), 6, 8, 9, 10, or 12(e).

(c) Whoever knowingly or willfully gives false information as to his name, address, or period of residence in the voting district for the purpose of establishing his eligibility to register or vote, or conspires with another individual for the purpose of encouraging his false registration to vote or illegal voting, or pays or offers to pay or accepts payment either for registration to vote or for voting shall be fined not more than $10,000 or imprisoned not more than five years, or both. . . .

(d) Whoever, in any matter within the jurisdiction of an examiner or hearing officer knowingly and willfully falsifies or conceals a material fact, or makes any false, fictitious, or fraudulent statements or representations, or makes or uses any false writing or document knowing the same to contain any false, fictitious, or fraudulent statement or entry, shall be fined not more than $10,000 or imprisoned not more than five years, or both.

. . .

Section 13

Listing procedures shall be terminated in any political subdivision of any State (a) with respect to examiners appointed . . . whenever the Attorney General notifies the Civil Service Commission . . . [that] the Director of the Census has determined that more than 50 percentum of the nonwhite persons of voting age residing therein are registered to vote, (1) that all persons listed by an examiner for such subdivision have been placed on the appropriate voting registration roll, and (2) that there is no longer reasonable cause to believe that persons will be deprived of or denied the right to vote on account of race or color in such subdivision. . . . A political subdivision may petition the Attorney General for the termination of listing procedures . . . and . . . to request the Director of the Census to take such survey or census as may be appropriate for the making of the determination provided for in this section. . . .

Section 14

(c) (1) The terms "vote" or "voting" shall include all action necessary to make a vote effective in any primary, special, or general election, including, but not limited to, registration, listing pursuant to this Act, or other action required by law prerequisite to voting, casting a ballot, and having such ballot counted properly and included in the appropriate totals of votes cast with respect to candidates for public or party office and propositions for which votes are received in an election. (2) The term "political subdivision" shall mean any county or parish, except that, where registration for voting is not conducted under the supervision of a county or parish, the term shall include any other subdivision of a State which conducts registration for voting.

. . .

Section 17

Nothing in this Act shall be construed to deny, impair, or otherwise adversely affect the right to vote of any person registered to vote under the law of any State or political subdivision. . . .

Vote Dilution and the Shift from At-Large to Single-Member Districts: *Allen v. State Board of Elections*

By the mid-1970s, vote denial was largely a thing of the past. All bets were off, however, when the issue moved from denying minorities the vote to diluting the effect of their vote. What use was a right to vote if it did no appreciable good? This was the dilemma facing the nation as race-based and other forms of vote denial were eradicated. Merely getting excluded groups the vote was not enough. If the meaning and purpose of having the vote were to be sustained, then vote dilution techniques had to go.

The federal courts struggled with this problem for years. How did one define vote dilution? What remedies were effective, or even appro-

priate, once one determined that vote dilution existed? Was vote dilution even covered by federal law? In 1969's Allen v. State Board of Elections, *the Supreme Court finally answered these questions—vote denial was not permitted under the Constitution and the VRA of 1965. Four years later, in* White v. Regester, *the high Court called on the lower courts to attack the problem of vote dilution and provided standards for proving vote dilution's existence. The Court also hinted at the proper remedy for vote dilution—the adoption of single-member districts so as to empower local majorities of minority residents. Reorganized by the Fifth Circuit in* Zimmer v. McKeithen, *the standards and remedies as set out by the Supreme Court in* White *became a virtual call to arms. Over the next decade, minorities filed hundreds of vote dilution suits. By the mid-1980s, this flood of litigation had brought about a near revolution of U.S. political forms as hundreds of cities, counties, and other kinds of jurisdictions across the South and the nation moved away from at-large elections toward single-member districts—districts designed with the deliberate intent of empowering minority votes by creating what came to be called "minority-majority" districts. Remarkable gains in minority officeholding were the inevitable result.*

Excerpted below is one of the most important decisions that shaped this process: Allen v. State Board of Elections. *As you read this decision, note the commitment on the part of the federal bench to intrusive action on the part of the federal courts in forcing compliance with the law. Yet at the same time, note also the struggle on the part of these judges in defining the proper limits of federal power in these matters. Action was necessary, but the courts were still uncertain just how far they could go in defining the problem and providing a solution to that problem. However, where in the past this uncertainty would have lead to inaction, now it was not allowed to stand in the way of change.*

Allen v. State Board of Elections

Supreme Court of the United States
393 U.S. 544
March 3, 1969
Opinion By CHIEF JUSTICE WARREN:
These four cases, three from Mississippi and one from Virginia, involve the application of the Voting Rights Act of 1965 to state election laws and regulations. . . .
In *South Carolina v. Katzenbach,* . . . we held the provisions of the

Act involved in these cases to be constitutional. These cases merely require us to determine whether the various state enactments involved are subject to the requirements of the Act. . . .

Under § 5, if a State covered by the Act passes any "voting qualification or prerequisite to voting, or standard, practice, or procedure with respect to voting different from that in force or effect on November 1, 1964," no person can be deprived of his right to vote "for failure to comply with" the new enactment "unless and until" the State seeks and receives a declaratory judgment in the United States District Court for the District of Columbia that the new enactment "does not have the purpose and will not have the effect of denying or abridging the right to vote on account of race or color." . . .

However, § 5 does not necessitate that a covered State obtain a declaratory judgment action before it can enforce any change in its election laws. It provides that a State may enforce a new enactment if the State submits the new provision to the Attorney General of the United States and, within 60 days of the submission, the Attorney General does not formally object to the new statute or regulation. . . . Once the State has successfully complied with the § 5 approval requirements, private parties may enjoin the enforcement of the new enactment only in traditional suits attacking its constitutionality; there is no further remedy provided by § 5.

In these four cases, the States have passed new laws or issued new regulations. The central issue is whether these provisions fall within the prohibition of § 5 that prevents the enforcement of "any voting qualification or prerequisite to voting, or standard, practice, or procedure with respect to voting" unless the State first complies with one of the section's approval procedures.

. . .

I

These suits were instituted by private citizens; an initial question is whether private litigants may invoke the jurisdiction of the district courts to obtain the relief requested in these suits. . . .

The Act was drafted to make the guarantees of the Fifteenth Amendment finally a reality for all citizens. . . . Congress realized that existing remedies were inadequate to accomplish this purpose and drafted an unusual, and in some aspects a severe, procedure for insuring that States would not discriminate on the basis of race in the enforcement of their voting laws.

The achievement of the Act's laudable goal could be severely hampered, however, if each citizen were required to depend solely on litigation instituted at the discretion of the Attorney General. . . . The Attorney General has a limited staff and often might be unable to uncover quickly new regulations and enactments passed at the varying levels of state government. It is consistent with the broad purpose of the Act to allow the individual citizen standing to insure that his city or county government complies with the § 5 approval requirements. . . .

The guarantee of § 5 that no person shall be denied the right to vote for failure to comply with an unapproved new enactment subject to § 5, might well prove an empty promise unless the private citizen were allowed to seek judicial enforcement of the prohibition.

. . .

IV

Finding that these cases are properly before us, we turn to a consideration of whether these state enactments are subject to the approval requirements of § 5. These requirements apply to "any voting qualification or prerequisite to voting, or standard, practice, or procedure with respect to voting . . . ." The Act further provides that the term "voting" "shall include all action necessary to make a vote effective in any primary, special, or general election, including, but not limited to, registration, listing . . . or other action required by law prerequisite to voting, casting a ballot, and having such ballot counted properly and included in the appropriate totals of votes cast with respect to candidates for public or party office and propositions for which votes are received in an election." . . . Appellees . . . maintain that § 5 covers only those state enactments which prescribe who may register to vote. While accepting that the Act is broad enough to insure that the votes of all citizens should be cast, appellees urge that § 5 does not cover state rules relating to the qualification of candidates or to state decisions as to which offices shall be elective. . . .

Appellees [further] . . . argue that § 5 was not intended to apply to a change from district to at-large voting, because application of § 5 would cause a conflict in the administration of reapportionment legislation. They contend that under such a broad reading of § 5, enforcement of a reapportionment plan could be enjoined for failure to meet the § 5 approval requirements, even though the plan had been approved by a federal court. Appellees urge that Congress could not have intended to force the States to submit a reapportionment plan to two different courts.

We must reject a narrow construction that appellees would give to § 5. The Voting Rights Act was aimed at the subtle, as well as the obvious, state regulations which have the effect of denying citizens their right to vote because of their race. Moreover, compatible with the decisions of this Court, the Act gives a broad interpretation to the right to vote, recognizing that voting includes "all action necessary to make a vote effective." . . . We are convinced that in passing the Voting Rights Act, Congress intended that state enactments such as those involved in the instant cases be subject to the § 5 approval requirements.

. . .

VI

Appellants . . . have asked this Court to set aside the elections conducted pursuant to these enactments and order that new elections be held under the pre-amendment laws. The Solicitor General has also urged us to order new elections if the State does not promptly institute § 5 approval proceedings. We decline to take corrective action of such consequence, however. These § 5 coverage questions involve complex issues of first impression—issues subject to rational disagreement. The state enactments were not so clearly subject to § 5 that the appellees' failure to submit them for approval constituted deliberate defiance of the Act. Moreover, the discriminatory purpose or effect of these statutes, if any, has not been determined by any court. We give only prospective effect to our decision, bearing in mind that our judgment today does not end the matter so far as these States are concerned. They remain subject to the continuing strictures of § 5 until they obtain from the United States District Court for the District of Columbia a declaratory judgment that for at least five years they have not used the "tests or devices" prohibited by § 4 [of the 1965 Voting Rights Act].

. . . All four cases are remanded to the District Courts with instructions to issue injunctions restraining the further enforcement of the enactments until such time as the States adequately demonstrate compliance with § 5.

It is so ordered.

The Conservative Reaction to Expanded Voting Rights:
Dissents in *Reynolds* and *Allen;* Majority in *Shaw*

By the early 1990s, the voting rights revolution in U.S. politics was largely complete. With the exception of felony exclusions, age-based limits, and citizenship requirements, vote denial was no more. Even the more diffuse forms of vote denial were abandoned. The victory against vote dilution was also near complete. Organized around the concept of proportional representation through majority-minority districts, racial and ethnic minorities across the country were electing group members to positions of power in numbers near proportional to their percentages within the population. Yet no voting rights victory has been without its contradictions and counterreactions. The application of race-conscious districting to combat group-based vote dilution was no exception.

For years, a growing segment within the governing elite of this country—especially conservative judges—worried about the implications and justifications behind the federal courts' anti–vote dilution efforts. As early as 1962, in his dissent to Baker v. Carr, *Justice Frankfurter had warned that "such a massive repudiation of the experience of our whole past in asserting destructively novel judicial power . . . may well impair the Court's position as the ultimate organ of 'the supreme Law of the Land' in that vast range of legal problems, often strongly entangled in popular feeling, on which this Court must pronounce." Apportionment, Justice Frankfurter concluded, was too complex a process to be standardized within a simple numerical formula. Yet the lack of such a unifying methodology doomed the endeavor to inevitable failure. "To promulgate jurisdiction in the abstract is meaningless, ... as devoid of reality as 'a brooding omnipresence in the sky,' for it conveys no intimation what relief, if any, [the courts are] capable of affording." Without a consistent remedy to offer, the courts were likely to do more harm than good by their actions.*

In the years that followed, many judges echoed Justice Frankfurter's words of warning and dissent. The appointment of conservative judges in the 1980s only made such views even more popular. By the early 1990s, what had once been in dissent had become the dominant perspective of the Supreme Court. In 1993 in Shaw v. Reno, *the entire structure of minority-majority districting was challenged. As these justices saw things, minority-majority districting was nothing more than racial gerrymandering—and hence impermissible under the Constitution.*

As you read the two dissents by Justice Harlan and the majority decision in Shaw v. Reno *excerpted below, note both the strong feelings these matters raised as well as the evolving nature of the debate. For, as you will see, what changed over time was not the arguments made, but the success these arguments had in shaping judicial policy. Why do you think it took so long for these views to move from minority to majority status? What factors might explain the shift?*

Dissent in *Reynolds v. Sims*

Supreme Court of the United States
  377 U.S. 533
  June 15, 1964
  MR. JUSTICE HARLAN, dissenting.

Preliminary Statement

Today's holding is that the Equal Protection Clause of the Fourteenth Amendment requires every State to structure its legislature so that all the members of each house represent substantially the same number of people; other factors may be given play only to the extent that they do not significantly encroach on this basic "population" principle. Whatever may be thought of this holding as a piece of political ideology—and even on that score the political history and practices of this country from its earliest beginnings leave wide room for debate . . .—I think it demonstrable that the Fourteenth Amendment does not impose this political tenet on the States or authorize this Court to do so.

The Court's constitutional discussion, . . . is remarkable . . . for its failure to address itself at all to the Fourteenth Amendment as a whole or to the legislative history of the Amendment pertinent to the matter at hand. Stripped of aphorisms, the Court's argument boils down to the assertion that appellees' right to vote has been invidiously "debased" or "diluted" by systems of apportionment which entitle them to vote for fewer legislators than other voters, an assertion which is tied to the Equal Protection Clause only by the constitutionally frail tautology that "equal" means "equal."

Had the Court paused to probe more deeply into the matter, it would have found that the Equal Protection Clause was never intended to inhibit the States in choosing any democratic method they pleased for the apportionment of their legislatures. This is shown by the language of the Fourteenth Amendment taken as a whole, by the understanding of those who proposed and ratified it, and by the political practices of the States at the time the Amendment was adopted. It is confirmed by numerous state and congressional actions since the adoption of the Fourteenth Amendment, and by the common understanding of the Amendment as evidenced by subsequent constitutional amendments and decisions of this Court before *Baker v. Carr* made an abrupt break with the past in 1962.

The failure of the Court to consider any of these matters cannot be excused or explained by any concept of "developing" constitutionalism. It is meaningless to speak of constitutional "development" when both the language and history of the controlling provisions of the Constitution are wholly ignored. Since it can, I think, be shown beyond doubt that state legislative apportionments, as such, are wholly free of constitutional limitations, save such as may be imposed by the Republican Form of Government Clause (Const., Art. IV, § 4), the Court's action now bringing them within the purview of the Fourteenth Amendment amounts to nothing less than an exercise of the amending power by this Court.

So far as the Federal Constitution is concerned, the complaints in these cases should all have been dismissed below for failure to state a cause of action, because what has been alleged or proved shows no violation of any constitutional right.

. . .

II

The Court's elaboration of its new "constitutional" doctrine indicates how far—and how unwisely—it has strayed from the appropriate bounds of its authority. The consequence of today's decision is that in all but the handful of States which may already satisfy the new requirements the local District Court or, it may be, the state courts, are given blanket authority and the constitutional duty to supervise apportionment of the State Legislatures. It is difficult to imagine a more intolerable and inappropriate interference by the judiciary with the independent legislatures of the States.

. . .

Conclusion

With these cases the Court approaches the end of the third round set in motion by the complaint filed in *Baker v. Carr.* What is done today deepens my conviction that judicial entry into this realm is profoundly ill-advised and constitutionally impermissible. As I have said before, *Wesberry v. Sanders*, ... I believe that the vitality of our political system, on which in the last analysis all else depends, is weakened by reliance on the judiciary for political reform; in time a complacent body politic may result.

These decisions also cut deeply into the fabric of our federalism. What must follow from them may eventually appear to be the product of state legislatures. Nevertheless, no thinking person can fail to recognize that the aftermath of these cases, however desirable it may be thought in itself, will have been achieved at the cost of a radical alteration in the relationship between the States and the Federal Government, more particularly the Federal Judiciary. Only one who has an overbearing impatience with the federal system and its political processes will believe that that cost was not too high or was inevitable.

Finally, these decisions give support to a current mistaken view of the Constitution and the constitutional function of this Court. This view, in a nutshell, is that every major social ill in this country can find its cure in some constitutional "principle," and that this Court should "take the lead" in promoting reform when other branches of government fail to act. The Constitution is not a panacea for every blot upon the public welfare, nor should this Court, ordained as a judicial body, be thought of as a general haven for reform movements. The Constitution is an instrument of government, fundamental to which is the premise that in a diffusion of governmental authority lies the greatest promise that this Nation will realize liberty for all its citizens. This Court, limited in function in accordance with that premise, does not serve its high purpose when it exceeds its authority, even to satisfy justified impatience with the slow workings of the political process. For when, in the name of constitutional interpretation, the Court adds something to the Constitution that was deliberately excluded from it, the Court in reality substitutes its view of what should be so for the amending process.

I dissent in each of these cases, believing that in none of them have the plaintiffs stated a cause of action. To the extent that *Baker v. Carr*, expressly or by implication, went beyond a discussion of jurisdictional doctrines independent of the substantive issues involved here, it should be limited to what it in fact was: an experiment in venturesome constitutionalism....

Dissent in *Allen v. State Board of Elections*

Supreme Court of the United States
393 U.S. 544
March 3, 1969
MR. JUSTICE HARLAN, concurring in part and dissenting in part.

The Court's opinion seeks to do justice by granting each side half of what it requests. The majority first grants appellants all they could hope for, by adopting an overly broad construction of § 5 of the Voting Rights Act. As if to compensate for its generosity, the Court then denies some of the same appellants the relief that they deserve. Section 5 is thereby reduced to a dead letter in a very substantial number of situations in which it was intended to have its full effect.

I

I shall first consider the Court's extremely broad construction of § 5. . . . We are in agreement that in requiring federal review of changes in any "standard, practice, or procedure with respect to voting," Congress intended to include all state laws that changed the process by which voters were registered and had their ballots counted. The Court, however, goes further to hold that a State covered by the Act must submit for federal approval all those laws that could arguably have an impact on Negro voting power, even though the manner in which the election is conducted remains unchanged. I believe that this reading of the statute should be rejected on several grounds. It ignores the place of § 5 in the larger structure of the Act; it is untrue to the statute's language; and it is unsupported by the legislative history.

A. First, and most important, the Court's construction ignores the structure of the complex regulatory scheme created by the Voting Rights Act. The Court's opinion assumes that § 5 may be considered apart from the rest of the Act. In fact, however, the provision is clearly designed to march in lock-step with § 4—the two sections cannot be understood apart from one another. Section 4 is one of the Act's central provisions, suspending the operation of all literacy tests and similar "devices" for at least five years in States whose low voter turnout indicated that these "tests" and "devices" had been used to exclude Negroes from the suffrage in the past. Section 5, moreover, reveals that it was not designed to implement new substantive policies but that it was structured to assure the effectiveness of the dramatic step that Congress had taken in § 4. The federal approval procedure found in § 5 only applies to those States whose literacy tests or similar "devices" have been suspended by § 4. As soon as a State regains the right to apply a literacy test or similar "device" under § 4, it also escapes the commands of § 5.

The statutory scheme contains even more striking characteristics which indicate that § 5's federal review procedure is ancillary to § 4's substantive commands. A State may escape § 5, even though it has consistently violated this provision, so long as it has complied with § 4, and has suspended the operation of literacy tests and other "devices" for five years. On the other hand, no matter how faithfully a State complies with § 5, it remains subject to its commands so long as it has not consistently obeyed § 4.

As soon as it is recognized that § 5 was designed solely to implement the policies of § 4, it becomes apparent that the Court's decision today permits the tail to wag the dog. For the Court has now construed § 5 to require a revolutionary innovation in American government that goes far beyond that which was accomplished by § 4. The fourth section of the Act had the profoundly important purpose of permitting the Negro people to gain access to the voting booths of the South once and for all. But the action taken by Congress in § 4 proceeded on the premise that once Negroes had gained free access to the ballot box, state governments would then be suitably responsive to their voice, and federal intervention would not be justified. In moving against "tests and devices" in § 4, Congress moved only against those techniques that prevented Negroes from voting at all. Congress did not attempt to restructure state governments. The Court now reads § 5, however, as vastly increasing the sphere of federal intervention beyond that contemplated by § 4, despite the fact that the two provisions were designed simply to interlock. The District Court for the District of Columbia is no longer limited to examining any new state statute that may tend to deny Negroes their right to vote, as the "tests and devices" suspended by § 4 had done. The decision today also requires the special District Court to determine whether various systems of representation favor or disfavor the Negro voter—an area well beyond the scope of § 4. Section 4, for example, does not apply to States and localities which have in the past permitted Negroes to vote freely, but which arguably have limited minority voting power by adopting a system in which various legislative bodies are elected on an at-large basis. And yet, . . . the Court holds that a statute permitting the at-large election of county boards of supervisors must be reviewed by federal authorities under § 5. Moreover, it is not clear to me how a court would go about deciding whether an at-large system is to be preferred over a district system. Under one system, Negroes have some influence in the election of all officers; under the other, minority groups have more influence in the selection of fewer officers. If courts cannot intelligently compare such alternatives, it should not be readily inferred that Congress has required them to undertake the task.

The Court's construction of § 5 is even more surprising in light of the Act's regional application. For the statute, as the Court now construes it, deals with a problem that is national in scope. I find it especially difficult to believe that Congress would single out a handful of States as requiring stricter federal supervision concerning their treatment of a problem that may well be just as serious in parts of the North as it is in the South.

The difficulties with the Court's construction increase even further when the language of the statute is considered closely. When standing alone, the statutory formula requiring federal approval for changes in any "standard, practice, or procedure with respect to voting" can be read to support either the broad construction adopted by the majority or the one which I have advanced. But the critical formula does not stand alone. Immediately following the statute's description of the federal approval procedure, § 5 proceeds to describe the type of relief an aggrieved voter may obtain if a State enforces a new statute without obtaining the consent of the appropriate federal authorities: "no person shall be denied the right to vote for failure to *comply* with such qualification, prerequisite, standard, practice, or procedure." (Emphasis supplied.) This remedy serves to delimit the meaning of the formula in question. Congress was clearly concerned with changes in procedure with which voters could comply. But a law, . . . which permits all members of the County Board of Supervisors to run in the entire county and not in smaller districts, does not require a voter to comply with anything at all, and so does not come within the scope of the language used by Congress. While the Court's opinion entirely ignores the obvious implications of this portion of the statute, the Solicitor General's amicus brief candidly admits that this provision is flatly inconsistent with the broad reading the Government has advanced and this Court has adopted. The Government's brief simply suggests that Congress' choice of the verb "comply" was merely the result of an oversight. I cannot accept such a suggestion, however, when Congress' choice of language seems to me to be consistent with the general statutory framework as I understand it.

. . .

C. Section 5, then, should properly be read to require federal approval only of those state laws that change either voter qualifications or the manner in which elections are conducted. This does not mean, however, that the District Courts in the four cases before us were right in unanimously concluding that the Voting Rights Act did not apply. Rather, it seems to me that only the judgment in *Fairley v. Patterson*, . . . should be affirmed, as that case involves a state statute which simply gives each county the right to elect its Board of Supervisors on an at-large basis.

. . .

II

After straining to expand the scope of § 5 beyond its proper limits, the majority surprisingly refuses to grant appellants in the Mississippi cases the only relief that will effectively implement the Act's purposes. As the Court recognizes, . . . the Voting Rights Act only applies to the States for a limited period of time—Mississippi may free itself from § 5's requirements in 1970. And yet the Court affords appellants in the Mississippi cases only declaratory relief, permitting state officials selected in violation of § 5 to hold office until their four-year terms expire in 1971. An election for these offices may never be held in compliance with Congress' commands. And of course, the Court's decision respecting relief does not only control these particular cases. There may have been hundreds of officials throughout the South who began serving long terms in office this November under procedures that have not been federally approved. As a result of this part of the Court's decision, the Voting Rights Act may never play the full role that Congress intended for it.

It seems clear to me that we should issue a conditional injunction in the Mississippi cases along the lines suggested by the Solicitor General, except of course in the *Fairley* case which I think should be affirmed. Unless Mississippi promptly submits its laws to either the Attorney General or the District Court for the District of Columbia, new elections under the pre-existing law should be ordered. Of course, if the laws are promptly submitted for approval, a new election should be required only if the District Court determines that the statute in question is discriminatory either in its purpose or in its effect. . . .

Majority in *Shaw v. Reno*

Supreme Court of the United States
509 U.S. 630
June 28, 1993
JUSTICE O'CONNOR delivered the opinion of the Court.

This case involves two of the most complex and sensitive issues this Court has faced in recent years: the meaning of the constitutional "right" to vote, and the propriety of racebased state legislation designed to benefit members of historically disadvantaged racial minority groups. As a result of the 1990 census, North Carolina became entitled to a 12th seat in the United States House of Representatives. The General Assembly enacted a reapportionment plan that included one majority-black congressional district. After the Attorney General of the United States objected to the plan pursuant to § 5 of the Voting Rights Act of 1965, ... the General Assembly passed new legislation creating a second majority-black district. Appellants allege that the revised plan, which contains district boundary lines of dramatically irregular shape, constitutes an unconstitutional racial gerrymander. The question before us is whether appellants have stated a cognizable claim.

I

. . .

The first of the two majority-black districts . . . , District 1, is somewhat hook shaped. Centered in the northeast portion of the State, it moves southward until it tapers to a narrow band; then, with finger-like extensions, it reaches far into the southernmost part of the State near the South Carolina border. District 1 has been compared to a "Rorschach ink-blot test," . . . and a "bug splattered on a windshield." . . .

The second majority-black district, District 12, is even more unusually shaped. It is approximately 160 miles long and, for much of its length, no wider than the I–85 corridor. It winds in snakelike fashion through tobacco country, financial centers, and manufacturing areas "until it gobbles in enough enclaves of black neighborhoods." Northbound and southbound drivers on I–85 sometimes find themselves in separate districts in one county, only to "trade" districts when they enter the next county. Of the 10 counties through which District 12 passes, 5 are cut into 3 different districts; even towns are divided. At one point the district remains contiguous only because it intersects at a single point with two other districts before crossing over them. . . .

The Attorney General did not object to the General Assembly's revised plan. But numerous North Carolinians did. The North Carolina Republican Party and individual voters brought suit in Federal District Court, alleging that the plan constituted an unconstitutional political gerrymander under *Davis v. Bandemer*. . . . That claim was dismissed . . . and this Court summarily affirmed. . . .

Shortly after the complaint . . . was filed, appellants instituted the present action in the United States District Court for the Eastern District of North Carolina. Appellants alleged not that the revised plan constituted a political gerrymander, nor that it violated the "one person, one vote" principle, . . . but that the State had created an unconstitutional racial gerrymander. . . .

II

A. "The right to vote freely for the candidate of one's choice is of the essence of a democratic society . . . ." For much of our Nation's history, that right sadly has been denied to many because of race. The Fifteenth Amendment, ratified in 1870 after a bloody Civil War, promised unequivocally that "the right of citizens of the United States to vote" no longer would be "denied or abridged . . . by any State on account of race, color, or previous condition of servitude." . . .

But "[a] number of states . . . refused to take no for an answer and continued to circumvent the fifteenth amendment's prohibition through the use of both subtle and blunt instruments, perpetuating ugly patterns of pervasive racial discrimination." Ostensibly race-neutral devices such as literacy tests with "grandfather" clauses and "good character" provisos were devised to deprive black voters of the franchise. Another of the weapons in the States' arsenal was the racial gerrymander—"the deliberate and arbitrary distortion of district boundaries . . . for [racial] purposes." . . . In the 1870's, for example, opponents of Reconstruction in Mississippi "concentrated the bulk of the black population in a 'shoestring' Congressional district running the length of the Mississippi River, leaving five others with white majorities." . . . Some 90 years later, Alabama redefined the boundaries of the city of Tuskegee "from a square to an uncouth twenty-eight-sided figure" in a manner that was alleged to exclude black voters, and only black voters, from the city limits. . . .

Congress enacted the Voting Rights Act of 1965 as a dramatic and severe response to the situation. The Act proved immediately successful in ensuring racial minorities access to the voting booth; by the early 1970's, the spread between black and white registration in several of the targeted Southern States had fallen to well below 10%....

But it soon became apparent that guaranteeing equal access to the polls would not suffice to root out other racially discriminatory voting practices. Drawing on the "one person, one vote" principle, this Court recognized that "the right to vote can be affected by a dilution of voting power as well as by an absolute prohibition on casting a ballot." ... Where members of a racial minority group vote as a cohesive unit, practices such as multimember or at-large electoral systems can reduce or nullify minority voters' ability, as a group, "to elect the candidate of their choice." ... Accordingly, the Court held that such schemes violate the Fourteenth Amendment when they are adopted with a discriminatory purpose and have the effect of diluting minority voting strength.... Congress, too, responded to the problem of vote dilution. In 1982, it amended § 2 of the Voting Rights Act to prohibit legislation that results in the dilution of a minority group's voting strength, regardless of the legislature's intent....

B. It is against this background that we confront the questions presented here. In our view, the District Court properly dismissed appellants' claims against the federal appellees. Our focus is on appellants' claim that the State engaged in unconstitutional racial gerrymandering. That argument strikes a powerful historical chord: It is unsettling how closely the North Carolina plan resembles the most egregious racial gerrymanders of the past.

An understanding of the nature of appellants' claim is critical to our resolution of the case. In their complaint, appellants did not claim that the General Assembly's reapportionment plan unconstitutionally "diluted" white voting strength. They did not even claim to be white. Rather, appellants' complaint alleged that the deliberate segregation of voters into separate districts on the basis of race violated their constitutional right to participate in a "color-blind" electoral process....

Despite their invocation of the ideal of a "color-blind" Constitution, ... appellants appear to concede that race-conscious redistricting is not always unconstitutional.... That concession is wise: This Court never has held that race-conscious state decision-making is impermissible in all circumstances. What appellants object to is redistricting legislation that is so extremely irregular on its face that it rationally can be viewed only as an effort to segregate the races for purposes of voting, without regard for traditional districting principles and without sufficiently compelling justification. For the reasons that follow, we conclude that appellants have stated a claim upon which relief can be granted under the Equal Protection Clause. . . .

III

A. The Equal Protection Clause provides that "no State shall . . . deny to any person within its jurisdiction the equal protection of the laws." . . . Its central purpose is to prevent the States from purposefully discriminating between individuals on the basis of race. . . . Laws that explicitly distinguish between individuals on racial grounds fall within the core of that prohibition.

. . .

B. Appellants contend that redistricting legislation that is so bizarre on its face that it is "unexplainable on grounds other than race," . . . demands the same close scrutiny that we give other state laws that classify citizens by race. Our voting rights precedents support that conclusion.

. . .

In some exceptional cases, a reapportionment plan may be so highly irregular that, on its face, it rationally cannot be understood as anything other than an effort to "segregate . . . voters" on the basis of race. . . . [In] *Gomillion*, in which a tortured municipal boundary line was drawn to exclude black voters, was such a case. So, too, would be a case in which a State concentrated a dispersed minority population in a single district by disregarding traditional districting principles such as compactness, contiguity, and respect for political subdivisions. We emphasize that these criteria are important not because they are constitutionally required—they are not . . . —but because they are objective factors that may serve to defeat a claim that a district has been gerrymandered on racial lines. . . .

Put differently, we believe that reapportionment is one area in which appearances do matter. A reapportionment plan that includes in one district individuals who belong to the same race, but who are otherwise widely separated by geographical and political boundaries, and who may have little in common with one another but the color of their skin, bears an uncomfortable resemblance to political apartheid. It reinforces the perception that members of the same racial group—regardless of their age, education, economic status, or the community in which they live—think alike, share the same political interests, and will prefer the same candidates at the polls. We have rejected such perceptions elsewhere as impermissible racial stereotypes. . . . By perpetuating such notions, a racial gerrymander may exacerbate the very patterns of racial bloc voting that majority-minority districting is sometimes said to counteract.

The message that such districting sends to elected representatives is equally pernicious. When a district obviously is created solely to effectuate the perceived common interests of one racial group, elected officials are more likely to believe that their primary obligation is to represent only the members of that group, rather than their constituency as a whole. This is altogether antithetical to our system of representative democracy. . . .

For these reasons, we conclude that a plaintiff challenging a reapportionment statute under the Equal Protection Clause may state a claim by alleging that the legislation, though race neutral on its face, rationally cannot be understood as anything other than an effort to separate voters into different districts on the basis of race, and that the separation lacks sufficient justification. It is unnecessary for us to decide whether or how a reapportionment plan that, on its face, can be explained in nonracial terms successfully could be challenged. Thus, we express no view as to whether "the intentional creation of majority-minority districts, without more," always gives rise to an equal protection claim. . . . We hold only that, on the facts of this case, appellants have stated a claim sufficient to defeat the state appellees' motion to dismiss.

. . .

V

Racial classifications of any sort pose the risk of lasting harm to our society. They reinforce the belief, held by too many for too much of our history, that individuals should be judged by the color of their skin. Racial classifications with respect to voting carry particular dangers. Racial gerrymandering, even for remedial purposes, may balkanize us into competing racial factions; it threatens to carry us further from the goal of a political system in which race no longer matters—a goal that the Fourteenth and Fifteenth Amendments embody, and to which the Nation continues to aspire. It is for these reasons that race-based districting by our state legislatures demands close judicial scrutiny.

The Debate over Nationalization of Voting Rights:
Bush v. Gore

The legal aftermath of the 2000 presidential election exposed the fundamental tensions posed by voting rights in the United States. The conflict between equal protection and equal impact, localism and national supremacy, and the negative effects of increased voter dissatisfaction with the political process—all central issues in the 2000 election controversy—are critical to the ongoing evolution of voting in the United States. Despite 200-plus years of debate and change, the problem of who can and cannot vote in this country remains unsolved. The answers chosen to these questions will define voting rights' future, and with it the future of democracy in the United States, for generations to come.

Included here are selections from the litigation that settled the 2000 election controversy: the majority opinion in the Florida Supreme Court's ruling in Gore v. Harris; *the U.S. Supreme Court's stay of proceedings in* Bush v. Gore; *and the substantive opinions (majority, concurrence, and dissents) in* Bush v. Gore. *As you read these opinions and rulings, note the ongoing debate among the judges as to the primary objectives in voting rights matters, the requirements for resolving the presidential election dispute, and the proper limits to judicial authority in political matters.*

Gore v. Harris

> Supreme Court of Florida
> 772 So. 2d 1243
> December 8, 2000
> PER CURIAM

> . . . .
> Through no fault of appellants, a lawfully commenced manual recount in Dade County was never completed and recounts that were completed were not counted. Without examining or investigating the ballots that were not counted by the machines, the trial court concluded there was no reasonable probability of a different result. However, the proper standard required by section 102.168 was whether the results of the election were placed in doubt. On this record there can be no question that there are legal votes within the 9,000 uncounted votes sufficient to place the results of this election in doubt. We know

this not only by evidence of statistical analysis but also by the actual experience of recounts conducted. The votes for each candidate that have been counted are separated by no more than approximately 500 votes and may be separated by as little as approximately 100 votes. Thousands of uncounted votes could obviously make a difference.

Although in all elections the Legislature and the courts have recognized that the voter's intent is paramount, in close elections the necessity for counting all legal votes becomes critical. However, the need for accuracy must be weighed against the need for finality. The need for prompt resolution and finality is especially critical in presidential elections where there is an outside deadline established by federal law. Notwithstanding, consistent with the legislative mandate and our precedent, although the time constraints are limited, we must do everything required by law to ensure that legal votes that have not been counted are included in the final election results. . . .

Only by examining the contested ballots, which are evidence in the election contest, can a meaningful and final determination in this election contest be made. As stated above, one of the provisions of the contest statute, . . . provides that the circuit court judge may "fashion such orders as he . . . deems *necessary* to ensure that each allegation in the complaint is investigated, examined or checked, to prevent any alleged wrong, and to provide any relief appropriate under such circumstances (emphasis supplied).

In addition to the relief requested by appellants to count the Miami-Dade undervote, claims have been made by the various appellees and intervenors that because this is a statewide election, statewide remedies would be called for. . . . [W]e agree. While we recognize that time is desperately short, we cannot in good faith ignore both the appellant's right to relief as to their claims concerning the uncounted votes in Miami-Dade County nor can we ignore the correctness of the assertions that any analysis and ultimate remedy should be made on a statewide basis.

We note that contest statutes vest broad discretion in the circuit court to "provide any relief appropriate under the circumstances." Section 102.168(5). Moreover, . . . the circuit court has jurisdiction, as part of the relief it orders, to order the Supervisor of Elections and the Canvassing Boards, as well as the necessary public officials, in all counties that have not conducted a manual recount or tabulation of the undervotes in this election to do so forthwith, said tabulation to take place in the individual counties where the ballots are located.

Accordingly, for the reasons stated in this opinion, we reverse the final judgment of the trial court dated December 4, 2000, and remand this cause for the circuit court to immediately tabulate by hand the approximate 9,000 Miami-Dade ballots, which the counting machine registered as non-votes, but which have never been manually reviewed, and for other relief that may thereafter appear appropriate. The circuit court is directed to enter such orders as are necessary to add any legal votes to the total statewide certifications and to enter any orders necessary to ensure the inclusion of the additional legal votes for Gore in Palm Beach County and the 168 additional legal votes from Miami-Dade County.

Because time is of the essence, the circuit court shall commence the tabulation of the Miami-Dade ballots immediately.... Moreover, since time is also of the essence in any statewide relief that the circuit court must consider, any further statewide relief should also be ordered forthwith and simultaneously with the manual tabulation of the Miami-Dade undervotes.

In tabulating the ballots and in making a determination of what is a "legal" vote, the standards to be employed is that established by the Legislature in our Election Code which is that the vote shall be counted as a "legal" vote if there is "clear indication of the intent of the voter." . . .

It is so ordered.

Bush v. Gore (Stay of Florida Recount)

Supreme Court of the United States
　　121 S. Ct. 512
　　December 9, 2000
　　PER CURIAM
　　The application for stay . . . is granted, and it is ordered that the mandate of the Supreme Court of Florida, . . . is hereby stayed pending further order of the Court. In addition, the application for stay is treated as a petition for a writ of certiorari, and petition for writ of certiorari granted. . . .
　　JUSTICE SCALIA, concurring.
　　Though it is not customary for the Court to issue an opinion in connection with its grant of a stay, I believe a brief response is necessary to JUSTICE STEVENS' dissent. I will not address the merits of

the case, since they will shortly be before us in the petition for certiorari that we have granted. It suffices to say that the issuance of the stay suggests that a majority of the Court, while not deciding the issues presented, believe that the petitioner has a substantial probability of success.

On the question of irreparable harm, . . . the issue is not, as the dissent puts it, whether "counting every legally cast vote can constitute irreparable harm." One of the principal issues in the appeal we have accepted is precisely whether the votes that have been ordered to be counted are, under a reasonable interpretation of Florida law, "legally cast votes." The counting of votes that are of questionable legality does in my view threaten irreparable harm to petitioner, and to the country, by casting a cloud upon what he claims to be the legitimacy of his election. Count first, and rule upon legality afterwards, is not a recipe for producing election results that have the public acceptance democratic stability requires. Another issue in the case, moreover, is the propriety, indeed the constitutionality, of letting the standard for determination of voters' intent—dimpled chads, hanging chads, etc.— vary from county to county, as the Florida Supreme Court opinion, as interpreted by the Circuit Court, permits. If petitioner is correct that counting in this fashion is unlawful, permitting the count to proceed on that erroneous basis will prevent an accurate recount from being conducted on a proper basis later, since it is generally agreed that each manual recount produces a degradation of the ballots, which renders a subsequent recount inaccurate.

For these reasons I have joined the Court's issuance of stay, with a highly accelerated timetable for resolving this case on the merits.

JUSTICE STEVENS, with whom JUSTICE SOUTER, JUSTICE GINSBURG, and JUSTICE BREYER join, dissenting.

To stop the counting of legal votes, the majority today departs from three venerable rules of judicial restraint that have guided the Court throughout its history. On questions of state law, we have consistently respected the opinions of the highest courts of the States. On questions whose resolution is committed at least in large measure to another branch of the Federal Government, we have construed our own jurisdiction narrowly and exercised it cautiously. On federal constitutional questions that were not fairly presented to the court whose judgment is being reviewed, we have prudently declined to express an opinion. The majority has acted unwisely.

Time does not permit a full discussion of the merits. It is clear, however, that a stay should not be granted unless an applicant makes a substantial showing of a likelihood of irreparable harm. In this case, applicants have failed to carry that heavy burden. Counting every legally cast vote cannot constitute irreparable harm. On the other hand, there is a danger that a stay may cause irreparable harm to the respondents—and, more importantly, the public at large—because of the risk that "the entry of the stay would be tantamount to a decision on the merits in favor of the applicants." . . . Preventing the recount from being completed will inevitably cast a cloud on the legitimacy of the election.

It is certainly not clear that the Florida decision violated federal law. . . . In its opinion, the Florida Supreme Court['s] . . . ruling was consistent with earlier Florida cases that have repeatedly described the interest in correctly ascertaining the will of the voters as paramount. . . . Its ruling also appears to be consistent with the prevailing view in other States. . . . As a more fundamental matter, the Florida court's ruling reflects the basic principle, inherent in our Constitution and our democracy, that every legal vote should be counted. . . .

Accordingly, I respectfully dissent.

Bush v. Gore

Supreme Court of the United States
531 U.S. 98
December 12, 2000
PER CURIAM

The petition presents the following questions: whether the Florida Supreme Court established new standards for resolving Presidential election contests, thereby violating . . . the United States Constitution . . . and whether the use of standardless manual recounts violates the Equal Protection and Due Process Clauses. With respect to the equal protection question, we find a violation of the Equal Protection Clause.

. . .

The individual citizen has no federal constitutional right to vote for electors for the President of the United States unless and until the state legislature chooses a statewide election as the means to implement its power to appoint members of the Electoral College. . . . When the state legislature vests the right to vote for President in its people, the right to vote as the legislature has prescribed is fundamental; and one source of its fundamental nature lies in the equal weight accorded to each vote and the equal dignity owed to each voter. . . .

The right to vote is protected in more than the initial allocation of the franchise. Equal protection applies as well to the manner of its exercise. Having once granted the right to vote on equal terms, the State may not, by later arbitrary and disparate treatment, value one person's vote over that of another. . . . It must be remembered that "the right of suffrage can be denied by a debasement or dilution of the weight of a citizen's vote just as effectively as by wholly prohibiting the free exercise of the franchise."

. . .

There is no difference between the two sides of the present controversy on these basic propositions. Respondents say that the very purpose of vindicating the right to vote justifies the recount procedures now at issue. The question before us, however, is whether the recount procedures the Florida Supreme Court has adopted are consistent with its obligation to avoid arbitrary and disparate treatment of the members of its electorate.

Much of the controversy seems to revolve around ballot cards designed to be perforated by a stylus but which, either through error or deliberate omission, have not been perforated with sufficient precision for a machine to count them. In some cases a piece of the card—a chad—is hanging, say by two corners. In other cases there is no separation at all, just an indentation.

The Florida Supreme Court has ordered that the intent of the voter be discerned from such ballots. For purposes of resolving the equal protection challenge, it is not necessary to decide whether the Florida Supreme Court had the authority under the legislative scheme for resolving election disputes to define what a legal vote is and to mandate a manual recount implementing that definition. The recount mechanisms implemented in response to the decisions of the Florida Supreme Court do not satisfy the minimum requirement for non-arbitrary treatment of voters necessary to secure the fundamental right. Florida's basic command for the count of legally cast votes is to consider the "intent of the voter." . . . This is unobjectionable as an abstract proposition and a starting principle. The problem inheres in the absence of specific standards to ensure its equal application. The formulation of uniform rules to determine intent based on these recurring circumstances is practicable and, we conclude, necessary.

The law does not refrain from searching for the intent of the actor in a multitude of circumstances; and in some cases the general command to ascertain intent is not susceptible to much further refinement. In this instance, however, the question is not whether to believe a witness but how to interpret the marks or holes or scratches on an inanimate object, a piece of cardboard or paper which, it is said, might not have registered as a vote during the machine count. The factfinder confronts a thing, not a person. The search for intent can be confined by specific rules designed to ensure uniform treatment.

The want of those rules here has led to unequal evaluation of ballots in various respects. . . . As seems to have been acknowledged at oral argument, the standards for accepting or rejecting contested ballots might vary not only from county to county but indeed within a single county from one recount team to another. . . .

The State Supreme Court ratified this uneven treatment. It mandated that the recount totals from two counties, Miami-Dade and Palm Beach, be included in the certified total. The court also appeared to hold sub silentio that the recount totals from Broward County, which were not completed until after the original November 14 certification by the Secretary of State, were to be considered part of the new certified vote totals even though the county certification was not contested by Vice President Gore. Yet each of the counties used varying standards to determine what was a legal vote. Broward County used a more forgiving standard than Palm Beach County, and uncovered almost three times as many new votes, a result markedly disproportionate to the difference in population between the counties. . . .

In addition to these difficulties the actual process by which the votes were to be counted under the Florida Supreme Court's decision raises further concerns. That order did not specify who would recount the ballots. The county canvassing boards were forced to pull together ad hoc teams comprised of judges from various Circuits who had no previous training in handling and interpreting ballots. Furthermore, while others were permitted to observe, they were prohibited from objecting during the recount.

The recount process, in its features here described, is inconsistent with the minimum procedures necessary to protect the fundamental right of each voter in the special instance of a statewide recount under the authority of a single state judicial officer. Our consideration is limited to the present circumstances, for the problem of equal protection in election processes generally presents many complexities.

The question before the Court is not whether local entities, in the exercise of their expertise, may develop different systems for implementing elections. Instead, we are presented with a situation where a state court with the power to assure uniformity has ordered a statewide recount with minimal procedural safeguards. When a court orders a statewide remedy, there must be at least some assurance that the rudimentary requirements of equal treatment and fundamental fairness are satisfied.

Given the Court's assessment that the recount process underway was probably being conducted in an unconstitutional manner, the Court stayed the order directing the recount so it could hear this case and render an expedited decision. The contest provision, as it was mandated by the State Supreme Court, is not well calculated to sustain the confidence that all citizens must have in the outcome of elections. The State has not shown that its procedures include the necessary safeguards. . . .

Upon due consideration of the difficulties identified to this point, it is obvious that the recount cannot be conducted in compliance with the requirements of equal protection and due process without substantial additional work. It would require not only the adoption (after opportunity for argument) of adequate statewide standards for determining what is a legal vote, and practicable procedures to implement them, but also orderly judicial review of any disputed matters that might arise. . . .

The Supreme Court of Florida has said that the legislature intended the State's electors to "participate fully in the federal electoral process," as provided in 3 U.S.C. § 5. . . . That statute, in turn, requires that any controversy or contest that is designed to lead to a conclusive selection of electors be completed by December 12. That date is upon us, and there is no recount procedure in place under the State Supreme Court's order that comports with minimal constitutional standards. Because it is evident that any recount seeking to meet the December 12 date will be unconstitutional for the reasons we have discussed, we reverse the judgment of the Supreme Court of Florida ordering a recount to proceed.

Seven Justices of the Court agree that there are constitutional problems with the recount ordered by the Florida Supreme Court that demand a remedy. . . . The only disagreement is as to the remedy. Because the Florida Supreme Court has said that the Florida Legislature intended to obtain the safe-harbor benefits of 3 U.S.C. § 5, JUSTICE BREYER's proposed remedy—remanding to the Florida Supreme Court for its ordering of a constitutionally proper contest until December 18—contemplates action in violation of the Florida election code, and hence could not be part of an "appropriate" order authorized by Fla. Stat. § 102.168(8) (2000).

. . .

None are more conscious of the vital limits on judicial authority than are the members of this Court, and none stand more in admiration of the Constitution's design to leave the selection of the President to the people, through their legislatures, and to the political sphere. When contending parties invoke the process of the courts, however, it becomes our unsought responsibility to resolve the federal and constitutional issues the judicial system has been forced to confront. . . .

It is so ordered.

CHIEF JUSTICE REHNQUIST, with whom JUSTICE SCALIA and JUSTICE THOMAS join, concurring.

We join the per curiam opinion. We write separately because we believe there are additional grounds that require us to reverse the Florida Supreme Court's decision.

. . .

In most cases, comity and respect for federalism compel us to defer to the decisions of state courts on issues of state law. That practice reflects our understanding that the decisions of state courts are definitive pronouncements of the will of the States as sovereigns. . . . Of course, in ordinary cases, the distribution of powers among the branches of a State's government raises no questions of federal constitutional law, subject to the requirement that the government be republican in character. . . . But there are a few exceptional cases in which the Constitution imposes a duty or confers a power on a particular branch of a State's government. This is one of them. Article II, § 1, . . . provides that "each State shall appoint, in such Manner as the *Legislature* thereof may direct," electors for President and Vice President. (emphasis added) Thus, the text of the election law itself, and not just its interpretation by the courts of the States, takes on independent significance.

. . .

If we are to respect the legislature's Article II powers, therefore, we must ensure that postelection state-court actions do not frustrate the legislative desire to attain the "safe harbor" provided by § 5 [of the federal election laws].

In Florida, the legislature has chosen to hold statewide elections to appoint the State's 25 electors. Importantly, the legislature has delegated the authority to run the elections and to oversee election disputes to the Secretary of State (Secretary), . . . and to state circuit courts. . . . Isolated sections of the code may well admit of more than one interpretation, but the general coherence of the legislative scheme may not be altered by judicial interpretation so as to wholly change the statutorily provided apportionment of responsibility among these various bodies. In any election but a Presidential election, the Florida Supreme Court can give as little or as much deference to Florida's executives as it chooses, so far as Article II is concerned, and this Court will have no cause to question the court's actions. But, with respect to a Presidential election, the court must be both mindful of the legislature's role under Article II in choosing the manner of appointing electors and deferential to those bodies expressly empowered by the legislature to carry out its constitutional mandate.

. . .

[A]s we indicated in our remand of the earlier case, in a Presidential election the clearly expressed intent of the legislature must prevail. And there is no basis for reading the Florida statutes as requiring the counting of improperly marked ballots, as an examination of the Florida Supreme Court's textual analysis shows. We will not parse that analysis here, except to note that the principal provision of the election code on which it relied, . . . was, as the Chief Justice pointed out in his dissent from Harris II, entirely irrelevant. . . . The State's Attorney General (who was supporting the Gore challenge) confirmed in oral argument here that never before the present election had a manual recount been conducted on the basis of the contention that "undervotes" should have been examined to determine voter intent. . . . For the court to step away from this established practice, prescribed by the Secretary of State, the state official charged by the legislature with "responsibility to . . . obtain and maintain uniformity in the application, operation, and interpretation of the election laws," . . . was to depart from the legislative scheme.

. . .

The scope and nature of the remedy ordered by the Florida Supreme Court jeopardizes the "legislative wish" to take advantage of the safe harbor provided by 3 U.S.C. § 5. . . .

Surely when the Florida Legislature empowered the courts of the State to grant "appropriate" relief, it must have meant relief that would have become final by the cut-off date of 3 U.S.C. § 5. In light of the inevitable legal challenges and ensuing appeals to the Supreme

Court of Florida and petitions for certiorari to this Court, the entire recounting process could not possibly be completed by that date. Whereas the majority in the Supreme Court of Florida stated its confidence that "the remaining undervotes in these counties can be [counted] within the required time frame," . . . it made no assertion that the seemingly inevitable appeals could be disposed of in that time. Although the Florida Supreme Court has on occasion taken over a year to resolve disputes over local elections, . . . it has heard and decided the appeals in the present case with great promptness. But the federal deadlines for the Presidential election simply do not permit even such a shortened process.

. . .

For these reasons, in addition to those given in the per curiam, we would reverse.

JUSTICE STEVENS, dissenting.

The Constitution assigns to the States the primary responsibility for determining the manner of selecting the Presidential electors. . . . When questions arise about the meaning of state laws, including election laws, it is our settled practice to accept the opinions of the highest courts of the States as providing the final answers. On rare occasions, however, either federal statutes or the Federal Constitution may require federal judicial intervention in state elections. This is not such an occasion.

The federal questions that ultimately emerged in this case are not substantial. Article II provides that "each *State* shall appoint, in such Manner as the Legislature thereof may direct, a Number of Electors." (emphasis added). It does not create state legislatures out of whole cloth, but rather takes them as they come—as creatures born of, and constrained by, their state constitutions. . . ."[W]hat is forbidden or required to be done by a State" in the Article II context "is forbidden or required of the legislative power under state constitutions as they exist." . . . [W]e also observed that "the [State's] legislative power is the supreme authority except as limited by the constitution of the State." . . . The legislative power in Florida is subject to judicial review pursuant to Article V of the Florida Constitution, and nothing in Article II of the Federal Constitution frees the state legislature from the constraints in the state constitution that created it. Moreover, the Florida Legislature's own decision to employ a unitary code for all elections indicates that it intended the Florida Supreme Court to play the same role in Presidential elections that it has historically played in resolving electoral disputes. The Florida Supreme Court's exercise of appellate jurisdiction therefore was wholly consistent with, and indeed contemplated by, the grant of authority in Article II.

It hardly needs stating that Congress, pursuant to 3 U.S.C. § 5, did not impose any affirmative duties upon the States that their governmental branches could "violate." Rather, § 5 provides a safe harbor for States to select electors in contested elections "by judicial or other methods" established by laws prior to the election day. Section 5, like Article II, assumes the involvement of the state judiciary in interpreting state election laws and resolving election disputes under those laws. Neither § 5 nor Article II grants federal judges any special authority to substitute their views for those of the state judiciary on matters of state law.

Nor are petitioners correct in asserting that the failure of the Florida Supreme Court to specify in detail the precise manner in which the "intent of the voter," . . . is to be determined rises to the level of a constitutional violation. We found such a violation when individual votes within the same State were weighted unequally, . . . but we have never before called into question the substantive standard by which a State determines that a vote has been legally cast. And there is no reason to think that the guidance provided to the factfinders, specifically the various canvassing boards, by the "intent of the voter" standard is any less sufficient—or will lead to results any less uniform—than, for example, the "beyond a reasonable doubt" standard employed everyday by ordinary citizens in courtrooms across this country.

Admittedly, the use of differing substandards for determining voter intent in different counties employing similar voting systems may raise serious concerns. Those concerns are alleviated—if not eliminated—by the fact that a single impartial magistrate will ultimately adjudicate all objections arising from the recount process. Of course, as a general matter, "the interpretation of constitutional principles must not be too literal. We must remember that the machinery of government would not work if it were not allowed a little play in its joints." . . . If it were otherwise, Florida's decision to leave to each county the determination of what balloting system to employ—despite enormous differences in accuracy—might run afoul of equal protection. So, too, might the similar decisions of the vast majority of state legislatures to delegate to local authorities certain decisions with respect to voting systems and ballot design.

Even assuming that aspects of the remedial scheme might ultimately be found to violate the Equal Protection Clause, I could not subscribe to the majority's disposition of the case. As the majority explicitly holds, once a state legislature determines to select electors through a popular vote, the right to have one's vote counted is of constitutional stature. As the majority further acknowledges, Florida law holds that all ballots that reveal the intent of the voter constitute valid votes.

Recognizing these principles, the majority nonetheless orders the termination of the contest proceeding before all such votes have been tabulated. Under their own reasoning, the appropriate course of action would be to remand to allow more specific procedures for implementing the legislature's uniform general standard to be established.

In the interest of finality, however, the majority effectively orders the disenfranchisement of an unknown number of voters whose ballots reveal their intent—and are therefore legal votes under state law—but were for some reason rejected by ballot-counting machines. It does so on the basis of the deadlines set forth in Title 3 of the United States Code. . . . But, as I have already noted, those provisions merely provide rules of decision for Congress to follow when selecting among conflicting slates of electors. . . . They do not prohibit a State from counting what the majority concedes to be legal votes until a bona fide winner is determined. . . . [N]othing prevents the majority, even if it properly found an equal protection violation, from ordering relief appropriate to remedy that violation without depriving Florida voters of their right to have their votes counted. As the majority notes, "[a] desire for speed is not a general excuse for ignoring equal protection guarantees." . . .

Finally, neither in this case, nor in its earlier opinion in *Palm Beach County Canvassing Bd. v. Harris,* . . . did the Florida Supreme Court make any substantive change in Florida electoral law. Its decisions were rooted in long-established precedent and were consistent with the relevant statutory provisions, taken as a whole. It did what courts do—it decided the case before it in light of the legislature's intent to leave no legally cast vote uncounted. In so doing, it relied on the sufficiency of the general "intent of the voter" standard articulated by the state legislature, coupled with a procedure for ultimate review by an impartial judge, to resolve the concern about disparate evaluations of contested ballots. If we assume—as I do—that the members of that court and the judges who would have carried out its mandate are impartial, its decision does not even raise a colorable federal question.

What must underlie petitioners' entire federal assault on the Florida election procedures is an unstated lack of confidence in the impartiality and capacity of the state judges who would make the critical decisions if the vote count were to proceed. Otherwise, their position is wholly without merit. The endorsement of that position by the majority of this Court can only lend credence to the most cynical appraisal of the work of judges throughout the land. It is confidence in the men and women who administer the judicial system that is the true backbone of the rule of law. Time will one day heal the wound to that confidence that will be inflicted by today's decision. One thing, however, is certain. Although we may never know with complete certainty the identity of the winner of this year's Presidential election, the identity of the loser is perfectly clear. It is the Nation's confidence in the judge as an impartial guardian of the rule of law.

I respectfully dissent.

JUSTICE SOUTER, dissenting.

The Court should not have reviewed either *Bush v. Palm Beach County Canvassing Bd.*, . . . or this case, and should not have stopped Florida's attempt to recount all undervote ballots . . . by issuing a stay of the Florida Supreme Court's orders during the period of this review. . . . If this Court had allowed the State to follow the course indicated by the opinions of its own Supreme Court, it is entirely possible that there would ultimately have been no issue requiring our review, and political tension could have worked itself out in the Congress following the procedure provided in 3 U.S.C. § 15. The case being before us, however, its resolution by the majority is another erroneous decision.

. . .

It is only on the third issue before us [Equal Protection] that there is a meritorious argument for relief. . . . It is an issue that might well have been dealt with adequately by the Florida courts if the state proceedings had not been interrupted, and if not disposed of at the state level it could have been considered by the Congress in any electoral vote dispute. But because the course of state proceedings has been interrupted, time is short, and the issue is before us, I think it sensible for the Court to address it.

Petitioners have raised an equal protection claim (or, alternatively, a due process claim), . . . in the charge that unjustifiably disparate standards are applied in different electoral jurisdictions to otherwise identical facts. It is true that the Equal Protection Clause does not forbid the use of a variety of voting mechanisms within a jurisdiction, even though different mechanisms will have different levels of effectiveness in recording voters' intentions; local variety can be justified by concerns about cost, the potential value of innovation, and so on. But evidence in the record here suggests that a different order of disparity obtains under rules for determining a voter's intent that have been applied (and could continue to be applied) to identical types of ballots used in identical brands of machines and exhibiting identical physical characteristics (such as "hanging" or "dimpled" chads). . . . I can conceive of no legitimate state interest served by these differing treatments of the expressions of voters' fundamental rights. The differences appear wholly arbitrary.

In deciding what to do about this, we should take account of the fact that electoral votes are due to be cast in six days. I would therefore remand the case to the courts of Florida with instructions to establish uniform standards for evaluating the several types of ballots that have prompted differing treatments, to be applied within and among counties when passing on such identical ballots in any further recounting (or successive recounting) that the courts might order.

Unlike the majority, I see no warrant for this Court to assume that Florida could not possibly comply with this requirement before the date set for the meeting of electors, December 18. . . . To recount these [votes] manually would be a tall order, but before this Court stayed the effort to do that the courts of Florida were ready to do their best to get that job done. There is no justification for denying the State the opportunity to try to count all disputed ballots now.

I respectfully dissent.

JUSTICE GINSBURG, dissenting.

The CHIEF JUSTICE acknowledges that provisions of Florida's Election Code "may well admit of more than one interpretation." . . . But instead of respecting the state high court's province to say what the State's Election Code means, THE CHIEF JUSTICE maintains that Florida's Supreme Court has veered so far from the ordinary practice of judicial review that what it did cannot properly be called judging. My colleagues have offered a reasonable construction of Florida's law. Their construction coincides with the view of one of Florida's seven Supreme Court justices. . . . I might join THE CHIEF JUSTICE were it my commission to interpret Florida law. But disagreement with the Florida court's interpretation of its own State's law does not warrant the conclusion that the justices of that court have legislated. There is no cause here to believe that the members of Florida's high court have done less than "their mortal best to discharge their oath of office," . . . and no cause to upset their reasoned interpretation of Florida law.

This Court more than occasionally affirms statutory, and even constitutional, interpretations with which it disagrees. . . . Surely the Constitution does not call upon us to pay more respect to a federal administrative agency's construction of federal law than to a state high court's interpretation of its own state's law. And not uncommonly, we let stand state-court interpretations of federal law with which we might disagree. . . .

In deferring to state courts on matters of state law, we appropriately recognize that this Court acts as an "'outsider' lacking the common exposure to local law which comes from sitting in the jurisdiction." . . . That recognition has sometimes prompted us to resolve doubts about the meaning of state law by certifying issues to a State's highest court, even when federal rights are at stake. . . . Notwithstanding our authority to decide issues of state law underlying federal claims, we have used the certification device to afford state high courts an opportunity to inform us on matters of their own State's law because such restraint "helps build a cooperative judicial federalism."

. . .

THE CHIEF JUSTICE says that Article II, by providing that state legislatures shall direct the manner of appointing electors, authorizes federal superintendence over the relationship between state courts and state legislatures, and licenses a departure from the usual deference we give to state court interpretations of state law. . . . The Framers of our Constitution, however, understood that in a republican government, the judiciary would construe the legislature's enactments. . . . In light of the constitutional guarantee to States of a "Republican Form of Government," U.S. Const., Art. IV, § 4, Article II can hardly be read to invite this Court to disrupt a State's republican regime. Yet THE CHIEF JUSTICE today would reach out to do just that. By holding that Article II requires our revision of a state court's construction of state laws in order to protect one organ of the State from another, THE CHIEF JUSTICE contradicts the basic principle that a State may organize itself as it sees fit. . . . Article II does not call for the scrutiny undertaken by this Court.

The extraordinary setting of this case has obscured the ordinary principle that dictates its proper resolution: Federal courts defer to state high courts' interpretations of their state's own law. This principle reflects the core of federalism, on which all agree. "The Framers split the atom of sovereignty. It was the genius of their idea that our citizens would have two political capacities, one state and one federal, each protected from incursion by the other." . . . THE CHIEF JUSTICE's solicitude for the Florida Legislature comes at the expense of the more fundamental solicitude we owe to the legislature's sovereignty. . . . Were the other members of this Court as mindful as they generally are of our system of dual sovereignty, they would affirm the judgment of the Florida Supreme Court.

. . .

The Court assumes that time will not permit "orderly judicial review of any disputed matters that might arise." . . . But no one has doubted the good faith and diligence with which Florida election officials, attorneys for all sides of this controversy, and the courts of law have performed their duties. Notably, the Florida Supreme Court has produced two substantial opinions within 29 hours of oral argument. In sum, the Court's conclusion that a constitutionally adequate recount is impractical is a prophecy the Court's own judgment will not allow to be tested. Such an untested prophecy should not decide the Presidency of the United States.

I dissent.

JUSTICE BREYER, dissenting.

The Court was wrong to take this case. It was wrong to grant a stay. It should now vacate that stay and permit the Florida Supreme Court to decide whether the recount should resume.

. . .

[T]here is no justification for the majority's remedy, which is simply to reverse the lower court and halt the recount entirely. An appropriate remedy would be, instead, to remand this case with instructions that, even at this late date, would permit the Florida Supreme Court to require recounting all undercounted votes in Florida, including those from Broward, Volusia, Palm Beach, and Miami-Dade Counties, whether or not previously recounted prior to the end of the protest period, and to do so in accordance with a single-uniform substandard.

The majority justifies stopping the recount entirely on the ground that there is no more time. In particular, the majority relies on the lack of time for the Secretary to review and approve equipment needed to separate undervotes. But the majority reaches this conclusion in the absence of any record evidence that the recount could not have been completed in the time allowed by the Florida Supreme Court. The majority finds facts outside of the record on matters that state courts are in a far better position to address. Of course, it is too late for any such recount to take place by December 12, the date by which election disputes must be decided if a State is to take advantage of the safe harbor provisions of 3 U.S.C. § 5. Whether there is time to conduct a recount prior to December 18, when the electors are scheduled to meet, is a matter for the state courts to determine. And whether, under Florida law, Florida could or could not take further action is obviously a matter for Florida courts, not this Court, to decide. . . .

By halting the manual recount, and thus ensuring that the uncounted legal votes will not be counted under any standard, this Court crafts a remedy out of proportion to the asserted harm. And that remedy harms the very fairness interests the Court is attempting to protect. The manual recount would itself redress a problem of unequal treatment of ballots. As JUSTICE STEVENS points out, . . . the ballots of voters in counties that use punch-card systems are more likely to be disqualified than those in counties using optical-scanning systems. According to recent news reports, variations in the undervote rate are even more pronounced. . . . Thus, in a system that allows counties to use different types of voting systems, voters already arrive at the polls with an unequal chance that their votes will be counted. I do not see how the fact that this results from counties' selection of different voting machines rather than a court order makes the outcome any more fair. Nor do I understand why the Florida Supreme Court's recount order, which helps to redress this inequity, must be entirely prohibited based on a deficiency that could easily be remedied.

. . .

[T]he Court is not acting to vindicate a fundamental constitutional principle, such as the need to protect a basic human liberty. No other strong reason to act is present. Congressional statutes tend to obviate the need. And, above all, in this highly politicized matter, the appearance of a split decision runs the risk of undermining the public's confidence in the Court itself. That confidence is a public treasure. It has been built slowly over many years, some of which were marked by a Civil War and the tragedy of segregation. It is a vitally necessary ingredient of any successful effort to protect basic liberty and, indeed, the rule of law itself. We run no risk of returning to the days when a President (responding to this Court's efforts to protect the Cherokee Indians) might have said, "John Marshall has made his decision; now let him enforce it!" ... But we do risk a self-inflicted wound—a wound that may harm not just the Court, but the Nation.

I fear that in order to bring this agonizingly long election process to a definitive conclusion, we have not adequately attended to that necessary "check upon our own exercise of power," "our own sense of self-restraint." ... Justice Brandeis once said of the Court, "The most important thing we do is not doing." ... What it does today, the Court should have left undone. I would repair the damage done as best we now can, by permitting the Florida recount to continue under uniform standards.

I respectfully dissent.

number of disputed county returns used these IBM voting machines and where determining the intent of the voter based on "hanging" or "dimpled" chads lay at the heart of the equal protection arguments that ended the election (see also *Bush v. Gore; Gore v. Harris;* Overvotes; Undervotes).

Circuit Court of Appeals

Middle level of the federal judicial system, the thirteen federal circuit courts hear appeals from the federal district courts (trial courts). Broken down into eleven geographic regions (plus two specialized courts in Washington, D.C.) the circuit courts of appeals provide the first appellate review of most civil rights matters, including the right to vote.

Colegrove v. Green

1946 Supreme Court case in which the Court ruled that determining the proper application of state legislative districting was beyond the scope of the federal courts. "The remedy for unfairness in districting is to secure State legislatures that will apportion properly, or to invoke the ample powers of Congress," not to turn to the courts, which lacked the authority to enforce the remedies sought, the Court ruled. "The Constitution has many commands that are not enforceable by courts because they clearly fall outside the conditions and purposes that circumscribe judicial action"—and legislative districting was definitely one of them. "Courts ought not to enter this political thicket" (see also *Baker v. Carr;* Gerrymandering).

Constitutional Conventions

Special assemblies called to write or rewrite a state's basic foundational laws (its constitution). Constitutional conventions are primary forums for debating voting restrictions, especially in the nineteenth century. Between 1790 and 1860, for instance, most of the thirty-one states held at least one constitutional convention. Each dealt with the linked problems of representation (the apportionment of power in the form of legislative seats) and franchise (who could vote). The answers these conventions arrived at, in turn, lay a foundation for all subsequent debate over voting rights and the proper extent of the franchise.

Democracy

Technically, a form of government in which all forms of political power are held and applied by the entire population of a state or nation. More generally, democracy stands for any governing system in which the will and opinion of the people serve as the foundation of government formation and policy. In the United States, democratic principles began to shape the political and governing process beginning in the 1830s. Today, the United States has a democratic society and political system grafted on the republican structures of government implemented by the Constitution (see also Republic/Republicanism).

Dependency

Justification for eighteenth and early nineteenth century property qualifications for voting. At that time, established wisdom held that being dependent on others for the necessities of life—food, shelter, clothing—robbed an individual of the independence of spirit necessary to make the sort of "selfless" decisions necessary for popular government to work. Most colonies therefore imposed specific property qualifications for voting. Only those who owned property, especially tangible property like land, were felt to have made the solid commitment to society so necessary if they were to say no to the seductive inducements of faction and greed. Hence, only property holders were fit voters (see also Freeholders; Paupers; Property Qualifications).

Disenfranchisement (also Disfranchisement)

Process of denying a particular individual or group the vote. Also the process of taking the right to vote away from an individual or group that formerly had this right.

District Courts

Lowest level of the federal judicial system, district courts are trial courts, headed by a single judge and holding hearings to determine both the facts and the application of the law in individual cases. Federal district courts are the primary implementers of federal judicial rulings and policy in voting rights matters.

Eight-Box Rule

An 1882 South Carolina rule under which ballots for individual offices had to be placed in separate ballot boxes. Put a ballot in the wrong box, and it would not be counted. This was intentionally applied to disenfranchise illiterate black voters, for although the boxes were usually labeled properly, this meant little to illiterate black voters unable to read the labels. And, as if this were not enough, many election supervisors would shift the boxes around periodically resulting in countless misplaced—and hence uncounted—ballots (see also Disenfranchisement; Vote Denial).

Electoral College

Organized in Article II, sections 2 and 3 of the U.S. Constitution, the electoral college is the name given to the two-tiered system used to choose the president of the United States. As laid out by these sections, each state is assigned electors equal in number to its representatives and senators. In most states, electors are chosen by a *popular* vote. (Currently, all but two states appoint as their electors nominees who have promised to vote for the presidential candidate that received the *most* popular votes in that state, winner take all, even if by just one vote). A majority of electoral votes are required to win the presidency. Currently, the magic number for presidential victory is 270 electoral votes.

Elk v. Wilkins

An 1884 Supreme Court ruling refusing to extend the privileges and protections of the Fourteenth Amendment as regarded citizenship and voting rights to Indians despite the Fourteenth Amendment's explicit wording that "All persons born or naturalized in the United States, and subject to the jurisdiction thereof, are citizens of the United States and of the state wherein they reside." One of a series of Supreme Court rulings in the late nineteenth and early twentieth centuries refusing to apply the Fourteenth Amendment to enhance minority voting rights (see also Fourteenth Amendment; *Minor v. Happersett*).

Equal Protection

Legal/constitutional concept growing out of the Fourteenth Amendment's order that no state shall "deny to any person within its jurisdiction the equal protection of the laws." This means that no state law or procedure can treat or affect one group or segment of the population any differently than any other group or population segment—the law must be evenhanded in its actions. This does not mean that a state cannot discriminate in how it treats its residents; just that either (a) the discrimination has to affect all residents equally or (b) the state can show that this discrimination was both necessary and the only practical way that the state could fulfill a required governmental function. In practical terms this means that some variation of treatment under the law is acceptable if the state can prove to the courts the overriding need for disparate action. Foundation to the Supreme Court's ruling in *Bush v. Gore* (see also *Bush v. Gore;* Fourteenth Amendment).

Federalism

The political concept of split sovereignty or governmental authority. Specifically, the system of shared power between the states and the national government as set up by the Constitution. In practical terms, the idea that some matters of public business are *not* the concern of the national government (or alternately, of the state governments). This split authority includes jurisdiction over voting where, for most of United States history, state authority to regulate the election process was held supreme and controlling. This constitutional understanding only changed in the mid to late twentieth century (see also *Baker v. Carr; Colegrove v. Green; Smith v. Allwright*).

Felony Restrictions

Prohibitions on convicted felons voting. Before the Civil War, twenty-five state constitutions instituted bans on felons voting. The common consensus was that criminals forfeited their rights to independence, and hence the vote, by their acts against the community. By the early twentieth century, all forty-eight states applied some sort of voting proscription for criminal activity. Many included all convicted felons. Most left the date of redemption undetermined. In most states, they continue in force today, widely seen as a legitimate retribution for past acts and essential deterrence against future wrongs.

Fifteenth Amendment

Adopted in 1870, this amendment to the U.S. Constitution ordered that "the right of citizens of the United States to vote shall not be denied or abridged by the United States or by any state on account of race, color, or previous condition of servitude." Currently, along with the Fourteenth Amendment, serves as the constitutional source of the national government's power to regulate the election process.

Fourteenth Amendment

Adopted in 1868, this amendment to the U.S. Constitution ordered, among other provisions, that "All persons born or naturalized in the United States, and subject to the jurisdiction thereof, are citizens of the United States and of the state wherein they reside. No state shall make or enforce any law which shall abridge the privileges or immunities of citizens of the United States; nor shall any state deprive any person of life, liberty, or property, without due process of law; nor deny to any person within its jurisdiction the equal protection of the laws." Currently, along with the Fifteenth Amendment, serves as the constitutional source of the national government's power to regulate the election process.

Franchise

Technical term for the right to vote and the process of voting.

Frankfurter, Felix

Supreme Court justice appointed to the Court in January, 1939, by President Franklin D. Roosevelt, Frankfurter was a vocal opponent of judicial intervention in the voting rules and procedures of the states. Author of the Court's opinion in *Colegrove v. Green* and a strong dissent in *Baker v. Carr,* Frankfurter is most famous in the realm of voting rights for his depiction of voting rights litigation as a "political thicket."

Freeholders/Non-Freeholders

Technical term for those owning real property (for example, land), and thus permitted under colonial and early U.S. state laws to vote.

Those lacking property and thus the right to vote were known as non-freeholders.

Gerrymander/Gerrymandering

Process of shifting a legislative district's borders to achieve a specific electoral result. When done for reasons of political advantage (for example, to help one political party gain electoral success over another), gerrymandering is constitutionally acceptable. When done to keep unpopular minority groups from voting, or to dilute the political clout of a particular minority group, gerrymanders are constitutionally prohibited (see also Legislative Redistricting).

Ginsburg, Ruth Bader

Supreme Court justice appointed to the Court on June 22, 1993, by President William J. Clinton, Ginsburg was part of the dissent in *Bush v. Gore*. Angrily taking the majority in this case to task, Ginsburg complained that "the extraordinary setting of this case has obscured the ordinary principle that dictates its proper resolution: Federal courts defer to state high courts' interpretations of their state's own law." That they did not do this—and in fact, did not for as limited a reason as "time will not permit an 'orderly judicial review of any disputed matters that might arise'"—was improper. "No one has doubted the good faith and diligence with which Florida election officials, attorneys for all sides of this controversy, and the courts of law have performed their duties." Yet, the Court has adopted a conclusion that "is a prophecy the Court's own judgment will not allow to be tested." Such untested prophecies, Justice Ginsburg concluded, "should not decide the Presidency of the United States." Lacking all respect for the majority's logic, and perhaps distrusting their motives, Justice Ginsburg broke with tradition and ended her views in *Bush v. Gore* bluntly: "I dissent" (see also *Bush v. Gore*).

Gray v. Sanders

A 1963 Supreme Court ruling overturning Georgia's county-unit method of primary elections that gave rural voters a significantly heavier weight than urban voters. "How then can one person be given twice or ten times the voting power of another person in a statewide election merely because he lives in a rural area or because he lives in the smallest rural county?" The Court's answer was that one cannot. "Once the geographical unit for which a representative is to be chosen is designated, all who participate in the election are to have an equal vote—whatever their race, whatever their sex, whatever their occupation, whatever their income, and wherever their home may be in that geographical unit. . . . The concept of 'we the people' under the Constitution visualizes no preferred class of voters but equality among those who meet the basic qualifications. The idea that every voter is equal to every other voter in his State, when he casts his ballot in favor of one of several competing candidates, underlies many of our decisions." The standard to be applied in such cases, the Court concluded, was a simple, yet effective one—"one person, one vote" (see also *Baker v. Carr;* "One Man/One Vote"; *Reynolds v. Sims*).

Harlan, John Marshall

Supreme Court justice appointed to the Court on January 10, 1955, by President Dwight Eisenhower, Harlan was a vocal opponent of the Supreme Court's foray into voting rights litigation. Dissenting in *Baker v. Carr,* the justice agreed with Justice Felix Frankfurter's assessment as to the dangers of the Court entering the political thicket of legislative districting, arguing that the "lack of standards by which to decide such cases as this, is relevant not only to the question of 'justiciability,' but also, and perhaps more fundamentally, to the determination whether any cognizable constitutional claim has been asserted in this case." (His answer was no). In *Reynolds v. Sims,* Harlan supported Justice Potter Stewart's attack on the one person/one vote concept as uncalled for and dangerous. In the years that followed, Justice Harlan continued his vocal opposition to the one person/one vote concept. In 1969's *Allen v. State Board of Elections,* he expressed reservations about the extension of section 5 preclearance to include "all those laws that could arguably have an impact on Negro voting power, even though the manner in which the election is conducted remains unchanged." As he read the VRA, this was much too wide an interpretation of Congress's intent and, worse yet, "require[d] a revolutionary innovation in American government that goes far beyond that which was accomplished by [section] 4." Troubling as it might be, vote dilution—such as that imposed by at-large voting systems—was beyond the proper scope of the VRA, Harlan concluded. To force preclearance beyond its proper scope was not only to grant the federal courts a power they did not rightly have, but to empower one segment of the population (southern blacks) with protections they did not need, nor properly have claim to, as the law was currently written (see also *Allen v. State Board of Elections; Baker v. Carr; Gray v. Sanders; Reynolds v. Sims*).

Harris, Katherine

Florida secretary of state during the 2000 election, Harris was that state's primary election official, and as such, was caught in the middle of the entire Florida election controversy. A Republican (and, in fact, co-chair of George W. Bush's election team in Florida), Harris's rulings against hand recounts in November 2000 led to charges of bias and improper action. She was also named defendant in the Florida Supreme Court case, *Gore v. Harris,* that preceded the U.S. Supreme Court's ruling in *Bush v. Gore* (see also *Bush v. Gore; Gore v. Harris*).

Legislative Districting/Redistricting

Process of redrawing the borders of a legislative or other governmental voting district. Under federal law, states must redraw their congressional district lines following the national census every ten years. Currently, states are also required to redistrict state and local political boundaries in compliance with the judicial doctrine of one person/one vote (see also "One Man/One Vote"; Gerrymandering; *Reynolds v. Sims*).

Literacy Requirements

Rules denying the vote to those unable to read. The uneducated, the argument went, lacked the intelligence, knowledge, and mental capacity necessary to be a proper voter. Reading requirements thus had the same general intent of excluding those deemed "unfit" by nature of their personal status to vote (in this case as an illiterate) as did earlier property qualifications and later "understanding" rules (see also Paupers; Property Qualifications; "Understanding" Rules; Vote Denial).

Majority Vote Requirements

Rules requiring that candidates for any state office receive a *majority* of the votes cast to win their seat, not merely a plurality (the largest number) of those cast—a common occurrence in at-large election systems wherein multiple candidates run for the same office. This requirement was specifically designed to undermine the chances that large black pluralities could slip in a candidate in at-large elections through single-shot voting (see also Single-Shot Voting; Vote Dilution).

Majority-Minority Districts/Districting

Voting districts deliberately structured to ensure that a majority of voters within a district were of a single minority group. In practical terms, the creation of minority-majority districts involved subdividing large, heterogeneous districts (usually those applying at-large voting systems) into smaller, homogeneous, single-member districts wherein minority voters were the majority. The expectation was that bringing together minority voters into a single district would allow these voters to effectively elect candidates of their choice in numbers roughly proportional to their percentages in the general population. Adopted as part of the federal courts' ongoing efforts to give practical meaning to the voting rights of long excluded minorities, majority-minority districts have become the primary mechanism used to combat minority vote dilution (see also At-Large Elections; Gerrymandering; Single-Member Districts).

Marshall, Thurgood

Supreme Court justice appointed to the Court on June 13, 1967, by President Lyndon Baines Johnson, Marshall was a strong supporter of expanded judicial review of voting rights matters. Earlier in his career, as chief counsel of the NAACP's Legal Defense Fund, Marshall served as lead counsel in *Smith v. Allwright* (see also *Smith v. Allwright*).

McKay v. Campbell

An 1871 Federal District Court of Oregon case challenging rules denying citizenship, and hence the right to vote, to Indians despite the explicit wording of the Fourteenth Amendment that "All persons born or naturalized in the United States, and subject to the jurisdiction thereof, are citizens of the United States and of the state wherein they reside." Ruling in this matter, District Judge Matthew Deady upheld the ban on Indian citizenship. "Being born a member of 'an independent political community' [McKay] was not born subject to the jurisdiction of the United States—not born in its allegiance." As such, McKay could not be a citizen without being naturalized first. The decision as to naturalization, in turn, was "a matter within the exclusive cognizance of congress," and hence beyond the scope of judicial remedy. One of a series of federal court rulings in the late nineteenth and early twentieth centuries refusing to apply the Fourteenth Amendment to enhance minority voting rights (see also *Minor v. Happersett,* Vote Denial).

Minor v. Happersett

An 1874 Supreme Court ruling denying women the vote under the Fourteenth Amendment. "There is no doubt that women may be citizens. They are persons, and by the fourteenth amendment 'all persons born or naturalized in the United States and subject to the jurisdiction thereof' are expressly declared to be 'citizens of the United States and of the State wherein they reside'," the Court ruled. Yet to say that women are citizens did not mean that they were necessarily empowered to vote. Voting was not a "privilege or immunity" granted by the Constitution. "For nearly ninety years the people have acted upon the idea that the Constitution, when it conferred citizenship, did not necessarily confer the right of suffrage." Therefore, the "Constitution of the United States does not confer the right of suffrage upon any one, and that the constitutions and laws of the several States which commit that important trust to men alone are not necessarily void," the justices concluded. One of a series of Supreme Court rulings in the late nineteenth and early twentieth centuries refusing to apply the Fourteenth Amendment to enhance minority voting rights (see also *Elk v. Wilkins;* Fourteenth Amendment; Nineteenth Amendment).

Nineteenth Amendment

Adopted in 1920, this amendment to the U.S. Constitution ordered that "the right of citizens of the United States to vote shall not be denied or abridged by the United States or by any state on account of sex." The result was the enfranchisement of most of the nation's adult women.

Nixon v. Herndon and Nixon v. Condon

The 1927 and 1932 Supreme Court rulings attacking aspects of the Texas all-white primary as unconstitutional discriminations. "While states may do a good deal of classifying that is difficult to believe rational," wrote Justice Oliver Wendell Holmes in 1927, "there are limits [to this power], and it is too clear for extended argument that color cannot be made the basis of a statutory classification affecting the right" to vote in a primary election. Five years later, Justice Benjamin N. Cardozo again held that Texas Democratic Party was not a simple voluntary association in primary elections. Rather, its organization and control of these elections derived directly from a "grant of power" from the state, and hence was a prohibited "state action" under the Fourteenth Amendment. In both cases, however, these rulings proved limited in their impact. Both Holmes and Cardozo left loopholes that allowed Texas Democrats to continue their all-white primaries. Not until 1944's *Smith v. Allwright* would the all-white primary be finally defeated (see also All-White Primary; *Smith v. Allwright*).

O'Connor, Sandra Day

Supreme Court justice appointed to the Court on August 19, 1981, by President Ronald Reagan, O'Connor was the lead author in 1993's *Shaw v. Reno*, arguing that "reapportionment is one area in which appearances do matter." A reapportionment plan "that includes in one district individuals who belong to the same race, but who are otherwise widely separated by geographical and political boundaries, and who may have little in common with one another but the color of their skin, bears an uncomfortable resemblance to political apartheid. . . . By perpetuating such notions, a racial gerrymander may exacerbate the very patterns of racial bloc voting that majority-minority districting is sometimes said to counteract." In fact, wrote O'Connor, in some "exceptional cases, a reapportionment plan may be so highly irregular that, on its face, it rationally cannot be understood as anything other than an effort to 'segregate . . . voters' on the basis of race." For these reasons, the majority in *Shaw* concluded that "a plaintiff challenging a reapportionment statute under the Equal Protection Clause may state a claim by alleging that the legislation, though race neutral on its face, rationally cannot be understood as anything other than an effort to separate voters into different districts on the basis of race, and that the separation lacks sufficient justification." Where a state "concentrated a dispersed minority population in a single district, disregarding traditional districting principles such as compactness, contiguity, and respect for political subdivisions," a red flag of warning demanded a close examination to ensure that race was not the only determinant in creating the district (see also Gerrymandering; "One Man/One Vote"; Redistricting).

"One Man/One Vote"

Constitutional doctrine first promoted by the Supreme Court in 1963's *Gray v. Sanders* wherein the Court argued that "the concept of 'we the people' under the Constitution visualizes no preferred class of voters but equality among those who meet the basic qualifications. The idea that every voter is equal to every other voter in his State, when he casts his ballot in favor of one of several competing candidates, underlies many of our decisions." The standard to be applied in such cases was "one person, one vote." One year later in *Reynolds v. Sims* (1964) the Court took this concept and applied fully to the issue of legislative redistricting, ruling that "the Equal Protection Clause requires both houses of a state legislature to be apportioned on a population basis." The "fundamental goal" and "plain objective" of the Constitution, the Court explained, demanded the application of the "easily demonstrable" standard of one person/one vote. Anything less than "an honest and good faith effort" on the part of the State to reach this goal was constitutionally inadequate. The effect of this ruling was electric. Combined with 1965's Voting Rights Act, one person/one vote became the constitutional foundation for most of the judicial reform of voting rights in the late twentieth century (see also *Reynolds v. Sims* and *Gray v. Sanders*).

Overvotes

When a voter places a mark next to the names of more than one candidate for the same office. Such overvotes invalidate a ballot for that electoral race.

Ozawa v. United States

A 1922 Supreme Court case wherein the Court refused the plea of a Japanese immigrant challenging his denial of citizenship and hence the vote, noting how Asians were "clearly of a race [that] is not Caucasian and therefore belongs entirely outside the zone" of legal inclusion—at least pending a change in the laws. One of a series of Supreme Court rulings in the late nineteenth and early twentieth centuries refusing to apply the Fourteenth Amendment to enhance minority voting rights (see also *Elk v. Wilkins; Minor v. Happersett*).

Paupers

Individuals unable to financially support themselves and thus placed under the protection and control of government. By definition, paupers were felt to be dependent people unfit for public office and voting. As property owning requirements for voting were ended in the early nineteenth century, states replaced them with rules explicitly denying paupers the vote (see also Dependency; Property Qualifications).

Poll Tax

Rules imposing payment of a specific tax on voting. Originally adopted as either a revenue measure or an alternative to property owning requirements for the franchise, by the mid-nineteenth century, poll taxes had become primarily a technique of vote denial applied most stringently in the South where poll taxes served as the capstone to the region's race-based vote denial efforts. Declared unconstitutional for federal elections in 1964 by the Twenty-fourth Amendment, and for all elections by the Supreme Court in *Harper v. Virginia Board of Elections* (1966).

Preclearance

Rule imposed by section 5 of the 1965 VRA requiring that any state or county covered by the act's special provisions (prior to 1975 these included just southern states) seeking to modify its voting laws had to "preclear" these changes by submitting the proposed revision to the Justice Department and proving that the planned changes did "not have the purpose and . . . [would] not have the effect of denying or abridging the right to vote on account of race or color." All changes not precleared by the Justice Department (which had sixty days to object) were legally barred from implementation. Alternately, a state could file for a declaratory judgment with the U.S. District Court for the District of Columbia; a positive response by this court served the same purpose as preclearance by the Justice Department (see also Voting Rights Act of 1965).

Property Qualifications

Rules limiting the vote to only those who own a certain amount and/or type of property. Common in the Colonial, Revolutionary, and Early National periods of American history, property qualifications for voting were phased out in the first half of the nineteenth century (see also Dependency; Freeholders; Paupers).

Purging Laws

Rules that allowed either local election officials or a set number of qualified voters to challenge the status of any voter on the voting rolls and demand that this name be dropped from the election rolls. Though originally designed to promote the clearing out of nonvoters from the election lists, as applied in the South in the 1950s and 1960s, purging rules became another tool of vote denial aimed at excluding blacks from the polls (see also Disenfranchisement; Vote Denial).

Rehnquist, William H.

Supreme Court justice first appointed to the Court as associate justice on October 22, 1971, by President Richard M. Nixon and later appointed as chief justice on June 20, 1986 by President Ronald Reagan, Rehnquist is a strong conservative jurist and supporter of federalism who has voted in both the dissent and the majority against expansion of the judicial role in voting rights matters. Member of the majority in *Bush v. Gore*, Rehnquist wrote the strong concurrence (in which Justices Scalia and Thomas joined) defending the Court's actions in halting the recounts on equal protection and judicial activism grounds (see also *Bush v. Gore; Shaw v. Reno*).

Republic/Republicanism

Technically, a form of government in which political power rests in the hands of a select number of representatives of the wider population. More generally, republicanism stands for any form of representative government in which the will of the people is expressed by popularly elected representatives. Republicanism is thus the foundation of American governing/political doctrine, its concepts infusing the writing of the U.S. Constitution and the subsequent formation of U.S. government (see also Democracy).

Reynolds v. Sims

A 1964 Supreme Court case in which the Court held that "[l]egislators represent people, not trees or acres. . . . As long as ours is a representative form of government, and our legislatures are those instruments of government elected directly by and directly representative of the people, the right to elect legislators in a free and unimpaired fashion is a bedrock of our political system." The Court therefore ruled that "the Equal Protection Clause requires both houses of a state legislature to be apportioned on a population basis." The "fundamental goal" and "plain objective" of the Constitution demanded the application of the "easily demonstrable" standard of one person/one vote. Applied in future cases, the one person/one vote doctrine became the constitutional foundation for most of the judicial reform of voting rights in the late twentieth century (see also *Baker v. Carr; Gray v. Sanders;* Legislative Districting; "One Man/One Vote").

Scalia, Antonin

Supreme Court justice appointed to the Court on June 24, 1986, by President Ronald Reagan, Scalia is a strong conservative jurist and supporter of federalism who has voted in both the dissent and the majority against expansion of the judicial role in voting rights matters. Member of the majority in *Bush v. Gore,* Scalia joined in Chief Justice Rehnquist's concurrence defending the Court's actions in halting the recounts on equal protection and judicial activism grounds. Scalia also wrote a strong concurrence to the Court's earlier stay order halting the Florida recount and accepting jurisdiction over *Bush v. Gore,* which implied his precommitment to ending the election quickly (see also *Bush v. Gore*).

Shaw v. Reno

A 1993 Supreme Court legislative redistricting case wherein the Court ruled that "reapportionment is one area in which appearances do matter" and that "a reapportionment plan that includes in one district individuals who belong to the same race, but who are otherwise widely separated by geographical and political boundaries, and who may have little in common with one another but the color of their skin, bears an uncomfortable resemblance to political apartheid." For these reasons, the majority in *Shaw* concluded that "a plaintiff challenging a reapportionment statute under the Equal Protection Clause may state a claim by alleging that the legislation, though race neutral on its face, rationally cannot be understood as anything other than an effort to separate voters into different districts on the basis of race, and that the separation lacks sufficient justification." Where a state "concentrated a dispersed minority population in a single district, disregarding traditional districting principles such as compactness, contiguity, and respect for political subdivisions," a red flag of warning demanded a close examination to ensure that race was not the only determinant in creating the district. Though subsequent litigation at the trial level would determine that the district in question was properly organized, the concept that districts organized solely on the basis of race were unconstitutional violations of equal protection called into question the validity of twenty years of majority-minority districting (see also Gerrymandering; Legislative Redistricting; Majority-Minority Districting; O'Connor, Justice Sandra Day).

Single-Shot Voting

Under an at-large election system, all candidates run against each other, with the top vote-getters filling the available seats. Single-shot voting occurs where a particular subgroup withhold some of their votes to ensure that their preferred candidate is one of the top vote-getters. Beginning in the 1950s, most southern states passed laws ordering that all ballots failing to include a full slate of preferences were disqualified, making single-shot voting impossible, and thus undermining the ability of blacks to elect even one candidate in an at-large election.

Smith v. Allwright

A 1944 Supreme Court case wherein the Supreme Court ruled that all-white primaries were unconstitutional violations of the Fifteenth Amendment. Political parties were agencies of the state when they ran primary elections, and as such fully contained within the Constitution's prohibitions against discriminatory treatment based on race. The culmination of a twenty-five year fight to end this vote denial scheme, the ruling in *Smith* was the first step in what became a slow, but ever-quickening judicial attack on vote denial and dilution.

Souter, David H.

Supreme Court justice appointed to the Court on July 25, 1990, by President George H. W. Bush, Souter is a moderate jurist who was troubled by the equal protection implications in the Florida recount process and thus voted with the majority in ordering a halt to recounts pending the establishment of uniform standards as to what was a proper vote. Souter was in the dissent, however, on the issue of remedy. Along with Justice Breyer, Souter strongly felt that the proper remedy was to return the case to the Florida Supreme Court for the creation of uniform voting standards. "If this Court had allowed the State to follow the course indicated by the opinions of its own Supreme Court," wrote Justice Souter, "it is entirely possible that there would ultimately have been no issue requiring our review, and political tension could have worked itself out in the Congress following the procedure provided in 3 U.S.C. § 15." Sadly it had not. And having wrongly taken up the case, the "resolution by the majority" was producing "another erroneous decision" (see also *Bush v. Gore*).

Stevens, John Paul

Supreme Court justice appointed to the Court on November 28, 1975, by President Gerald Ford, Stevens is a moderate to liberal jurist who opposed the Supreme Court's actions in *Bush v. Gore*. Stevens dissented both to the stay order (arguing that "to stop the counting of legal votes, the majority today departs from three venerable rules of judicial restraint that have guided the Court throughout its history. . . . The majority has acted unwisely") and the majority's per curiam ruling (concluding that "one thing, . . . is certain. Although we may never know with complete certainty the identity of the winner of this year's Presidential election, the identity of the loser is perfectly clear. It is the Nation's confidence in the judge as an impartial guardian of the rule of law") (see also *Bush v. Gore*).

Suffrage

The right to vote. Also the process of applying one's vote.

Terry v. Adams

Cases out of the Federal District Court for the Southern District of Texas (1950), the Fifth Circuit Court of Appeals (1952), and the Supreme Court (1953) that ultimately overturned the Texas Jaybird primary as an unconstitutional attempt to continue the all-white primaries prohibited by 1944's *Smith v. Allwright*. One of a series of lower federal court cases in the 1950s and early 1960s that struggled with the proper limits of race-based vote discrimination.

Thomas, Clarence

Supreme Court justice appointed to the Court on July 8, 1991, by President George H. W. Bush, Thomas is a conservative jurist who opposes expansion of judicial oversight of the voting rights process and any application of minority-majority legislative districting.

Three-Judge Courts

Special federal trial courts organized where a suit challenged the constitutionality of a state law or constitutional provision, three-judge courts were presided over by three judges drawn from both the district and circuit court levels and decisions were based on a majority vote. Appeals from three-judge courts go directly to the Supreme Court. Three-judge courts were a primary way that important voting rights litigation was litigated at the trial level.

"Understanding" Rules

Election rules limiting registration to only those able to "understand and explain" a specific public document, usually the state or federal constitution, as proof of their fitness to be a voter. Most common in the South (where they were employed to keep blacks from voting), enforcement of so-called good character and understanding tests were normally left to the discretion of unsympathetic, and usually hostile, local election officials whose standards were so demanding that even educated blacks had trouble passing these tests; for illiterate blacks, they proved to be an almost insurmountable barrier (see also Vote Denial; Vote Dilution).

Undervotes

When no mark is made by a voter for a particular electoral race. Such nonvotes are not counted in the final vote tallies.

United States v. Classic

A 1941 Supreme Court decision that Article I, Section 4 of the U.S. Constitution gave Congress the power to regulate primary elections "where the primary is by law made an integral part of the election machinery." An important first step in the Supreme Court's decision to invalidate the all-white primary in 1944's *Smith v. Allwright* (see also *Smith v. Allwright; Nixon v. Herndon*).

Universal Suffrage

Concept in which nearly everyone can vote. Over time, universal suffrage has become the ideal goal in voting rights matters. Historically, this term was used to denote what more accurately could be called "universal white manhood suffrage." Even today, the term allows for suffrage restrictions on the young, aliens, and felons.

Vote Denial

Concept and practice of excluding individuals or groups from the election process due to a perceived incapacity on the part of these individuals or group members to properly fulfill the role of voter.

Vote Dilution

Process wherein those in the majority systematically use voting rules, procedures, or practices to diminish the ability of a particular group or subgroup to vote for candidates of its choice. Vote dilution takes place when those in charge make is so difficult to vote, or make the voting process so complicated, that certain voters find that their vote has no meaning—and thus are effectively disenfranchised.

Voter Intimidation

The use of force or threats of force to keep the members of a particular group or subgroup from applying their franchise (see also Vote Denial).

Voter Registration

Rules regulating the voting process that all potential voters must follow if they are to legitimately apply their franchise and vote. In most cases, registration rules set a deadline prior to the election by which all voters must prove their qualifications to vote (residency requirements; citizenship requirements; age requirements) and be placed on the official voting rolls. Failure to register prior to an election disqualifies an otherwise lawful voter from voting in a particular election. Perfectly legitimate in the abstract, in the past voter registration rules have been made so complicated as to effectively exclude certain voters from the polls (see also Purging Laws; Vote Denial; Vote Dilution).

Voting Rights Act of 1965 (VRA)

Signed into law on August 6, 1965, the VRA was expressly designed to attack the race-based vote denial and vote dilution then prevalent across the South. The nineteen sections of the VRA imposed a new enforcement methodology for combating voting rights violations. Not only did it outlaw vote denial based on race or color (and later ethnicity) in section 2, it also gave both the executive branch and the courts a powerful new set of tools for voting rights enforcement. Among them were the power to appoint federal examiners and observers in whatever numbers the president felt necessary, prohibitions on literacy tests and poll taxes, and rules outlawing any action "under color of the law" that prevented qualified voters from voting or having their votes fairly counted. Most powerful were the "preclearance" provisions of section 5. Combined with the one person/one vote doctrine imposed on state legislative redistricting by

Reynolds v. Sims, the VRA is the foundation for most of the reform of voting rights in the late twentieth century (see also "One Man/One Vote"; "Preclearance"; Vote Denial; Vote Dilution).

White v. Regester

A 1973 Supreme Court case challenging at-large voting districts as unconstitutionally discriminatory denials of equal protection to minority voters. Growing out of Texas's long-standing denial of political power to blacks and Mexican Americans, *White* generated a trial record cataloging many and varied economic, social, educational, and political discriminations that combined to dilute minority voting strength. Swayed by the sheer bulk of discriminations— including such factors as the long history of state-sanctioned discrimination against blacks and Mexican Americans in Texas, the small number of blacks and Mexican Americans elected to office, and the existence of majority-vote and numbered-place rules designed to maintain white electoral dominance—the Supreme Court ruled that, viewed in the "totality of the circumstances," these factors were more than adequate to prove the existence of unconstitutional discriminations. In sum, Texas blacks and Mexican Americans "had less opportunity than did other residents in the district to participate in the political processes and to elect legislators of their choice." Hence, although multimember districts were still not unconstitutional per se, and disproportionate representation was not by itself evidence of a discriminatory intent, they could be determinative when viewed in the context of other "intensely local" factors. In so ruling against Texas's at-large voting system, the Supreme Court provided trial courts with both standards and a test for proving vote dilution (see also At-Large Voting; Vote Dilution).

Chronology

1619	Virginia planters vote for first time, electing members to the Colony's lower representative assembly (the House of Burgesses).
1715	Connecticut imposes first property qualifications for voting, demanding that voters own a freehold estate worth 40 shillings per year or £40 in personal property.
1727	New Hampshire becomes second colony to adopt laws grounding franchise on landownership, in this case land worth £50 or more.
1762	Virginia adopts a law requiring voters to own 50 acres of unimproved land to vote or, alternatively, 25 acres if the land is improved and has a house on it. This statute is updated by constitutional amendment in 1776.
1776	Declaration of Independence states principles of Revolution, in particular the concept "That all men are created equal; that they are endowed by their Creator with unalienable rights; that among these are life, liberty and the pursuit of happiness . . . that to secure these rights, governments are instituted among men, deriving their just powers from the consent of the governed." These egalitarian concepts are not, however, carried over into the new state constitutions, all of which continue to impose bans on voting based on class, gender, and race.
1776–1781	Eleven of the original thirteen states hold constitutional conventions in which they struggle with the problem of access to the franchise. All impose limits based on property ownership and bans on women voting. Most

	impose formal limits on voting by people of color, and all impose informal limits on blacks voting.
1786	"Independent Republic" of Vermont adopts universal white manhood suffrage without any property owning requirements.
1787	Constitutional Convention convenes in Philadelphia ultimately producing the U.S. Constitution. Troubled by the issue of who should vote for the new national government, the Convention compromises, allowing the states to determine who is an eligible voter in national elections and the rules under which such voters vote. This compromise effectively severs national citizenship from state citizenship as related to voting. The Constitution also sets up a two-tiered system for choosing president, soon known as the electoral college.
1788	Constitution ratified.
1788–1789	First national elections under the authority of the Constitution held over a three month period. George Washington elected first U.S. president.
1789	First national government formed under the authority of the Constitution convenes in New York City. Bill of Rights is passed by Congress and sent to states for ratification.
1790-1860	Eighteen new states enter union, each without property requirements for voting. (They either adopted universal white manhood suffrage or employed limited poll taxes in setting franchise requirements.) Old states begin to repeal property rules and either open polls to all free white male voters or, more common, impose poll tax requirements. Most states also impose pauper and felony voting restrictions.
1792	Kentucky bans those convicted of "bribery, perjury, forgery or other high crimes or misdemeanors" from voting.
1801	Maryland drops all property owning requirements for voting.
1810	South Carolina adopts rules banning paupers from the polls.
1818	Illinois adopts explicit ban on black voting. Connecticut adopts ban on voting by blacks and felons in revised state constitution.

1819	Alabama adopts explicit ban on black voting. Maine excludes "Indians not taxed" from the polls.
1820	New Jersey, Maryland, and Connecticut adopt laws expressly limiting the vote to whites. Missouri bans all those convicted of electoral bribery from voting for ten years.
1821	New York, while removing property qualifications for white males, imposes them (along with residency requirements) for blacks—in the process disenfranchising most of the state's African American residents. New York also adopts felony voting exclusion rules. Massachusetts drops all property owning rules for the franchise but imposes a poll tax requirement and adopts rules explicitly banning paupers from the polls.
1830	The U.S. Supreme Court, in *Cherokee Nation v. Georgia,* declares Indian tribes "domestic dependent nations" subject to the control and authority of the United States government in the same way that a "ward" was subject "to his guardian." This concept becomes a foundation for the ongoing denial of the franchise to Native Americans.
1831	Delaware adopts rules banning paupers and felons from the polls.
1835	North Carolina's 1835 Convention added the word *white* to its constitutional voting requirements to explicitly exclude black voting.
1838	Kentucky allows widows and unmarried women who own property subject to taxation to vote in school elections.
1840	Tennessee limits the vote to whites, but allows that "no person shall be disqualified from voting in any election on account of color, who is now a competent witness in a court of justice against a white man" (which, as blacks were barred from testifying in court against whites, still effectively excluded blacks from the polls).
1844	New Jersey adopts rules banning paupers and felons from the polls.
1845	Connecticut adopts universal manhood suffrage, dropping all property owning requirements to vote. Texas and Florida adopt new constitutions that explicitly ban black voting. Louisiana bans any person "under convic-

tion of any crime punishable with hard labor" from the polls.

1849   California adopts constitutional provision banning all persons convicted of any infamous crime from polls.

1850   Virginia drops all property owning and poll tax requirements for voting.

1855   Connecticut imposes literacy test for voting. Michigan allows women who are taxpayers to vote in school elections.

1857   Massachusetts imposes literacy test for voting.

1865   Missouri imposes literacy test for voting.

1867   Alabama imposes voting ban for "those convicted of treason, embezzlement of public funds, malfeasance in office crime punishable by imprisonment in penitentiary or bribery." Maryland adopts similar ban for those convicted of larceny or other infamous crimes.

1868   Passage of the Fourteenth Amendment (which reads in part, "All persons born or naturalized in the United States, and subject to the jurisdiction thereof, are citizens of the United States and of the state wherein they reside. No state shall make or enforce any law which shall abridge the privileges or immunities of citizens of the United States; nor shall any state deprive any person of life, liberty, or property, without due process of law; nor deny to any person within its jurisdiction the equal protection of the laws"). In time, this amendment would become one of the foundations of vote expansion. Mississippi excludes "Indians not taxed" from the polls.

1869   Territory of Wyoming extends complete franchise to women. Texas excludes from franchise all "Indians not taxed."

1870   Passage of the Fifteenth Amendment (which reads in part that "[t]he right of citizens of the United States to vote shall not be denied or abridged by the United States or by any state on account of race, color, or previous condition of servitude"). In time, this amendment would become one of the foundations of vote expansion. Territory of Utah extends full franchise to women. (This grant is annulled by Congress in 1887.) Missouri requires that immigrants seeking the vote declare their intent to become citizens (and thus to vote) "not less than one year nor more than five years before he offers to vote." Congress passes Civil Rights Enforcement Act to implement Fifteenth Amendment.

1871 Judge Matthew Deady of the District Court of Oregon holds in the case of *McKay v. Campbell* that, as Indian tribes were "independent political communities," their members were not fully covered by U.S. legal jurisdiction—including the right to citizenship based on place of birth. Congress passes Ku Klux Klan Act to combat racial violence intended to stop African American voting in the South.

1872 Supreme Court rules in *Minor v. Happersett* that the Fourteenth Amendment does not require the states to grant the vote to women. "There is no doubt that women may be citizens," argues the unanimous Court. "They are persons, and by the fourteenth amendment 'all persons born or naturalized in the United States and subject to the jurisdiction thereof' are expressly declared to be 'citizens of the United States and of the State wherein they reside.'" Yet to say that women are citizens did not mean that they were necessarily empowered to vote. The term "citizen" merely denotes "membership of a nation," identifying those who "owe [the nation] allegiance and [are] entitled to its protection . . . nothing more." Voting was not a "privilege or immunity" granted by the Constitution.

1873 Pennsylvania bars any person convicted of willful violation of election laws from the franchise. In an effort to disenfranchise black voters, Georgia passes a law permitting local election supervisors to close their registration rolls to new applicants *except* during those times when black farmers were too busy to register, such as planting or harvest time.

1874 Arkansas imposes voting ban on all convicted felons.

1875 Alabama excludes education requirements (literacy tests; understanding requirements) for voting. This provision is repealed in 1901.

1876 Colorado requires that naturalization has to take place at least four months before an election for a newly declared citizen to vote.

1877	In a compromise worked out to settle the disputed presidential election of 1876, northern Republicans agree to end their Reconstruction efforts in return for southern Democratic acceptance of Republican candidate Rutherford B. Hayes's victory. This compromise set the stage for the eventual disenfranchisement of blacks by southern states lasting through the 1950s and 1960s. In an effort to disenfranchise black voters, Georgia increases the amount of its poll tax, making payment of the tax cumulative before voters were permitted to cast their ballots. As a result, voters not only had to pay the present year's tax to vote, but all the accumulated back taxes imposed by state law—miss one year, and the cumulative and indefinite nature of the poll tax made it near impossible for poor black voters (and many white voters) ever to vote again.
1879	California requires that naturalization has to take place at least ninety days before an election for a newly declared citizen to vote.
1880	Mississippi allows women who were "heads of families" to vote in school elections. New York and Vermont allow all women citizens to vote in school elections.
1882	South Carolina implements the "Eight-Box Ballot Law." Under this rule, ballots for individual offices had to be placed in separate ballot boxes. Put a ballot in the wrong box, and it would not be counted. The result was the effective disenfranchisement of illiterate South Carolina blacks.
1883	Territory of Washington extends full franchise to women. (Declared unconstitutional by state supreme court in 1887.)
1884	The Supreme Court concludes in *Elk v. Wilkins* that the Fourteenth Amendment does not include Indians, even those who had assimilated into white society. Merely severing one's ties to the tribe of one's birth by "fully and completely surrender[ing]" to the "jurisdiction of the United States," was not enough for a Native American to claim citizenship, the justices ruled. Without explicit action on the part of Congress or the president, Indians were not citizens and as such, lacked all citizenship rights—especially the right to vote

1887	Territory of Montana extends full franchise to women. Kansas allows women to vote in municipal elections. Congress passes the General Allotment (or Dawes) Act, breaking up reservations and parceling the land among the individual tribe members with the intention of forcing the Indians to adopt "the habits of civilized life" by becoming landowners and farmers and thus become fit for citizenship and the franchise.
1889	Wyoming becomes first state to extend full franchise to women. Montana allows women to vote in elections involving taxation. Idaho excludes "Indians not taxed, who have not severed their tribal relations and adopted the habits of civilization" from the polls. North Dakota adopts similar provisions, as does Washington state.
1890	Mississippi implements the "Mississippi Plan" to disenfranchise blacks. It includes (1) a $2 poll tax payable before registration; (2) a literacy test in which voters had to read, understand, or interpret any section of the state constitution to the satisfaction of a white (and usually hostile) election official; (3) long-term residency rules demanding two years domicile within the state and one year within the voting district; and (4) permanent disenfranchisement for crimes felt most likely to be committed by blacks. States across the South soon adopt similar comprehensive disenfranchisement plans. Territory of Oklahoma and Washington allow women to vote in school elections.
1893	Colorado becomes second state to extend full franchise to women. Michigan allows literate women to vote in school, village, and city elections.
1895	In an effort to disenfranchise black voters, South Carolina requires all potential voters to read and explain any section of the state constitution provided by the local voting registrar prior to being allowed to register to vote. Utah continues grant of full franchise for women upon becoming a state and excludes from franchise all persons convicted of treason.
1896	Idaho extends full franchise to women. Washington amends its constitution to read that "Indians not taxed shall never be allowed the elective franchise." North Dakota allows Indians who have severed ties to their

tribes to vote. Texas requires that immigrants seeking the vote declare their intent to become citizens (and thus to vote) not less than six months before an election.

1896–1915   Adoption of all-white primaries in states across the South.

1898   Louisiana imposes a literacy test as a prerequisite for voting. Concerned with the potential of these rules to expel poor and illiterate whites from the polls, the state also adopts a grandfather clause, which allows those who had voted before 1867 (when blacks could not vote) or whose fathers and grandfathers had voted then, to waive the new requirements.

1900   North Carolina imposes a poll tax and adopts literacy tests administered by local registrars (who had full discretion as to which parts of the state constitution applicants had to read) as its primary tool of vote denial. In an effort to protect illiterate white voters, the state adds a grandfather clause similar to Louisiana's.

1901   Alabama imposes literacy test for voting.

1902   Virginia and New Hampshire impose literacy tests for voting.

1904   Texas imposes literacy test for voting.

1907   Georgia requires that voters "must be able to read in English any paragraph of state or U.S. Constitution and write the same in English." Oklahoma extends franchise to "persons of Indian descent" who are also "native of the United States."

1908   Georgia imposes literacy test for voting.

1910   Arizona and Washington extend full franchise to women. New Mexico excludes "Indians not taxed" from the polls.

1911   California extends full franchise to women, imposes literacy requirements for voting.

1912   Kansas and Oregon extend full franchise to women.

1913   Illinois passes law allowing women to vote in presidential elections.

1914   Montana and Nevada extend full franchise to women.

1917   New York extends full franchise to women. Indiana, Michigan, Nebraska, North Dakota, and Rhode Island pass laws permitting women to vote in presidential elections. Arkansas allows women to vote in primary elections only. Minnesota requires that Indians sever all ties to their tribe before being allowed to vote.

1918   Michigan, Oklahoma, and South Dakota extend full franchise to women. Texas allows women to vote in primary elections and nominating conventions.

1919   Indiana, Iowa, Maine, Minnesota, Missouri, Ohio, Tennessee, and Wisconsin pass laws permitting women to vote in presidential elections.

1920   Passage of Nineteenth Amendment (which reads that "[t]he right of citizens of the United States to vote shall not be denied or abridged by the United States or by any state on account of sex") extends a full franchise to all adult American women.

1922   The Supreme Court in *Ozawa v. United States* holds that as Asians are "clearly of a race [that] is not Caucasian," and hence, "belong entirely outside the zone" of legal inclusion—at least pending a change in the laws' content. The Court therefore holds that Asians have no constitutional claim under the Fourteenth or Fifteenth Amendments to demand that the states grant them the right to vote.

1923   Supreme Court in *Nixon v. Herndon* holds Texas's 1923 voting rights law imposing an all-white primary an unconstitutional violation of the Fourteenth Amendment. "It seems . . . hard to imagine a more direct and obvious infringement of the Fourteenth Amendment," the justices rule. Unfortunately, as this opinion dealt only with the explicit prohibition of black voting by the legislature, the Court's ruling left a loophole within which the state could continue the all-white primary by devolving this power back to the Democratic Party. In fact, soon after the Supreme Court's ruling, a special session of the state legislature amended Texas's primary voting law, deleting provisions explicitly barring black voting, and allowing the Democratic Party Executive Committee to impose any new rules it saw fit—rules that, when adopted by that committee, produced the same results as the law just repealed.

1924　Indian Enfranchisement Act grants all Native Americans, assimilated or not, full citizenship including the right to vote.

1932　In *Nixon v. Condon,* the Supreme Court rules that the Texas Democratic Party was not a simple voluntary association—at least as regards primary elections. Rather, the party was an agent to the state, deriving its authority directly from a "grant of power" from the state, and as such, its imposition of an all-white primary was a form of prohibited "state action" under the Fourteenth Amendment. However, as with the Court's earlier opinion attacking the Texas all-white primary, this ruling left a loophole through which the Texas Democrats could circumvent the Court's intent, permitting in the process the Democratic Party convention to legally impose these same restrictions on black voting. As the justices pointed out, this body had never declared its "will to bar negroes of the state from admission to the party ranks." Soon thereafter, the state Democratic Party did just this, voting to exclude black members.

1935　Supreme Court in *Grovey v. Townsend* accepts the Texas Democratic Party convention's updated rules barring blacks from the Democratic primary. This permits the practice of all-white primaries to continue for another twelve years.

1941　Supreme Court rules in *United States v. Classic* that Article I, Section 4 of the U.S. Constitution gives Congress the power to regulate primary elections "where the primary is by law made an integral part of the election machinery." This ruling paves the way for the subsequent invalidation of the all-white primary in 1944's *Smith v. Allwright.*

1944　Supreme Court invalidates the all-white primary in Texas (and by implication, across the South) in *Smith v. Allwright.* The Court holds that, in light of *United States v. Classic's* holding that primary elections do come under the Fifteenth Amendment's purview, the Texas Democratic Party's control of the state's primary system is evidence that it operated as an "agency of the state"—even with the vote by the party's full membership that they did not want black members—and hence is prohibited by the Constitution.

1946   Supreme Court rules in *Colegrove v. Green* that the determination of the proper application of state legislative districting rules is a matter beyond the scope of the federal courts. "Courts ought not to enter this political thicket," cautioned Justice Frankfurter for the Court. "The remedy for unfairness in districting is to secure State legislatures that will apportion properly, or to invoke the ample powers of Congress," not to turn to the courts which lacked the authority to enforce the remedies sought.

1947   U.S. District Judge J. Waties Waring declares South Carolina's attempt to rewrite its election laws to "completely renounce control of political parties and [the] primaries held thereunder" unconstitutional in *Elmore v. Rice*. As Judge Waring explains, "all citizens of this State and Country are entitled to cast a free and untrammeled ballot in our elections . . . and if the only material and realistic elections are clothed with the name 'primary,' they are equally entitled to vote there."

1949   Georgia state legislature passes a "registration and purge" law. Under this statute, any voter who fails to vote at least once in a two-year period was to be automatically expunged from the voter rolls. Further, anyone reregistering following removal from the election lists (or registering for the first time) had to pass either the state's existing literacy test, or to answer ten of thirty questions allegedly aimed at proving their good character and their understanding of the duties of citizenship. As applied by largely biased local election registrars, this law effectively excludes most blacks from the polls.

1950   Southern District of Texas Judge Thomas Kennerly in *Terry v. Adams* holds the segregated Jaybird Democratic Association (a purportedly self-governing voluntary private club, which put forth a slate of candidates that "nearly always" ran unopposed in the Democratic primaries) "a political organization or party" and rules "that its chief object had always been to deny Negroes any voice or part in the election of county officials." Judge Kennerly therefore holds the association's racial discriminations invalid and enters judgment accordingly. In *South v. Peters* the Supreme Court upholds a district court's refusal to review Georgia's county election system (even though charges of unfair discrimination had been made), noting how "federal courts consistently refuse to exercise their equity powers in cases posing political issues arising from a state's geographical distribution of electoral strength among its political subdivisions."

1952   The Fifth Circuit Court of Appeals reverses the district court ruling in *Terry v. Adams*, holding that "there was no constitutional or congressional bar to the admitted discriminatory exclusion of Negroes because Jaybird's primaries were not to any extent state controlled."

1953   The Supreme Court reverses the Fifth Circuit in *Terry v. Adams*, supporting instead the district court's ruling declaring the Jaybird primary an impermissible racial discrimination.

1957   The Alabama state legislature gerrymanders the municipal boundaries of Tuskegee, Alabama, to exclude all but four or five of the city's four hundred or so qualified black voters (but none of the whites) from city elections. Suit is filed in the Middle District of Alabama, but the judge holds that (given Supreme Court precedents) he lacks the power to review and reverse the legislature's districting decisions. Congress passes a civil rights act that grants the Justice Department authority to intervene in voting rights matters.

1960   In *Gomillion v. Lightfoot* (an appeal of the Middle District of Alabama's refusal to rule on the racially biased gerrymander of the municipal boundaries of Tuskegee, Alabama) the Supreme Court rules that "[l]egislative control of municipalities, no less than other state power, lies within the scope of relevant limitations imposed by the United States Constitution. . . . The opposite conclusion, urged upon us by respondents, would sanction the achievement by a State of any impairment of voting rights whatever so long as it was cloaked in the garb of

the realignment of political subdivisions." This was constitutionally impermissible. When a "State exercises
power wholly within the domain of state interest, it is
insulated from federal judicial review. But such insulation is not carried over when state power is used as an
instrument for circumventing a federally protected
right." Congress passes a civil rights act that increases
the powers of the Justice Department in voting rights
suits.

1962   Reviewing Tennessee's unequal distribution of legislative seats, the Supreme Court holds in *Baker v. Carr*
that "the fact that the suit seeks protection of a political
right does not mean it presents a political question" (and
hence would be beyond the scope of judicial review).
The right of individuals and groups to equal protection
of the law, the justices argued, was supreme, and matters
of this sort were well within the purview of the courts.
Baker v. Carr opened the door for numerous voting
rights suits challenging unequal or discriminatory legislative districting.

1963   The Supreme Court in *Gray v. Sanders* begins to apply
the activist logic behind *Baker v. Carr,* overturning
Georgia's county-unit method of primary elections that
gave rural voters a significantly heavier weight than
urban voters.

1964   In *Reynolds v. Sims,* the Supreme Court holds that
"Legislators represent people, not trees or acres. . . . As
long as ours is a representative form of government, and
our legislatures are those instruments of government
elected directly by and directly representative of the
people, the right to elect legislators in a free and unimpaired fashion is a bedrock of our political system." The
Court therefore rules that "the Equal Protection Clause
requires both houses of a state legislature to be apportioned on a population basis." The "fundamental goal"
and "plain objective" of the Constitution demands the
application of the "easily demonstrable" standard of one
person/one vote, the justices concluded. Applied in
future cases, the one person/one vote doctrine became
the constitutional foundation for most of the judicial

reform of voting rights in the late twentieth century. Congress passes a civil rights act aggressively attacking most forms of race-based discrimination. Voting rights, however, are not explicitly covered under the new law.

1965   Congress passes the Voting Rights Act of 1965 (VRA), in the process vastly expanding the range of powers available to the federal courts and the Justice Department in attacking vote denial and vote dilution. Combined with the one person/one vote doctrine imposed on state legislative redistricting by *Reynolds v. Sims,* the VRA becomes the foundation for most voting rights reforms in the late twentieth century.

1966   The Supreme Court in *South Carolina v. Katzenbach* upholds the VRA as a valid exercise of Congress's plenary power to enforce the Fifteenth Amendment. In *Harper v. Virginia Board of Elections,* the Court declares poll taxes unconstitutional. In *United States v. Mississippi* and *United States v. Louisiana* separate district courts order state officials "to provide to each illiterate voter who may request it such reasonable assistance as may be necessary to permit such voter to cast his ballot in accordance with the voter's own decision" (quoting from *United States v. Mississippi*).

1967   The Supreme Court declares literacy tests unconstitutional in *Gaston County v. United States.*

1968   In *Brown v. Post* Judge Benjamin C. Dawkins of the Western District of Louisiana overturns a 1966 school board election due to voter fraud by local officials in this case involving the refusal to provide absentee ballots to qualified black voters. In *United States v. Post* he declares an election for parish sheriff null and void after the parish registrar left a black candidate for office off the Democratic Party slate and yet informed voters that by casting a straight Democratic Party ticket vote they would be voting for their desired nominee (the result was that the black candidate was not elected).

1969   In *Allen v. State Board of Elections* (challenging Virginia's and Mississippi's election law reforms, including the shift to at-large county elections following passage of the VRA of 1965) the Supreme Court holds that sec-

tion 5 of the Voting Rights Act encompasses vote dilution as well as vote denial discriminations. Invoking the
one person/one vote requirement of *Reynolds v. Sims,*
the Court rules that "the right to vote can be affected by
a dilution of voting power as well as by an absolute prohibition on casting a ballot. . . . Voters who are members
of a racial minority might well be in the majority in one
district, but in a decided minority in the county as was
whole. This type of change could therefore nullify their
ability to elect the candidate of their choice just as
would prohibiting them from voting." Laws seeking to
dilute the voting strength of minorities, the justices conclude, were thus constitutionally impermissible.

1970   The Supreme Court upheld the VRA's suspension of literacy tests in *Oregon v. Mitchell.*

1973   In *White v. Regester* the Supreme Court holds that
where the "totality of the circumstances" shows a pattern of economic, social, educational, and political discriminations all combining to dilute minority voting
strength—causing minorities, in other words, to have
"less opportunity than did other residents in the district
to participate in the political processes and to elect legislators of their choice"—then multimember districts
elected at-large could be unconstitutional denials of
equal protection of the law. Hence, while multimember
districts were not unconstitutional per se, and disproportionate representation was not by itself evidence of a
discriminatory intent, viewed in the context of other
intensely local factors, courts could determine such discrimination to exist and then apply appropriate remedies. Although an awkward standard to apply, the
"totality of the circumstances" test becomes the standard of proof in vote dilution litigation through the
1970s and beyond. In *Zimmer v. McKeithen,* the Fifth
Circuit simplifies the district judges' job in vote dilution
cases by reorganizing the standards of proof of discrimination proposed by the Supreme Court in *White v.
Regester* into a more useful set of four "primary" and
four "enhancing" tests to determine illegal discriminations. (Among the criteria were the inability of minori-

ties to have "access . . . [to] the process of slating candidates," legislative unresponsiveness "to their particularized interests," "a tenuous state policy [in] . . . preference for multi-member or at-large districting," and the existence of past discriminations that precluded "the effective participation [by minorities] in the election system.") However, just as in *White,* the *Zimmer* tests still do not specify at what point violations of the prescribed factors demanded action. Rather, like the Supreme Court in *White,* the Fifth Circuit falls back on a preponderance of the evidence standard: "The fact of dilution is established," the court rules, "upon proof of the existence of an aggregate of these factors." Judge Benjamin Dawkins of the Southern District of Louisiana in *Wallace v. House* holds at-large elections in Louisiana unconstitutional violations of equal protection.

1974   Congress renews VRA of 1965, in the process amending it to include "language minorities" (Hispanics, Asian Americans, etc) within the special provisions of the act (in particular section 5's preclearance requirements). In *Stewart v. Waller,* a three-judge district court strikes down Mississippi's election laws requiring at-large municipal and county elections "as a purposeful device conceived and operated to further racial discrimination in the voting process" and therefore not allowed under the Fourteenth and Fifteenth Amendments. Judge Newell Edenfield of the Northern District of Georgia rules in *Pitts v. Busbee* that Fulton County's at-large elections system, though not intentionally discriminatory, had the effect of "grossly minimiz[ing] the possibility of blacks fully participating in their county government and particularly in the election of county commissioners of their choice." He therefore declares the law implementing at-large elections unconstitutional and imposes a new approach (requiring single-member districts) for selecting candidates in the next election.

1978   Objecting to the extension of the one person/one vote doctrine, four justices of the Supreme Court dissent to the majority ruling in *Wise v. Lipscomb,* criticizing the "preponderance of the evidence" standard used in these matters as an "amorphous theory."

1979   In *United Jewish Organizations v. Carey,* a legislative districting case from New York, a highly divided Supreme Court carries out a dialogue of concurring opinions that hints at a growing movement on the Court toward applying some form of intent standard to rein in the excesses in vote dilution litigation. The District Court of Connecticut in *Baker v. Regional High School Dist. No. 5* holds that "where there is an indication of racial bias, scrutiny of apportionment of elective state bodies [should be] particularly strict, and even generally acceptable apportionment procedures may be invalid in such circumstances."

1980   In *City of Mobile v. Bolden,* the Supreme Court demands that a "plaintiff must prove that the disputed plan was 'conceived or operated as [a] purposeful device to further racial discrimination' . . ." in voting dilution matters. This ruling throws a shadow over voting rights litigation until Congress's 1982 revision of section 2 of the VRA reimposing an "effects" standard of proof in these matters returns voting rights litigation to its pre-*City of Mobile* status.

1982   Congress renews VRA of 1965, in the process amending section 2 to the effect that proof of an intent to discriminate (as demanded by the Supreme Court in 1980 in *City of Mobile v. Bolden*) was not necessary to initiate reform, merely proof of discriminatory "effect." (If the effects were discriminatory in their impact, treating minorities differently from whites, then the voting structure was constitutionally unacceptable whatever the original intent in creating the voting structure.) This revision had the immediate impact of opening the door to literally hundreds of vote dilution suits.

1983   In *Major v. Treen,* an Eastern District of Louisiana three-judge panel holds that state's 1981 redistricting plan unconstitutional. (In its effort to split the mostly black Orleans parish in two, the legislature's plan so contorted the boundary lines of the new Second Congressional District that it resembled nothing so much as a duck.) Disregarding arguments that these changes were merely the result of a color-blind effort to protect incumbent positions, the court rules that "the protection of existing relationships among incumbents and their constituents, and the benefits accruing to the state from the seniority its delegation may have achieved in Congress, are pragmatic considerations which often figure prominently in the drawing of congressional districts. These considerations are not talismanic, however, and may not serve to protect incumbents by imposing an electoral scheme which splinters a geographically concentrated black populace within a racially polarized parish, thus minimizing the black citizenry's electoral participation."

1984   Judge James Fox of the Eastern District of North Carolina in *Johnson v. Halifax County* imposes a preliminary injunction halting voting under Halifax County's at-large voting system. Soon after, a consent decree produces a more acceptable election system. In *Jordan v. Winter*, the Northern District of Mississippi implements an interim redistricting plan in place of a state plan that had unconstitutionally diluted black voting strength by splitting black populations among multiple congressional districts. The result was the creation of a black-majority Second Congressional District and the election of Mississippi's first black representative since Reconstruction.

1985   In *Butts v. City of New York*, black and Hispanic voters in New York City challenge the state's primary runoff law (requiring a second round of voting if no candidate won a majority vote in the primary, and which applied only to the City of New York, and then only to the three citywide offices of mayor, city council, and comptroller). Their contention, to which the judge hearing the case agreed, was that "the operation of the runoff statute was intended to . . . make it more difficult for a Black or Hispanic candidate to emerge as the party nominee." An order to change the system to allow victory on a plurality of the votes soon followed.

1986	Though technically in line with the 1982 revision of the VRA, the Supreme Court's ruling in *Thornburg v. Gingles* imposes a new standard in vote dilution cases, one demanding that "the minority group . . . demonstrate that it is sufficiently large and geographically compact to constitute a majority in a single-member district." The Court reasons that any district failing this test, "as would be the case in a substantially integrated district," meant "the multi-member form of the district cannot be responsible for minority voters' inability to elect its candidates." And if race was not the cause of electoral failure, then race-conscious districting was obviously not the proper remedy.
1989	In *Jeffers v. Clinton,* a three-judge panel of the District Court of Arkansas, strikes down a 1989 state reapportionment plan (which had included five black-majority districts) as not proportional enough. Finding that voting in the state was "markedly polarized by race," the court argues that, as currently constructed, state legislative district lines made "it very difficult [for blacks] to elect more than six black legislators, out of a total in both houses of 135 members." Given that blacks made up "about 16 per cent" of the State's population, this was not enough to meet section 2's nonexclusionary requirements. "We find," ruled the court, "that a total of 16 such districts . . . could have been created" given state populations and residential patterns. And, while the judges would not require "the creation of any particular number of majority-black districts," they did make clear "a sort of presumption that any plan adopted should contain that number of majority-black districts." A revised districting plan soon followed.
1990	In *Garza v. County of Los Angeles,* Hispanic voters charge that the Los Angeles County Board of Supervisors' 1981 redistricting plan impaired Hispanics' chances to gain representation on the board. Taking note of "the explosive and continuous growth of the Los Angeles County Hispanic community, . . . the steady decline of the County's non-Hispanic white population," and the "long and painful history of discrimi-

nation against Hispanics in this County," the judge rules "that the Los Angeles County Board of Supervisors knew that by adopting the 1981 redistricting plan, they were further impairing the ability of Hispanics to gain representation on the Board"—an action for which "no legal justification, including "the protection of" an incumbent's job, was justified. An order for revisions of the county election system, soon followed.

1993   Supreme Court rules in *Shaw v. Reno* that "reapportionment is one area in which appearances do matter," for "a reapportionment plan that includes in one district individuals who belong to the same race, but who are otherwise widely separated by geographical and political boundaries, and who may have little in common with one another but the color of their skin, bears an uncomfortable resemblance to political apartheid." For these reasons, the majority in *Shaw* concludes that "a plaintiff challenging a reapportionment statute under the Equal Protection Clause may state a claim by alleging that the legislation, though race neutral on its face, rationally cannot be understood as anything other than an effort to separate voters into different districts on the basis of race, and that the separation lacks sufficient justification." Where a state "concentrated a dispersed minority population in a single district, disregarding traditional districting principles such as compactness, contiguity, and respect for political subdivisions," a red flag of warning demanded a close examination to ensure that race was not the only determinant in creating the district. Though subsequent litigation at the trial level would determine that the district in question was properly organized, the concept that districts organized solely on the basis of race were unconstitutional violations of equal protection calls into question the validity of twenty years of majority-minority districting.

2000   Extremely close presidential election contest between Republican George W. Bush and Democrat Al Gore produces a result too close to call in Florida. (Eventually, the difference in Florida would prove to be fewer than five hundred votes out of a total of some six million cast—less than a .005 percent difference). Given Florida's twenty-five electoral college votes, however, the outcome of the Florida vote was key in determining the election's winner. Following thirty-six days of political, legal, and constitutional contest over the need and form of a Florida vote recount, the ultimate result was the Supreme Court's ruling in *Bush v. Gore* that a lack of uniform standards in determining a properly submitted ballot invalidated the Florida recount process under the equal protection clauses of the Constitution. The Court also, in response to perceived stringent time constraints, refuses to allow hand recounts to continue even under uniform standards. In so ruling, the Court effectively ends the election, determining by its highly controversial ruling that the winner of the election was George W. Bush.

Table of Cases

Elmore v. Rice, 72 F. Supp. 516 (1947)

Fortson v. Dorsey, 379 U.S. 433 (1965)

Garza v. County of Los Angeles, 756 F. Supp. 1298 (1990)

Gaston County v. United States, 395 U.S. 285 (1969)

Gomillion v. Lightfoot, 364 U.S. 339 (1960)

Gore v. Harris, 772 So. 2d. 1243 (Florida Sup Ct, 2000)

Gray v. Sanders, 372 U.S. 368 (1963)

Grigsby v. Harris, 27 F. 2d 942 (1928)

Grove v. Townsend, 295 U.S. 45 (1935)

Hannah v. Larche, 363 U.S. 420 (1960)

Harper v. Virginia Board of Elections, 383 U.S. 663 (1966)

Jeffers v. Clinton, 730 F. Supp. 196 (1989)

Johnson v. Halifax Co., 594 F. Supp. 161 (1984)

Jordan v. Winter, 604 F. Supp. 807 (1984)

Kidd v. McCanless, 352 U.S. 920 (1956)

Kirkpatrick v. Preisler, 394 U.S. 526 (1968)

Kirksey v. Board of Supervisors of Hinds County, 528 F. 2d 536 (1976)

Lassiter v. Northampton County Board of Elections, 360 U.S. 45 (1959)

Love v. Griffith, 266 U.S. 32 (1924)

Lucas v. Forty-Fourth General Assembly of Colorado, 377 U.S. 713 (1964)

Major v. Treen, 574 F. Supp. 325 (1983)

Marbury v. Madison, 5 U.S. 137 (1803)

McKay v. Campbell, 16 F. Cas. 166 (1871)

Miller v. Johnson, 115 S. Ct. 2475 (1995)

Minor v. Happersett, 88 U.S. 162 (1874)

Mitchell v. Wright, 154 F. 2d 924 (1946)

Mitchell v. Wright, 62 F. Supp. 580 (1945)

Morris v. Fortson, 261 F. Supp. 538 (1966)

Myers v. Anderson, 238 U.S. 368 (1915)

Nixon v. Condon, 286 U.S. 73 (1932)

Nixon v. Herndon, 273 U.S. 536 (1927)

Oregon v. Mitchell, 400 U.S. 112 (1970)

Ozawa v. United States, 260 U.S. 178 (1922)

Pitts v. Busbee, 395 F. Supp. 35 (1975)

Plessy v. Ferguson, 163 U.S. 537 (1896)

Pope v. Williams, 193 U.S. 621 (1904)

Reno v. Bossier Parish School Board, 117 S. Ct. 1419 (1997)

Reynolds v. Sims, 377 U.S. 533 (1964)

Annotated Bibliography

Ball, Howard, Dale Krane, and Thomas P. Lauth. *Compromised Compliance: Implementation of the 1965 Voting Rights Act* (Westport, CT: Greenwood Press, 1982).

    Highly critical discussion of the Voting Rights Act of 1965 and its subsequent implementation and evolution by judicial and administrative means.

Basch, Norma. **"Reconstructing Female Citizenship:** *Minor v. Happersett,"* in Donald Nieman, ed., *The Constitution, Law, and American Life: Critical Aspects of the Nineteenth-Century Experience* (Athens: University of Georgia Press, 1992): 52–66.

    Analysis of *Minor v. Happersett* in the context of the women's rights movement's effort to employ the Fourteenth Amendment as ammunition against state bans on women voting.

Belknap, Michal R. *Federal Law and Southern Order: Racial Violence and Constitutional Conflict in the Post-Brown South* (Athens: University of Georgia Press, 1987).

    Discusses federal efforts to control racial violence from the 1950s through the 1970s. Useful for its descriptions of the violent context in which voting rights litigation took place.

Bernstein, Richard B. *Amending America: If We Love the Constitution So Much, Why Do We Keep Trying to Change It?* (New York: Times Books, 1993).

    One of the very best books on the amendment process. Bernstein's sections on the civil rights amendments (Thirteenth–Fifteenth) and the Nineteenth Amendment (granting women the vote) are exceptionally concise summaries of the forces that shaped the formation and evolution of these amendments. The book is even more useful for its explanation of the amendment process, in particular the forces and preconditions necessary if constitutional change by amendment is to take place.

Binion, Gayle. "The Implementation of Section 5 of the 1965 Voting Rights Act: A Retrospective on the Role of Courts," *Western Political Quarterly* 32 (1979): 154–173.

Detailed description of litigation to enforce section 5 of the Voting Rights Act of 1965. Argues that, on the whole, federal judges remained opposed to all efforts to end race-based vote discrimination, and points to the actions of the Justice Department as the primary source of reform in voting rights matters.

Blacksher, James U., and Larry T. Menefee. "From *Reynolds v. Sims* to *City of Mobile v. Bolden:* Have the White Suburbs Commandeered the Fifteenth Amendment?" *Hastings Law Journal* 34 (September 1982): 1–64.

Extremely useful article on the evolution of the one person/one vote doctrine. Blacksher and Menefee argue that in its drive for manageable standards in combating vote dilution (a drive that they argue was ultimately unsuccessful), the Supreme Court distorts its proper constitutional priorities as it attempted to balance the "implied constitutional right of majority rule with the explicit constitutional demand for the protection of racial groups."

Carter, Dan T. *When the War Was Over: The Failure of Self-Reconstruction in the South, 1865–1867* (Baton Rouge: Louisiana State University Press, 1985).

Detailed description of the failure of Reconstruction policies and reforms. Explores both the causes and effects of this failure.

Chayes, Abram. "The Role of the Judge in Public Law Litigation," *Harvard Law Review* 89 (May 1976): 1281–1316.

Analytical discussion of the changing roles and functions of judges in the litigation process from the nineteenth to the twentieth century. In particular, Chayes argues that with the rise of institutional reform litigation (represented, among other matters, by voting rights suits with their long life span and need for the judge to constantly intervene in the dispute resolution process), judges shifted their role from that of neutral adjudicator to interactive and interventionist case manager. One of the most important theoretical works in the field of judicial politics.

Chute, Marchette Gaylord. *The First Liberty: A History of the Right to Vote in America, 1619–1850* (New York: Dutton, 1969).

Basic history of voting rights from the colonial period through the antebellum years. Contains solid materials that can also be found in Alexander Keyssar's *The Right to Vote*, Chilton's *American Suffrage: From Property to Democracy*, and Porter's *A History of Suffrage in the United States*.

Cogan, Jacob K. "Note: The Look Within: Property, Capacity, and Suffrage in Nineteenth-Century America," *Yale Law Journal* 107 (November 1997): 473–498.

This law review Student Note looks at suffrage reform from the late eighteenth century to the adoption of the Fifteenth Amendment and argues that during this period voting rights reformers were obsessed with the "inner qualities of persons," not their external qualifications. Hence, whereas the eighteenth century located a person's capacity to vote in material things, such as property, the nineteenth century found these qualities in "innate and heritable traits," such as intelligence or personal independence. The result was the rise of felon, pauper, and literacy franchise exclusions.

Davidson, Chandler. **"Minority Vote Dilution: An Overview,"** in Chandler Davidson, ed., *Minority Vote Dilution* (Washington, DC: Howard University Press, 1984): 1–23.

Very well written and argued summary of the problem of race-based vote dilution. A very good place to start for anyone seeking a deeper understanding of this issue.

————. *Race and Class in Texas Politics* (Princeton: Princeton University Press, 1990).

Useful analysis of the role of class and race in shaping the political process, examined through the example of Texas, but applicable to evaluating the role of class and race in shaping the political process across the South and even the nation. In terms of voting rights, Davidson's book provides useful information on the state's struggles with vote dilution and denial, and a more general analytical foundation by which to evaluate the experiences of other states.

————. **"The Voting Rights Act: A Brief History,"** in Bernard Grofman and Chandler Davidson, eds., *Controversies in Minority Voting: The Voting Rights Act in Perspective* (Washington, DC: The Brookings Institution, 1992): 7–51.

Useful description of the Voting Rights Act of 1965, its origins, forms, and subsequent evolution through legislative revision and judicial enforcement. A useful first start for anyone wishing to know more about the issue of race-based vote denial and especially of race-based vote dilution.

————. **"The Recent Evolution of Voting Rights Law Affecting Racial and Language Minorities,"** in *Quiet Revolution in the South: The Impact of the Voting Rights Act, 1965–1990* (Princeton: Princeton University Press, 1994): 21–37.

One of the best short summaries of the legal issues and problems associated with vote dilution, in particular since the passage of the Voting Rights Act of 1965. Read in context with the other articles in this book, it provides the most complete analysis to date of the impact of the VRA on southern politics and society.

————, "The Voting Rights Act and the Second Reconstruction," in *Quiet Revolution in the South: The Impact of the Voting Rights Act, 1965–1990* (Princeton: Princeton University Press, 1994): 378–388.

Concluding chapter to Davidson's and Grofman's analysis of the Voting Rights Act of 1965 and its impact on southern politics and society. Argues for the need for a historical perspective in analyzing the VRA and its effects.

————, eds., *Quiet Revolution in the South: The Impact of the Voting Rights Act, 1965–1990* (Princeton: Princeton University Press, 1994).

A compendium of original articles, Davidson and Grofman's book examines the history and impact of voting rights litigation in reshaping southern politics and society. Collectively, the authors conclude that voting rights litigation (brought mostly by private litigants under the provisions of the VRA) effectively transformed the nature of southern life and politics—in the process producing what the editors call a "quiet revolution." This book is one of the best places to start any examination of the VRA and of the fight against race-based vote dilution in the last third of the twentieth century.

Derfner, Armand. **"Racial Discrimination and the Right to Vote,"** *Vanderbilt Law Review* 26 (1973): 523–584.

Inclusive and exhaustive description and analysis of published and unpublished voting rights cases from the 1940s through the early 1970s.

Dionne, E. J., Jr., and William Kristol, eds. **Bush v. Gore:** *The Court Cases and the Commentary* (Washington, DC: Brookings Institution Press, 2001).

Compendium of reprinted judicial opinions and op-ed columns associated with the 2000 presidential election controversy and the judicial responses to this controversy. Useful as an easily acquired source of the judicial opinions generated by the 2000 election, the book is even more helpful for its collection of editorial commentary, communicating the diversity of opinions (often by the same commentator over time) and the confusion and discomfort caused by these events.

DuBois, Ellen C. *Feminism and Suffrage: The Emergence of an Independent Women's Movement in America* (Ithica, Cornell University Press, 1978).

Informative survey of the rise of the women's rights movement and its fight for the franchise. One of the better and more complete sources on the topic of women's suffrage.

————. **"Outgrowing the Compact of the Fathers: Equal Rights, Women Suffrage, and the United States Constitution, 1820–1876,"** *Journal of American History* 74 (1987): 836–862.

Analysis of women's rights movement, including the fight for the vote, in the context of the radical tradition of equal rights theory in U.S. political and constitutional discourse.

————. **"Taking Law into Their Own Hands: Voting Women during Reconstruction,"** in Donald W. Rogers, ed., *Voting and the Spirit of American Democracy* (Urbana: University of Illinois Press, 1992): 67–80.

Short survey of early efforts by women to apply the Fourteenth Amendment to the issue of women's voting rights. DuBois argues that the women's rights movement had its origins in the Fourteenth Amendment's ideal of national citizenship and that despite the unwillingness of the courts to accept such arguments, this effort laid a foundation for the successful campaign that resulted in the Nineteenth Amendment.

Fleming, Walter C. **"Politics in the Mainstream: Native Americans as the Invisible Minority,"** in Wilber C. Rich, ed., *The Politics of Minority Coalitions: Race, Ethnicity, and Shared Uncertainties* (Westport, CT: Praeger, 1996): 233–246.

Short article describing the forces shaping Native American civil rights (among them citizenship rights and the right to vote) from the early nineteenth century to the present.

Foner, Eric. *Reconstruction: America's Unfinished Revolution, 1863–1877* (New York: Harper & Row, 1988).

A remarkable synthesis of historical understanding of Reconstruction. Foner places race and class at the center of the story, and while law and the Supreme Court play minimal roles in Foner's narrative, it is still the best single source for understanding the forces shaping the origins of race-based vote denial in the South.

————. **"From Slavery to Citizenship: Blacks and the Right to Vote,"** in Donald W. Rogers, ed., *Voting and the Spirit of American Democracy* (Urbana: University of Illinois Press, 1992): 55–65.

Exceptionally lucid short survey of the African American community's fight for the franchise during Reconstruction.

————. *The Story of American Freedom* (New York: W. W. Norton, 1998).

Survey of the influence the idea of freedom has had on U.S. history. Useful as a general background to the debates and intellectual forces surrounding voting rights conflicts.

Goldman, Robert M. *Reconstruction and Black Suffrage: Losing the Vote in* Reese *and* Cruikshank (Lawrence: University of Kansas Press, 2001).

Well-written and accessible account of two early voting rights cases wherein the Supreme Court refused to extend the reach of the Fourteenth and Fifteenth Amendments to protect black voting rights. Places the Supreme Court's rulings on the right to vote in the context of failed federal enforcement efforts to promote actual voting.

Greenfield, Jeff. *"Oh, Waiter! One Order of Crow!": Inside the Strangest Presidential Election Finish in American History* (New York: G. Putnam and Sons, 2001).

Pithy and insightful description of the 2000 presidential election and its legal aftermath.

Grofman, Bernard. **"Would Vince Lombardi Have Been Right If He Had Said: 'When It Comes to Redistricting, Race Isn't Everything, It's the Only Thing'?"** *Cardozo Law Review* 14 (April 1993): 1237–1276.

Article exploring the role of race as the primary factor in legislative redistricting matters in the context of (1) the growing number of redistricting suits; (2) the government's strong support for tough voting rights enforcement; and (3) the rising scholarly and public backlash to the VRA and its primary enforcement technique, minority-majority districting. Grofman argues that voting rights, though a civil rights matter, are structurally different from other types of civil rights reforms such as affirmative action, and that this explains the three trends explored in his article.

Guinier, Lani. *The Tyranny of the Majority: Fundamental Fairness in Representative Democracy* (New York: Free Press, 1994).

Controversial analysis of minority voting rights that adopts a highly critical approach (from a radical perspective) to minority-majority districting. Guinier argues that such race-conscious efforts to elect minority government officials have not been matched with real power-sharing and, as such, have been a failure. In its place, Guinier calls for more effective forms of proportional representation of minorities.

Hainsworth, Robert. **"The Negro and the Texas Primaries,"** *Journal of Negro History* 18 (October 1933): 426–450.

Dated but still useful description of early black efforts to attack the all-white primary in Texas.

Hamilton, Charles V. *The Bench and the Ballot: Southern Federal Judges and Black Voters* (New York: Oxford University Press, 1973).

Well-reasoned and somewhat critical appraisal of the mixed role of southern federal district judges in voting rights cases from the 1940s to the early 1970s. Hamilton argues that the perspective of judges on segregation was a major determining factor in the impact of the federal courts on voting rights matters. He contends that for real change to occur, administrative as well as judicial reforms are necessary.

Harvey, Anna L. *Votes without Leverage: Women in American Electoral Politics, 1920–1970* (Cambridge: Cambridge University Press, 1998).

Analysis of the impact of women's right to vote on the electoral process and on resulting governmental policy. Harvey argues that one can only understand the impact (or lack of impact) of women's voting by examining the role of intermediate political organizations (such as political parties or the women's movement).

Hays, Samuel P. "The Politics of Reform in Municipal Government in the Progressive Era," reprinted in Barton J. Bernstein and Allen J. Matusow, *Twentieth Century America: Recent Interpretations* (New York: Harcourt, Brace & World, 1969): 34–58.

Influential article on the rise of at-large elections in the Progressive Era. Hays argues that these electoral reforms had class and ethnic bias aimed primarily at diluting the electoral impact of immigrants and other distrusted groups.

Hench, Virginia, "The Death of Voting Rights: The Legal Disenfranchisement of Minority Voters," *Western Law Review* 48 (Summer 1986): 730–788.

Useful, if somewhat negative, analysis of voting rights litigation from the mid-nineteenth century to the late twentieth century. Especially good for its analysis of the Supreme Court's logic in such recent cases as *Shaw v. Reno.*

Hine, Darlene Clark. *Black Victory: The Rise and Fall of the White Primary in Texas* (Millwood, New York: KTO Press, 1979).

Exceptionally rich description and analysis of the all-white primary in Texas. Best source for information and insight on the campaigns that ended this practice.

Hodes, W. William. "Women and the Constitution: Some Legal History and a New Approach to the Nineteenth Amendment," *Rutgers Law Review* 25 (1970): 26–53.

Law review Student Note analyzing the Nineteenth Amendment by means of a direct comparison of African Americans' and women's struggles for the franchise. Hodes argues that as a result of such a comparison, the Nineteenth Amendment must be seen as more than just the realization of women's suffrage, but rather as an extension to women of the full range of the civil rights amendments' protections and provisions.

Issacharoff, Samuel. "Groups and the Right to Vote," *Emery Law Journal* 44 (Summer 1995): 869–909.

Discussion of the problems associated with group-based rights and the vote, in particular the dilemma faced in enforcing minority voting rights against group-based vote dilution techniques such as at-large elections and majority vote requirements.

Kerber, Linda. *No Constitutional Right to Be Ladies: Women and the Obligations of Citizenship* (New York: Hill and Wang, 1998).

Exceptional study of the constitutional limits and duties imposed upon women, and the fight by women to exceed the limits and partake of the duties of citizenship. In terms of voting rights, Kerber's book provides an invaluable description of early efforts by women's rights advocates to employ the Fourteenth Amendment as ammunition against state bans on women voting.

Keyssar, Alexander. *The Right to Vote: The Contested History of Democracy in the United States* (New York: Basic Books, 2000).

Simply the best monograph on voting rights to date. Both a synthesis of existing historical research and an innovative reworking of this research, Keyssar's book covers the entire topic in depth and with insight.

Klarman, Michael J. *"Bush v. Gore:* **Through the Lens of Constitutional History,"** (Unpublished manuscript, January 30, 2001).

Insightful article (no doubt forthcoming in a law review) analyzing the Supreme Court's ruling in *Bush v. Gore.* Klarman stresses the constitutional failure of the majority's ruling in this case.

Kousser, J. Morgan. *The Shaping of Southern Politics, Suffrage, and the Establishment of the One-Party South* (New Haven: Yale University Press, 1974).

Well-written narrative and analysis of the rise of the one-party South by means of black disenfranchisement following Reconstruction. Best read in conjunction with Perman's *Struggle for Mastery,* which seeks to update Kousser's arguments and conclusions.

———. *Colorblind Injustice: Minority Voting Rights and the Undoing of the Second Reconstruction* (Chapel Hill: University of North Carolina Press, 1999).

Rich and very detailed discussion of the evolution and impact of voting rights litigation in the late twentieth century. Kousser, who often serves as an expert witness for minority litigants in voting rights cases, seeks to "set voting rights policy straight by getting its history right." Kousser hopes to show the powerful impact Supreme Court rulings have in shaping minority voting rights and, in particular, to undermine the Supreme Court's constitutional logic attacking the concept of majority-minority districting applied in 1993's *Shaw v. Reno.*

Lawson, Steven F. *In Pursuit of Power: Southern Blacks and Electoral Politics, 1965–1982* (New York: Columbia University Press, 1985).

Continuation of the narrative started in *Black Ballots.* This book focuses on the African American community's attack on vote dilution and its attempt to gain actual political power, not just the right to vote. Also evaluates the impact of the revolution in voting rights after 1965.

———. *Black Ballots: Voting Rights in the South, 1944–1969* (Lanham, MD: Lexington Press, 1999 [originally published in 1976]).

Rich and useful description of the African American fight against race-based vote denial from *Smith v. Allwright* to *Allen v. State Board of Elections.* Especially helpful in its portrayal of the black community's role in shaping the fight for race-neutral voting. Best read in conjunction with Lawson's 1985 sequel, *In Pursuit of Power,* and Davidson and Grofman's *Quiet Revolution in the South.*

McCarty, L. Thorne, and Russell B. Stevenson. **"The Voting Rights Act of 1965: An Evaluation,"** *Harvard Civil Rights–Civil Liberties Law Review* 2 (Spring 1968): 357–413.

Detailed description of the various provisions of the Voting Rights Act of 1965 and an analysis of early litigation under this act.

Montejano, David. *Anglos and Mexicans in the Making of Texas, 1836–1987* (Austin: University of Texas Press, 1987).

History of white and Hispanic interactions in Texas from statehood to the late twentieth century. Places Mexican American disenfranchisement (and ultimate enfranchisement) into the larger context of ethnic relations in the Southwest.

Parker, Frank R. **"Racial Gerrymandering and Legislative Reapportionment,"** in Chandler Davidson, ed., *Minority Vote Dilution* (Washington, DC: Howard University Press, 1984): 85–117.

Useful summary of the problem of race-based gerrymandering and efforts to deal with this problem through race-conscious legislative redistricting. Parker is in favor of race-conscious redistricting efforts, arguing that "a racially neutral remedy [often] may be no remedy at all."

———. *Black Votes Count: Political Empowerment in Mississippi after 1965* (Chapel Hill: University of North Carolina Press, 1990).

Narrative and analytical account of Mississippi's struggles with voting rights following passage of the Voting Rights Act of 1965. Parker's book explores the sources of white resistance to change, the efforts of the black community to force change, the judicial and political responses to these struggles, and evaluates the impact of voting rights legislation and litigation on Mississippi politics and race relations. Parker also places these changes in the context of the national political and constitutional scene. Especially useful for its description of the background and consequences of *Allen v. State Board of Elections.*

Perman, Michael. *Struggle for Mastery: Disenfranchisement in the South, 1888–1908* (Chapel Hill: University of North Carolina Press, 2001).

Recent survey of the process of African American disenfranchisement in the late nineteenth century. Perman argues that the process by which blacks were denied the vote was complex and varied, involving: (1) informal action, statutory legislation, and constitutional revision; (2) constant political infighting as to objectives and results; and (3) regional variations as to origins, forms, and sources of white participation between and within the southern states. Very useful read in context with Kousser's *The Shaping of Southern Politics, Suffrage, and the Establishment of the One-Party South* and Keyssar's *The Right to Vote.*

Pildes, Richard H., and Richard G. Niemi. **"Expressive Harms, 'Bizarre Districts,' and Voting Rights: Evaluating Election-District Appear-**

ances after *Shaw v. Reno,*" *Michigan Law Review* 92 (December 1993): 483–587.

Law review article analyzing in a largely positive manner the constitutional logic and likely impacts of *Shaw v. Reno.*

Piven, Frances Fox, and Richard A. Cloward. *Why Americans Don't Vote* (New York: Pantheon, 1988).

Analysis of the growing trend of poor and minority citizens to not vote at a time when their access to the polls was increasing. The authors place this trend into the context of vote denial and dilution, arguing that "the methods by which people are made into nonvoters matter" and that much of the blame for nonvoting lies with society and the prevalent voting system, not the nonvoters themselves.

———. *Why Americans Still Don't Vote* (Boston: Beacon Press 2000).

Updated version of their 1988 book, *Why Americans Don't Vote,* takes the discussion of the topic up to the present, in particular exploring the origins and impacts of the National Voter Registration Act of 1993 (Motor Voter Act).

Porter, Kirk Harold. *A History of Suffrage in the United States* (New York: AMS Press, 1971 [1918]).

Reprint of a dated, yet fact-filled book on the evolution of voting rights legislation and practice in the late eighteenth and nineteenth centuries. Most of the information made available here can also be found in Alexander Keyssar's *The Right to Vote.*

Rakove, Jack N. *Original Meanings: Politics and Ideas in the Making of the Constitution* (New York: Alfred A. Knopf, 1996).

Informative and well-argued book on the formation and evolution of the Constitution. A good place to start any exploration of the original meanings of the Constitution. In terms of voting rights, a useful source for information on the compromises struck in regard to who controls the voting process as well as on the adoption of the electoral college in presidential elections.

Rogers, Donald W., ed. *Voting and the Spirit of American Democracy* (Urbana: University of Illinois Press, 1992 [reprint of 1990 ed.]).

Short yet informative survey of the evolution of the right to vote by some of the top historians of the periods explored. A useful start for those interested in the history of voting rights.

Steinfeld, Robert J. **"Property and Suffrage in the Early American Republic,"** *Stanford Law Review* 41 (January 1989): 335–376.

Law review article exploring the evolution and ultimate decline of property qualifications for voting. Steinfeld argues that nineteenth-century Americans concurrently held two contradictory visions of the political world: one that viewed a political realm in which all men, whether or not they owned property, should have a voice in the political process, and one that stressed the necessary power gap between property owners and the propertyless. The move to end property qualifications, Steinfeld explains, took place in the context of a struggle between these two inconsistent perspectives. The ultimate resolution of this conflict was found in the adoption of franchise exclusions for paupers—the ideal that all men did have the right to full participation in politics unless they showed some special failing that excluded them from this right. Extreme poverty was deemed to be one of these forms of special failing.

Stern, Gerald E. **"Judge William Harold Cox and the Right to Vote in Clarke County, Mississippi,"** in Leon Freidman, ed., *Southern Justice* (Cleveland: Meridian Books, 1965): 165–186.

Article describing the obstructionist actions of extreme segregationist federal district judge William Harold Cox of the Northern District Court of Mississippi.

Stevens, Doris. *Jailed for Freedom: American Women Win the Vote* (Troutdale, OR: New Sage Press, 1995 [1920]).

Reprint of 1920 history of the fight for the franchise by the women's movement by a participant in the process.

Taylor, Jeremy M. **"Comment: The Ghost of Harlan: The Unfulfilled Search for Judicially Manageable Standards in Voting Rights Litigation,"** *Mississippi Law Journal* 65 (Winter 1995): 431–461.

Law review Student Note discussing the Supreme Court's ongoing difficulties in establishing coherent and easily enforceable standards in voting rights litigation. Taylor argues that the original concept of one person/one vote was adopted in regard to "starkly unjust misapportionment and voter dilution situations," and that this fact resulted in a judicial policy that proved inappropriate for most other types of voting rights cases.

Wilentz, Sean. **"Property and Power: Suffrage Reform in the United States, 1787–1860,"** in Donald W. Rogers, ed., *Voting and the Spirit of American Democracy* (Urbana: University of Illinois Press, 1992): 31–42.

Short yet informative survey of the efforts by reformers to end property-based vote restrictions prior to the Civil War. Wilentz argues that the successful movement toward a more universal franchise had its origins in a transatlantic traffic in political ideas and the rise of a market economy that transformed U.S. politics and social relations.

Wilkins, David. **"An Inquiry into Indigenous Political Participation: Implications for Tribal Sovereignty,"** *Kansas Journal of Law and Public Policy* 9 (Summer 2000): 732–749.

Law review article exploring the issue of Native American sovereignty and patriotism. Includes a useful summary of Indian voting rights from the early nineteenth century to the present.

Williamson, Chilton. *American Suffrage: From Property to Democracy, 1760–1860* (Princeton: Princeton University Press, 1960).

Fact-filled book on the evolution of voting rights legislation and practice in the late eighteenth and early nineteenth centuries. The primary secondary source of information on early voting rights prior to the publication of Keyssar's *The Right to Vote;* most of the information made available here can also be found in Keyssar's book.

Wolfley, Jeannette. **"Jim Crow, Indian Style: The Disenfranchisement of Native Americans,"** *American Indian Law Review* 16 (1991): 167–202.

Detailed summary of government efforts to disenfranchise Native Americans. Best available source of information on this topic.

Index

About the Author

Charles L. Zelden is associate professor of history at Nova Southeastern University. He is the author of *Justice Lies in the District: The United States District Court for the Southern District of Texas, 1902-1960* (1993), and the series editor for ABC-CLIO's On Trial series.